Overcoming Borderline Personality Disorder

A Family Guide for Healing and Change

VALERIE PORR, M.A.

OXFORD
UNIVERSITY PRESS

2010

OXFORD
UNIVERSITY PRESS

Oxford University Press, Inc., publishes works that further
Oxford University's objective of excellence
in research, scholarship, and education.

Oxford   New York
Auckland   Cape Town   Dar es Salaam   Hong Kong   Karachi
Kuala Lumpur   Madrid   Melbourne   Mexico City   Nairobi
New Delhi   Shanghai   Taipei   Toronto

With offices in
Argentina   Austria   Brazil   Chile   Czech Republic   France   Greece
Guatemala   Hungary   Italy   Japan Poland   Portugal   Singapore
South Korea   Switzerland   Thailand   Turkey   Ukraine   Vietnam

Published by Oxford University Press, Inc.
198 Madison Avenue, New York, New York 10016
www.oup.com

Library of Congress Cataloging-in-Publication Data

Porr, Valerie.
    Overcoming borderline personality disorder : a family guide for healing
and change / Valerie Porr.
        p. cm.
    Includes bibliographical references and index.
    ISBN 978-0-19-537958-7
    1. Borderline personality disorder—Popular works. I. Title.
    RC569.5.B67P67 2010
    616.85'852—dc22

                                                          2010009506

7 9 8
Typeset by Glyph International, Bangalore, India
Printed in the United States of America
on acid-free paper

Overcoming Borderline
Personality Disorder

*This book is dedicated to
a very special
TARA
who taught me to understand suffering and
compassion and motivated me to find a way to
help people onto the path out of suffering*

Contents

ONE   Loving Someone with Borderline Personality Disorder: The Family Experience   3

TWO   The Science of Borderline Personality Disorder   37

THREE   The Principles of Behavior Change   77

FOUR   Understanding Dialectical Behavior Therapy   105

FIVE   Understanding and Applying Validation   129

SIX   Mindfulness   189

SEVEN   Grieving and Radical Acceptance   215

EIGHT   Dialectical Behavior Therapy Skills for Behavior Change: Interpersonal Relationships, Emotion Regulation, and Distress Tolerance   245

NINE   Mentalization: Understanding
       Misunderstandings   287

TEN   Putting It All Together: Integrating Skills
       for Acceptance and Change   329

       Afterword: For Clinicians   347

       Resources   351

       Bibliography   353 .

       Index   375

Foreword

IF YOU ARE READING THIS BOOK, CHANCES ARE THAT YOU, LIKE Valerie, come to this moment and these pages not by choice. You come desperate, having already traveled a long and arduous road as you sought answers, explanation, and the possibility of real help for your loved one with borderline personality disorder (BPD). You seek an understanding that is only possible among those who have stood in your shoes, who need no words to truly *get* the horrors you have faced, the fear as you consider the future, the profound sadness and grief, and the yearnings of your heart. You come hoping against hope that perhaps you will find the way out of the hell you and your loved one have endured.

However you got here, whatever your own path has been, you have arrived well. You can take comfort in knowing that your guide, Valerie Porr, has devoted decades of her life scaling the mountain tops far and wide, also searching for answers and explanations about BPD, and for a way out, for those she loves and for those she may never meet. She has applied her brilliant and creative mind, her seemingly endless and bountiful energy, and a determined passion to the pursuit of gathering, piecing together, distilling, and disseminating all that is known scientifically about BPD. This book, a compilation of all she has learned and now teaches to those in her family classes, is a labor of love if there ever was one. Valerie has read scientific journals copiously, often making connections unseen by researchers themselves until hearing her astute observations. She and her members attend scientific conferences throughout the world on an annual basis (American Psychiatric Association, American Psychological Association, Association of Behavioral and Cognitive Therapy, International Society for the Study of Personality Disorders, to name a few). She engages deeply in these meetings, fearlessly asking hard questions, and reminding the scientific community that our research "subjects" are her and her members' sons, daughters, wives, and husbands. You can expect to find Valerie seated near the front, with camera in hand, taking digital images of the presenter's slides so she can immediately incorporate what she has learned into her next class or workshop. There is no time to wait. People are dying and lives are being destroyed by the disorder of BPD.

I originally met Valerie shortly after she formed TARA, her nonprofit organization that seeks to assist and support loved ones of those afflicted with BPD. She had applied to attend a 10-day Intensive Training in Dialectical Behavior Therapy (DBT), a scientifically proven treatment for BPD developed by Marsha M. Linehan, Ph.D. at the University of Washington. Her application sparked a number of interesting and important conversations for our training organization about the role of families in "treating" individuals with BPD. DBT, like those it seeks to treat, is difficult to learn, even for well-trained mental health professionals. DBT is a comprehensive treatment built on multiple theories, containing numerous principles, strategies, procedures, and skills. Linehan's primary treatment manual (Linehan, M.M., *Cognitive and Behavioral Treatment of Borderline Personality Disorder*, New York: Guilford Press, 1993) is thick, tedious, and technical. How could family members with no training in mental health treatments be expected to learn DBT, let alone use it well? Furthermore, was it even ethical for them to do so? Over time, I discovered how naïve and wrong I was. I learned that in fact the most ethical and effective approach to treatment is, when possible, to actively engage families who seek to help in the treatment. Indeed, few others will go the distance as will family members of those with BPD.

The contents of this book have their roots in that DBT intensive. Valerie's team returned to the second part of the DBT Intensive Training having established TARA's first DBT psychoeducational program for family members. Through her tireless actions and her commitment to rigorous scientific research and evidence-based therapies, she has the ear of the scientific community and has helped those who treat BPD to understand the rightful place of family members in treatment. As she has told me and other treatment professionals on many occasions, while we therapists can go home at night and observe our limits with respect to responding to our clients' crises, family members of individuals with BPD are never off duty. My time with a particular patient is limited to an hour or two a week, whereas a family member's contact may fill the remaining hours, to care for and coach in more effective ways of responding.

You arrive on this scene at a very exciting time, as many advancements have been made in the understanding and treatment of BPD over the past two decades. BPD is no longer the life sentence it once was. Those who receive an evidence-based therapy can expect very positive outcomes, including full remission from the disorder. There are now several manualized and empirically supported psychosocial therapies for BPD, including DBT and mentalization, the two therapies described within these chapters. Valerie's emphasis on DBT is rightly placed, as it is the treatment most rigorously researched to date. Currently, there are over ten published randomized controlled trials conducted by a number of different investigators from around the globe demonstrating that DBT works. Having now proven that DBT significantly improves the lives of those with BPD, the research has advanced to examination of those elements and isolating specific DBT treatment modes that give DBT the greatest impact. Linehan's 1993 treatment manuals, *Cognitive Behavioral Treatment for Borderline Personality Disorder* and *Skills Training Manual for Borderline Personality Disorder* have been identified as the most widely read and influential books in psychology (Cook, Bivanova, & Coyne, 2009). Anyone who questions the scientific advances in the treatment of BPD or the efficacy of DBT can now download the United Kingdom's National Institute for Health and Clinical Excellence (NICE) Clinical Guidance #78, entitled, "Borderline Personality Disorder: Treatment and Management." Four primary documents exist, including a 559-page review of the research literature, a 20-page reference guide, and a 15-page document for individuals with BPD and their families.

There is good cause for hope and optimism.

You have come to the right place. Learning what is known about the neurobiological basis of BPD, the efficacious psychosocial treatments for BPD, and what you can do is the critical (though, perhaps daunt-ing) first step. Fortunately, Valerie has distilled the latest of the late research within the pages of this book and provides very concrete suggestions and tips for what to do and not do. She will teach you DBT skills and other techniques that will allow you to find new ways to respond to and help your loved one. Building on DBT's emphasis on non-judgmental stance, she will help you to see the world of your loved one in a way that will help engender compassion toward your-self and your loved one.

As long as individuals meet criteria for BPD, there will be work for all of us to do. Reading this book is a terrific first step. As you read, consider identifying a DBT skill or two that you might pass along to your loved one with BPD in the near future. Eventually, you might decide next to read Linehan's (1993) treatment manuals, watch her lectures and those of other senior BPD researchers on YouTube, take a TARA class, and/or join Valerie and her colleagues in the front rows of presentations on BPD at scientific conferences.

May the pages of this book sustain you on the next leg of your journey.

Linda A. Dimeff, Ph.D.
Seattle, WA

Preface: Why Me?

IN 1990, A PERSON I LOVE WAS DIAGNOSED WITH BORDERLINE personality disorder (BPD). Although I have a degree in psychology, I had never heard of BPD. My first response was to research the disorder, hoping to find information that could help me make sense of the tsunami that had swept over my family and torn our lives apart. I hoped that understanding the diagnosis would guide me toward finding a way to help.

By 1994, I had not yet found any answers that made sense to me. I was desperate for help. My quest eventually led me to attend a lecture in Kingston, New York, a small city about 100 miles north of my New York City home. Marsha Linehan, PhD, was giving a talk about Dialectical Behavior Therapy (DBT), a treatment for BPD that was the subject of her recently published book. I found that DBT explained BPD in a way that differed from everything else I had learned. Her descriptions and explanations of confusing BPD behaviors resonated with my experiences with my loved one and offered a methodology that gave me hope. I left Kingston determined to bring Dr. Linehan to New York City so that this treatment would be available for people with BPD. I set about organizing a conference that would introduce Dr. Linehan and DBT to New York professionals. The conference, funded by the New York City Department of Mental Health and the New York State Office of Mental Health, took place in December of 1994 at the New York Academy of Medicine.

The Treatment and Research Advancements National Association for Personality Disorders (TARA NAPD, or TARA) was founded in February of 1995 as a consequence of this first New York City DBT conference. We were the first national organization to focus exclusively on BPD, and for the past 15 years have operated the only National BPD Helpline and Resource and Referral Center.

The helpline calls we have received over the years have made me acutely familiar with the experiences of people with BPD within the mental health system. I learned about what helped or hurt them and about what they felt they needed. I spoke with countless family members searching for a way to help or to simply understand their loved one's quixotic, often abusive behaviors. I spoke with many clinicians who had provided patients with misinformation as to the etiology of or prognosis for BPD, and who did not know about or utilize evidence-based BPD treatments. These clinicians were usually unsuccessful in helping the person with BPD and consequently felt as frustrated and disheartened as did the family members.

Speaking to students and graduate students I found that they had minimal exposure to personality disorder in their classes, and generally had not been informed of the existence of evidence-based BPD treatments. Among the mental health policy makers I have met with, from the local to the national level, I have found that many questioned the authenticity of BPD as a real diagnosis, even though the research findings they themselves had funded clearly demonstrated that BPD is a distinct disorder that, untreated, leads to enormous public health costs. The BPD researchers and clinicians I have met over the years at the research conferences I attend have become my friends and mentors, informing my ideas and interpreting my observations. In turn, I have given them the opportunity to learn about families' experiences raising children who later met criteria for BPD. Our helpline is a window onto the frontline of BPD community experience.

The Family Experience

What families experience in trying to cope with a loved one with BPD is not well researched and is not generally considered except in reference to pathology. Family members are usually blamed for the disorder. As a result, effective ways to help them have not been developed.

I realized that family members were virtually invisible. A voice was needed to express the frustration and despair they endured in their quest to cope with and to find help for their loved ones with BPD. They needed help that acknowledged the impotence they felt at being unable to ease the suffering of a person they cared for so much, with the grief they felt for their loved one's suffering and for their own suffering, and with their inability to maintain a sense of safety in their homes for all members of the family. I realized that family members did not know how to be effective or how to ameliorate daily stressors for the person they loved.

These husbands, wives, partners, siblings, fathers, mothers, and children of people with BPD are usually extremely intelligent people and are highly motivated to help. They need to know the most recent and cutting-edge findings of the burgeoning BPD research community and how to translate this information into practical skills. They need hands-on how-to skills for improving and reconciling their relationships. They need guidance that respects and echoes their long-term experiences with BPD. The pain and frustration that I was hearing every day motivated me to develop a concrete, practical, understandable method for families to help that was based on DBT and mentalization-based therapy (MBT), both evidence-based treatments.

What Is Psychoeducation?

Family psychoeducational programs are research-based psychosocial interventions that offer state-of-the-art biological and pharmacological information, providing families with accurate information about a disorder as well as family coping skills. These programs value family participation as an adjunct to treatment rather than seeing the family as the cause of the illness. Families learn evidence-based problem-solving strategies and management techniques to decrease stress and tension in their natural environment. The goal is to prevent relapse, stabilize symptoms, reinforce effective use of problem-solving strategies, and improve functioning. Psychoeducation can be focused on either patient outcome or on family well-being—in the latter, improvement of the person with the disorder is a secondary consideration.

These programs are usually taught in groups, as group classes help reduce stigma and provide support to families. The participants share experiences and understand each other with a kind of empathy that is not available within their usual social networks. They encourage one another to try different ways to deal with problems, reinforced by successful practice exercises within the group and the experiences of participants and teachers. These groups are safe places that offer the beleaguered family members a new social circle of survivors and copers. Research has demonstrated the efficacy of family psychoeducation programs for people with schizophrenia and their families. William McFarlane, MD, has found that treatment outcomes improve, relapse declines, medication compliance increases, and patients are rehospitalized less often when families learn about schizophrenia, are taught appropriate and effective coping techniques, and are offered emotional support from peers. A study by David Miklowitz, MD, produced similar findings regarding families of people with bipolar disorder. He found that outcomes and medication compliance improved and patients did better when their families participated in a psychoeducation program. Finally, in a study of people with BPD and their families, Jill Hooley, DPhil, found that people with BPD did better with increased family involvement. These evidence-based studies showed me the potential for psychoeducational programs to benefit both people with BPD and their families.

BPD psychoeducation teaches family members the neurobiology underlying BPD behaviors, what treatments are effective, why past treatments were not effective, and how Dialectical Behavior Therapy and mentalization-based therapy (MBT) can be reinforced and modeled by families. It gives families a path out of the morass of daily BPD struggles and shows them how to restore balance to their lives. It teaches them how to implement DBT and MBT methods to help their loved ones navigate their own lives. When a person with BPD is not in any treatment, the family is her lifeline. Clearly, these incredibly motivated family members spend more time than anyone else with the person with BPD. Every interaction can be an opportunity to decrease outbursts or to teach a coping skill. This is the philosophical approach that underlies treatment for autistic children, too, and it works.

What Is Available for Families Now?

Very little accurate educational material is currently available for the loved ones of people with BPD. At the present time, across the nation, there are likewise very few support or psychoeducational programs for families or loved ones of people with BPD. Most people with BPD are not in treatment, and when they are, the treatment does not usually involve their families. Programs that do involve families generally do so only when the loved one with BPD is already in treatment. In these cases, families and patients participate in groups together, facilitated by clinicians. Generally, professionally developed programs patronize family members by underestimating their ability to be effective agents of change.

I believe that families are competent, motivated, and capable of teaching and reinforcing the effective behaviors found in DBT and MBT; they can learn and reinforce DBT skills; they can provide home "schooling" when it is needed. Where can the families of people with BPD go for help when their loved one believes there is nothing wrong with him, is presently not in any treatment, refuses to go to treatment, drops out of treatment, or has given up hope of ever finding someone who can help him? Most people with BPD have seen too many therapists, been rejected or thrown out of therapy and programs too many times, have "failed at therapy" too often. Why should they entertain the idea of trying again? Who can blame them?

What Is Dialectical Behavior Therapy (DBT)?

When I first heard Marsha Linehan speak, I realized that if I had been aware of DBT methodology, I could have prevented some of the painful experiences in my loved one's life that came about because of my own ignorance and following of inept advice. Dialectical Behavior Therapy is a method of treatment based on the principles of Behavioral Therapy and elements of Buddhist philosophy pertaining to acceptance and compassion. At the present time, DBT has a strong foundation of randomly controlled clinical trials demonstrating its efficacy in improving treatment outcomes for persons with BPD, and therefore qualifies as an evidence-based method of BPD treatment. It was developed by Marsha Linehan of the University of Washington in Seattle.

Family DBT Skills Training

When I developed TARA's family DBT skills course into a manual, it was my hands-on experiences with families that led me to understand what skills in particular would be useful in addressing family needs. TARA's family DBT skills training aims to decrease family stress, increase communication, rebuild trust, diminish stressors or behaviors that maintain BPD behaviors, and improve troubled relationships. The overarching goal is to motivate the person with BPD to enter into effective, evidence-based treatment, such as DBT, so that she can have a life worth living.

Lack of understanding and frustration at not knowing how to help can often be expressed as anger. It is not hard to understand how families' repeated exposure to what seem to be irrational behaviors can lead them to a pattern of negative interactions. Loved ones are dealing with out-of-control situations while trying to control or suppress their own painful emotions. They, too, become emotionally dysregulated; family members may be best described as living with perpetual traumatic stress disorder. They are exhausted and feel defeated after years of trying to find logical explanations for illogical behaviors. When families learn DBT skills, they have the tools they need to reduce the number and intensity of aggressive incidents in the home, decreasing the pathos of their lives and the suffering of their loved ones. Family members who learn more appropriate means of coping become effective and actually see positive changes in their relationships. When families understand and know what to do, their anger can metamorphose into acceptance and compassion. Most important, they can hope once again.

TARA's program is primarily focused on patient outcome and, as John Gunderson advises, "customizes the BPD family environment to make it less stressful for the person with BPD." Family well-being is our secondary goal, although we aim for synthesis of the two. When your loved one does better, so do you. When the person with

BPD is not in treatment, applying DBT skills and MBT skills and attitudes can lead to changes in the home environment that foster trust so that your loved one can believe that he can get better and be motivated to seek evidence based treatment—the ultimate objective of TARA workshops. The family can reinforce DBT skills, can become on-site DBT coaches, and be important adjuncts to treatment. As Marsha Linehan stated at the 2004 annual meeting of the American Association of Behavior Therapy, "Families are an untapped resource for reinforcing DBT skills." Outcome data derived from pre- and post-TARA workshop surveys have shown that family members can learn to be effective parents and partners. This book explains DBT in detail, skill by skill, and will guide you in implementing these skills within your own family.

Additionally, I have adapted techniques based on my application of MBT, developed by Peter Fonegy and Anthony Bateman. Mentalization is an interactive treatment based on meticulous monitoring of moment-by-moment interactions. Whereas DBT focuses on how an individual can learn to regulate his own emotions and change his own behaviors, MBT focuses on how each person in an interaction is thinking and perceiving the situation, moment-by-moment, so as to clarify each person's intentions within the relationships and keep people connected. These mentalization skills will provide you with tools to use to avoid dysregulations and to handle eruptions that are in progress. Graduates of TARA's mentalization program have found these skills to be extremely helpful. Both DBT and MBT rest on acceptance and compassion for the person with BPD.

Whenever a new TARA family DBT workshop begins I am always touched by the body language, facial expressions, and attitudes of the participants. The tension is palpable. I know they are asking themselves, "Why am I here? How is this class going to help my loved one? Or me? What do these strangers know about my pain or how miserable my life has become?" As the first class unfolds they are transformed; they begin to relax, to trust and become hopeful. Participants briefly introduce themselves and describe their situation. The others hear reflections of their own experiences, frustrations, fears, despair, and anger. As participants relate what they do professionally, I can see that the others are stunned. "A lawyer can't solve this problem, this CEO is stressed the same way I am, this medical doctor with all his education doesn't know the answer. I am not the only one struggling to cope with BPD!" Borderline personality disorder is an equal opportunity disease. It is the great leveler, a common denominator among a disparate group of people who begin our workshops as strangers and leave bonded, as new friends. Although participation in the class may not have solved all their problems, they are no longer alone and isolated. They have a path to follow, a community where they are accepted, and, most important, they have new hope.

For all the readers of this book: I too am a family member, and have walked in your shoes. I have endured all that you are enduring. I have been able to reconcile with a loved one in what seemed to be a hopeless relationship. If I was able to do this, so can you! If you are willing to do the hard work it takes to change yourself, this book can serve as your guide for repairing your relationship with someone with BPD. This requires learning about DBT and MBT, applying new coping strategies in your own environment, and having the compassion and humility to try new ways to help your loved one. This book can be your lifeline out of suffering; all you need to do is grab on and hold tight. My sincerest hope is that it will help both you and your loved one.

Acknowledgments

WITH SPECIAL THANKS TO REGINA PISCITELLI, GLEN FEINBERG, Sondra Boone, Sarah Piscitelli, and Leena Newcomb for their encouragement, support, generosity, patience, loyalty, and trust in me;

Thanks to Marsha Linehan, Anthony Bateman, and Peter Fonagy for teaching me how to help;

Thanks to Linda Dimeff, for her guidance and wise counsel;

Thanks to Larry Siever, Martin Bohus, Antonia New, Barbara Stanley, Harold Koenigsberg, Emil Cocarro, and Christain Schmahl for honoring my biological understanding of BPD with their wisdom;

Thanks to Roger Peele for his unwavering professional advocacy;

Thanks to Shari Manning for her help in getting it right;

And especially, thank you to all the TARA graduates, TARA members, BPD sufferers, TARA Callers, and the clinicians who have shared their experiences with me.

Overcoming Borderline Personality Disorder

Loving Someone with Borderline Personality Disorder

The Family Experience

ARE YOU PERPETUALLY STRESSED BECAUSE YOU LOVE SOMEONE who disrupts your life and causes you endless worry? Does it seem as if the person you love can shift from calm to rage to despair in an instant? Do his moods change so rapidly, from angry one moment to composed the next, that you find yourself completely confused, wondering if you have imagined what you have just experienced? Your loved one changes moods as quickly as a cloud moves across the sky on a windy day, appearing happy or calm one moment and suddenly, for no reason apparent to you, becoming angry or completely hopeless a moment later. A mental health professional would describe these mood changes as *lability* or *affective dysregulation*.

Does the person you love seem to lack emotional or behavioral control so that you constantly worry about her safety? Does she engage in myriad dangerous behaviors such as self-injury, eating disorders, addiction to drugs, alcohol, risky sex, gambling, excessive spending, or suicide attempts? Does she drive recklessly or have problems with the law because of her aggressive behaviors? A clinician would describe this behavior as *impulsivity*.

Do you love someone who describes his life as one of daily frustration, unhappiness, and stress, yet seems unable to do anything, to make even the slightest change, to improve matters? Everyday life decisions seem to be major challenges for the person you love. Do you watch helplessly as he makes one bad choice after another? Do his daily struggles with decision making result in crippling inertia, excessive perfectionism, and paralyzing anxiety? Is this complicated by what seems to be an inability to learn from past mistakes or to connect cause with effect? Does he seem as if he is trapped within his own life, locked inside his own brain, like a fly stuck to flypaper? The fly buzzes frantically, but no matter what it does it cannot free itself from the sticky glue. Although this person you love is aware that he is in his own mental prison, he refuses entry to anyone who might help him get free. A clinician would describe this as *difficulty with decision making*, coupled with *inflexible thinking*.

For the person you love, relationships are minefields, veritable disaster areas. She seems to live in an "either-or," "black-white" world where gray does not exist and compromise is an impossibility. Any attempt to negotiate interpersonal conflicts is guaranteed to fail because of her rigid approach to relationships. As suddenly as she may have a new best friend or "love of her life", the relationship will end. She either loves or hates you. She seems unable to find solutions to problems that include compromise, or alternate interpretations of interpersonal interactions. Although she perceives herself as being problem free, she also experiences herself as the perpetual victim of the "bad" behavior of others. *Responsibility* seems to be a word in a remote foreign language, while blaming others and "it's your fault" are her daily mantra. A clinician would describe this as *interpersonal relationship problems*.

Do you love someone who, probably since early childhood, is supersensitive to noise, voice tones, smells, light, clothing textures, or foods? Is he sensitive to the emotional nuances of others? Is he extremely vulnerable to others' responses? Even the slightest hint of criticism, blame, or rejection can evoke a strong reaction, so much so that sometimes he will isolate himself to avoid social interactions. Because you are so close to him, you are often seen as his "judge," "chief criticizer," or "constant blamer." Does your loved one distrust you? Is your life permeated with tension arising from fear of saying or doing the wrong thing? Do you find it impossible to be spontaneous for fear of how your actions may be interpreted? A clinician would describe this as *hypersensitivity* and *hypervigilance*.

Are you frightened by your loved one's intense reactions? Is she so hyperbolic, so extreme, that your home feels like a soap opera set with your loved one cast as the drama queen? Is there a crisis of the day, like the flavor of the week? Do you fear your loved one's behaviors will lead to tragic consequences? Unfortunately, your fears may be justifiable.

Does the person you love taunt you with painful memories? No matter how much time has passed since an incident occurred, no matter how often you have apologized or how many explanations you have offered, or how you have tried to make amends, painful memories do not seem to abate. You are forced to relive distressing events over and over again, with no resolution or forgiveness. These memories seem to have an emotional life of their own.

When the person you love describes an incident from the past, her memory or recollection does not correlate with your own memory of the same event. Her perception is so markedly different from what everyone else in the family recalls that it is as if you were each describing a totally different event. When your loved one recalls her childhood or past experiences, your intuition tells you there is a reason to doubt the validity of her memories. They do not seem to be a reflection of reality as you experienced it. Arguments over what is "true" become family exercises in futility. You are sure your interpretation of the situation is accurate and are determined to prove you are "right." You marshal all the logical reasons you can come up with to prove your point. Consequently, you become willful, and invalidate the perceptions or memories of the person you love. You may even say, "No, that never happened!" Your loved one is now perceived as a liar or manipulator. No one trusts anyone, adding additional strain to your already fragile relationship. A clinician would describe these memory problems as *memory dysregulation* or *cognitive distortions*.

Does your loved one live a life permeated with regrets for what he should have done, fears of "what if's," or anticipation of the imagined consequences of actions he might take? Do you get frantic calls from him all through the day or emergency calls in the middle of the night? A clinician would describe this as *anxiety*.

Does she sleep most of the day and stay awake most of the night, possibly disturbing others? Has this been a problem since infancy or is it a recent development? Are you at your wit's end trying to get her to get out of bed, participate in family life or do something during the day such as go to school, work, or therapy? A clinician would call this a *sleep disorder*.

Thus far you have felt powerless to protect this person you love so much from harm and have been unable to find an effective way to help. You probably feel confused, frustrated, and stressed, and do not know what to do to improve the situation. You are also likely to be bearing the brunt of what appears to you as irrational, manipulative, dangerous, or abusive behaviors. You are frantic with worry that he may be arrested, thereby involving the family with the police, law-yers, and the criminal justice system. You may be financially liable for the consequences of his poor choices and capricious behaviors, such as drunken driving or compulsive shopping. Your pervasive sense of impotence leaves you feeling defeated. You may be angry at yourself, the situation, or at your loved one. Anger may disguise your frustration, fears, and feelings of helplessness. Or, you may react by imposing limits and boundaries, rules and regulations to control his behavior while criticizing, judging, or blaming him for the trouble he got himself into. You may even choose to cut off all contact.

Your efforts to help, to offer support or suggestions for solutions to problems, only seem to aggravate matters. Daily interactions have turned your kitchen into a war zone, you car into a deadly weapon, and your bedroom into a fortress. You have no idea what it is that you say or do that seems to trigger intense mood shifts, explosive erup-tions, sudden rage attacks, retreats from the relationship, or suicide attempts. Sometimes, without any reason apparent to you, your loved one will cut off all communication, completely isolating herself. This can be just as troubling because you sense she is very unhappy and in extreme psychic pain, but you are clueless as to how to ameliorate the situation. This is tantamount to watching helplessly as your loved one is swept away by a giant wave. You see the wave approaching, try to warn her of the impending danger, and are ignored, misunder-stood, or told "don't tell me what to do." You stand by helplessly as the wave engulfs her, unable to prevent a catastrophe that could have been avoided.

Just what is going on here? Whatever it is, it seems to have com-pletely changed your son, daughter, husband, wife, or sibling. The person you knew and loved seems to have disappeared, vanished in a puff of smoke, leaving behind a hollow shell that looks like the person you care so much about—but certainly does not act like he or she once did. You would like someone to wave a magic wand, "fix" your loved one, restore him to "normal," to the way you thought he would be, the way you think he should be. You are desperate to find information, an expert, or an effective treatment that will lift the dark cloud hanging over your family.

If these experiences resonate with you or are descriptions of scenes from your life, it is possible that the apparently competent, intelligent, and talented adolescent or adult that you love may have an emotional disability, may actually be suffering from a diagnosable mental disorder.

It is possible that the apparently competent, intelligent and talented adolescent or adult that you love may be suffering from a diagnosable mental disorder.

What Is Borderline Personality Disorder?

Perhaps, while you described your loved one's behavior, a friend or a clinician may have said, "it sounds like she may have borderline characteristics or traits." Curious, you probably searched the Web for information or looked for books that could help you understand this tornado whirling through your life. Maybe, while looking for something else online, you came across borderline personality disorder (BPD) by accident and realized that the criteria aptly described the person you love. Could all these confusing behaviors actually be indications of a real sickness?

Your loved one may meet criteria for BPD, a severe and persistent psychiatric illness characterized by extreme impulsivity, mood instability, and problems with interpersonal relationships. BPD is classified as one of several personality disorders in the *Diagnostic and Statistical Manual of Mental Disorders, Fourth Edition, Text Revision* (DSM-IV-TR, or DSM for short). The DSM is a publication of the American Psychiatric Association; its most recent edition was released in 2000. The DSM is a universally used system of nomenclature for psychiatric disorders employed for diagnosis and reimbursement by insurance companies, government agencies, and psychiatrists all over the world. For each psychiatric diagnosis, the DSM names, assigns a code number, classifies, and describes symptoms and evidence-based (supported by scientific research) treatments. It can be considered as the bible of the psychiatric community.

The diagnostic criteria for BPD as provided in the DSM-IV-TR are listed in the box on page 9. To meet criteria for the official diagnosis of BPD, a person must have any five out of the nine symptoms; this means that at present there are at least 198 possible combinations of these nine BPD symptoms. According to the DSM, adolescents can be diagnosed with BPD only if they have five of the nine criteria for a sustained period of time (1 year). For adults, no such time requirement exists. The DSM is currently being revised, with the next edition slated for completion in 2013. This means that the criteria for BPD will probably change.

Marsha Linehan, the developer of the most researched, evidence-based treatment for BPD, describes the disorder in a way that may be easier for families to understand than the official language of the DSM. Those with BPD exhibit emotional dysregulation (angry outbursts, emotional instability), interpersonal dysregulation (unstable relationships, trying to avoid loss), behavioral dysregulation (suicide threats or suicidal behaviors), impulsive behaviors (impaired functioning), cognitive dysregulation (poor problem solving, rigid black-white thinking, paranoid ideation, and self-referential thinking), and self-dysregulation (identity confusion, pervasive sense of emptiness, and dissociation).

Can a list of symptoms possibly describe what it is like to live with someone with BPD? How can knowing the symptoms of a disorder help you cope with the daily chaos? Many family members are unaware that the troubling behaviors they struggle with each day are actually the symptoms of a specific disorder called BPD. While it is obvious that the person you love is emotionally distressed, clinicians often do not tell families that their loved one meets the criteria for BPD, what the symptoms are, or how BPD can affect them. You probably have not had access to reliable information, needed coping skills, or any support to alleviate stress or guide you onto a helpful path. You have tried to cope as well as you can, without benefit of supportive help, and mistakes have probably been made. Most family members desperately seek out any professional who will offer them even a scintilla of hope. Somewhere, you believe, there must be a magic pill or a method of treatment that can relieve your loved one's distress

Diagnostic Criteria for Borderline Personality Disorder

A pervasive pattern of instability of interpersonal relationships, self-image, and affects, and marked impulsivity beginning by early adulthood and present in a variety of contexts, as indicated by five (or more) of the following:

1. Frantic efforts to avoid real or imagined abandonment. Note: Do not include suicidal or self-mutilating behavior covered in Criterion 5.
2. A pattern of unstable and intense interpersonal relationships characterized by alternating between extremes of idealization and devaluation.
3. Identity disturbance: markedly and persistently unstable self image or sense of self.
4. Impulsivity in at least two areas that are potentially self-damaging (e.g. spending, sex, substance abuse, reckless driving, binge eating). Note: Do not include suicidal or self-mutilating behavior covered in Criterion 5.
5. Recurrent suicidal behavior, gestures, or threats, or self-mutilating behavior.
6. Affective instability due to a marked reactivity of mood (e.g., intense episodic dysphoria, irritability or anxiety usually lasting a few hours and only rarely more than a few days).
7. Chronic feelings of emptiness.
8. Inappropriate, intense anger or difficulty controlling anger (e.g. frequent displays of temper, constant anger, recurrent physical fights).
9. Transient, stress-related paranoid ideation or severe dissociative symptoms.

Reprinted with permission from the Diagnostic and Statistical Manual of Mental Disorders, Text Revision, Fourth Edition, (Copyright 2000). American Psychiatric Association.

and improve her life. But despite all your efforts, you fail to find a way to make her symptoms go away or even abate. Your loved one will usually refuse to go into treatment, will drop out of treatment, or will not seem to be helped by her current treatment. Or her therapist may refuse to continue treating your loved one, or may even be making things worse. Your personal efforts to help may often backfire as you are attacked for your good intentions.

One out of four people in the general population will suffer with a mental illness at some time in their lives. For most people, mental illness is synonymous with depression, bipolar disorder, or schizophrenia—disorders characterized by behaviors that are in stark contrast to what is considered "normal." If you have difficulty understanding depression, it can be explained by the talking white clouds in the Zoloft commercials, by the national ad campaign that states, "Depression Hurts," or by the numerous celebrities who have come forward to talk about their personal bouts with the illness.

This experience contrasts sharply with that of a family coping with a loved one with BPD. Many people have never heard of BPD, despite recent research by the National Institute on Alcohol Abuse and Alcoholism that indicates as many as 5.9% of the general population meet criteria for BPD. Professionals do not talk much about this disorder on television; your friends may not believe it exists; even Oprah does not discuss it. There is no poster person for BPD rallying support, no telethon to help raise money. No medication approved by the federal Food and Drug Administration has been designated as a "cure" for BPD, and there are no public education campaigns. You and your loved one find yourself adrift in the stormy sea of psychiatry without anything to hold on to or a compass for direction.

Families struggling with BPD feel isolated because the public is largely unaware of BPD, its diagnosis is murky, evidence-based treatments are unavailable in most communities, and support, educational material, and understanding are often unavailable. These factors can help explain the difficulty family members have accepting the diagnosis of BPD. Public perception of BPD can be likened to the plight of AIDS 25 years ago, before it was accepted and understood. At the present time, BPD is treated like psychiatry's stepchild, receiving very little research funding considering the havoc that it wreaks and the prevalence of the disorder. While it is excruciatingly painful to accept that someone you love has BPD, it is easier to cope with a problem when you face and try to understand it.

Apparent Competence

In a famous Carl Sandburg poem, the fog is compared to a cat, moving in furtively, casting a sudden chill into the air, and then, just as suddenly, moving on. BPD, like the fog, is insidious. Painful symptoms can dissipate as quickly as dew evaporating in the morning sun only to creep back, stealthily when you least expect them. BPD can hide from public scrutiny yet suddenly reveal itself within the safety of intimate relationships. Many people with BPD are able to control their behavior in public situations or among strangers. They have the ability to appear calm and competent to outsiders, to act "as if" they are "okay"; but they seem unable to maintain this behavior within intimate relationships with partners or close family members. For families, this *apparent competence* is one of the most frustrating, perplexing, and confusing aspects of BPD. Family members observing the rapid switches from dysregulated, high emotionality at home to seemingly calm and regulated behaviors in public situations have doubts about their own perceptions. They may believe they are imagining the illness. It is in part this apparent competence that can make it so difficult for you and others to accept or believe that the person you love is truly feeling the extreme emotional pain that characterizes BPD.

For families, this apparent competence is one of the most frustrating, perplexing, and confusing aspects of BPD.

The intellectual abilities of most BPD sufferers are not generally affected by the disorder. They can earn university degrees, become doctors, lawyers, CEOs, and have successful careers. Many are very gifted creatively. Despite their intellectual competence, their painful emotional symptoms persist. This dilemma is summed up eloquently by Elinor, a medical student with BPD. "BPD is a monster. It is just so brutal. How can I pass my medical boards one day only to find myself in a psychiatric emergency room just a week later? How can I have a medical degree yet qualify for disability? It is so unfair, so painful, this is not the way it should be." Many people with BPD have never been hospitalized, attempted suicide, or engaged in self-injury. However, despite their "high functioning" ability or apparent competence, people with BPD often do not achieve a high degree of satisfaction in their lives, and instead seem to live lives of quiet desperation. It is baffling to live with a person who can function so well in social situations, is so capable of high functioning behavior in public, and yet who is irrational and abusive in the privacy of your home. When you experience this duality, it is hard to maintain a supportive and compassionate stance toward your loved one. When a stranger enters the room or the telephone rings, your loved one seems to be able to turn off her anger, rage, or despair as quickly as you can channel surf with your remote. Data collected by the Treatment and Research Advancements National Association for Personality Disorder (TARA) through its telephone helpline reveal that such apparent competence is the norm for those with BPD.

Many public figures suffer with BPD but do not publicly acknowledge having the disorder. Owing to their ability to "act as if," it is not surprising that many people with BPD become actors. Unknown to her many admirers, Princess Diana was diagnosed with BPD.[1] She is an example of a public figure who experienced excruciating private psychic pain, despite all of her advantages of wealth and privilege. She employed various maladaptive coping methods, such as self-injury, anorexia-bulimia, compulsive shopping, excessive exercise, stormy relationships with friends, and stalking of her romantic partners. Diana's extreme vulnerability could be sensed in her photographs as well as in her empathetic responses to those in pain. This may have accounted for her enormous public appeal. Despite Diana's masterful apparent competence in public, her grasp of herself and her emotional control crumbled in her private life. Those close to her were just as confused by the secret collapse of her public persona as you probably are by similar situations with your loved one.

The Raised Eyebrow Effect and the Gaslight *Syndrome*

When you describe the explosive, abusive behaviors you have experienced to a spouse, partner, family member, relative, friend, colleague, or professional, when you seek support or advice, you may be surprised when you meet with responses such as, "What are you talking about?

---

[1] Smith, 1999.

He's fine with me!" Or, "I never saw her act like that!" People who are less emotionally involved with the person have probably never witnessed the full-blown BPD behaviors and cannot imagine the apparently sweet or nice person they know as being the hurtful, insulting, abusive, raging, or withdrawing person you are describing. They have had a completely different experience of the person with BPD than you have. They give you a look of incredulousness, a "raised eyebrow," because they doubt the accuracy of your account or narrative, and cannot believe the situation is as bad as you say it is.

This raised eyebrow response from those who have never witnessed BPD behaviors causes you, too, to doubt your own perceptions and feel that it must be you who has the problem. This can be described as the *Gaslight* syndrome, after the classic film of that name. In this movie, Ingrid Bergman plays an heiress who notices that the gaslight is constantly dimming over the dinner table. Each evening she points out the dimming gaslight to her husband, played by Charles Boyer. His response is, "No, darling, the gaslights are certainly not dimming, you are imagining things." As the heiress's perceptions of reality are persistently challenged and invalidated, she begins to believe she is going mad. (It turns out that her husband has been dimming the gaslights in order to make her question her own sanity so that he can steal her fortune.)

When what you perceive is not seen by others, causing you to doubt your own perceptions and intuitions, you too will suffer from the *Gaslight* syndrome. This experience is all too familiar to most family members coping with a loved one with BPD. Have you ever called the police for help or taken your out-of-control loved one to the emergency room only to find that the troublesome behavior seems to disappear when outside help arrives? As you describe the problem that now seems nonexistent, you begin to wonder whether it is you who is overreacting. You may feel foolish and embarrassed, and lose credibility with the very people you turned to for help. You feel as though you are dining with Boyer and Bergman, watching the gaslights dim.

Only when family or friends actually witness the behaviors you have described do they begin to understand. They will then become fountains of potentially harmful advice. They may tell you to "Get tough! His behavior is awful, he needs to be held responsible for what he does." "No wonder she acts like that, you are too lenient. You are enabling her." You are told to set rigid rules, enact severe punishments, boundaries, or limits, and apply "tough love." Desperate parents may be uncomfortable utilizing these methods, but because they have run out of alternatives, they capitulate. They may know intuitively that these punitive methods are inappropriate, but they implement them anyway because they do not know what else to do and are overwhelmed by fear, frustration, and feelings of powerlessness. Partners are often advised to leave their spouses. After all, why would anyone put up with such behavior? Although partners may love their significant other and want to make their relationship work, they just do not know how. They may be embarrassed in front of others because they choose to remain in the relationship; there may also be children to think of.

It probably seems as if no one understands what you are going through. You are correct; most people have no idea what it is like to cope with this very difficult, emotionally debilitating disorder. You are a member of a club no one wants to join.

BPD and Family Relationships

Coping with an adolescent, adult child, parent, sibling, spouse, partner, friend, or colleague with BPD is very difficult. It puts great pressure on any relationship and on all the members of a family. People with BPD are often extremely self-involved, due in part to their neurobiological deficits (see Chapter 2), and do not realize how hard you are trying to help them. They often reject your concerns and offers of help, perceiving these as efforts to control them. As a consequence, you feel hurt, disappointed, neglected, unappreciated, tired, sick, or sad. Life with someone with BPD often feels like a one-way street of giving. When Jessica, a TARA family group participant, heard the sagas of other group members, she would repeat, over and over again, "Don't you realize? You just don't count!" Family members live in an invalidating environment where their love and concern is rejected, distrusted or criticized and is unacknowledged.

Family members live in an invalidating environment where their love and concern is rejected, distrusted or criticized, and is unacknowledged.

Every relationship has different expectations and responsibilities and is affected differently by BPD. The quality and dynamics of the relationship are dependent on how close you are to the person with BPD and by the support and understanding available to you.

Parents of Those with BPD

The way parents cope with their child with BPD is a reflection of their personalities and their styles of handling all aspects of their lives. One parent may be permissive and conflict aversive (avoiding conflict at all costs), while the other may tend to be more critical, aggressive, and prone to utilizing *aversive control* (controlling behavior that is hurtful, punishing, and eventually harmful). One parent may jump when her son with BPD has a crisis while the other will respond by imposing "rules" and "boundaries." Two distinct coping styles within one family sends a very confusing message to the person with BPD.

Picture a type-A alpha male, a highly successful and well-respected businessman with a lifetime record of solving problems very well. The buck stops with him, he gets things done, resolves disputes, protects and provides. He believes that by making things easier for his daughter with BPD, he is helping her recover. He provides apartments and jobs, and bails her out of all her financial difficulties. When his daughter has arguments with his wife, his solutions to the problems are in direct opposition to his wife's position. After all, he is the one who knows how to "fix" problems—that is his job. When he applies his philosophy to his BPD daughter, it does not work; instead of improving, she gets worse. His wife feels that by solving all of his daughter's problems he is preventing her from experiencing the natural consequences of her own behavior. The husband refuses to back up his wife's attempts to impose any consequences on his daughter because he is sure his methods will eventually prevail, even though his wife is frequently the target of the girl's abusive behavior. He cannot accept that he is up against a situation that he cannot control. His wife resents his refusal to try her way. She has researched BPD, consulted with experts, and is learning as much as she can. She believes that following Dialectical Behavior Therapy principles will help her daughter and motivate her to consult a therapist. Her husband's behavior invalidates her efforts to protect herself from her daughter's unrelenting abuse and help her daughter to solve her own problems.

Each partner feels his or her coping style is best and would be effective if only the other would be more supportive. Their ensuing power struggle and reciprocal invalidation leads to continuous arguments. This schism in attitude leads to seismic disturbances, threatening the core foundation of their relationship. The frustration and sense of failure each parent experiences when coping with BPD can make or break a marriage. This couple may very well find themselves on the verge of divorce.

Blame often plays a significant role in the life of a parent, especially when a child has a mental illness. The working mother may believe that these problems would not have happened if she had stayed home with her child. The stay-at-home mom may believe the illness was caused by her being around all the time. If she had gone to work, the situation would have been better. The lenient parent might believe he should have been stricter, enforced more rules, set more limits, while the disciplined parent blames himself for not giving the child more "space." Some parents vacillate between leniency and authority, blaming each other. The divorced parent blames the divorce for BPD; the parents with adopted children blame BPD on the adoption. Many parents are guilt-ridden, thinking that something they did or did not do might have prevented the disorder, but this is not so.

If family and friends have never witnessed the BPD storms of a teenager, the parents coping with an adolescent with BPD will get responses such as "you're overreacting, it's just typical adolescent behavior!" Are the rages, mood changes, withdrawals, and offensive behaviors simply indications of typical teenage rebellions or impulsive behaviors? Does any situation merit so intense an outburst or justify so virulent a response? A teenager with BPD, struggling with emotional pain and isolation, tries to cope as "best" as he can but does not know what to do to reduce his aversive feelings. Peer pressure and social standards are powerful motivators. The most readily available ways for teenagers to cope with and decrease their pain will often be drugs, alcohol, sexual promiscuity, or risky, dangerous, and impulsive behaviors. You fear for the safety of your child yet you are advised that you are making a fuss over trivial issues. The not-so-hidden message here is that your responses are "excessive, inappropriate, or extreme." You are seen as pathologizing normalcy—making up a disease where none exists. You are persuaded to doubt your own perceptions and deny your intuitions, to oversimplify how you ought to respond to these difficult or dangerous BPD behaviors. It is very hard to stand up to this pressure. "He'll outgrow it." "She'll get a job, then everything will be okay." "As soon as she meets someone, she'll be fine." "This is just a phase." If one parent sees it this way and you do not, even if you are divorced, you are in for a bumpy ride. You are, in essence, coping alone while having to justify your responses to the other parent.

Time and again the TARA helpline receives phone calls from concerned family members who believe their teenager is exhibiting behaviors symptomatic of BPD, or meets criteria for BPD, but who are told that BPD cannot be diagnosed in children or adolescents. Before it was revised 10 years ago, the DSM-IV stated that adolescents could not be diagnosed with BPD until they were 18 years of age. At 18, they had a psychiatric "bar mitzvah" and became official BPD sufferers.

Fortunately, this is no longer true today as the DSM-IV-TR clearly states that children or adolescents can be diagnosed with BPD if their symptoms persist for at least 1 year. Many professionals are either unaware of the DSM-IV-TR classification or are just leery of diagnosing BPD in children or adolescents. Thus, many adolescents are misdiagnosed and slip through the cracks of the mental health system. Again, parents are left in confusion as the diagnosis is not verified, and yet they know something is not right. But they have no credibility. When diagnosis and treatment of BPD in adolescents is avoided or delayed, future treatment is compromised, especially when the person is treated for a diagnosis he or she does not have. Early intervention and access to treatment would probably prevent development of harmful coping methods such as substance abuse, driving while intoxicated, unsafe sex, and unwanted pregnancies. At the present time, failure to diagnose and treat adolescents, along with the paucity of evidence-based treatments available in most communities, can be very harmful.

> At the present time, failure to diagnose and treat adolescents, along with the paucity of evidence-based treatments available in most communities, can be very harmful.

Many school counselors are generally not well informed about BPD, resulting in the school system's failure to meet the needs of adolescents with this disorder. At school, a student's maladaptive attempts to cope are usually treated as discipline problems. When attempting to control their teenagers' acting out behavior and keep them safe, many parents elect to send them to highly structured wilderness programs or residential treatment programs. Unfortunately, parents learn through sad experience that these programs and residential treatment facilities, usually costing outrageous amounts, do not teach their teenagers how to control their impulsive behaviors and moods, or how to solve problems effectively, as they are not providing the evidence-based treatment shown to be effective for BPD. While the teens may do well while they are in the program, they quickly regress to maladaptive and dangerous behaviors as soon as they return to their home environment. Sadly, many teenagers end up in the juvenile justice system as a consequence of their aggressive coping behaviors.

Paula's 18-year-old daughter Lilly was diagnosed with BPD as well as a severe addiction to alcohol. Lilly had spent much of the last 4 years hospitalized, a major portion of this time in seclusion and restraint because she became violent when she drank. Somehow, Lilly always seemed to be able to obtain alcohol, even when hospitalized. Instead of treating Lilly's alcoholism and BPD, the various hospitals simply locked her up. What effect did seclusion and restraint have on this very intelligent and sensitive young woman? The only way Lilly knew how to cope with her emotional pain was to drink, yet none of her hospitalizations helped this condition. She had not learned how to live outside of a hospital setting, so the vicious cycle repeated itself. Desperate for help, the parents, both of whom were medical doctors, brought her to a hospital famous for treating people with BPD. Unfortunately, once again she found alcohol while there, once again became violent, and was placed in seclusion and restraint. The hospital decided she was too difficult to treat and discharged her without a treatment plan in place. The parents asked, "If you won't treat Lilly, who will? What do you suggest we do to help our daughter?" They were told that that they would treat Lilly's BPD when alcoholism was no longer a problem. Lilly was treated as though she were a throw-away person. Her parents were left to cope with Lilly on their own, at home.

Parents of an adolescent are on the first rung of the BPD ladder, at the very beginning of the BPD roller coaster ride. You will need to be persistent in finding effective treatment for your teenager rather than wasting years on harmful, ineffective therapies that leave everyone feeling defeated and hopeless.

Senior parents of an adult child with BPD are faced with a heartbreaking dilemma. You must acknowledge to yourself that you are not going to live forever. At the same time you must face the fact that, at the present time, your son or daughter with BPD lacks the skills to provide for himself or herself. Older parents are terrified that no one will be there to help their son or daughter when they are gone. This is a valid fear. Some parents attempt to solve this problem by establishing trusts administered by lawyers or mental health agencies. Martha and Sid established such a trust with the intention of providing for Helen, their daughter with BPD. Unfortunately, instead of consulting Helen while making these arrangements, they imposed them upon her. When Helen discovered what her parents had done, she was enraged. She severed her relationship with her parents and even refused to visit her father when he suffered a heart attack. Helen believed that her parents were trying to control her from their grave and were labeling her as incompetent in perpetuity. Helen perceived her exclusion from these arrangements as proof that her parents viewed her as helpless and hopeless. When interacting with someone with BPD, your intentions are not nearly as important as how you actually act upon them. Had Martha and Sid consulted Helen while they were planning the trust, given her the opportunity to make choices and have some control of her own life, they might have negotiated a solution that was acceptable to all of them. A great deal of relationship repair was needed to reestablish communication in this family.

Parents of older adults have been seeking help and ways to cope for a very long time. They probably began their search before BPD was identified or effective treatments were developed. Most blame themselves for the problem. They have accumulated many, many years of stress, fear, and failure. Their concern, love, and feelings of powerlessness to help their loved one over so much time leave them either emotionally burnt out or even more vulnerable to the caprices of BPD behaviors. If you are an older parent, you need to know that your loved one will be safe and independent when you are no longer around to solve problems and provide financial support.

Siblings of Those with BPD

The plight of brothers and sisters of those with BPD has been neglected by the mental health community. To date, sibling relationships and BPD have not been the subject of significant research. While coping with a brother or sister with BPD, siblings are often deeply affected and conflicted, as they may also be dealing with a family that has itself been disrupted and dysregulated by the myriad problems brought about by coping with BPD. A brother or sister with BPD is like a black hole in space that absorbs so much of the family's attention and concern that the needs of the other children (even when they are adults) are often overlooked. Their excellent achievements may fail to garner the attention and recognition they deserve because their parents are too absorbed with keeping the sibling with BPD safe, and putting out the "crisis of the day fires." Their own problems may be neglected as a consequence of their parents' focus on the BPD sibling. Siblings are pressured to be perfect, to be "the good one" and to do the "right thing" to compensate for the "wrong" behavior of the BPD sibling. They realize their parents are suffering and do not want to add to their burden, hence the pressure to be "perfect." They may be scrutinized and encouraged to be perfect to such a degree that the family pathologizes their normalcy out of fear that they may "become" like their BPD sibling. They may be very angry at their BPD sibling for the pain he or she has caused their parents. They may express their anger and resentment with passive aggression or by being rebellious themselves and acting out.

When siblings are close in age, others in the community are probably aware of the unusual or dangerous behaviors of the sibling with BPD, causing embarrassment in front of peers, in school, and in the community. This can foster enough anger and resentment that they may eventually cut off contact with the entire family. Some siblings take on the responsibility of caring for their BPD sibling as they realize that their parents are aging and that their brother or sister cannot cope with life very well on his or her own. They accept that they will have to shoulder this burden when their parents pass on. Siblings are also put in difficult positions regarding loyalty to their parents or loyalty to their sibling with BPD, whom they may love and look up to, particularly when their BPD sibling is the eldest. They live on an emotional diet of ambivalence and conflict as they struggle to come to terms with a relationship that baffles adults.

How can children raised in the same family environment have such marked contrasts and different outcomes? Barbara, a delightful, well-adjusted young woman, has an older sister with BPD who is also addicted to heroin. Barbara feels that "I won the family gene lottery. It is not my sister's fault that she didn't get the good genes." At the age of 15 Barbara attended the TARA family DBT workshop with her parents. She realized that the problems of coping with a sibling or a parent with BPD were unique and, with TARA's help, she developed a sibling program teaching teens relevant coping skills while giving them an opportunity to express their concerns and frustrations and share their feelings. Barbara's insights have informed this discussion of siblings. Another family has two sons who are very close, yet their daughter with BPD is estranged from them and has been out of their lives for over 10 years. Another family has seven successful sons, all of whom attended TARA classes to learn how to help their sister with BPD. She perceives herself as alone and isolated despite the support and concern of her seven brothers.

Partners and Spouses

People with BPD have many positive qualities. They are often exciting, challenging, interesting, artistically talented, very sensitive, and highly intelligent. Women who like to be taken care of can be very appealing and attractive to the type of man who likes to be the problem solver and family "fixer." You may really love your partner or spouse. However, partners or spouses of someone with BPD have very different problems, needs, expectations, and options from those of parents who have a child with BPD. A parent may be able to accept giving unconditional love without reciprocity since this is part of having children. For a partner or spouse, however, this is much more difficult. You have a right to expect a reciprocal relationship. However, most people with BPD are unable to maintain one. This is devastating, hurtful, and baffling for a partner. Initially, most partners will go to extreme lengths to work at their relationships, are determined to find a way to "fix" them, and would feel like quitters or failures if they did not try. While you have the option of leaving, severing the relationship, or getting a divorce, if you do decide to leave, you need to know you have done all you could to resolve the relationship. Leaving in anger can result in stalking, domestic violence, or combative, exhaustive, revengeful divorces.

Carla tried to cope with Ben, her partner with BPD. As time passed, his volatile symptoms and acting-out behaviors became more and more severe. Ben was jealous, controlling, prone to temper tantrums, financially irresponsible, and verbally abusive. As the stress within the relationship increased, Carla herself became more and more dysfunctional. She was less able to cope or protect herself and began exhibiting battered wife symptoms. Carla was no longer behaving or thinking like the competent, hopeful person she had been. She was burned out. Their relationship spiraled into violence, the police arrested Ben, and an order of protection was issued by the courts. At this point she remarked, "BPD may have genetic components but, for me, it is contagious."

Divorcing a person with BPD usually results in complex and lengthy court battles, orders of protection, nasty custody fights, allegations of abuse and domestic violence, stalking, and/or frequent change of attorneys resulting in added expenses and delays as well as prolongation of acute emotional distress. When children are involved, the situation becomes extremely complicated as the children also become victims of the resulting stressors.

Spouses are devastated by untrue accusations their BPD spouses may make and will obsessively defend themselves. Most confusing are the frequent declarations of love from a BPD partner in the midst of a retributional, revengeful divorce. Divorcing someone with BPD usually ends up with pain, unhappiness, and a high degree of dysfunction for the other partner. Professional help is usually needed to overcome the trauma of these painful divorces. It would be helpful if lawyers and judges dealing with these cases were knowledgeable about BPD so they could make more informed decisions. Although you may justifiably feel duped, cheated, or betrayed, the person who is suffering the most in this divorce is the partner with BPD. No matter what she may have done or failed to do, surely it was not her intention to do so, as she has so little control over her impulsive behaviors. When you understand BPD, you can try to integrate compassion into your attitude toward your spouse and negotiate a separation or divorce with greater sensitivity to your partner's needs, leaving the marriage with less anger and resentment. Afterward, you will need to find a way to rebuild your life without anger or bitterness, and you may have great difficulty trusting another partner.

Children of Those with BPD

A child whose parent has BPD is dependent on a person who is mercurial and impulsive, yet the child may be too young to understand
that his parent has a mental disorder. The suffering experienced
by children of someone with BPD is tragic. They generally blame
themselves for their parent's quixotic mood changes and emotional
outbursts. They grow up thinking they are never good enough or are
"bad" because their parent is so often upset with them. They do not
have the opportunity to be children because they have to learn how
to keep their parent with BPD calm and avoid conflict rather than
receiving the unconditional love, acceptance, and concern children are
entitled to. As adults they may be burdened with anger and resentment. Children of a parent with BPD need help in radically accepting
their parent's illness and understanding that they do not have to take
personal responsibility for it. They must also allow themselves to
experience grief for their thwarted childhoods. They also need the
guidance and support of the other parent to balance this painful and
unfair situation.

Often, the parent without BPD is angry with his partner and may
turn the child against the parent with BPD. While this is logically understandable, it ignores the important attachment relationship that exists
between a child and a parent, an attach-
ment that is real and vital to the child
and should not be minimized, no matter
what the parent's diagnosis may be. The
child of a parent with BPD needs to
develop compassion for his parent as
well as for himself. Many self-help books
and Internet resources available for the general public tend to vilify the
BPD parent, as if her intention was to harm her child. They blame the
BPD parent for the problems the adult child may now have. People do
not ask to have BPD, nor do they intentionally hurt their children.

The child of a parent with BPD needs to develop compassion for his parent as well as for himself.

Although a parent plays a crucial role in the emotional well-being
of a child or adult child, the existence of BPD in a parent calls for
forgiveness, compassion, and acceptance if the troubled relationships
are to find any resolution. It is certainly not fair to a child to have a
parent with BPD, but unfortunately, this is the way it is. Surely there

are some positive qualities in the parent, and a great deal can be gained by accepting that the parent with BPD is doing the best he or she can.

What Families Need

After a while it can become difficult to discern who in the family actually has BPD, as dysfunctional and maladaptive coping has become the family style. Which comes first, the chicken or the egg? Did the family always behave in this dysfunctional manner, or have unsuccessful attempts to cope with a loved one with BPD over time and continuous invalidation of their efforts led to this level of burnout and despair? It is at this point, usually in the midst of a major family crisis that has escalated to operatic, epic proportions, that a clinician will meet the family for the very first time.

To improve the situation you will need to acknowledge the illness, as well as the fear, pain, disappointment, and loss you have experienced as you struggled to cope with your loved one with BPD. When you understand BPD, learn hands-on methods for decreasing the stress you live with each and every day, and learn effective means of coping with "irrational" BPD behaviors, your fears will decrease. Face the facts and acknowledge that you are incapable of solving the problems of your loved one's dysregulated and dangerous behaviors. This problem is over your head and you need help.

You need the support of your friends and relatives, for them to realize that you are a beleaguered family member doing the best you can in the moment. This may mean that you will have to educate them about BPD, just as you are educating yourself. Additionally you will have to reflect on what you have endured over the years as you have tried to cope with this painful disorder and confront the sadness you feel for what your loved one, you, and your family have lost because of living with BPD; then you must grieve your invalidated losses. You also need your grief to be acknowledged and validated by the psychiatric community, which often fails to recognize the struggles of BPD families, even going so far as to blame them for the illness. The perpetual state of traumatic stress that you have been living in merits recognition by clinicians as well as by relatives and friends.

Sometimes you cannot do any more than what you are presently doing because you are burned out by the constant effort and energy you have expended over a very long time in coping with your loved one's BPD symptoms and behaviors. You have been "on duty" 24 hours a day for many years. Few professionals could maintain so rigorous a schedule. You probably spend more time with the person with BPD than anyone else. You, too, are burned out, yet your needs usually go unmet. You are left feeling isolated and overwhelmed. You need the emotional support to be found in BPD support groups and the real- ization that you are not alone, that other people have faced the same problems, changed their behavior, and improved their relationships and family functioning. You need to read stories of improvement and recovery. This is essential and invaluable.

Many of the difficult experiences described in this book might have been minimized or avoided if those with BPD had been cor- rectly diagnosed in a timely manner, received evidence-based treat- ments early on, and if the family had known what environmental conditions needed to change and how to change them. When pre- sented with concrete evidence of the disorder and what is needed, families can make positive changes and repair their relationships. You did not intentionally harm your loved one with BPD, but neverthe- less mistakes have almost certainly been made.

Milk is the universal nourishment for babies. In every culture in the world as well as in the animal kingdom, just moments after emerging from the womb, infants suckle at their mothers' breasts because milk makes babies healthy and strong. If you deprived a baby of milk you would be seen as a cruel and neglectful parent. Since you believe that milk is good for a child, you nurse her, give her milk. You include milk in your child's diet, in desserts, sauces, cereals, and soups. Believing you are doing the best you can for your baby, you supplement her diet with yogurt, cream, ice cream, cheeses, sheep, or goat milk, which you believe are essential for her healthy devel- opment. Despite all your good intentions, your child becomes sickly. Unbeknownst to you, it is drinking milk that is causing her rashes, colic and illness. Your pediatrician never suggested that your baby might be allergic to milk (lactose intolerant). Are you a bad parent? If you had been aware that the baby was allergic to milk, would you have continued to give her milk? Despite your love and concern, whatever you do seems to cause your loved one more pain. You have been doing the wrong thing over and over again for the right reasons.

Getting Help

How can you be certain that a given treatment will be helpful? How can you separate evidence-based treatments from those that are not proven effective? How can you ensure that a therapist is qualified to treat BPD? First, you need to educate yourself about this disorder, but you must be selective about where you get your information. You may have read self-help books or searched the Internet, or attended 12-step meetings or support groups, or even visited chat rooms specializing in BPD. But this can be problematic; for instance, many Internet chat rooms are not supervised or monitored by anyone trained in effective methodology or evidence-based treatment. You may have acted on bad advice and incorrect information from well-meaning family and friends who are also not experts on BPD. This is the blind leading the blind.

The process of finding a therapist usually begins by asking friends for recommendations, but the results may be poor. Most of us do not know how specialized and trained a clinician must be to help someone with BPD. Instead, we unconditionally accept with blind faith whatever mental health professionals tell us because we believe that such professionals do not make mistakes. After all, lawyers, doctors, or accountants can solve your problems—they are professionals, they know what to do. Unfortunately, we are not generally aware of the difference between one kind of mental health professional and another, between one diagnosis and another, or one treatment approach and another.

Instead of relying on family and friends' recommendations and word-of-mouth, seek out experts who have written books on BPD, have done research on the disorder, or are heads of psychiatry in teaching hospitals, medical schools, and universities. You want to be sure that your loved one gets the very best help (especially as you may be paying for this treatment, which is often not covered by insurance)—and not every therapist is an expert in diagnosing and treating BPD.

Challenges of the BPD Diagnosis

Clinicians are often reluctant to diagnose BPD, circumventing the diagnosis by saying that the person has BPD "features" or "traits" but does not meet full criteria for BPD. What does this mean? Is this the equivalent of telling someone they are just a little bit pregnant?

Clinicians will often advise families that it is better not to "label" their loved one with the diagnosis of BPD, perhaps fearing that knowing she meets criteria for a specific mental illness called BPD will result in your stigmatizing her. How can you think badly about something you have never heard of before and know nothing about?

Clinicians are often reluctant to diagnose BPD, circumventing the diagnosis by saying that the person has BPD "features" or "traits" but does not meet full criteria for BPD.

Sometimes clinicians treating your loved one or consulted for advice on how to handle your family problems will not tell you the diagnosis, nor will they explain the symptoms, etiology, or prognosis for BPD because they are constrained by regulations of confidentiality. If your loved one had a heart condition or multiple sclerosis or any other physical disorder, you would certainly be informed. You would be offered literature on the disorder and would be considered an adjunct to treatment. When the diagnosis of BPD is only hinted at, downplayed, or not revealed at all, the family continues in its uninformed emotional maze, searching for ways to cope and help.

People with BPD engage in many dangerous behaviors and are at high risk for suicide. Family members cannot deal effectively with safety issues when the psychiatric world they turn to for help avoids, minimizes, or trivializes the problem. This is not helpful. Families need to know the truth. Presumably, clinicians justify not giving the person the actual diagnosis so as to soften the "blow" of acknowledging BPD. Or they are told that BPD is a "garbage bag" or "waste basket" diagnosis and cannot be treated. Conversely, some clinicians treat people with BPD for years and years without any real improvement. Marsha Linehan has repeatedly stated at professional conferences that "if your patient isn't better in a year, you should find another therapist for your patient."

A great deal of confusion surrounds the diagnosis of BPD partly because an easily administered, universally accepted, comparably validated instrument for diagnosing BPD has not yet been developed, such as are used with other mental disorders. For example, the Hamilton Beck Inventory is one of several instruments used to diagnose depression. Anxiety is diagnosed with what is known as the Barrett scale. This situation is further complicated by the fact that BPD symptoms overlap or co-occur with many other disorders.

Misdiagnosis

Many clinicians diagnose BPD as bipolar disorder to ensure that the person receives insurance coverage. But this is problematic because bipolar medication is then prescribed, which is not effective and often makes people with BPD feel worse. This also contributes to the problem of *polypharmacy*, wherein patients are prescribed multiple medications that do not work, and then become reluctant to take any medications at all. Furthermore, Medicare does not have a billing code for BPD, thus BPD is generally described by its co-occurring disorders such as substance abuse, anxiety, and/or depression. This results in the lack of funding for research on new treatment programs as the data for the incidence of BPD do not justify such funding. This is a catch 22 situation that only continuous advocacy will change.

Not all misdiagnosis of BPD is intentional. People with BPD are often misdiagnosed as having an array of other disorders before an eventual diagnosis of BPD is made. Analysis of data collected from thousands of family members who have called the TARA helpline reveals that a person diagnosed with BPD has generally had at least five prior diagnoses, including attention-deficit hyperactivity disorder (ADHD), depression, bipolar disorder, anxiety disorder, posttraumatic stress disorder (PTSD), oppositional defiant disorder (ODD), intermittent explosive disorder, (IED) conduct disorder (CD), narcissism, substance abuse and/or alcoholism, and eating disorder. While many disorders can coexist with BPD, other disorders often tend to mask BPD so that it remains undiagnosed.

Anna's 9-year-old son Sean exhibited extremely difficult behaviors. A renowned psychiatrist diagnosed him with bipolar disorder and prescribed mood stabilizers. When Anna and her husband read books and professional journals on bipolar disorder, they felt this diagnosis did not describe Sean's behavior. The boy did not improve with this treatment. In fact, he got worse. They consulted another esteemed doctor who proclaimed that the boy had ADHD and prescribed medication. As Anna and her husband became experts on ADHD, they realized that this diagnosis did not explain Sean's behavioral problems, either—did not fit their son as they knew him. Again, their son's behavior did not improve. The next doctor they consulted diagnosed Sean with Asperger's syndrome. Again, they studied everything they could find, consulted books, professional articles, and

Web sites. The boy continued to have impulsive outbursts and nothing Anna and her husband were advised to do seemed to help. They tried again. This time it was suggested that Sean met criteria for BPD. At this point the family was shell-shocked, traumatized by a psychiatric community that, in all its erudition, had not offered them any hands-on skills to help the boy or themselves. These caring, intelligent parents gave up on finding a specific diagnosis or label that described their son's behavior and concentrated, instead, on teaching him the skills that could help him control his behavior and tolerate distress. They taught him DBT skills (see Chapter 4). As the boy learned how to control his behavior, the explosive episodes began to abate. Although he was by no means "cured," he was finally able to go back to school. This devoted and perseverant family, working together in an informed manner, managed to dramatically improve the situation.

Each new diagnosis brings the hope that you have found the answer, that the problem can now be dealt with and your loved one will finally get the help he needs. With each new diagnosis, you read books or search the Web for information. By the time your loved one is diagnosed with BPD, you have probably become an expert on many disorders.

Iatrogenic Advice: Tough Love

Mental health professionals counseling family members of people with BPD often advise them to implement "tough love," "set boundaries, sign contracts, and impose limits" as a means of making the person responsible for herself and her actions. They are told to "just walk away, take care of yourself, you are entitled to your life. Mourn her and move on." Much of the advice you may have received from clinicians, self-help books, and chat rooms, as well as from family and friends, extols iatrogenic measures that almost always do more harm than good. *Iatrogenic* is a term meaning harm that is doctor-generated. These methods generally lead to worsening or actual severing of family relationships, leading to catastrophic consequences for the person with BPD and the family. Tough love type actions usually destroy whatever fragile remnants of trust remain in your relationship with your loved one with BPD. How can someone ever trust a parent who refuses to help her, throws her out, has her arrested, or locks her away in an institution, all in the name of love? The person with BPD interprets these actions as a rejection and betrayal. From her perspective, it certainly is.

Research does not demonstrate that tough love is effective in bringing about positive changes for people with BPD. Families will act upon this advice even though it is usually counterintuitive to what their hearts tell them to do because they are desperate for a solution and they are unaware of other alternatives. Spouses or partners are often advised to leave their significant other leading to lengthy, costly, and emotionally draining divorce actions with often irreparable and disastrous consequences to both the relationship and their children. Without intending to, family members have hurt their loved one with BPD. Tough love techniques move them further and further away from the compassionate understanding that can ameliorate the situation. What other illness is treated so cruelly? How can we justify punishing people for their symptoms as a means of helping them? Public health policy no longer supports seclusion and restraint as an effective treatment for mental disorders. It is being abolished all over the nation—and yet it is still used as a means to prevent BPD suicides. Surely there is a better way to help people in pain who cannot control their impulsive behaviors than to reject and punish them.

> *Research does not demonstrate that tough love is effective in bringing about positive changes for people with BPD.*

BPD Stigma

Many clinicians will limit the number of BPD patients they will treat or will outright refuse to treat patients with BPD because they find these patients too needy, difficult, or time-consuming. Ineffective advice is generally given and little hope for improvement is offered. The person with BPD usually senses the clinician's negative attitude toward him. He not only fails to improve but may even get worse. As his symptoms escalate, he is fulfilling the clinician's prophecy about how difficult it is to treat someone with BPD. The clinician may attribute his failure to improve as an indication that the patient is simply a "bad patient" or is "treatment resistant" and will abruptly drop him. When the patient exhibits acting-out behaviors or threatens suicide, the very behaviors that led him to seek treatment in the first place, some programs may declare, "We can't help you, your problems are too severe." Imagine a mother watching while her child climbs a tree. Worried that the child might fall, she says, "If you fall and break your leg, don't come running to me." Can you imagine a kidney specialist telling the patient whose kidney disease is not responding to treatment that he is treatment resistant, and therefore the physician will no longer treat him?

When professionals blame an illness on a "bad patient" they crush the person's hope of ever finding help. This is devastating to both patients and their families. The implied message is that if he were a "good" patient, he would get better. The "bad patient" has not responded to treatment even though there may not be any scientific evidence that the treatment offered is actually effective. The idea that the treatment failed, not the patient, is generally not considered. When family members concur with this point of view, they become complicit with the professional community in dooming the person with BPD, depriving him of hope and nailing him into an emotional coffin.

BPD is a disorder that can polarize clinicians into behaviors that can be described as stigmatizing, or just plain "I can't stand this patient." The response of a mental health professional treating a patient with BPD without training in effective methods such as DBT (see Chapter 4) or mentalization (see Chapter 9) is akin to a family member's response. Frustration can make clinicians feel as uncomfortable, ineffective, impotent, and inadequate as family members do. However, they can attribute their unpleasant feelings to the "treatment resistant patient" and/or her "dysfunctional" family. Difficult BPD behaviors can certainly justify clinicians' decision to give up on the patient. If angry, frustrated family members walk out on the person with BPD, they are more likely to experience guilt, blame, and failure. They will also run the risk of being demonized by the person with BPD. With evidence-based treatment and compassionate support, people with BPD can and do get better. Without hope, families will be far less helpful and less likely to have compassion for their loved one.

When your loved one has BPD and you seek help from a mental health professional, you yourself will often meet with negative and judgmental attitudes. If you consult with a clinician on your own for help with coping with your BPD relative, you will probably be treated as a victim of BPD behaviors and encouraged to set limits and create boundaries—after all you have a right to your own life. If you meet with a clinician in conjunction with your loved one's treatment, such as in multi-family groups, be aware that most of the clinicians you consult are generally accustomed to blaming you for causing BPD. Prevailing unsubstantiated theories regarding the origins of BPD view the disorder as the inevitable result of sexual, physical, or emotional abuse, or of the child's failure to attach to the parent as she developed. When you are in a clinician's office, you are generally being observed for pathology to confirm how you and the family must have contributed to the disorder. Clinicians often presume that somehow you must have abused your child, thereby causing BPD. Latest research indicates that abuse is not a prerequisite for BPD; all people with BPD have not been abused. Sometimes it is important to remember that the perception of an experience is not the same as the actual experience.

Most of these accusations are based on reports from the person with BPD, on the perceptions of someone who has cognitive distortions and overreactions to her own life that are not corroborated. Or, parents are told that they enabled the person, did not allow her to grow up, separate, and individuate. This is so painful for a parent to experience; it is as if a flash flood has occurred, your child is drowning, and as you are trying to save her, you are accused of causing the flood. For family members, it is devastating to be treated without compassion, to be blamed for causing the problem while you feel guilty for failing to keep your loved one safe or finding a means to help her. Your efforts to help are invalidated by your loved one, other family and friends, and the very professionals you thought would help you. Psychiatric literature is replete with these theories, thus far lacking sufficient data to substantiate or corroborate this hypothesis.

A single mother was desperate for help because her 17 year-old daughter was out of control. Her daughter's behavior ran the gamut from abuse toward her mother to drug use, shop lifting, and sexual promiscuity. Frantic with worry about how to keep her daughter safe, the mother brought her daughter to a therapist recommended by a friend. In a subsequent family session, the clinician informed the two that this was "the worst mother and daughter relationship" he had ever seen. As a consequence of the therapist's insensitive and iatrogenic remark, it became even more difficult for the mother to keep her daughter safe than it had been before she had sought professional help. The daughter, vindicated by the therapist's comment, felt justified in disregarding her mother's attempts to control her behavior and often quoted the therapist. Her out-of-control behavior escalated, and their relationship deteriorated at a rapid pace, resulting in this young girl's leaving home and having no contact with her mother for many years. The mother was billed for the treatment that alienated her daughter.

When a clinician alienates a person from his family or fosters the development of negative feelings, and subsequently drops him from treatment because he is "treatment resistant" or because his family is no longer paying the bill, the person with the disorder usually returns to the only support available to him, the demonized family that was trying to help him in the first place. At this point the family dynamic is even more difficult because the therapist has fostered development of even more negative feelings toward the patient's family.

In the grand scheme of societal stigma toward mental disorders, families of people with BPD presently rank number one, overtaking their predecessors, the "schizophrenogenic mothers" purported to cause their children's schizophrenia or the "ice-box" or "refrigerator mothers" of autistic children whose cold and nonbonding behavior supposedly caused their children's autism. These attitudes have been responsible for causing enormous pain to families who struggled valiantly to deal with extraordinary problems and did not give up trying.

Families as Adjuncts to Treatment

Though it is best if your loved one seeks formal treatment for BPD from a qualified therapist, she need not be in formal treatment in order for you to help her. Aspects of DBT and mentalization can be learned and applied by family members outside of formal therapy in order to improve family functioning and interpersonal relationships.

Aspects of Dialectical Behavior Therapy (DBT) and mentalization can be learned and applied by family members outside of formal therapy in order to improve family functioning and interpersonal relationships.

A New York City department store's ads proclaim, "An educated consumer is our best customer!" As a family member, you must become an educated consumer so you can act as an advocate in seeking the best possible treatment for your loved one. You need to empower yourself and spare others from experiencing what you have experienced. To help your loved one have a better quality of life, you must seek out evidence-based treatments, such as DBT, that have been shown to be effective in clinical trials. Apply the same standards of care and decision making to mental health treatment as you would do to any other health condition, including seeking a second opinion. When you are aware of the neurobiology that underlies BPD (discussed in Chapter 2) you will be able to understand and predict many of the BPD behaviors that now baffle you. Concrete scientific evidence and research findings reported in professional journals can transpose the "bad" person with BPD into someone suffering with a disorder, and restore your compassion so you can relieve the frustration and anger you feel toward your loved one and rekindle hope.

Be warned: Family members trying to learn the ins and outs of BPD are often looked upon suspiciously and may be described as "enmeshed" or over-involved in their loved one's illness. A double standard seems to operate when looking at the concern you express for a loved one with a physical illness versus a mental illness. When an adult or child is sick; has a physical illness or a broken limb; needs medication, special care, exercise regimes, or bandage changing, the parent or partner does whatever is necessary to provide needed care. Doctors count on family assistance in the treatment of many disorders, such as cystic fibrosis or diabetes. When your loved one is on the verge of an asthma attack or is going into anaphylactic shock, you must take action and know how to provide a life-saving intervention, give needed medication, or get him to an ER so as to save his life. Parents or partners who can recognize signs of suicide risk need to be able to take actions to save their loved one's life. They need to know how to intervene effectively so as to prevent death, hospitalizations, and trauma.

It would be unthinkable to tell the parent or partner, "You are not a doctor or a nurse, you cannot help." Why, then, is helping a loved one suffering with a mental disorder such as BPD met with so much resistance and stigma? Why is it considered such a travesty when parents or partners of someone with BPD teach or reinforce life skills that will increase their loved one's ability to handle her own problems? Why is a well-informed parent or partner who knows what to do and what not to do so threatening? Why is there such a taboo against including loved ones in the process of helping someone with a mental illness? Your efforts to understand and be helpful may go unacknowledged, unappreciated, and unencouraged.

Family members are amazingly motivated to help their loved one. They desperately need to access the kinds of coping skills that will enable them to transform their concern, compassion, and grief into effective strategies. Their love and frustration need to be channeled so that they can help their loved ones. A knowledgeable family member may be able to help motivate a loved one into effective treatment despite countless prior therapy failures. A potential liability can become an amazing asset when families are taught how to become therapeutic family members. Withholding the skills a family needs to help a loved one with BPD is iatrogenic and stigmatizing. The psychiatric community must learn to harness family energy and convert families into clinical allies and treatment reinforcers.

This book is a road map for those of you who want to learn how to help. It will guide you along the path of compassionate understanding of daily relationship challenges. It will teach you how to change your own behavior and how to apply practical skills to improve the life of your loved one as well as your own. The ultimate goal is to motivate your loved one to enter effective, evidence-based treatment, to reinforce the treatment she is already receiving, or to guide her toward implementing more effective methods of coping with her pain. A fringe benefit of using compassionate and skillful methods will be the decrease of your own distress and frustration and discernible progress toward relationship repair.

The Science of Borderline Personality Disorder

Facts do not cease to exist because they are ignored.

—Aldous Huxley

UNDERSTANDING THE CUTTING-EDGE RESEARCH ON THE NEURO-
BIOLOGY underlying borderline personality disorder will help
you understand how behaviors that wreak havoc on family life are
probably your loved one's maladaptive attempts to cope with
enormous emotional pain. This new understanding may be very painful for you to accept, as it may challenge your long-held beliefs about
your loved one's with BPD. You may suddenly find that what you
always thought to be true is not true, what you have learned is not quite
true, and what you were advised to do
was not the best thing you could have
done. Or, this new information may confirm your own experience with this disorder, what you knew intuitively deep
inside you, that no one else confirmed
or validated. You may even become very
angry with yourself or with the professionals you consulted in the past.

Understanding the biology of BPD can help you make positive changes if you work at applying this new information instead of focusing energy on what you did not do.

Remember, you did the best you could with what you knew at the time. However, that was then and this is now. We cannot change the past, but we can use this new information to bring about changes for the better in the future. Understanding the biology of BPD can help you make positive changes if you work at applying this new information instead of focusing energy on what you did not do. If you find neurobiology confusing, think of it as a Russian novel that you have to reread over and over again so that you can understand who the characters are and what roles they play in the saga.

It may be hard for you to believe that the moodiness, poor judgment, and dangerously impulsive or willful behaviors you are struggling to cope with can be biologically based. As a family member, acceptance of this information can help you, to feel less angry and fearful, reduce the sense of guilt or responsibility you may feel, and encourage you to accept that your loved one is doing the best she can. This chapter will help you understand BPD so that feelings of anger and disappointment can be replaced with compassion for the pain your loved one endures on a daily basis. It will also help you change beliefs you might have held, such as believing that your loved one is an evil manipulator or a demon from whom you need to be protected. Hope can be restored when you understand that she has neurobiological systems that are dysregulated, and that there are treatments that numerous clinical trials have demonstrated to be actually effective. These are called evidence, based treatments.

The Current State of BPD Research

Borderline personality disorder is a scientific enigma that pathbreaking neuroscientists are trying to decipher. Thus far, research on BPD has revealed problems or irregularities in several important areas of functioning, such as impulse control and mood regulation. However, understanding the cause or etiology of BPD at the present time is like working on a complex jigsaw puzzle that has pieces missing when you have never seen a picture of the completed puzzle. Various scientific communities are engaged in research on different areas of the brain, on chemicals in the brain called *neurotransmitters*, on the anatomical architecture of the brain, and on how specific parts of the brain function and interact with each other. Current research is exploring specific behaviors as well as the functions and reactions of distinct areas of the brain. Researchers are piecing together what seem to be snippets of data, finding some answers in research from other disciplines such as neurology and addiction. As of now, we do not know precisely how all these new findings fit together to explain this disorder, nor do we know what destabilizes the person, what actually triggers the emotional dysregulation that characterizes or actually drives BPD symptoms, what starts the cascade that leads to the emotional outbursts or suicide attempts. What we are missing is a clear overview, a theory to integrate all these diverse observations. How does information about specific structures of the brain, functional abnormalities, or neurotransmitter increases or decreases add up to explanations that can account for BPD behaviors? How do we connect the dots to see how research in one area of neuroscience fits into research in other areas? The scientific findings brought together here will help you reframe BPD as a mental disorder with real, tangible biological underpinnings rather than a "character flaw" or a matter of "bad" personality.

Imagine a doctor who is trying to treat a person with a "fever" in the year 1200. He would see a patient who was hot to the touch, shaking with chills, possibly red in the face, sweating profusely, or very pale with parched lips, perhaps afflicted with hives, spots, or pustules. The doctor would diagnose the person as having a fever. Today we would describe the person with much more refined terminology, as having an infection caused by strep, staph, or other bacteria or viral in origin. The patient would then receive a specific treatment.

BPD research is still in the Middle Ages, so to speak. If a group of blindfolded scientists were on various ladders around an elephant and were asked to describe only what they feel and smell directly in front of them, each one would be sure that the part he is describing is the whole. Research on BPD is in a similar place. It has been looking at facets of the disorder—such as mood dysregulation, impulsivity, or addictive behaviors—rather than the disorder as a whole. As a result, BPD is generally described by its symptoms in a dimensional way. We do not know for sure how to effectively decrease or prevent the situations that trigger the behaviors nor do we have a panacea drug to cure BPD, as penicillin cures infection or chicken soup "cures" the common cold. What we do have is burgeoning neurobiological research that is giving us new areas to study, vital clues about the disorder, and new directions as to how to treat it.

Changing the Brain Changes Behavior

Phineas Gage was a railroad worker who lived from 1823 to 1860. Gage was a responsible, reliable, well-liked, nondrinking, and considerate family man. He was not aggressive, nor did he get into arguments or barroom brawls. He was in charge of a work crew that blasted rocks to clear a path for railroad tracks. They drilled holes in the rocks, pushed gunpowder and a fuse into the hole, added sand, then pushed it all down with an iron tamping rod. One day, Gage was somehow distracted and a terrible accident occurred. The fuse was ignited while the tamping rod was still in place. The resulting explosion blew the tamping rod out of the hole and into Gage's skull, entering under his eye socket and coming out through the area at the top of his skull above his eye—the region called the prefrontal cortex (PFC).

Miraculously, Gage survived his injury. The hole in his head managed to heal, yet he seemed to turn into a completely different person. His personality changed so drastically that he became irresponsible, made very bad decisions, could not get along with his crew or his family, was aggressive and careless, fought with everyone, drank heavily, and eventually abandoned his family. He died destitute and homeless.

Antonio Damasio, in his book *Descartes' Error*, described the actual area where Phineas Gage's skull was injured; his prefrontal cortex had suffered devastating damage. This is of particular interest to neuroscientists today because it documents a radical change in a person's personality and behavior that corresponds with damage to a specific part of the brain, the prefrontal cortex. Long before we had functional magnetic resonance imaging (fMRI) machines with which to observe how the brain functions, Gage's injury demonstrated the interconnection between the architecture, or *neuroanatomy*, of the brain, and actual behavior. Dr. Damasio studies people with brain injuries and tumors, relating how the exact location of a brain injury, tumor, or lesion affects a person's behavior. It seems that Phineas Gage developed many symptoms of BPD after his prefrontal cortex was damaged; certainly he became impulsive and exhibited poor judgment.

Behavioral Aspects of BPD

You have no doubt seen a juggler in a circus or magic act tossing five or six colored balls into the air in different combinations and rhythms that constantly vary. Sometimes all the balls are moving in a circle, sometimes two may be up in the air from the juggler's right hand while the others remain low in his left hand. Or, two are up and three down, four up and one down. There does not seem to be a logical plan as to how the juggler tosses these balls. You are always anticipating what he will do next, ready for a surprise.

Now, imagine that each one of the colored balls the juggler tosses into the air is a behavioral aspect of BPD caused by a neurobiological system in dysregulation. Keep the image of the juggler in your mind as we discuss how different neurobiological systems work, how they affect behavior, and how they can help to explain BPD. This metaphor will help you understand the mercurial behavior of people with BPD and how the nine symptoms of BPD in the DSM-IV-TR can combine or morph into so many different variations, yet still meet criteria for a single disorder.

Latest research findings on various neurobiological systems explain some of the apparently irrational BPD behaviors from a neurobiological and genetic point of view, minus guilt or blame. Have you ever noticed the cacophony when an orchestra is tuning up before a performance? Like the juggler's balls, each section of the orchestra can be thought of as a neurobiological system in dysregulation. When the orchestra is in tune you will not hear an individual flute or an out-of-tune violin. When tuned up, each section is in harmony with the others and you hear beautiful music. When the brain is in tune, when moods are regulated, and sleep is not troubled, a person will be in harmony and will function well in most situations. His behavior will tend to be predictable and generally stable.

People with BPD have been found to have neurobiological vulnerabilities that are likely genetic in origin yet are probably exasperated or mitigated by environmental influences. Study your family members and try to create your own family tree. You will probably find an impulsive uncle, an aunt who suffered from depression, someone else who was painfully shy, a brother who suffered with addictions, a distant cousin who was emotionally volatile and another who was extremely sensitive. People who develop BPD seem to have lost at the genetic lottery. They have inherited a combination of dysregulations that have reached a critical mass of system dysregulations that seems to add up to the disorder. If one were to inherit these traits separately, they could be considered as assets—such as a very sensitive person who becomes an artist, an impulsive person who is fun to be around, or a highly successful business person who enjoys taking risks. But the combination of these elements, the pileup, so to speak, in one person, can result in BPD. Sometimes BPD affects more than one child in a family or both a parent and child in family. BPD can be found in both biological and adopted children. In one family, a mother may have BPD, as well as four out of five of her daughters. Studies with twins have shown that BPD runs in families, and that 69% of the variance in the likelihood of someone having BPD can be explained by inherited genetic factors.[1]

What this all means is that there is no simple explanation for BPD. It will be easier for you to understand this disorder if you consider each behavioral component as a symptom. Each symptom described here is represented by one of the nine colored balls our juggler is tossing into the air. Here is a key to each symptom, each colored ball of the juggler:

- #1 blue: impulse control dysregulation
- #2 red: mood or affective dysregulation
- #3 purple: sensitivity dysregulation
- #4 green: cognitive dysregulation
- #5 yellow: emotion processing dysregulation
- #6 orange: sleep dysregulation
- #7 black: pain dysregulation
- #8 white: memory dysregulation
- #9 pink: anxiety

Impulsivity—Blue Ball

Impulsive people seem to act without thinking. Impulsivity can be defined as a tendency toward an action with little or no planning to reduce the impact of aversive stimuli. Impulsivity can be vital for survival as it can get you out of danger in a hurry. However, depending on the context and intensity of the response, impulsivity can be a dysfunctional characteristic that can get a person into trouble. Impulsive people seem to have a lower threshold for what can trigger their responses, particularly aggressive responses; they are often unable to curb or inhibit their reactions.

---

[1] Siever, 1997; Siever et al., 2002.

Impulsivity is a key component of BPD. People with BPD seem to live life in perpetual "knee-jerk" mode. Something happens and they react—they do not know how to slow down or control their reactions. People with BPD may engage in dangerous or reckless behaviors such as unsafe sex, gambling, excessive spending, shoplifting, road rage, stalking,[2] or domestic violence.[3] They may be extremely volatile, or say or do things that have negative consequences, ranging from quitting a job and ending a relationship to physical violence resulting in their arrest and incarceration.[4] Many people with BPD end up in the criminal justice system. Robert Trestman studied the prison population in Connecticut and found that 28% of the inmates met criteria for BPD. Impulsiveness is also associated with substance abuse and alcoholism as well as eating disorders such as binging, purging, and anorexia.[5]

"The threshold for impulsive or aggressive acts is more easily crossed in a person of highly changeable emotions and moods." –Larry Siever and Harold Koenisberg

THE PREFRONTAL CORTEX

You have learned how severe damage to a specific area of the brain, the prefrontal cortex, changed Phineas Gage from a responsible, well-liked man to an irascible, impulsively aggressive person with poor judgment. The prefrontal cortex is the place in the brain where impulsive behavior is regulated. We can liken this system to the brakes in a car. Driving a car without brakes is an accident waiting to happen, a sure-fire way to commit suicide. This system, which suppresses or controls aggressive or impulsive behaviors in the brain, seems to function less effectively in people with BPD so that they seem to be negotiating daily life without a behavioral brake to regulate their impulses or to slow down their responses.

The prefrontal cortex, located approximately behind the eyebrows or forehead, is the area of the brain where judgment and decision making seems to occur. Areas of the pre frontal cortex are also responsible for higher cognitive functioning, such as planning and reasoning,

[2] Meloy, 1998.
[3] Dutton, 1998.
[4] Trestman, 2000; Trestman et al., 2005.
[5] Siever & Koenisberg, 2000.

and play an important role in inhibiting aggression. What are the specific brain circuits involved in inhibiting behaviors or controlling impulses? Martin Bohus, a researcher at Germany's University of Heidelberg and Central Institute of Mental Health, University of Mannheim, conducted fMRI studies of activity in a part of the prefrontal cortex in people with BPD and found strong evidence that the volume of regions of the prefrontal cortex was smaller than those of people without BPD.[6] If this region of the brain controls impulses and decision making and is smaller in people with BPD, one can see why it might be more difficult for people with BPD to control their impulses. Again using fMRI, Dr. Bohus studied the activation of the prefrontal cortex in response to stories (or scripts) that were about abuse and also involved abandonment memories in people with and without BPD. The response to these scripts in people with BPD appeared to be the opposite to how people without BPD (normal controls) reacted. Antonia New and Larry Siever, brilliant psychiatrists at New York's Mount Sinai School of Medicine, found that the prefrontal cortex normally modulates a person's response to negative emotion and that this ability to modulate responses may be disrupted in people with BPD. In other words, when people with BPD try to step on their emotional brakes, their brains do not respond as they should so that their emotional cars keep going.[7]

SEROTONIN

A neurotransmitter is a chemical that relays signals in the brain. Serotonin is described as a modulatory neurotransmitter. If the prefrontal cortex is the brain's brake, serotonin can be thought of as the brain's brake fluid. It moderates activity in the prefrontal cortex. Serotonin is also associated with social behaviors. Low serotonin levels seem to be related to difficulty in suppressing certain behaviors. Increasing the amount of serotonin can decrease aggression. Self-destructive acts, like cutting and suicide attempts, are considered self-directed aggression. Researchers have found that serotonin system activity is blunted or diminished in people with BPD. This may explain their angry outbursts, impulsive self-destructive behaviors, and suicide attempts, as well as the high irritability that characterizes people with BPD.

---

[6] Bohus, Schmahl, & Lieb, 2004.
[7] New et al., 2004; Hazlett et al., 2005; Frankle et al., 2005.

Serotonin-enhancing drugs known as selective serotonin reuptake inhibitors (SSRIs) such as Prozac, Lexapro, and Zoloft, have been found to be moderately effective in treating depression in those with BPD and can also help in treating anger/impulse dyscontrol. These drugs generally have limited side effects and can therefore be well tolerated by people with BPD. Research has found that the prefrontal cortex becomes more active on SSRIs, so it is possible that these medications may be helping people have better behavioral control.

Psychiatrist Hans Steiner of Stanford University treated an impulsive teenager with BPD. He suggested that the young man count to 10 to help him control his impulsive anger. The young man stated that, on his own, he could barely manage to count to 2. When he took medication, he could count up to 8. However, he complained, he did not know what to do with his anger once he got to 8. The medication may have slowed down this young man's reaction, but it did not take away his anger or help him deal effectively with it. It is important to understand that medication can dampen BPD symptoms like impulsivity but does not provide the sufferer with the coping skills needed to manage his emotions. Medication alone is clearly not the solution to the problem.

Mood or Affective Dysregulation—Red Ball

Affective or mood dysregulation is another key neurobiological symptom of BPD, another of the juggler's balls spinning in the air. This is also called *lability*. Mood changes happen so fast that it is hard to keep track of them. They are as quick as the sudden chill you feel when a cloud passes over the sun on a hot summer day. Larry Siever describes people with BPD as unusually emotionally reactive.

Rapid mood changes are a core feature of BPD that Marsha Linehan describes as emotional dysregulation. Dr. Linehan posits first that people with BPD are highly sensitive to emotional cues and have a low threshold for emotional reaction; therefore, they react very quickly. They are supersensitive to criticism, judgment, and blame, and seem to perceive negative cues before others even notice them— if they notice them at all. Secondly people with BPD exhibit very high reactivity, meaning their reactions are extreme. Their high arousal interrupts their cognitive processing, their ability to think logically. Thirdly, they have slow returns to baseline, meaning their reactions are long lasting. This contributes to a high sensitivity to the next emotional trigger that may come along. A person with BPD can be in a fine mood, then, suddenly, become furiously angry or terribly anxious without your being aware of any apparent trigger to account for the change in behavior. Once aroused, your loved one can remain in this heightened state for a few hours or a day.[8] Martin Bohus describes people with BPD as emotionally vulnerable, with enhanced sensitivity, enhanced reactivity, difficulty in regulating their emotions, and needing a prolonged amount of time to return to baseline once they have been dysregulated.

Bonnie, a young woman who volunteered at the TARA offices, revealed that her mood could change as many as 27 times in one day. Can you imagine how painful and frightening it must feel to have absolutely no control over your moods? This renders people with BPD unable to control their lives; surely this must fill them with anxiety and shame. This can be equally painful for you as a family member, as you do not know what triggers the mood changes, nor do you know what to do about them once they occur. Your loved one may be busy doing something, perhaps getting ready to go somewhere, when suddenly, for no reason that you are aware of, she is in a state of despair. Or, even worse, she is angry to the point of rage. She usually has no idea why this has happened and cannot control how she feels, yet this is how she is now feeling. She may not show up for appointments because she is either too mad or too sad and does not know how to deal with either state. After missing her appointment, her mood can suddenly switch; she is now embarrassed, ashamed, or guilty, and she will have to deal with the consequences or repercussions of her own behavior even though she does not have a clue as to what to do next. You, on the other hand, may be feeling manipulated and angry because you believe she is just trying to get your attention. You may feel personally responsible for causing the mood changes, or criticize and judge your loved one because of her sudden shifts in mood. You probably mean well when you tell your loved one to "snap out of it." The problem is she cannot; she does not know how. Nothing in her environment that you can see easily explains these capricious changes in mood.

---

[8] Koenigsberg et al., 2003; Koenigsberg et al., 2002.

THE AMYGDALA

Understanding the *limbic system,* located in the deep center of the brain, can help you to demystify erratic BPD behaviors. The amygdala, a part of the limbic system, seems to be involved in the affective/mood dysregulation of BPD. Emotional states result from the specific patterns of activation within this brain system as well as interaction with the environment. The dysregulations appear as an abrupt change in emotional states and behaviors, especially those that have adverse interpersonal consequences. These interconnected systems react like a machine in a Rube Goldberg cartoon or a cascade of dominoes falling, one after the other. How can your car function if too much gas goes into the engine, or if only two out of eight cylinders are operating? The challenge is to identify each system and how functional impairments in certain parts dysregulate the entire system.

The amygdala is a small, almond-shaped structure whose primary function is the processing of emotions and storing of emotional memories. It is the place in the brain that processes negative emotions such as fear, as well as pleasure responses. This is the brain's alarm system, where "fight or flight" reactions take place. The amygdala receives sensory input from the body through the thalamus and sends messages to many other areas, including the face, activating facial expressions. The amygdala is also associated with areas of the brain that are concerned with the sense of smell. The amygdala has been found to function abnormally in anxiety disorders, autism, posttraumatic stress disorder, phobias, and BPD. The amygdalae of people with BPD have been shown to be smaller in volume than in healthy controls on some, not all, studies. If the prefrontal cortex is likened to the brain's brake, the amygdala can be described as the brain's gas pedal.

It is important to remember that the amygdala is a component of a complex, highly interconnected set of brain structures. In people with BPD, this circuitry does not seem to be functioning as it should. Functional magnetic resonance imaging (fMRI) studies show us that when emotional reactions are evoked, activity increases in the amygdala. In people with BPD, the amygdala seems to be working overtime—in fact, it seems to be working

People with BPD seem to have a heightened emotional response to almost all situations and can be described as being hypervigilant.

overtime almost all of the time. People with BPD seem to have a heightened emotional response to almost all situations and can be described as being *hypervigilant*.

AVERSIVE AROUSAL

Aversive arousal describes the feeling of being repelled by something and having a desire to avoid it. It is having unpleasant, uncomfortable feelings in your body and in your mind. Aversive feelings make you want to turn away from what you perceive as painful or punishing stimuli. These feelings include tension, stress, stomach pains, anxiety, shame, anger, or fear. There is strong evidence that people with BPD experience aversive emotions and arousal more frequently than do healthy control subjects, that they experience these aversive feelings more intensely and rapidly, and that the unpleasant feelings endure for longer periods of time. These feelings can be so aversive that they can lead to dissociative responses.

Martin Bohus found that people with BPD undergo sudden intense arousal that is experienced as being extremely aversive, but that they have difficulty assigning or describing these feelings to a specific emotion. He gave handheld computers, like BlackBerrys, to healthy controls and persons with BPD and beeped them periodically throughout the day. When the subjects got the signal they rated and recorded their own feelings. The results showed that people with BPD experienced aversive feelings more frequently than did healthy controls. These aversive feelings were also more intense and persisted for a longer period of time. What does this mean to you as a family member? It means that the person you love with BPD is feeling badly almost all of the time and is usually receiving the message from her body and her mind that her inner state is aversive or painful. This is a real feeling that does not depend on what is going on around her at the moment or on what is happening according to your evaluation of the situation. If you want to be helpful to your loved one it is vital that you have compassion for this constant pain.

SHAME

Intense emotional reaction is another facet of affective dysregulation in BPD. Martin Bohus compared the intensity and frequency of various emotional reactions of people with and without BPD. He found that people with BPD experience anxiety, anger, and grief almost nine times more often than those without BPD, whereas those without

BPD experience twice the level of joy and interest than do people with BPD.

One of Bohus's most startling findings has been that people with BPD experience chronic feelings of shame while healthy controls do not. Shame is an extremely aversive sensation arising from the feeling that one is a "bad" person. A typical response to most situations for the person with BPD is a pervasive feeling of badness or unworthiness. Shame is often confused with guilt; however, they are two very distinct emotions. Guilt is feeling bad about having done something wrong and experiencing regret. It was the action or behavior that was wrong—not the person. Guilt is what most people feel if they break something belonging to someone else, forget someone's birthday, or are late to an appointment. You have done something you see as "bad," but you do not necessarily see yourself as bad. Guilt is a negative feeling about a specific *event* rather than about the self. Shame, conversely, is a global negative feeling about the self, the feeling that one is a "completely bad" or "awful" person, especially in the eyes of others. Being prone to feeling shame can radically change a person's interpretations of his life experiences.

If a person breaks a dish at a friend's house or forgets a friend's birthday, he realizes that the friendship is still intact and he will apologize or make amends. A shame-prone person with BPD might instead think, "I am a bad person because I broke the dish. David will not want me as a friend any more, I am a loser." This feeling is so aversive to a person with BPD that he may self-injure; make a suicide attempt; or use drugs, alcohol, or other maladaptive, harmful behaviors to escape his painful feelings. Experiencing shame has been found to be a predictor of multiple parasuicidal episodes.[9]

A shame-prone person fails to complete a required report at work. He might think, "I'm such a loser; I just can't get it together. I let everyone down. I am going to lose my job; everyone already knows I am incompetent, I might as well quit." A guilt-prone person would more likely think, "I feel bad for not doing my work, I let my co-workers down, I'll stay late tonight and finish the work." Intensely painful feelings of shame do not seem to motivate people into constructive directions. Feelings of guilt are painful but seem to be less disabling and are more apt to motivate a person toward taking

---

[9] Bohus, Schmahl, & Lieb, 2004; Tangney & Mashek, 2004.

responsibility for his actions and to attempt reparations. Because experiencing shame can be so painful, the person with BPD may often deflect blame onto other people.

Psychologist June Price Tangney found that shame-prone people will often become dependent on alcohol or drugs to reduce the painful and debilitating feelings they experience in their core sense of self. There seems to be a relationship between the amount of alcohol consumed, the risk for alcohol dependence and alcohol-related problems, and using alcohol to cope with negative emotions. For shame-prone people such as those with BPD, the alcohol or drugs then set off a vicious cycle that fosters continued use of alcohol; more alcohol or drugs are used to cope with the new pain and shame so that alcohol or drug dependency is a likely outcome. Little wonder that substance abuse programs focusing on shame inducement fail to help people with BPD and can actually do more harm than good. Failing in these programs reinforces feelings of failure, humiliation, and worthlessness in those with BPD, inducing self-defeating cycles of negative feelings and even more shame.

Painful feelings of shame about the self cut to our core, and, rather than motivating reparative action, motivate denial, defensiveness, anger, and aggression. Shame impairs a person's ability to generate effective solutions to interpersonal problems and can diminish confidence in the person's ability to implement solutions. Shame can be thought of as the common denominator of BPD responses to most situations and experiences, a component of the red ball that is mood dysregulation. It is very hard for family members to integrate the pervasive, chronic, and unremitting sense of shame their loved one is feeling into their own thinking because shame is generally not in their experiential repertoire. Adults tend to experience feelings of guilt but will not generally experience feelings of shame—though they may have shame memories connected to early childhood memories such as wetting the bed or forgetting lines in an elementary school play. When you are trying to decipher BPD behavior, you can probably presume that your loved one's response to most situations is the feeling of shame. Additionally, shame prone people are more sensitive to rejection. Geraldine Downey at Columbia University has found that people prone to rejection sensitivity often have BPD.

Bipolar Disorder and BPD

The rapid mood shifts that people with BPD experience often lead to their being misdiagnosed with bipolar disorder. It is important to make the distinction between the mood shifts that characterize BPD and those of bipolar disorder. In bipolar disorder, emotion may vary slightly over the course of a day; the shifts must last for days, weeks, or months in order to qualify for this diagnosis. Bipolar diagnoses are generally made based on the length of time the person experiences these extreme moods. A person has to experience being depressed for a minimum of three to four weeks to receive the diagnosis of depression, whereas a bipolar state is a rapid change from depression to mania or euphoria. Rapid in this case can mean over weeks. Rapid cycling bipolar disorder refers to three to four switches of mood in a year. In contrast, people with BPD often experience this number of shifts in a day. People with BPD do not generally become manic as those with bipolar disorder do. Furthermore, it has been demonstrated that people with bipolar disorder worsen on antidepressants known as SSRIs,[1] whereas borderline patients can improve on SSRIs. Conversely, people with BPD do not benefit from mood stabilizers such as lithium. In 2006, John Gunderson of Harvard University and Mclean Hospital in Boston pointed out the relationship between bipolar disorder and BPD. Marc Zimmerman, director of a research project known as the Rhode Island Methods to Improve Diagnostic Assessment and Services (MIDAS), has found that 25% of patients diagnosed with bipolar disorder meet criteria for BPD, and 40% of patients in his study who were diagnosed with BPD were misdiagnosed as having bipolar disorder.

As described in Chapter 1, clinicians may misdiagnose BPD as bipolar disorder intentionally to ensure that the person with BPD receives insurance coverage. Medicare does not have a billing code for BPD. Up to now, the classification of mental disorders has been divided into axes in the DSM. Mental illnesses such as schizophrenia, bipolar disorder, major depression, substance abuse, and other disorders are on Axis I, while all personality disorders are currently on Axis II—despite the fact

---

[1] Rinne, T et al, 2002.

(Continued)

that severity and degree of disability of personality disorders is the same or more severe that the Axis I disorders. No scientific research justifies the segregation of personality disorders onto a separate axis; psychiatrist Roger Peele has advocated tirelessly to move personality disorders to Axis I. The DSM V, although not slated to be published until 2013, finally seems to be changing the Axis II placement of personality disorders. Disorders such as substance abuse, anxiety, eating disorders, and depression can actually be considered as symptoms of BPD, therefore treating these symptoms alone without treating the underlying BPD will not be effective. If BPD is consistently misdiagnosed, these other symptomatic disorders will not improve and the expenditure for new treatment programs and more research is not seen as justified.

BPD and Suicide

By observing someone with major depression you may realize that he is planning suicide. He may have been feeling hopeless and depressed over a long period of time, have decided to end his life, prepared and made a plan; he may even have warned you.

Suicide attempts by people with BPD are very different. They are usually more spontaneous, impulsive, behavioral responses to unbearable pain, in the moment. They may not be actual attempts to die but maladaptive efforts to find immediate relief for emotional pain. Marsha Linehan discourages hospitalizing people with BPD when they make suicide attempts unless there has been serious injury. Hospitalizing someone with BPD can have unintended negative consequences such as becoming fearful of being outside the hospital and becoming dependent on external aide in a crisis. Rushing to the person's side and giving her attention and acknowledgment when she threatens suicide actually reinforces suicidal behavior. At no time should a suicide attempt be trivialized. Clearly, there needs to be greater availability of informed assistance for people with BPD when they are in crisis. The following example illustrates the impulsive nature of a BPD suicide attempt and how distraction in the moment can sometimes discourage the behavior. Loren, a young woman with BPD, had just had an argument with her partner on the cell phone that ended their relationship. Loren was walking across a bridge at that time, was in enormous emotional pain, and was in despair. She was sure that she was a loser, all her friends would make fun of her; she would never again have another boyfriend. She felt she could not bear her pain for another moment and, impulsively, decided to jump off the bridge. She was approaching the bridge railing when a car came along and stopped besides her. The driver got out and asked Loren for directions to a local club. He invited Loren to join him. Distracted, Loren was no longer thinking about dying.

Sensitivity Dysregulation—Purple Ball

Larry Siever has done extensive neurobiological studies of BPD and is committed to unraveling the enigma that is this disorder. He describes these patients as "exquisitely sensitive," extremely responsive to stimuli, and sensitive to changes in medication. Dr. Siever's description resonates with the experiences of families across the country. Parents of those with BPD often observe that their children were extremely sensitive, sometimes beginning in infancy. Parents often report children's sensitivity to textures as so severe that they could not wear certain clothing because it was "too itchy." This sensitivity often persists into adulthood.

Many people with BPD are also supersensitive to sound. Your loved one may complain that someone is screaming at her when others experience the person as talking in a normal tone. Some find music is blaringly loud, saying that it hurts their ears while others in the family do not find this to be so. The tastes or smells of certain foods may be so offensive that many become picky eaters. Some may complain that light hurts their eyes.

People with BPD are also acutely sensitive to emotional nuances and facial expressions. Parents, often out of ignorance or simply from not understanding, generally do not acknowledge this sensitivity. Pediatricians and other medical professionals generally overlook or dismiss these parental observations. Children are not generally tested for their levels of sensory sensitivity. *Sensory processing disorder*, while not currently well understood, may very well be an early

"Psychic blindness: Perfectly good visual acuity but blind to the psychological significance of stimuli."
—Joseph LeDoux[10]

indication of something awry in development leading to future difficulties like BPD.

In a study of 4-month-old infants, Harvard researcher Jerome Kagan found that some of the infants were highly reactive and had a more intense response to the sound of a handclap or loud noise (known as startle response). He studied these same children in infancy, at 7 years of age, and into early adolescence. He found their temperamental characteristics were generally stable. The highly reactive babies were more likely to become subdued, anxiety prone, shy, and timid—the kind of adults who avoid people, objects, and situations that are unique, innovative, or unfamiliar. The lower reactive babies were uninhibited children and became bolder, more spontaneous, and less socially inhibited adults. A high startle response seems to correlate with a person's being more sensitive to perceived fearful situations and might be an early predictor of the hypervigilance that characterizes people with BPD. Dr. Kagan studied pregnant women and was able to identify children with a high startle responses in utero, that is, before they were born. Clearly we come into the world with a specific temperament for how we will respond to stressors. This can be seen as an early risk factor for later behavioral difficulties. Identifying high sensitivity in children at an early age would afford us the opportunity to modify their environments and to teach coping skills that would enable them to overcome their natural or genetic temperaments, thereby circumventing the development of maladaptive responses.

Some children can be thought of as hyperallergic to their environments, as if they had severe immune deficiency disorders. To survive, they might have to live in specially controlled environmental bubbles. Perhaps extremely sensitive children who have a genetic proclivity to BPD need to grow up in a similar protected, structured environmental bubble where they are exposed to as little stress as possible. Unfortunately, such an environment does not exist.

---

[10] LeDoux, 1996.

Cognitive Dysregulation—Green Ball

Cognitive and emotion processing, or information processing, is a neu-robiological system represented by the green ball that our juggler is tossing into the air. This system, to date, has received the least amount of research attention in BPD. However, it is irregularities in cognition that are often the first sign of the development of BPD apparent to family members. They describe difficulties they have and have always had in communicating with their loved ones. Here again it appears that there is a neurobiological system that is not operating as it should.

It also seems that statements that are neutral or logical to you are interpreted emotionally by the person with BPD—perhaps as judg-mental, critical, or blaming statements. A simple statement like "Pass the butter" can elicit a retort like, "Why? Don't you want me to eat?" "Why ask me? I'm not the maid!" Think of BPD as a language disorder, as emotional dyslexia.[11] Each area of the brain has a unique function and must be precisely interconnected to an appropriate brain area so as to function optimally.[12] Much more research is needed to find the neuroanatomical locations in the brain that may be malfunctioning or, where the actual miswiring is that could lead to the development of BPD to guide researchers in developing more effective treatments.

There seems to be a consistent pattern of misunderstandings that takes place between you and the person you love with BPD, almost as if you are speaking different languages. You are speaking French; your loved responds in Chinese, while everyone else is speaking English. It is as though you are not reading the subtitles in the movie that is your life. The person with BPD does not trust you, doubting what you say and your intentions. Latest research by Larry Siever and Barbara Stanley indicate that brain chemicals such as oxytocin and the endogenous opioid system may be involved in your loved one's difficulties in trusting and forming connections.

Each area of the brain has a unique function and must be con-nected to specific neuroanatomical locations in order for the systems to function optimally. Additionally, many neurotransmitters and neu-ropeptides (hormones) are involved with regulating these systems.

---

[11] Kiehl et al., 2004; Hare & Jutai, 1988; Kuperberg et al., 2000; Kuchinke et al., 2005.
[12] Poldrack et al., 1999.

The following examples demonstrate malfunctions in the brain in dyslexia, auditory processing disorder, and facial recognition in autism. These will help you to understand how brain misconnectivity can lead to behavioral dysfunction.[13]

DYSLEXIA

People with dyslexia have difficulty sounding out words or matching the sounds of words to the letters, therefore have difficulty reading. Using MRI, Sally Shaywitz, a researcher at Yale, mapped the brains of people with and without dyslexia. She found that in dyslexic people, the part of the brain responsible for viewing and processing the printed word did not connect with the other areas of the brain that processed reading as it did in normal readers. These people showed increased activity in the region of the brain associated with spoken language. This irregularity in brain circuitry explains how an otherwise intelligent person, who understands and speaks language very well, can have difficulty reading. People with BPD can be very intelligent yet seem to misinterpret what you say. Bennett A. Shaywitz, also at Yale, developed a method of teaching dyslexic children that helped "rewire" their brains so that they could read. When it was recognised that dyslexic brains were not wired the same way as everyone else's brain, different teaching methods to help dyslexics learn to read were developed. Teaching coping skills to similarly "miswired" people with BPD may also help develop new neuronal circuitry.[14]

AUDITORY PROCESSING DISORDER

Auditory processing disorder affects how the brain processes auditory information. The ear drum and other ear structures, as well as the auditory nerve seem to be intact, yet people with APD have difficulty processing what they hear, distinguishing between similar sounds or words, separating speech from background noise, and recalling what they have heard. Although it is a hearing disorder, APD is referred to as an information processing disorder because sufferers have an intermittent inability to process verbal information. APD is sometimes misdiagnosed as attention-deficit hyperactivity disorder (ADHD) as these people have difficulty tuning out other noises and therefore may

---

[13] Grant J. E. et al. 2007; Rusch N et al. 2003.
[14] Herpertz S. et al. 1997.

have trouble concentrating. They may lose the message or meaning of the words they have heard, although they are able to repeat the words back to you. Because people with APD frequently guess at what they think they are hearing, they may not realize that they have misunderstood what was said. APD is described as an "invisible disability." It, too, can be alleviated by learning new coping skills.

APD seems to parallel aspects of BPD cognition. If a person with APD also has difficulty controlling impulses and regulating mood, she might appear to have the characteristics of someone with BPD. In fact, many callers to TARA's Helpline tell us about family members having BPD along with APD. Research on APD is conducted at the National Institute for Deafness and Communication, whereas the National Institute of Mental Health oversees and funds much of the research on BPD. As a result, APD researchers do not typically meet with BPD researchers so the connection between the two disorders has not been studied.

FACIAL PERCEPTION IN AUTISM

Using fMRI studies, Robert T. Schultz, a researcher at the Yale Child Study Center, mapped the brains of people with and without autism while they were looking at various inanimate objects and faces. These scans showed that normal control subjects processed faces in an area of the brain known as the *fusiform* "face area" of the ventral temporal lobe whereas people with autism processed faces in that part of the brain where the normal controls processed inanimate objects. These findings could explain why autistic children do not respond to their mothers' faces, or any face displaying emotion. Their brains are seeing or processing their mothers' faces as inanimate objects, like a chair or a stone. Their brains do not seem to be wired so as to process a face. How can they bond with a chair? This is like plugging a European appliance into an American socket. Or, like the inability of a color-blind person to distinguish between red and green. Or, like the person with BPD who reads negative emotional meaning into neutral situations or statement, like "pass the butter." Are they processing a benign statement in a part of their brain that monitors threats?

Emotion processing dysregulation—yellow

Emotions are processed within specific brain areas. Behavior is affected by dysfunctions in brain circuitry, by the anatomical size of brain structures, or by too many or too few specific neurotransmitters in pre-cise locations. We know that neuronal circuits used in processing emotions need to be connected to precise areas in the brain to function appropriately. The circuits going from the amygdala to the prefrontal cortex are different from those going from the prefrontal cortex to the amygdala. These circuits account for the greater influence the amygdala has on the prefrontal cortex than the prefrontal cortex has on the amygdala. Emotions and cognition are separate but interacting mental functions mediated by separate interacting brain systems. The part of the brain that actually generates emotions is not necessarily the same part that reads meanings into them and may also be affected by mood (affect). Circuits that do not connect to the specific area that fulfills an exact function will yield unpredictable results, like ringing the doorbell to find that the radio goes on while the doorbell ringer remains silent.

Research suggests that positive and negative emotions are processed differently in different neural structures and have different neural circuitry.[15] Different locations in the brain have been shown to respond to negative surprised faces compared to positive surprised faces; likewise, different brain circuits and regions seem to be involved in regulation of positive and negative affect. There seem to be different locations for processing positive and negative words. Negative triggers provoke more intense responses than do positive triggers. Processing of negative words seems to take more cognitive effort than do positive words. People with BPD seem to have a largely negative bias when processing information, accounting for their usual view of life's cup as half empty.

> People with BPD seem to have a largely negative bias when processing information, accounting for their usual view of life's cup as half empty.

This no doubt contributes to their difficulty with interpreting interpersonal interactions. Recall that the amygdala can be seen as the gas pedal of the brain, its alarm center, the prefrontal cortex as its brake, and serotonin as its brake fluid. In people with BPD, this circuitry does not seem to be functioning as it should.

SELF-REFERENTIAL PROCESSING

Understanding one's own and other people's states of mind is essential for survival. To know what others sense, want, believe, intend, or

---

[15] Fossatti et al., 2003.

think, and to maintain relationships, we need the ability to judge our own and other individuals' emotional states. The better we are at this, the better we are at negotiating daily life. A specific region of the *anterior cingulate* of the brain, part of the limbic system, is activated when we evaluate social situations and process information about emotional states, our own and others'. The specific areas involved in processing information or emotional stimuli about the self are called "self-referential areas."[16] Self-referential areas are influenced by the intensity of emotion, the strength of the stimuli, and the type of stimuli, such as a positive pleasurable emotion or a negative or aversive emotion, by the context of the situation, and the person with whom you are interacting in the moment.

Similarly, emotional stimuli that you believe are about you, that you associate with personally, are processed in different brain areas and have different patterns of activity than stimuli that arise from more objective or neutral sources. You would process a tsunami in Asia in a different part of your brain from the place in which you would process a fire in the house next door. Harold Koenigsberg of the Mount Sinai School of Medicine mapped the brains of people with BPD and normal controls in fMRI scanners while they looked at photographs from the International Affective Picture System (IAPS).[17] These are photos of situations that evoke emotional responses, such as pictures of children in a war-torn village or a happy family scene. Dr. Koenigsberg found that people with BPD processed more IAPS pictures as self-referential than did normal controls. Additionally, their emotional responses were more intense or heightened than those of normal controls. Their reactions to other people or situations may be due to their greater personalization of negative emotional situations. They may also have attempted to inhibit their emotional responses during the processing of negative words. Thus, a person with BPD personalizes a negative emotional situation, such as a fire next door or a tsunami in Asia, processesing it as self-referential. Personalizing experiences or self-referential processing leads to more intense reactions in specific areas of the brain and affects memory; self-referential words are remembered better than other words.[18] Perhaps that is why people with BPD seem to retain memories of

---

[16] Fossati et al., 2003.
[17] Koenigsberg et al., 2005.
[18] Fossati et al., 2003.

unpleasant events with an intensity that does not abate. Situations that may be perceived as neutral or insignificant by others are inappropriately experienced as self-referential, accounting for some of the general confusion family members have in understanding BPD reactions to benign situations.

A man walking beside his wife accidentally steps on her toe. She perceives this self-referentially, concluding that he has deliberately stomped on her foot. She reacts to this perceived aversive experience with great intensity, flies into a rage, and brings up the incident over and over again for many years afterward. A person with BPD seems to interpret much of what you say as being about him, as self-referential. He may become distraught at perceived criticism or react to a perceived minor slight with intense anger. He may be terrified if you go out for the newspaper as this can be self-referentially perceived as "abandonment." You may feel that your loved one is narcissistic because he seems to think that everything that happens is about him. This may be the result of how or where he processes his experiences in his brain. Once you realize how his miswiring may lead to perceiving so many events as self-referential, his behavior will make more sense to you.

NEUTRAL FACES

Nelson Donegan, a researcher at Yale, studied brain reactivity in the brains of people with and without BPD with fMRI scans as they looked at a series of photos of Ekman Faces showing different facial expressions, such as happy, sad, fearful, and neutral.[19] This series of photos, (the Ekman Faces) depicts faces showing various emotions that are recognized in every culture.[20] People with BPD showed greater left amygdala activation to facial expressions of emotion compared with normal controls. An interesting finding of this study was that people with BPD had the most intense reactions to the *neutral* faces, found them threatening and difficult to comprehend, and projected negative attributes onto them. This was the most striking difference between the two groups. In evaluating the ambiguous "neutral" expressions,

"Love me or hate me, but spare me your indifference." —John Galsworthy

[19] Donegan et al., 2003.
[20] Ekman, 2003.

BPD subjects tended to attribute explanations to the neutral faces by projecting emotions/intentions onto them. For example, "They look like mug shots, like someone who just got arrested." "They look fake, like a façade—they are hiding something." "They look like they are plotting something." "He looks angry and, if he knew me, he would be angry with me." Their explanations for the neutral faces were uniformly negative, threatening, and untrusting. Several of the BPD patients reported that they were trying to figure out what the individuals with neutral expressions were thinking as they looked at them.[21] Amy Wagner and Marsha Linehan found that, compared with control subjects, people with BPD were able to identify human facial expressions accurately in all cases except for neutral faces (the same Ekman faces), for which they tended to make errors and consign negative emotions.

This study has great significance for family members, as it demonstrates the importance of the nuances with which you respond to daily life or potential conflict. Many family members, faced with rage and verbal abuse from their BPD loved one, try not to get upset and to remain as calm as they can. This response usually backfires into escalations that can even lead to violence. Examination of these fMRI brain scans showed that the brains of people with BPD lit up like Christmas trees when viewing neutral faces. It seems they have difficulty dealing with any kind of ambiguity and, when in doubt, assign negative attributions to neutral faces. Therefore, when you respond with a calm, neutral face, without emotion, it is usually interpreted as meaning you do not care, you are upset with your loved one, or you think he has done something wrong. Responding with a neutral expression is like waving a red flag at a bull in the bull ring. Imagine the effect on a person with BPD when a therapist with a neutral face says, "uh hum" in a calm tone.

Most psychoanalysts are trained to be neutral and unresponsive when in session with a patient. In a study of people with BPD and their families, Jill M. Hooley, professor of psychology at Harvard University,[22] found that families exhibiting a high degree of "expressed emotions" were linked to better outcomes in BPD patients. As Hooley wrote, the "emotional temperament of the patient's family seems to

---

[21] Wagner & Linehan, 1999.
[22] Hooley & Hoffman, 1999; Hooley & Hiller, 2000.

influence the course of BPD treatment." Patients who were discharged from the hospital to families that showed a high degree of concern and identification were doing better 1 year later. "The more emotional over-involvement there was in the family, the better the patient did, and the less likely he or she was to be rehospitalized," Hooley wrote.[23] This study indicates that it is easier for someone with BPD to interpret a highly expressed emotion than a neutral response, as the high emotion communicates a clearer and more unambiguous message of concern and involvement. A mildly expressed emotional response may make a person with BPD feel as though she is being ignored. With appropriate training, family members can learn to recognize communication problems arising from their loved one's misreading of their facial expressions and emotional responses.

Sleep Dysregulation—Orange Ball

Though trouble sleeping is not one of the diagnostic criteria for BPD, many people with the disorder seem to struggle with sleep problems. Sleep dysregulation is an understudied component of BPD despite its prevalence among people with BPD, either beginning in infancy, in childhood, or as adults. Sleep problems range from sleeping during the day, being unable to sleep at night, not sleeping through the night, difficulty regulating sleep-wake cycles such as not sleeping more than 2 hours at a time, or just plain insomnia. Sleep deprivation can make anyone irritable and is even utilized as a method of torturing people. Add the problem of sleep deprivation to a highly reactive, highly sensitive individual and his entire system can become even more dysregulated. How do you feel when you do not get enough sleep? Insomnia is a very aversive experience leading to rumination, anxiety, and a sense of isolation. For many people with BPD, getting up in the morning is extremely difficult. In personal discussions with the author, Dr. Linehan noted that her patients who are just beginning Dialectical Behavior Therapy have so much difficulty getting to sleep that she tries to avoid scheduling them for early morning appointments. After having been in DBT for a

---

[23] Hooley, 2002.

while, they seem to be able to reset their body clocks or better regulate their circadian rhythms, and can keep morning appointments.

Marilaine Medeeiros, a researcher in the Department of Neurology at the Federal University of Sao Paulo, Brazil, studied children with sleep disorder compared to a control group of children ranging from 8 to 10 years of age. Disturbance in circadian rhythm alters sleep in impulsive individuals, causing a reduction in rapid eye movement (REM) sleep and a sleep phase known as slow wave sleep. There are also indications that impulsivity, anxiety, aggressiveness, and hyperactivity interfere with sleep in children and affect their performance at school. Dr. Medeeiros found a much greater incidence of impulsivity in children with sleep disorders, such as refusal to lie down, difficulties in falling asleep, and frequent nocturnal arousals. Here is another BPD dilemma: Which comes first, the impulsivity or the sleep problem?

Celyne Bastien of Laval University[25] has proposed a study of people with BPD who are hypervigilant or have heightened awareness and also suffer from insomnia, comparing them to controls. Hypervigilance can interrupt anyone's sleep; this could be a description of "light" sleepers. There are no studies to date that have looked at BPD hypervigilance and sleep. Dr. Bastien posits that the daily hypervigilance, so characteristic of people with BPD, may contribute to their sleep difficulties if it persists at night. It is as if they cannot shut off their high sensitivity and vigilance. This can then exacerbate their mood disorders and stress sensitivity.[26]

Alexandra Philipsen and Christian Schmahl studied sleep in people with BPD at the University of Freiburg, Germany, and found a discrepancy between objective (laboratory recordings of sleep) and subjective (sleep diaries kept by subjects) evaluation of sleep. This means that people with BPD may have an altered perception of how they sleep. When asked how they had slept, the people with BPD

> "With respect to insomnia, many of our borderline clients fight a never-ending battle in which pharmacotherapy often seems of little help."
> —Marsha Linehan[24]

---

[24] Linehan, 1993b.
[25] Bastien et al., 2004; Bastien, Vallières, & Morin, 2004.
[26] Vallières et al., 2005.

reported drastically impaired sleep quality for the 2 weeks before the study and during the two laboratory nights. This was not what the laboratory recordings showed. The underlying psychological and neurobiological mechanisms of these alterations are still unclear and need further study.

Many parents describe their children as having had sleep problems beginning in infancy. What significance can this have in the later development of BPD? REM sleep is a sleep phase important to the developing brain, providing the neural stimulation that newborns need to form mature neural connections, and is necessary for proper central nervous system development. Dysregulated sleep patterns in infancy might disrupt REM sleep. Sleep deprivation early in life can result in behavioral problems, permanent sleep disruption, decreased brain mass,[27] and an abnormal amount of neuronal cell death. Clearly, more research is needed to determine the relationship between BPD and sleep dysregulation. Again, sleep researchers work in a different National Institute of Health branch than do researchers who study BPD.

Pain Dysregulation—Black Ball

Are people with BPD dysregulated in the neuronal system that regulates pain? Is this another ball they are juggling? Pain is an unpleasant sensation associated with actual or potential tissue damage, like a cut or an injury to some part of the body. It is a subjective experience that has emotional and physical components. Pain can arise from a bodily injury or from an emotional experience, such as death or loss. Pain is transmitted over neuronal pathways; however, it needs to be perceived as pain, just as sound needs to be perceived appropriately. Here again we can see that it is the perception of the experience, as in auditory processing disorder, rather than the actual experience, that determines how we feel and react to pain. Pain serves a purpose in the body. It warns us of danger, signaling the body to minimize detected harm as when we move away from something very hot (a reflex). Short-term pain is acute pain. Chronic pain is pain that persists and has outlived its purpose in defending or protecting the body.

---

[27] Mirmiran, 1995.

Pain perception occurs in the *thalamus* of the brain and then goes to the *somatosensory cortex.*

Opioids are chemicals that are used to treat and relieve acute pain (analgesics). They have the ability to block physical and emotional pain, producing euphoria, a feeling of well-being. Morphine, heroin, and methadone are all opioids, as are Vicodin and Percocet. Desire for the euphoric feeling they bring can lead people to drug dependency and addiction. Addiction is both a psychological attachment and physiological need for the euphoric effects of opioids and can be complicated by the body's development of dependency on the substances. This results in the unpleasant feelings described as withdrawal syndrome. Additionally, the body begins to tolerate the opioids so that the desired euphoria requires increasing amounts of drugs. According to studies by Carlos Grilo at Yale University,[28] 67% of substance abusers meet criteria for BPD. If someone is in constant emotional pain, drug use can be seen as the person's attempt to self-medicate so as to relieve or manage his physical or emotional pain.

Opioids are also produced naturally in the body. These are predominately in the form of endorphins and enkephalins. They have the ability to produce natural pain relief and a sense of well-being— such as the "runner's high." It is thought that a runner's high results from the endorphins released as a result of the physical exertion of running.

People with BPD seem to have a different response to pain than do others. They seem to experience chronic emotional pain. Feeling socially excluded or feeling shame can trigger painful sensations even though there may be no actual physical pain. The common expression "a broken heart" is an example of emotional pain that is experienced as a physical pain.

Self-injurious behavior is dangerous and often life-threatening. It occurs in 70% to 80% of people who meet criteria for BPD.[29] Why would anyone want to inflict pain upon herself by cutting or burning? Studies have shown that 70% to 80% of women with BPD report perceiving less pain or greater insensitivity to pain when they self-injure. Studies by Barbara Stanley at Columbia University have shown that pain perception among those with BPD is actually altered

---

[28] Grilo, Sanislow, & McGlashan, 2002.
[29] Schmahl et al., 2004a; Russ et al., 1996.

during periods of self-injury, as are their endogenous (natural) opioid levels. Of people who self-injure, 60% report that they do not feel pain (analgesia) when they cut or burn themselves but, instead, feel a sense of relief. Christian Schmahl has studied how people with BPD perceive pain and has found that they do not seem to have difficulty discriminating the sensation of pain but differ in their subjective interpretation of the pain. Self-injurious behavior may relieve dysphoria (the state of feeling unwell or unhappy), as well as the sense of not feeling pain or just not feeling at all by releasing endogenous opioids. Martin Bohus[30] studied pain perception in people with BPD and normal controls. His studies showed that people with BPD have a "significantly reduced perception of pain." This reduced perception of pain is found in states of both calmness and distress, but is even greater when the person is distressed.

There seems to be an altered neurosensory aspect to the perception of pain in people with BPD. Dr. Bohus's latest research indicates that the difficulty in pain perception experienced by people with BPD may be due to their cognitive evaluation of pain. They perceive pain differently. Endogenous opioid receptors may be hyperactive in people with BPD and may lead to their need to reduce the experience of pain. This process, wherein the problem seems to arise from the cognitive interpretation of an experience, is similar to what happens in auditory processing disorder and in Schmahl's studies on BPD and sleep.

Some people with BPD report that they only feel "normal" when they are taking opioids such as heroin, Vicodin, Percodan, and other pain relievers. They do not describe getting high or feeling euphoric but state that taking these opioids gives them a sense of feeling "normal," not feeling high but a sense of well–being that helps them function. According to Larry Siever, reduced opioid levels may play a part in intensifying the experience of negative emotions so that having low opioids would lead to feeling a sense of inner deadness and chronic dysphoria or sadness. Perhaps this is why so many people with BPD report feeling depressed but do not respond to antidepressant medications and tend instead to overuse opiate pain medications. They are self-medicating.

---

[30] Bohus et al., 2000.

As these drugs are controlled substances, their use is viewed as addiction. Additionally, people who use them seem to develop dependency and, when the drugs are withdrawn, they experience withdrawal. Opioids have been used safely for years in management of chronic pain with a minimal risk of addiction and toxicity and a great increase in quality of life. Off-label (not recommended by the FDA) use of opioids for psychological relief, however can leave perscribers at risk for legal liability.[31]

Fibromyalgia is a disease of acute sensitivity to pain that seems to be of unknown origin. The TARA helpline has received many calls from people with BPD who also suffer with fibromyalgia. Is there a relationship between fibromyalgia and BPD? Surely, the person described by Larry Siever as exquisitely sensitive could be exquisitely sensitive to pain. It seems clear that the link between pain and BPD is another area that needs further research.

Memory Dysregulation—White Ball

When your loved one with BPD describes a past experience, you may find you have a very different recollection of the event than he has. Something seems to have been lost in translation over time or added on to the experience. His description is not quite the way you remember it, yet somehow there is a nugget of truth within his memory. Why has the story changed so much? Why does the story change with each progressive retelling? Is it his interpretation of the facts that is off or is it his actual recall of the emotions associated with the event? Is he fabricating the story? Is he lying? Each time the memory is brought up there is yet another change, another ratcheting up of the emotions experienced at the time, making the incident even more extreme, more unpleasant, more aversive.

Clinicians typically hear descriptions of events and experiences in the lives of their patients but these are generally uncorroborated by family members. Corroboration would probably reveal disparities between the memories of those with BPD and a family member's recall of the same event. The following explanation of memory and current directions in memory research may shed light on how and

---

[31] New et al., 1997; Philipsen, Schmahl, & Lieb, 2004.

Very little can be more painful for a family member who loves someone with BPD than an automatic insinuation or an actual accusation of abuse when it did not actually happen. what people with BPD remember and how these memories affect their relationships with the people who love them, as well as the clinicians who treat them. Understanding the process of memory might also explain some of the descriptions of abuse that people with BPD frequently report. Although, sadly, abuse does occur in some cases, not all people with BPD have been abused. Very little can be more painful for a family member who loves someone with BPD than an automatic insinuation or an actual accusation of abuse when it did not actually happen.

Memory is an area of study that falls within two areas of science: cognitive psychology and neuroscience. The marriage of these two fields is called cognitive neuroscience. Memory is the ability of the brain to store, retain, and subsequently recall information. The process of recalling memories is called retrieval. Memory is not a one-dimensional system. The brain has multiple memory systems, each devoted to different kinds of learning and memory function. Memory is generally classified in several different ways: by the duration of time the memory lasts, by the nature of the memory, by how it is retrieved, and by the type of information remembered. A full description of the way memory works is beyond the scope of this book, but the following points will give you important insights into how your loved one learns and remembers.

We remember information and we remember emotions. Sometimes we remember them together and sometimes they are separate; however, they seem to be moderated by different brain systems. People with BPD seem to remember the emotion of an experience more intensely than the explicit details of that experience. "You were horrible to me on my fifth birthday and I will never forgive you!" If you delve into their memory by exploring and asking what happened, the actual experience may not justify the intensity of their memory.

THE AMYGDALA AND MEMORY

The amygdala is the center of the emotional memory system. It forms and stores emotional memories and memories of emotions and emotional events.[32] The amygdala remembers emotional feelings, even those experienced in infancy. Infants can experience emotions such as fear or anger before they have learned a language or are able to name their feelings. The amygdala also seems to modulate memory consolidation. Emotional memories that are stored in the amygdala are relatively indelible. Other types of memory such as *conscious* awareness of stored information or experience of procedures are processed in another part of the limbic system called the *hippocampus*. From the hippocampus, they are encoded and sent to other parts of the brain to be stored. When you recall information or experiences, the hippocampus retrieves these stored memories. They are then re-encoded and stored again, somewhat the way your computer saves and retrieves information. Emotional arousal, especially when arousal involves aversive feelings such as fear or anger, causes memory to be enhanced. The greater the emotional arousal at the time of an event, the greater the intensity of emotion experienced, the greater the retention of that memory. These different memory systems produce *implicit* memories and *explicit* memories. Implicit memory is memory without conscious, awareness so that previous experiences inform current feelings or behavior. Implicit memory may likely occur in the amygdala. Explicit memory is the conscious, deliberate recollection of experiences and information, probably occuring in the hippocampus. Emotion-based learning is independent of the memory processes occurring in the hippocampus and other parts of the brain, so we often remember the feelings associated with a memory even if the facts do not correlate or justify them.

A stimulus or cue does not have to be consciously perceived to elicit a conditioned emotional response, such as avoiding a fearful cue, when you have not yet consciously realized you are feeling fear. With the passage of time, emotions associated with memories do not seem to diminish but rather to increase in strength. People also appear to be able to fuse conscious, explicit memories of past situations with present-day immediate emotional arousal—if, for example, we feel shame because of something that happened this morning, our past memories of shame are reawakened and seem to intensify our present feeling of shame. We are therefore forming new emotionally laden

---

[32] LeDoux, 2000.

memories of past situations whenever the past situation is recalled in a present emotional situation. It is as if the memory of an emotion from the past is augmenting and intensifying the emotion we are experiencing in the present. This then becomes part of our emotional repertoires.

In the present, Anne has to work late and is very upset because she had to cancel her birthday plans. She is disappointed, embarrassed, and ashamed in front of her friends and is also angry. The emotion she is feeling triggers her explicit memory of her fifth birthday party many years ago when she felt similar emotions because many kids did not show up. This old feeling is retrieved along with the associated explicit memory of her fifth birthday and joins with the aversive emotions of the present situation. The present situation will now feel much, much worse.

You were in a car accident, the car horn was stuck and kept going off while you were waiting for the ambulance. You were in pain and shock, and were very frightened. Now, every time you hear a car horn, your emotional memory system is triggered. Even if you do not want to think about it, your body will automatically respond to that emotion without your control and react as if you were in danger. The sound seems to go right to your amygdala; your emotional memory system does not forget the horn sound and recalls the emotion of the experience, the implicit emotional memory of fear. You have been conditioned to associate the sound of the horn with fear and pain. It is as if a dam has collapsed and the water released is the flood of emotional arousal that brings along all the body responses associated with fear and pain.

For someone with BPD, the emotion of an aversive situation from the past seems to become part of the present experience. The highly emotional memory has joined with the current experience of the horn to create a new, more intense aversive feeling. Now the current emotional arousal influences your conscious memory of the horn sound. To an observer, the emotion brought to the situation would be completely out of proportion to the actual situation—why would someone fear a car horn? Imagine trying to put out a fire without knowing it was being fed by an underground gas pipeline. This is the emotional memory system in the brain, and it is not under our voluntary control.

The sound of the horn is also remembered by the hippocampus and your temporal lobe—you know that you are hearing a car horn, and it triggers your memory of the actual accident—yet you know objectively that it should not make you fearful. This is an explicit memory, known as *declarative* memory, a remembrance of a fact. Other examples would be, "my mother died 20 years ago, my husband was injured in the war, our business failed last year." You have declarative memories of emotional experiences without having the emotional responses—these will not upset you as time has passed and you can deal with the memory when it arises. Somehow, people with BPD do not seem able to do this.

For people with BPD, this mechanism involved with of emotional memory seems to be more intense, to occur frequently, and affects many interactions that might otherwise be experienced as benign, especially with people closest to them. Joseph LeDoux of New York University notes that "the structure of the past imposes an interpretive landscape on the present."[33] This seems to be what happens when someone with BPD gets upset in the present over something that happened in the past. The amygdala hits the gas; emotional control in the prefrontal cortex is impaired (no brake), and the person is flooded with emotions he cannot control. Events in the present that are similar emotionally to past experiences seem to automatically arouse past emotions. If something in the environment of a person with BPD triggers an implicit memory or memory of an emotion, if something is self-referentially misinterpreted, emotions are aroused without the person knowing why, reactivating the past emotional experience over and over again. Past events or hurtful things you may have said seem to be recalled with the same degree of pain, suffering, and emotional intensity as if they had just happened, although the incident discussed may actually have occurred 10 or 20 years ago. They seems to combine with the present situation, and we are off to a full-fledged rage attack that seems to have appeared from nowhere, like the rabbit that a magician pulls out of his hat. The person is reacting to a present situation with an intensity that you cannot comprehend. You may believe you are talking about a present situation but, unbeknownst to you, you are actually strolling down memory lane. The passage of time seems to offer your loved one no relief; the pain never seems to abate. Any effort you make to reason with your loved one, explain the situation,

---

[33] LeDoux, 1996, p. 126.

defend yourself, or justify your actions at these times usually makes the situation worse. Even if you apologize, you are not forgiven.

This vicious cycle is especially prevalent when memories concern feelings of shame. As LeDoux writes, "Past painful memory plus present arousal fuse into a conscious experience of the moment."[34] This converts into a new memory that is similarly emotionally laden. We must have compassion for someone who is constantly reliving his past emotional pain. Most people can separate their emotional memories from their explicit memories; that is why we are able to recover from traumatic experiences and grief. It seems that people with BPD cannot do this so easily, if at all. The inability to let go of unpleasant memories contributes to living life in perpetual pain. Maybe this explains the invisible stone of pain that people with BPD carry around, dooming them to repeat past painful memories. Sadly, these painful memories do not seem to be modulated by memories of good times.

How does the memory system of people with BPD operate? Is it another neural network that is dysregulated? While research to decipher memory is ongoing, memory dysregulation as a specific BPD symptom has not yet been studied. The foregoing discussion of memory is based on the research on fear and memory of Joseph LeDoux.

Anxiety—Pink Ball

Anxiety can be described as a brooding fear of what might happen.[35] People with BPD generally suffer from anxiety. Hypervigilant and fearful, they live with persistent feelings of being out of control. Research points to a connection between anxiety, impulsivity, and mood disorders. People with BPD generally have all three. Anxiety is usually one of the first diagnoses that people with BPD receive on their journey through the psychiatric world. Anxiety can be seen in children at an early age but is not generally recognized or treated unless it is extreme. Perhaps greater public awareness of anxiety symptoms in children would bring about earlier diagnosis and exposure to coping skills that could prevent development of the maladaptive behaviors that characterize BPD.

---

[34] LeDoux, 1996.
[35] LeDoux, 1996.

The Big Picture

How can you be in control of yourself when you never know when your mood is going to switch, when an impulse that you cannot regulate will take over your life, you are hypersensitive to the world around you, and allergic to anything that sounds like criticism, blame, or judgment? You are always juggling those colored balls, always carrying the invisible stone of pain, always on your guard. Perhaps this is why people with BPD usually do well in highly structured environments. Take away the structure and they are unable to cope, as they lack everyday life skills. Feeling out of control, feeling insecure because you do not have a solid basis for your thoughts or actions, is like living your daily life on the rolling deck of a ship in a storm.

The TARA Tiara

As a visual cue to help you remember the many systems in dysregulation in BPD and to remind you that your loved one is doing the best he or she can, you can create a special TARA tiara to cue your memory. At Halloween or at birthday parties, children wear special headbands adorned with little springs attached to glittery hearts, balls, or crescents that stand up on the band. Tape several of these headbands together so that you have about 9 or 10 balls bopping in the air at once. Each one of these glittery balls represents a system in dysregulation, or one of the balls the juggler is tossing into the air. These tiaras are worn during role plays in TARA family workshops. Many a family member has described incidents like this: "I was with my son, and the situation was getting very tense when I suddenly pictured him wearing the TARA tiara. I stopped being angry, I stopped judging and criticizing, and was flooded with compassion. Then I knew just what to say to him. My son seemed to feel the change in me, got calmer, and the crisis was averted."

Looking Ahead: New BPD Research, New Hope

This chapter gives you an overview of what we know, what we are researching, and what we should be researching in the future with regard to BPD. In 2008, in response to TARA's Freedom of Information

Act inquiries, it was revealed that National Institute of Mental Health (NIMH)-funded studies on BPD amounted to approximately $7,000,000, or a little over one-half of 1% of that agency's total budget of over $1 billion. Schizophrenia receives approximately 14% of the total NIMH budget, depression 13.7%. All personality disorders combined receive only 1%. Is this sufficient for the 5.9% of the general population that has BPD (according to Bridget Grant's recent National Institute of Alcohol Abuse and Alcoholism epidemiological study of 34,500 people in the general population)? How long will it take to find a "cure" for BPD at this rate? You may have already spent huge sums of money on substance abuse facilities, rehabs, residential treatment facilities or eating disorder programs only to discover that these treatments were not effective because they did not treat the underlying BPD. They may often make the situation worse. Right now, the demand for evidence-based treatment for BPD and intensively trained clinicians in DBT or Mentalization-Based Therapy greatly exceeds availability. Clearly, the amount of research being done is paltry compared to the number of people affected by BPD.

Eric Kandel received a Nobel Prize for his work on memory, learning, and *neurogenesis*—the ability of the brain to grow new neuronal pathways, regardless of age.[36] This research is incredibly important because it shows us that *people can change*. Imagine that the highway you use is being repaired, lengthening your daily commute. Another road can get you to work but it is less direct and seems slower than the highway. As more and more cars begin to use the secondary road, signage and traffic lights are installed. Although at first the secondary road was frustrating and time-consuming, it now substitutes well for the highway, gets you to your destination, and is actually a shorter ride. It has replaced the highway. This is a metaphor for the brain's *neuroplasticity*.

The brain functions in a similar way. New neuronal networks develop with new learning as evidenced by the treatment of dyslexia. Sabine Herpertz, of the University of Heidelberg in Germany, conducted fMRI brain scans periodically on people with BPD who were in DBT (see Chapter 5) as their treatment progressed over 1 year. After intensive DBT treatment, the patients showed reduced activation in

---

[36] Kandel, 2000, 2005, 2006.

their amygdalas. This physical evidence that treatment can actually change the brains of people with BPD should give us hope for better lives for our loved ones. What is needed to decipher BPD and find better treatments are more studies like this one, and studies with larger numbers of patients. We need research to tell us what helps, why it helps, and what does not help.

Neurogenesis does not happen spontaneously. If a person with BPD wants to have a less stressful life and not be ruled by her emotions, she must work at learning new skills and at changing her own behavior. We do not judge a person if she has diabetes; however, the person has to take responsibility for her disorder and manage her daily sugar intake. She was not born knowing she had diabetes but must suffer the consequences of having diabetes until it is diagnosed and she and her family learn techniques to balance her diet and insulin intake. Your loved one did not ask to have a genetic vulnerability to BPD, yet she must learn how to live with it. Is it helpful to get angry at a diabetic person who falls into a coma because he ate too much or too little sugar? The person with BPD and her loved one's need to accept this disorder and work at learning coping skills and how to diminish daily stressors. Most importantly, we all need to cultivate compassion for our loved ones' pain.

> *Physical evidence that treatment can actually change the brains of people with BPD should give us hope for better lives for our loved ones.*

3

The Principles of Behavior Change

> They always say that time changes things but you actually have to
> change them yourself.
>
> —Andy Warhol

A S A CARING AND CONCERNED PERSON, YOU CLEARLY SEE THAT your loved one needs to do something differently, make better choices, and solve her own problems in order to have any financial or emotional security and a happier life. The person you love with borderline personality disorder is probably very intelligent, may have graduated from college, and may be artistically gifted; despite this, she may seem unable to achieve satisfaction in her life. It seems as if your loved one is not performing to her maximum capability or potential, like an eight-cylinder car operating on two cylinders. Somehow, the great things you thought she was capable of have never materialized. Her life is miserable as it is currently being led, and her misery is in turn making your life miserable. You and your family are suffering as a result of your loved one's rigid refusal or inability to change her behavior.

In order for you to help create changes in your family environment, you will need to learn the concepts underlying behavior change. Cognitive behavior therapy (CBT), which has been used to treat depression and other mental disorders, addresses the basic principles of changing behavior. You have already utilized CBT methods yourself when you learned various sports, a foreign language, how to play a musical instrument or drive a car, or when raising your children. Most parents are masters of CBT techniques. While you may not know it, you implemented CBT techniques when you toilet trained your children, taught them how to dress and feed themselves, taught them to ride a bicycle, roller-skate, swim, or play ball. Although these principles are simple, you probably already know they are not easy. The methods and actual procedures needed to help change behavior require a great deal of practice and persistence. When you first begin to use these behavioral change techniques with your loved one, they will seem counterintuitive and different from your usual responses to situations. Keep trying; in the long run, they will be effective. This chapter outlines the basics of how to change behavior and will inform the discussion of Dialectical Behavior Therapy in Chapter 4.

Have you ever smoked? Have you ever tried to quit? If so, was it easy? Have you ever been on a diet? Is it easy to pass up things you like to eat? Have you tried curbing how much money you spend? Maintaining an exercise regimen? Even when highly motivated, you probably found it difficult to change your own behavior. Most people do.

If you still believe changing behavior is easy, try the following: Look around your home or office environment; select an object that you use all the time and put it in a different place. Pick something you use frequently and automatically, something you do not generally think about. Change where you keep your alarm clock or recharge your cell phone. Move a chair, a television set, or your computer mouse. If all of this seems too complicated, simply wear your watch on your opposite wrist for a minimum of a week. This will allow you to experience the process of change so that you can see for yourself just how difficult it actually is to change a behavior. Notice how many times you looked at the wrong wrist when you wanted to know the time, how long it took you to remember that you moved your watch, or how you responded emotionally to not finding your watch where it was supposed to be. Do you still think it is so easy to change behavior?

You may very well have been trying to change your loved one's behavior for a long time. Whatever methods you have employed in the past have probably not succeeded; rules, boundaries, limits—none of these methods worked. Or maybe you tried a laissez-faire approach, allowing your loved one to do whatever it is he does just to avoid an argument, an angry scene, or another visit from the police. Or you may have quit trying altogether and given up doing anything to change his behavior. Having tried everything else, it is time for you to learn a completely new approach to behavior change, one based on changing your own behavior and responses in order to motivate and encourage your loved one to change. You may feel some indignation at this suggestion. After all, it is your loved one, not you, who has BPD, who is suffering or causing the problems; why should you change? A 12-step slogan applies here: "Insanity is doing the same thing over and over again and expecting different results."

Cognitive Behavior Therapy

Behavior is any activity, functioning, or reaction of an individual that includes an action or a response to a stimulus. Behavior can be overt, or public, so that other people can observe it, or it can be covert or private, observed only by the person doing the behavior. Physiological responses, such as rate of breathing, heart rate, sweating, or muscles tensing or relaxing are private or covert responses. Cognitive responses are what a person thinks, believes, expects, or hopes for and are

"We do not see things the way they are. We see them as we are."
–Talmud

also private or covert responses. Action behaviors such as smiling, crying, running, or tapping one's foot are overt, public behaviors.

A cognition is simply a thought or perception. Your thoughts and perceptions determine how you feel. The way you feel, your emotions, determine the way you act. The basic principle behind CBT is that your thinking patterns determine how you respond emotionally. Therefore if you are thinking negative thoughts, you will feel depressed, sad, or anxious. By changing the way they think about an experience, people can change how they feel about the experience and subsequently how they behave or act. The goal of CBT is to change thoughts and perceptions that are causing problems in a person's life.

Cognitive behavior therapy alters behavior by conscious imple-mentation of techniques such as behavioral modification, condition-ing, reinforcement theory, exposure therapy, operant conditioning, and behavioral analysis. These techniques require a person to learn new ways of thinking and acting. CBT is based on the research of well-known psychiatrists and psychologists such as B. F. Skinner, Abraham Lowe, Albert Ellis, Aaron Beck, and others. Many research studies have shown that CBT is more effective than other forms of psychotherapy or pharmacology in treating depression, as it brings about changes in the brain that are retained over time (known as *neurogenesis*)—whereas depression often returns when a medication is discontinued. CBT is widely practiced today.

Latest research demonstrates that behavioral change is best achieved by actually teaching someone how to change his behavior rather than trying to determine the origin or cause of his behavior. In CBT, a person learns how to reframe his thoughts about a situation in order to elicit different and effective responses. Cognitive behavior therapy focuses on a person's views and beliefs about his life, not on his personality traits or on events from the past that may have contributed to the current problem. Dr. Aaron Beck has had positive outcomes applying CBT to suicidal people with BPD.

In CBT, insight into oneself is developed through the discovery of behavioral patterns; progress happens by targeting specific behaviors to change and by learning new ways to react and respond. The aim of CBT is to replace maladaptive methods of coping by helping people define behavioral goals, determine what interferes with the attainment of those goals (what is reinforcing the old, dysfunctional behaviors and/or punishing the new behaviors), targeting specific behaviors to change, and moving toward those goals through the implementation of new, effective behaviors. It helps a person to get what he wants or needs while developing control of his life. Behavior therapy requires a person to change his life, to make a commitment to change, learn new behaviors, and have the willingness to practice them.

Cognitive Behavior Therapy versus Psychodynamic, or "Talk" Therapy

Most therapy practiced today is based on psychoanalytic or psycho-dynamic principles derived from Freud. It is commonly referred to as "insight" therapy. In the safety of the therapist's office, the patient is led to uncover buried childhood memories that established their lifelong patterns of behavior. Once the person understands their early memories, the insight derived will enable them to change their behavior.

Most people who call the TARA helpline have already been treated by an average of five to ten psychodynamically oriented therapists in their lifetime, all to no avail. This may include social workers, psychologists, psychiatrists, family therapists, members of the clergy, school guidance counselors, psychiatric nurses, probation officers, and so on. People with BPD are not generally helped by these methods of treatment, giving rise to the BPD myth of the "bad patient," or the "treatment resistant patient." How can the person needing help be blamed if the treatment fails to help him? Is it not more likely that the treatment itself or the person administering the treatment is ineffective? How does uncovering a childhood memory repair a specific brain circuit, repair an amygdala, or decrease responses in specific areas of the brain?

Many people, not only psychodynamic psychotherapists, believe that present-day behavior is caused by events that occurred in the past. In order to change behavior, this school holds, you must first gain understanding of the past. This idea, based on Freudian psychology, dominated the field of psychiatry for many years. As a result, people often jump to conclusions about a person's behaviors based on Freudian-like interpretations of past experiences. "She has problems because we had a difficult divorce." "He has BPD because I was not a stay-at-home mom but worked when he was a child." "She has BPD because she was raped at summer camp." "He has BPD because he was adopted."

A woman was working two full-time jobs: a stressful teaching job during the day and doing library research in the evenings, returning home near midnight each night. Although she was quite tired, she had difficulty falling asleep because she would be thinking about what she had researched. She consulted a psychiatrist about her sleep problem. In taking her history, the doctor asked her, "Did you have friends in high school?" He felt that long-forgotten childhood events, buried in her unconscious mind, were responsible for her current sleep problem. She, however, felt she was overworked and too mentally stimulated to fall asleep. His conclusion was based on his psychoanalytic training, not on the facts of the situation. Believing that past experiences are responsible for present-day behaviors leads people to believe that their feelings are unconsciously motivated therefore are out of their control.

Fortunately, we are now in the midst of a neurobiological revolution that is changing our thinking about the origin and development of mental disorders. How the brain functions is being revealed by new techniques such as magnetic resonance imaging (MRI), functional magnetic resonance imaging (fMRI), and positron emission tomography (PET) scans. Freud's theory that past experiences determine present behavior is an old paradigm that does not seem to be borne out by present-day scientific investigations.

Cognitive Behavior Change Techniques

CBT incorporates several strategies that, research shows, helps people learn new ways to think and behave. *Reframing* is a technique in which an alternate point of view is assigned to a certain situation or behavior—you can use this one yourself and you can model it for your loved one. *Reinforcement* is another technique you can use for encouraging particular responses and discouraging others. Also discussed below is *punishment,* which research shows does not generally work for those with BPD. *Extinction* is the process of gradually stopping a behavior by changing the expected response to that behavior. *Shaping* is gradually changing a behavior over successive trials by incrementally rewarding small amounts of progress toward the desired form of behavior.

REFRAMING

Learning to see situations in a different context is called *reframing.* If the way you think determines the way you feel and act, changing the way you think or the way you interpret experiences can change the way you feel and act. There are many ways to interpret situations or interactions with other people. A thought underlies the emotion that you feel. As Norman Vincent Peale said, "Change your thoughts and you change your world."

Reframing Cognitive Distortions Most negative thoughts or thinking patterns are based on distorted interpretations and will cause a person to feel negative emotions such as depression, sadness, shame, guilt, hopelessness, and anxiety. It is our own thoughts, beliefs, and attitudes about an event that upset us or determine how we feel, not the actual external event that occurred. Everyone, at some time or another, experiences cognitive distortions. When you are in a bad mood, upset, angry, or emotionally dysregulated, you may tell yourself things that are not necessarily true, leading to negative emotions.

People with BPD are prone to cognitive distortions, especially when they are emotionally dysregulated. They often "overgeneralize" a single negative event, which is seen as an indication of a never-ending pattern of negatives. If your loved one loses her job, for instance, she may think she will never get another one. People with BPD may also think in black-white, "all or nothing" terms: "If I don't get an A in this English course I am a complete failure and will have to drop out of college." Extreme or all-or-nothing thinking fosters knee-jerk reactions to situations and people, such as "he is mean," "she is bad."

> People with BPD are prone to cognitive distortions, especially when they are emotionally dysregulated.

Deciding outcomes in advance, or "crystal balling," is another cognitive distortion that you may recognize. "If I ask the professor for an extension to do my term paper, he will refuse, so I might as well drop the course." If she makes a superb seven-course dinner but the coffee is cold, she feels the dinner was a failure. This is another cognitive distortion—discounting the positive, minimizing the value or significance of anything positive that happens. Nothing she does is good enough, nothing she does counts. He wins a dance contest and says it is not important; he graduates cum laude and says, "So what? I still don't have a job."

Many of us "jump to conclusions" by presuming negative outcomes even though there are no facts to support these conclusions. If her date is late, she is sure he is not coming. When people believe their problems are worse than anyone else's, they are magnifying. When they are sure that the way they feel is the way things are, and their feelings *must* be justified, they are using emotional reasoning. If she feels jealous, her boyfriend must be cheating. Labeling is another harmful cognitive distortion: "If I make a mistake, I am a loser." Personalization and blame are other examples of distorted thinking: If her husband asks her for an aspirin it is because she gave him a headache. Family members of people with BPD are particularly prone to personalizing and blaming themselves for the behaviors or crises of the moment.

By learning to recognize when cognitive distortions like these are occurring in yourself and in others, by examining the situation at hand in a way that is grounded in reality, you will be able to help untwist those distortions. Changing thoughts to more positive, realistic thinking patterns can lead to hopeful, solution-oriented thinking.

Reframing Individual Perceptions Each person sees the world in her own way. We all perceive events and situations differently. Imagine two people in a room. One experiences the room as being too cold while the other person experiences the room as too warm. They both feel that their perception of the room's temperature is accurate. What seems like a distressing situation for one person can be a neutral or positive experience for someone else and a challenge for another. The real difference lies in how each of us interprets events. Some people get stuck in certain kinds of thinking patterns or attitudes that lead to endless cycles of difficulty, such as feeling incompetent or inadequate, unattractive, angry, guilty, anxious, ashamed, or lonely. If your loved one's expectations are unfulfilled, she feels frustrated. But if she can be helped to rethink her expectations, reframe the situation, examine the evidence to see if it supports her cognitive distortions, you will be able to help her feel less frustrated and negative. The old saying, "Is the glass half full or half empty?" describes how negative thinking patterns lead to negative responses and feelings.

It is important to acknowledge that your loved one's perceptions of events may not be the same as yours. To understand the reactions of those with BPD, we must put ourselves in their shoes, see the world as they see it, and evaluate their responses to events from their perspectives, not our own. Reframing the behavior of your loved one with BPD with an understanding of how his neurobiological systems are in dysregulation will help you to see situations from his point of view. People with BPD are exquisitely sensitive and extremely vulnerable to the emotions, attitudes, and behavior of others. They are super-responsive to almost any situation, and are easily emotionally dysregulated. Their reactions are quick and intense and will persist for a longer period of time than would your response to the same situation. They often misinterpret what you say or perceive things in a different context from the way you actually meant them. They are usually making self-referential interpretations that leave them feeling criticized, blamed, or judged. Remind yourself that feelings of shame are usually the primary BPD responses to most situations. Reframing BPD behavior with this knowledge will help you to deescalate and depersonalize your own negative reactions and respond with compassion to your loved one's unrelenting emotional suffering.

Reframing Social Interactions Mary and Alice both work for the same computer company. When their boss, Mr. Smith, comes into the office in the morning, he does not say good morning to either Mary or Alice. Mary thinks, "Oh my, Mr. Smith must have had a bad weekend." Alice, on the other hand, thinks, "Mr. Smith didn't say 'good morning' to me, so that means he doesn't like me. I must have done something wrong. He is going to fire me. What will I do now?" Mary has a productive day at work, while Alice is discouraged, ruminates on why the boss does not like her, feels tense and insecure about her job, and does not have a very productive day.

Mary and Alice had the very same experience yet each reacted to Mr. Smith's behavior in accordance with how she framed or interpreted the situation. Mary is the type of person who sees the glass as half full. She thinks positively, does not personalize, gave the situation a benign interpretation, and consequently was not disturbed or affected by Mr. Smith's rudeness. Alice, who generally thinks negatively and sees the glass half empty, personalized Mr. Smith's rudeness, ruminated on its possible negative implications and consequently had a very bad day at work.

Reframing Delays Sam wants to speak to his friend Frank about a matter that is very important to him. Sam calls Frank but he is not at home. Sam leaves a message saying, "This is Sam; please call me back as soon as possible. It is really important." Five days go by and Frank has not returned Sam's call. How would you interpret Frank's failure to call Sam? If you are a positive thinking person you will remind yourself that people can be overwhelmed by phone messages, e-mails, instant messages, letters, and cell phone calls and that it is very hard to keep up with the demands of today's hectic life. You assume that Frank is busy and will call Sam back when he can. Perhaps Frank is out of town. If you are a negative thinking person you would probably tell yourself that Sam does not count, that he is not important enough to Frank to warrant a call-back. You might assume that Frank does not want to talk to Sam any more. Some people might get angry and annoyed, "Why didn't he call me back? Who does he think he is?" Some people might feel sad, "Frank doesn't even remember me. I didn't make an impression on him at the party, my comments must have been so dumb. I am really embarrassed." Someone else might be concerned and wonder if something might have happened to Frank. The way we feel depends completely on the way we interpret a situation, the way we *frame* the situation. While the external event is the same in each scenario, it is our own thoughts and beliefs about a situation that determine our feelings and reactions.

Reframing Rejection Robert met Sue at a party. He thinks she is really special and would like to see her again. Sue gives him her phone number. Robert calls her a few days later and asks Sue out for Thursday evening. She turns him down because she already has plans. How does Robert interpret her response? He could think to himself, "Sue has no interest in seeing me ever again. She doesn't like me. I'm a loser." Or he could think, "Sue had someplace to go on Thursday night and couldn't make it. I'll call her again." Finally, he could think, "That bitch, she never really wanted to go out with me in the first place, she was only leading me on!"

If Robert thinks positively, he might try calling Sue again. After all, why would she give him her phone number if she was not interested in him? If instead he believes, "I'm a loser. Sue will never go out with me," the way Sue has responded will affirm Robert's thoughts about himself. He will never call her again and will continue to feel sorry for himself, thus reinforcing his own perception that he is a loser. If Robert is really trying to change his behavior patterns and is learning to reframe situations, this scenario could be a real challenge for him as he will have to take a risk and try a new behavior. He might be rejected again. However he might not. The action he takes will depend on how he thinks about the situation. By reframing, he can opt for a benign interpretation, give himself the benefit of the doubt, and try again. He will probably succeed in going out with Sue.

Reframing Manipulation Manipulation is defined as "to handle or manage especially with skill and dexterity, to treat or manage with mind and intellect, to control the action or course by management, to control, manage or play upon by artful, unfair or insidious means, especially to one's own advantage or to serve one's own purpose."

People with BPD have difficulty planning and executing actions because the way their prefrontal cortexes functions makes it very difficult for them to control their impulses. They have a hard time controlling this part of their brains, which also affects their judgment, and decision making ability. This is biological, not intentional. When you feel manipulated by your loved one with BPD, ask yourself, "What did he gain by this behavior? Was that his intention?" Is he capable of "skillfully, artfully handling a situation to achieve a goal"? When you reframe manipulation in this way, your loved one's actions will cease to seem manipulative.

Judith, a friend with BPD, calls you at work. She is extremely upset and begs you to meet her right away. You are very busy at work and, if you leave now, you will have to take work home and stay up very late this evening to meet a job deadline. Judith pleads with you. You capitulate, agreeing to meet her at a cafe. You arrive at the cafe on time and wait. Judith does not show up. When you call her, you get her answering machine. You are furious and feel completely manipulated. This is a typical experience for those involved with someone with BPD.

When you heard Judith's voice, it told you that she was extremely upset and emotionally dysregulated. You imagine her wearing the TARA tiara (see Chapter 2) and remind yourself that a person with BPD has a low tolerance for distress, is probably struggling with impulsive feelings, and needs immediate relief of her aversive feelings. Decision making is certainly not her strong suit when she is dysregulated. Judith truly wanted you to meet her to talk when she called. Perhaps while she was dressing she could not decide what to wear. She tried on different outfits and forgot about the time. She realized she could not possibly be ready on time and was too embarrassed and ashamed to call you. Or maybe she could not find her keys, could not face answering the phone, and avoided the whole painful experience by not showing up at all. She knows you will be angry with her and thinks that she is an irresponsible loser. Perhaps she received a phone call before leaving to meet you, was distracted, calmed down, and forgot that she had asked you to meet her in the cafe. Or she may have started to ruminate about what your conversation would be like, decided in advance how you would react to her problem, and felt so much shame that she was immobilized.

The questions you must ask yourself are these: Was her behavior in any way directed against you? Were you manipulated or are you dealing with someone who has a severe disability and is doing the best she can at that moment? By reframing the situation from a compassionate point of view, you can change your own response. What advantage has Judith gained by asking you to meet her somewhere and then not showing up? She probably realizes you will be angry with her and may not want to help her in the future, and that you may see her as selfish, unreliable, and irresponsible. What was her intent when she called you? How did she benefit by not showing up? It did not get her the help she needed with her problem. She is probably feeling shamed and guilty. Her handling of the situation was extremely *un*artful. In fact, it was inept. Why would anyone deliberately work toward this outcome?

Reframing a situation in no way endorses behavior, particularly negative or irresponsible behaviors. People do not want to be stood up, especially after they have put themselves out to get to an appointment. However, this behavior clearly was not directed against you or intended to hurt or annoy you. Although you may be justified in interpreting the situation as one in which you were manipulated, you were not manipulated. Feeling manipulated is not the same as being manipulated. A feeling is not a fact.[1] If you can reframe the situation by accepting your friend or loved one's emotional dysregulations and find compassion for her suffering, you will no longer feel manipulated.

> Feeling manipulated is not the same as being manipulated.

If you learn the principles underlying behavior change, such as reframing, interactions with your loved one can become opportunities to model new behaviors and reinforce positive changes. You are not "curing" BPD but are teaching him new ways to help himself cope with his own life.

REINFORCEMENT

Reinforcement is an action or behavior taken during or upon completion of another action or behavior that will increase the likelihood of that behavior occurring again. Reinforcement is defined by its results—if the behavior changes, reinforcement is successful.

---

[1] Linehan, 1993a.

Learners earn a reinforcer by what they do. Reinforcers can be positive or negative.

Positive Reinforcement A behavior followed by a pleasant consequence increases the likelihood of the behavior happening again. This is positive reinforcement. If what you are doing now is "good" and gets you something you want or like, something that gives you pleasure, such as a smile, praise, or a treat, the probability increases that you will repeat the behavior, some more. Therefore, the behavior increases. The behavior brings about or causes the reinforcement, and the reinforcement makes the behavior occur more frequently so that the person gets more reinforcement—a continuous feedback loop.

A dog likes dog biscuit treats. Each time the dog responds to the command "sit," you give him a biscuit treat. The dog wants more of the treats. When you say "sit" again, the dog responds quickly because he knows he will receive another biscuit. His new behavior is reinforced. Timing is crucial, as reinforcement must occur at the same time or in conjunction with the behavior being reinforced. This is particularly important when interacting with people with BPD. If the reinforcement or pleasant consequence does not occur at the same time as the behavior, the person with BPD will often misinterpret the omission of the positive reinforcement. Those with BPD may attribute their failure to receive a positive consequence or reinforcement as an indication that they performed a task incorrectly, as in "I did it wrong," or "You didn't notice how good a job I did so why should I ever try again?" The person learning needs immediate recognition that what he just did warrants a "prize," the prize being whatever the reinforcer is in the particular situation. Positive reinforcement tells the person that what he is doing now is good and will get him something that he wants, so he ought to do it some more. Behavior that is already occurring can be intensified with positive reinforcement, even if it is only occurring once in a while. If you try to reinforce behavior that has not yet occurred, you are not reinforcing, you are bribing. That is not an effective way to change behavior.

James is 18 years old. Whenever he goes out with his friends, he does not call his mother. She becomes frightened and anxious when she does not know where he is or when he will be home, and worries about his safety. She would like James's behavior to change so that he will call to touch base with her when he is out. When she asks him to call, his usual reply is, "You don't trust me and are just trying to control me!"

Positive reinforcement can be implemented to change James's behavior so that he will call his mother. After much discussion, James reluctantly agrees to call his mother by 11 P.M. when he is out with his friends. However, he fails to do so and it is midnight before James finally calls.

> MOM: "Oh James, I am so glad to hear from you. Thank you for checking in. I really appreciate the effort you are making to let me know where you are. I can only imagine how annoying it must be to call me when you are out with your friends. How is the dance? Are you having a good time?
>
> JAMES: Yes mom, it was great. I am at Sandy's house.
>
> MOM: I look forward to hearing all about it tomorrow. I am going to bed now, have fun, and thanks again for checking in. Good night.

In this exchange, James's mother let him know how happy she was to hear from him. Even though he called an hour later than they had agreed upon and was not where he said he would be, his mother did not judge or criticize him. She validated how annoying it must be for him to have to call her and told him how much she appreciated hearing from him. Because his mother trusted him, James felt good about himself, so the conversation was a positive experience for him. His own behavior brought him a positive consequence. This feeling was so good that James will now be much more likely to repeat the behavior so as to get more of this positive reinforcement.

Negative Reinforcement A negative reinforcer is something the learner wants to avoid, such as a blow, an annoying sound, a frown, or a displeased facial expression. When you get into a car, a nasty buzzer sounds if you fail to put on your seat belt. To make the sound go away, you must attach the seat belt as soon as you sit down. This is negative reinforcement. You increase a behavior, putting on the seat belt, to avoid something you do not want, listening to the unpleasant sound. To avoid negative reinforcers you need to change a behavior.

As soon as the new behavior starts, fastening the seat belt, the aversive response, the unpleasant sound, stops. Eventually you will put on your seat belt automatically upon getting into the car, even if the annoying noise is not present.

Negative reinforcement is not very effective with people with BPD because it gives them aversive feelings about their actions. As a result, they will not try to change their behavior but instead simply avoid the source of the aversive feelings. Let's look at James and his mother again. This time the interaction is an example of negative reinforcement.

MOM: James, it is midnight! You said you would call at 11 P.M. I've been worried about you. Where are you? Don't you realize I have to get up early in the morning?

JAMES: I didn't realize it was so late, I'm sorry. We are all at Sandy's house.

MOM: What are you doing at Sandy's house? You said you were going to the school dance. Why did you lie to me?

JAMES: Mom, I am not lying. You never trust me. I went to the dance and then everyone came over to Sandy's house to celebrate.

MOM: That is not what we agreed upon. You have broken your agreement with me. Don't forget your curfew. Besides, you have soccer practice tomorrow morning and have to get up early.

JAMES: I have to go mom. Bye.

Based on the response he received, James will probably not want to call his mother again unless he is really forced to because the conversation was an unpleasant, aversive experience that brought him negative feelings he would rather avoid. His mother criticized him, called him a liar, and made him feel incompetent. She is more concerned with being right than with being effective. What are his mother's short-term and long-term goals in this situation? Is the goal to improve her relationship with her son and the communication between them, or is it to get James home by curfew? Sometimes, to be effective, we must lose small battles so we can win the war.

Sometimes, to be effective, we must lose small battles so we can win the war.

Frequency of Reinforcing When you have identified a behavior to reinforce and have begun the process, you must reinforce that behavior every time the new behavior occurs. Once the skilled behavior happens frequently, indicating that change is occurring, you can begin to vary the reinforcement and gradually phase it out. Intermittent reinforcement means fading out reinforcement gradually, and eventually phasing it out altogether. This gradual process continues until your loved one has either learned the new behavior or phased out or extinguished the old unwanted behavior. Behavior the person has already learned does not need to be reinforced every time it is demonstrated. Once James begins to call his mom regularly, she will no longer need to reinforce him every time he calls.

On the other hand, if you are constantly reinforcing a newly learned behavior after it has already been learned, the person with BPD may interpret this as an indication that you feel he is incompetent. Once a behavior is learned, it is important not to reinforce it on a regular basis but instead, do so on a random or unpredictable basis. Skipping a reinforcer occasionally and selecting a stronger or better response to reinforce the next time is called *variable reinforcement*. For people with BPD, learning to tolerate an occasional failure, such as not being reinforced, can be a giant step forward. The goal for the person with BPD should be to maintain new behavior without constant reinforcement. Once a behavior has been reinforced, a new behavior to reinforce, such as establishing an appropriate time for James to come home, can be selected, and the entire process begins all over again. Slowly, step by step, change is achieved.

Reinforcers Relative to the Situation Reinforcers are relative. What is reinforcing for one person or in a certain situation may not be reinforcing for someone else or in another situation. A positive reinforcer must be something the person who is learning really wants. When selecting a reinforcer to use in a situation, it is important to know or to find out what the person wants. Food is reinforcing to someone who is hungry but not to someone who has just eaten. Ice cream is not a reinforcer to someone on a diet but may be for a child or someone trying to gain weight. If you are allergic to chocolate, it is not a good choice as a reinforcer. Praise can be a reinforcer, but not all the time. Sometimes praise can be given for the wrong reason. A teacher tells a student that he is very good at knowing when the other students are doing right or wrong. Although this may be true, the student's critical abilities did not make his classmates feel very good about him. In this case, praise from the teacher evoked a negative response from the class. Often what you think is reinforcing may be beneficial to you but not to the other person. This is often the case when family members tell their loved ones that they are "proud" of them. For the person with BPD, "I am proud of you" generally indicates that he has finally done something that meets with your approval, thereby meaning everything else he did was probably unacceptable to you. It would be more effective to say, "You must be so proud of yourself for having done that so well." Your knowledge of your loved one puts you in a good position to find effective reinforcers.

Self-Reinforcement Self-reinforcement is reinforcing yourself for good behaviors, efforts, or accomplishments. People with BPD have great difficulty doing this because they are generally supercritical of themselves and are often perfectionists. Imagine learning something new, such as how to dance the tango or play tennis. If each time you make a mistake you reprimand yourself with, "What an idiot I am, I'll never learn this," you will not improve. However, if you reinforce yourself with "that was terrific, that was a good step or a good shot, I am really getting it, and I am improving," you are positively self-reinforcing. You may not become Venus Williams or Fred Astaire, but you will certainly get more pleasure out of playing tennis or dancing. Demonstrate self-reinforcement by saying something like, "I learned to skateboard, I did it!" or "You're the kind of person who keeps trying and who doesn't give up. I admire your persistence." Reminders like this will help him learn self-reinforcement techniques of his own—which most people do naturally, but which is a challenge for those with BPD.

A visual record of improvement, or of tiny little changes (TLCs), is an effective means of self-reinforcement. Recording your performance at something you are trying to accomplish gives you visible proof of progress that can be seen at a quick glance. This provides motivation to continue trying. Dieters keep records of calories consumed per day or weight loss, students keep records of their grades, banks provide savings account books, and gyms give participants forms to track their progress. Charts, graphs, and diary cards are visible proof of improvement. Seeing an upward curving graph can help people to tolerate a particular day when they may have failed to improve. This can also help to counter the cognitive distortions such as all-or-nothing and black-white thinking that often characterizes the thought patterns of people with BPD.

Daily diary or record cards can be used to help a person monitor his own behavior. He can record the frequency and intensity of problem behaviors, allowing him to take stock of his positive behaviors and see his improvement over time. He can see increases in length of time between episodes of maladaptive behaviors, and decreases in the severity of slips. Total correction of a problem, all at once, is not expected or demanded. If a slip occurs, you must not "throw out the baby with the bathwater." Family members must learn to accept these baby steps as signs of progress. Other records can be extremely helpful for a person with BPD, such as listing the pros and cons associated with making a decision, writing out decision-making guides like short-term and long-term advantages versus short-term and long-term disadvantages, and *chain* or *behavioral analysis*. A chain or behavioral analysis is a step-by-step search for the incident that triggered an initial change in feeling or behavior and how that led up to the situation of the moment. This helps people learn how to organize their thoughts, make decisions, and monitor progress. Written records can help sharpen a person's ability to observe, describe, and be aware of the antecedents to and consequences of her behavior. This helps the person discriminate between inferences and observations of a situation or event. You can look at the record together and point out the progress the person has made if she fails to reinforce herself.

> Written records can help sharpen a person's ability to observe, describe, and be aware of the antecedents to and consequences of her behavior.

Remember, it is important to pay attention to the timing of reinforcements. Also, notice improvements in the behavior you have targeted for change, even if the improvement is only in baby steps. Be sure to reinforce these TLCs. Reinforce improved behavior as soon as possible; immediate reinforcement is more effective than delayed reinforcement.

Reinforce the Positive and Ignore the Negative If five out of 20 students do their homework, instead of scolding the 15 who did not do their homework, positively reinforce the five who did by focusing time and attention on them. Ignoring the students who did not do their homework is negative reinforcement. They want your time and attention and, by not doing their homework, they did not get it. They brought a consequence upon themselves they do not like therefore they will be more likely to do their homework next time. This approach will be more effective in motivating the 15 who did not do their homework than if you had punished them. When you respond minimally to harsh remarks and insults but reinforce any tendency to be pleasant and thoughtful with approval and attention, you will soon see changes in behavior. The trick here is to be persistent in ignoring the unpleasant behaviors. Be sure to overlook an occasional failure. Nobody is perfect!

Be ready to stop a negative reinforcer as soon as you see the behavior has changed. Do not dwell on the behavior, give lectures or speeches about the behavior, or even make a comment on the stopping of the behavior. Imagine you are discussing something that really frustrates your loved one. You are asking him what he can do about making friends. He gets so angry he breaks a dish. You insist he pick up the pieces and ask him to replace the dish for you as soon as possible. He bends down, picks up the pieces, and agrees to replace the dish. You say, "Thanks," and immediately return to the discussion of how he can make friends. Thus the inappropriate behavior is not permitted to deflect the discussion of how to create change and solve the problem. This requires you to be persistent and not to allow yourself to be distracted from your goal. If the desired result has been achieved and the negative reinforcement continues, you are no longer reinforcing the behavior and you will not be teaching the person anything. The reinforcement then becomes a meaningless and annoying noise, like a seat belt buzzer going off after the seat belt has been attached.

Beware of Reinforcing Harmful Behaviors Imagine a child in a supermarket. He sees CoCo Puffs, he wants them, and grabs them off the shelf. His mother says, "No, you cannot have the CoCo Puffs, they are too sweet and are not good for you." The child begins to scream and makes a scene. Everyone in the store comes running to see what is happening. The mother is mortified as people are staring at them. She does not know how to stop his tantrum so she buys him the CoCo Puffs. Although she gets short-term relief, this has long-term consequences. Because the mother could not tolerate the distress of her child throwing a tantrum in public, she reinforced the child's unacceptable behavior. He learned that tantrums get results; he got the CoCo Puffs, and this behavior is likely to recur. The "CoCo Puffs Syndrome" characterizes daily life for many families who live in fear of what their loved one might do if they say *no*. Caving in reinforces their loved one's dependency, abusive behaviors, and maladaptive coping.

The very maladaptive behaviors that people with BPD need to change are often unwittingly reinforced by family members and mental health professionals. When a person with BPD exhibits para-suicidal behaviors such as cutting, this is often not a wish to die but is a means of ending intolerably painful feelings in the moment. It is the person's maladaptive way of distracting herself or coping with aversive, unpleasant, and painful feelings. If the police are called she is taken to the hospital, family or partners rush over to see her, she is no longer alone, and she is distracted from the painful incident that caused the emotional pain in the first place. In the short run, the painful experience is certainly diluted. A person with BPD can often get more help by adopting a helpless or out-of-control emotional stance than by acting competently. Thus, helplessness and out-of-control emotionality are reinforced. The person has, in essence, received a positive reward or short-term immediate reinforcement for extremely maladaptive behavior. In the long run, she may experience negative or punishing outcomes such as finding herself in the hospital after a suicide attempt and being unable to get out, or becoming addicted to the drugs she used for relief, causing even more problems and negative consequences. Rocket science is not required to see where this road can lead. This situation is all too familiar to family members of people with BPD.

At the same time, this does not mean that talk of suicide should be ignored or downplayed. Do not assume that a suicide attempt was made just to get your attention, as you may be assuming intentions that were never there in the first place. Assuming intentions of behavior precludes observing and describing the behavior accurately. Thinking a person attempted or threatened suicide to get attention precludes finding or understanding the trigger that led to the behavior, the intensity of the emotional pain she was feeling, her inability to tolerate this emotional pain in the moment, and her lack of effective skills to reduce her painful feelings. These presumptions will prevent you (or a therapist) from understanding the significance of the behavior and from responding with compassion. Feelings or beliefs about causes of behavior that are not supported by facts will not tell you very much about what really influenced the behavior. Ask your loved one, "What happened?" and really listen for the answer before you jump to conclusions. Without knowing what actually happened, you lose the opportunity to explore alternative behaviors that could have been implemented.

PUNISHMENT

Punishment is any event that interrupts, suppresses, or stops behavior in a specific situation. The person being punished receives an aversive consequence that he does not want, such as being scolded in front of his siblings or friends, or loss of something he really wants, such as car privileges. The message is that what he is doing now is not good, and something bad will happen unless he stops. Punishment can stop a behavior from occurring in the moment; however, it does not improve or eliminate the behavior in the long run. It is for this reason that punishment does not generally work for people with BPD.

While reinforcers strengthen behavior in the future, so that a behavior can eventually be eliminated or extinguished, punishment in no way predicts that a behavior will stop in the future. Paradoxically, when punishment does not work, it is usually escalated—which also does not work. All punishment does is motivate a person to avoid that punishment in the future by any means possible. For someone with BPD, the behavior being punished is usually the result of skills deficits such as the inability to tolerate distress; how does punishing a person with BPD teach her distress tolerance skills? In particular, punishment that does not coincide in time with the actual behavior being punished, that occurs after the behavior has occurred, is also ineffective. The person does not connect the actual behavior she engaged in in the past with the punishment received in the present, and so learning does not occur.

Jessica, a 21-year-old college student with bulimia and BPD, lives at home with her parents. Jessica's boyfriend called her at 11 P.M. to break their date for the next evening because he had exams and needed more time to study. Jessica believes that her boyfriend is breaking up with her, has found another girl who she believes is thinner than she. She is convinced that she is unattractive and too fat, and that she will never have another boyfriend as long as she lives. As the evening wears on, all sorts of demons creep out of Jessica's emotional closet to torment her. Her anxieties spiral out of control. Lacking distress tolerance skills, Jessica goes to the kitchen and proceeds to binge on everything she can find, depleting all the food like an invading army of locusts. She then purges all she has eaten. She becomes physically sick and feels completely miserable and ashamed of her own behavior.

Myra, Jessica's mother, believes she is entitled to milk with her breakfast. This really matters to her. She makes sure there is always milk in the refrigerator before she goes to bed at night. The next morning Myra awakens to the telltale signs of her daughter's middle-of-the-night binge. The proverbial cupboard is bare; there is no milk in the refrigerator. Myra is furious and believes Jessica is selfish and inconsiderate. She decides to punish her by locking the refrigerator and considers protecting the family food from the marauding binger by moving the refrigerator into her bedroom closet.

Had Myra walked into the kitchen at the time Jessica was in the act of binging and purging to ease her distress, she might have been able to successfully stop the behavior. However, six hours later, Jessica's boyfriend has already called her to confirm their date for that evening and she is no longer dysregulated. She is in a completely different emotional state and does not connect her emotional pain of the night before with the lock her mother is threatening to place on the refrigerator door. Myra's and Jessica's behaviors resulted from unrelated triggers; think of their behaviors as parallel lines that will never meet. The punishment Myra is proposing will not be effective in stopping future binges because it has nothing to do with what triggered her daughter's dysregulated feelings of the night before.

EXTINCTION

Behaviors are maintained because they are reinforced; they will continue until you remove the reinforcers that maintain them. When you consistently remove reinforcers, over time, the behavior is extinguished. An *extinguished behavior* is one that is no longer occurring because it has not been reinforced. People with BPD often maintain maladaptive behavior patterns because they are constantly reinforced by their environments. If you can figure out precisely what these reinforcers are and systematically withhold them, you can extinguish the behavior and it will stop. Remember the child screaming for CoCo Puffs in the supermarket? His mother, embarrassed by his tantrum, bought the CoCo Puffs so that he would stop screaming, thereby guaranteeing that he will have another tantrum.

People with BPD often maintain maladaptive behavior patterns because they are constantly reinforced by their environments.

He learned that making a scene gets results. If the mother had been able to tolerate her son's first tantrum, there would not have been a second. Now she is faced with the task of extinguishing the behavior she created. She must endure the tantrums every time they go into the store and must persistently resist caving in. Slowly, the behavior (the tantrums) will stop.

Sue's daughter Ann habitually visited the emergency room in the middle of the night for conditions ranging from chronic pain, overdosing on prescription drugs, gastrointestinal problems, severe headache, and suicidal thoughts or threats. Ann would call in the middle of the night and demand that Sue come quickly and bring her to the hospital. Sue's life was falling apart. Her midnight rescues of Ann left her in a constant state of exhaustion. Her husband was furious because she was never at home, and her job was at risk because she could not keep up with the work she was missing. Her husband was talking about divorce.

Sue decided to target for extinction the middle-of-the-night calls to take Ann to the hospital. She began by responding to Ann's demanding calls with a theme and variation of this response: "Oh, Ann, it must be awful to feel so bad. No wonder you are calling me so late at night. What are you going to do about it?" Ann insisted that Sue bring her to the hospital, Sue consistently refused to do so and asked Ann, "How else can you get to the hospital?" Finally, Ann began calling 911. The police would arrive with an ambulance and bring Ann to the hospital. Afterwards, she would call Sue, demanding to be driven home. Sue responded with, "It must be awful to be in so much pain that you had to call 911. However, you are safe in the hospital now. You got yourself to the hospital, how do you think you can get home? I am sure you can get yourself home because you can do hard things. I have to get up for work in a few hours so I am going back to sleep now. I will call you later to see how you are." Sue persisted each and every time Ann called her in the middle of the night. She also stopped visiting whenever Ann was admitted to the hospital. At first, Ann was very angry with her mother. Sue did not cave in and was persistent in refusing to participate in the midnight rescues. After some time, Ann stopped calling her and then stopped going to the emergency room. The behavior was extinguished because Sue was no longer providing reinforcement for Ann's maladaptive method of coping.

Extinction Bursts An extinction burst is a temporary increase in the frequency and/or intensity of a behavior whose reinforcement has been withdrawn. It is the "last hurrah" before the behavior goes away. It is especially important not to cave in at these crucial times. An extinction burst means you are almost there. In the CoCo Puffs scenario, the mother was beginning to feel more relaxed when she went grocery shopping. There had not been a tantrum for weeks. Then, suddenly, it happened again. Her son demanded CoCo Puffs and made a major scene in the store. She endured the scene, refused to buy the CoCo Puffs and persistently said *no*. It was like Custer's last stand. This is an extinction burst—the "one more time to see if it works" effort. The same type of situation developed with Sue. Ann's middle-of-the-night calls began to decrease, and Sue felt that she had succeeded in extinguishing this troublesome behavior when suddenly the calls began increasing again. Nevertheless, Sue was able to hold her ground and did not reinforce Ann's renewed pleas to take her to the emergency room. Instead, Sue was a broken record, validating Ann's pain, then asking Ann how she could solve her own problem of getting herself to the hospital or getting home. Ann stopped using the emergency room as her evening social activity; Sue got some sleep and was able to repair her marriage. This may seem easy to do but it is not. At first, Sue was frightened and felt guilty. However, she received a great deal of cheerleading from her support team of caring friends and family, and stayed the course. She finally succeeded in extinguishing Ann's emergency room behavior.

SHAPING

Slow and steady progress when learning is called *shaping*. Shaping is the process of reinforcing small, successive responses toward a desired goal or behavior. Families need to accept change in small increments as a sign of progress.

Creating change requires acceptance of incremental goals and the persistence to keep working for those ever-important TLCs. Constant progress, even if only inch by inch, will get you to your ultimate goal faster than trying to force rapid change. Think about how we learn to play the piano. Remember how hard it was to wean or toilet train a child. These are all examples of learning through baby steps. How about the old fable about the tortoise and the hare? Slow and steady does win the race!

Shaping One Attribute at a Time We play scales before we play Bach or Mozart. We put training wheels on our bicycles before we ride the big two-wheelers. We learn to make omelets before we embark on a soufflé. We learn the basic steps of a dance before we try ballroom dancing. Shaping involves practicing only one attribute of a behavior at a time. You break down a desired behavior into small steps, each step is a separate component, you work on each component, separately, and teach the steps sequentially. Responses improve little by little until they reach a desired goal. Once the behavior is learned it becomes part of the person's repertoire of more complex behaviors. You then set a new behavioral goal to teach. Shaping involves recognizing tiny little changes. Sometimes you may need to hold up a magnifying glass to see progress more clearly. The essential element of shaping is to persistently reinforce each tiny effort that a person makes toward getting to a goal. Each time Sue refused to take Ann to the emergency room, she was shaping Ann's behavior.

Your husband Frank forages for food during the night, between meals, and when you are out. He leaves a trail of food debris and dirty dishes from one end of the kitchen to the other. You argue constantly about the mess in the kitchen. You demand that he clean it up, tell him he is inconsiderate, and punish him by refusing to cook the special dinners that he likes. He stares at you, blinking, as though he were a deer caught in your headlights. You are at your wit's end. One day you notice a dish and a spoon in the sink. "Frank, thanks for putting the dishes in the sink. I can see how hard you are trying to keep the kitchen clean and I really appreciate the effort you are making. It will be easier for me to get breakfast ready in the morning. Would you like your favorite pancakes?" This will be very hard to do because you are still looking at soda cans, juice containers, and dirty dishes. However, putting the dish and spoon in the sink is definitely an improvement over Frank's past behavior of doing absolutely nothing at all. The next morning you wake up to find your husband has put the dishes he used in to the sink. He has even thrown away some garbage. Again, "Frank, thank you for cleaning up the kitchen. You did a great job. I bet you really feel good about accomplishing this. I see how hard you are working." If you keep reinforcing his behavior this way, over time, you will no longer have to argue about what Frank is not doing.

If you asked Frank to clean the entire kitchen, the enormity of the job would be overwhelming. He simply would not know where to start and would feel hopeless and incompetent. Your expectation of Frank's ability, in the moment, exceeds his ability to accomplish the job. If you nagged him, he would probably feel guilty and ashamed and cover it up by getting angry at you. The anger in this case would be a secondary emotion. If you say, "Why did you only put one dish in the sink and leave the rest for me to clean up?" you would be punishing him for his efforts. Work on only one area at a time. Narrow the focus of your efforts into doable segments. Be patient. When one area improves and becomes part of his repertoire of daily behaviors, you can start on another area with new goals. If he fails to clean up one night, just ignore it. Do not start punishing again or you will lose the progress you have already made. What is needed is vigilance, determination, persistence, and a lot of energy.

> "Failure is the path of least persistence."
> —Anonymous

Shaping Breakthroughs A shaping breakthrough is a sudden leap forward that happens when a person realizes the point of what he is being asked to do. It indicates that the person has understood the principle underlying the method. Imagine learning to dance the tango. The tango is a very complex dance with precise steps. In each weekly class you are taught new steps. You count the beats in the music and try to remember the order and names of the steps, the routines to follow, how to stand, how to keep your balance, how to lead, or how to follow. You concentrate intensely, trying to learn all facets of the tango. One day, music is playing and you find yourself dancing. You are no longer memorizing the steps or counting the beats. You have learned the basic principles and can now dance the tango. When you realize that the steps are transferable, you can even improvise; you can develop a style of your own. When you have a moment of insight and suddenly "get it," there is sudden improvement. A shaping breakthrough indicates you are making a great deal of progress in a hurry, and it can be very exciting. This is how behavior changes, how your loved one will learn change skills and begin to use them.

A crucial factor required to shape behavior is for the person doing the shaping, you in this case, to be persistent and completely noncritical and nonjudgmental. Persistence makes all the difference. We can learn just about anything if we put in the time. Problems arise when we want immediate results, want to learn everything as fast as possible, and are bored by repetitions. However, reinforcement makes us feel good. We do the repetitions to get the reinforcement. Nonjudgmental persistence by the person doing the shaping is the key to success. Shaping is not just a verbal process but is a flow of interactive behavior over time. Make the amount of change or progress needed so small that the person has a real chance to achieve the new behavior. If only one dish goes into the sink, it is one dish more than none and the accomplishment needs to be reinforced

When using behavior change techniques, it is very important to keep in mind that your body language, facial expression, gestures, and tone of voice are just as important as what you say or what technique you use. You must learn to recognize when your loved one has distorted thoughts, and communicate in a way that conveys acceptance, care, concern, and interest rather than criticism, blame, or judgment. The quality of your relationship will determine how you go about using these techniques with your loved one. Being warm and genuine, and expressing closeness, can be helpful—but not if this behavior is viewed as threatening by your loved one. Generally, warmth and closeness are less effective with people who tend to use avoidance as their means of coping. Communicating that you like or admire the person and feel the person is competent and capable helps reinforce new behaviors. If your loved one is reassured that your concern and care signify unconditional acceptance rather than being contingent on "good" behavior, you will have more success. People with BPD need reassurance that you are dependable, reliable, and trustworthy and that your relationship with them is secure. When a positive relationship that includes trust has been developed,

Shaping Helpful Hints

- Focus on shaping only one small behavior at a time.
- Make it easy for the person to make steady improvements.
- Give up specific, long-term goals.
- Break down behavior into small steps, and work on one step at a time, sequentially.
- Practice is not shaping, as we may be repeating mistakes and ingraining mistakes.
- Understand the principle you are teaching rather than just the method.
- If no progress is being made, try a different method. There are many ways to reach the same goal. It is important to find a way that works for the person you are trying to teach.
- Be flexible and creative.
- Have patience. Don't push, don't pressure. Give up speed of progress and be willing to accept tiny little changes. Get rid of time limits in your own mind—shaping takes as long as it takes.
- Be prepared for sudden rapid progress and have the next goal waiting in the wings.
- Think like a Buddhist: quit when you are ahead, accept what's been accomplished in the moment.
- Trust that this process works. Nonjudgmental persistence is the key to success.

"We can do anything we want as long as we stick to it long enough."
—Helen Keller

the relationship itself can be used to bring about change. Family members need to combine acceptance with reinforcement to facilitate change. The distinction between unconditional love and unconditional acceptance will be discussed in Chapter 5.

4

Understanding Dialectical Behavior Therapy

DIALECTICAL BEHAVIOR THERAPY (DBT) IS A METHOD OF COGNITIVE behavioral therapy for treating people with borderline personality disorder; it was developed by Marsha Linehan in 1993 at the University of Washington in Seattle. Dr. Linehan studied chronically suicidal and self-harming women who met criteria for BPD. She realized that these women felt that their ability to change was overestimated, while their degree of suffering was underestimated. She saw their behaviors as maladaptive ways of coping with their constant emotional pain or as consequences of their inability to control their dysregulated emotions. Dr. Linehan formulated strategies to help these women tolerate their pain while working toward building "a life worth living." She developed a skills training program encompassing four modules that teach specific skills in the areas of Mindfulness, Interpersonal Effectiveness, Distress Tolerance, and Emotion Regulation and Self-Management. These skills teach people how to balance their emotions, thoughts, and overt behaviors so that they can enhance their lives without resorting to self-destructive behaviors. The concepts of compassion and acceptance, specific principles based on dialectics and Zen Buddhism are very important to the successful implementation of this treatment. This chapter will explain the general philosophy of DBT and describe how it is practiced. In Chapters 6 and 8 the DBT skill modules themselves will be described in greater detail so that family members can develop new, informed methods to help their loved ones most effectively, by modeling the skills and encouraging their loved ones to incorporate them into their own lives.

Dialectics

Dialectics is defined as a method of argument, persuasion, or debate that establishes the truths on both sides of an issue rather than disproving one argument or proving another. When you are thinking dialectically, you are recognizing that, in any situation, both points of view are valid and that opposites can coexist and be integrated. This necessitates redefining many words such as "right" or "wrong," "bad" or "good," "honest," "fair," "telling the truth," "telling a lie," or "manipulating." Thinking dialectically means accepting that there are absolute truths, such as the law of gravity; however, there are also relative truths. Thinking dialectically means avoiding polarized points of view, seeing both sides of any situation or the relative truths of each side, and seeking a synthesis or middle road. For loved ones of people with BPD, thinking dialectically means learning to see situations and relationships from the point of view of the person with BPD, without judgment, criticism, or blame. It also means giving up all efforts to control situations, to demand fairness or the "right" or "moral" solution. The "dialectic" in DBT arises from the principles and strategies used to balance "acceptance" with "change." Achieving this balance requires constant work, persistent effort, commitment, and recommitment to its goals.

The aim of a dialectic approach in DBT is to achieve a balance between the difficulty of a particular problem with thinking about how the problem can be overcome. Thinking dialectically helps a person with BPD overcome the tendency toward extreme, rigid, either-or, black-white thinking that so characterizes this disorder. Dialectics focuses on synthesizing opposite positions so as to accept that it is possible for opposites to exist simultaneously without negating

Thinking dialectically helps a person with BPD overcome the tendency toward extreme, rigid, either-or, black-white thinking that so characterizes this disorder.

either position. This can lead to a more balanced and integrative response to life. In Zen Buddhism, this approach is called the Middle Path.

Behavior Therapy

Behavior therapy looks at your present life situations rather than focusing on the past or searching for insightful conclusions. It aims to solve problems by teaching new ways of responding to situations. Change occurs when people define specific behavioral goals and determine what interferes with the attainment of those goals, such as what is reinforcing the old, dysfunctional behaviors and/or punishing the new behaviors. In DBT, behaviors to change are targeted and new ways to react and respond are learned to replace the maladaptive methods of coping. The person moves toward these goals through the implementation of new, effective behaviors. DBT helps a person get what he wants or needs while developing control of his life. Behavior therapy is all about changing your life by making a commitment to change, learning new behaviors, and being willing to practice them.

Implementing a Dialectic Approach

At first, thinking dialectically and implementing a DBT approach to relationships and behavior can be very difficult because it is counterintuitive to how most of us think, act, and are accustomed to living our lives. When you begin to learn and implement DBT techniques, you may feel as if you are reacting in a laissez-faire manner or endorsing anarchic or irresponsible behaviors in someone who is already prone to engaging in dangerous, impulsive, or avoidant behaviors. This can be frightening, especially if your loved one is very young and extremely impulsive. A dialectic approach requires learning to differentiate between consequences and punishments, tolerating not being "right" when you feel you are right, not "winning" even though your solution to a problem may be the better solution and be logically correct, and coping with the discomfort of change, contradictions, and inconsistencies. It means you must stop judging, criticizing, and blaming, and give up your efforts to control others.

Compassion is essential. Although implementing DBT requires learning definitive techniques and adhering to a treatment model that has been shown effective in many randomly controlled clinical trials, success in its implementation for both therapists and family members depends in large part upon the degree of compassion expressed toward the person with BPD. Compassion for the constant emotional pain the person with BPD experiences is a key tenet in the philosophy of DBT. Some family members and therapists learn DBT skills and ideas yet are unsuccessful at helping because they have not developed the compassionate stance that makes DBT so unique as both a treatment and a lifestyle.

The importance of developing compassion to successfully implement DBT skills is encompassed by the key DBT principles as described below. When you accept these principles you move toward a nonjudgmental and accepting way of living. The result is progress in overcoming pain, managing difficult lives, and improving relationships.

DBT is supportive. It helps people to identify their strengths, to build on them so as to develop mastery and a sense of competency, and to feel better about themselves and their lives.

DBT is collaborative. It requires that we pay constant attention to interpersonal interactions that can trigger stressful responses in a person with BPD. DBT encourages people to work out their relationship problems with their therapists as they arise and for the therapists to do the same with them. In general, family members try to avoid discussing difficult subjects that might lead to a confrontation with their loved one because they fear that any confrontation may lead to rage attacks, suicide attempts, or major episodes of avoidance or impulsivity. Family members must be vigilantly aware of the power of interactions to trigger responses. They need to learn new ways to interact with their loved ones that can enhance functionality. This is where and when families can apply DBT methods. Talking compassionately about relationship problems as soon as they arise can prevent the problems from transposing into enormous relationship roadblocks. When you do not deal with relationship discord as it arises, it is as if an elephant is stomping about your home while you pretend it is only the cat. It is crucial for relationship repair and development of trust that you engage in genuine discussions, especially when your points of view differ. Such conversations, though more stressful and fraught with more potential triggers than discussions about world peace or global warming, are opportunities to teach and practice more effective relationship skills.

DBT requires active commitment and participation by the patient. He must commit to attending therapy and to do the required work such as completing homework assignments, role-playing new ways of interacting with others, and practicing the skills he was taught in the classes in his own environment.

DBT and Improvisation

DBT is a principle-driven, flexible, and comprehensive treatment. It has a consistent philosophy at its core and is used to develop flexibility in inflexible people. The person with BPD suffers from being rigid and needs to learn how to be more flexible when making decisions, thinking, and living in general. Recognizing the inflexibility inherent in the person with BPD will enable families to relinquish control and be more willing to compromise in situations that could potentially lead to conflict.

Method Versus Principle

Practicing DBT is a bit like playing tennis. Tennis has strict rules, even a formal dress code, but every shot across the net requires the player to be able to improvise and respond with complete flexibility, in the moment, in order to hit the ball. Just like playing tennis, many different DBT techniques can be used strategically as long as they are consistent with the overall DBT philosophy. Practicing DBT can also be likened to learning to play music. There are many principles to learn in music. There is an underlying structure, a specific number of notes in an octave, a fixed number of octaves, major and minor keys, and a treble and a bass clef. There is a specific way to play each type of instrument. Once these principles are learned and the method is mastered, you can improvise any way you want to create music. Jazz musicians approach playing music with a similar methodology as a tennis player or a DBT therapist. In each case, improvisation and flexibility are integral. When you have learned DBT philosophy and methods, and practiced DBT skills until you really know them, you too will be able to improvise.

Skills are a crucial component of DBT and are taught to people undergoing therapy in weekly lectures, are reviewed in weekly homework assignments, and are referred to in every DBT group. In order to improve your life you have to stay alive, stay in therapy, come to group, and do your homework. The individual therapist will discuss the difficulties a person may have applying a particular skill but does not focus on the person's childhood or past experiences. The individual therapist helps the person to learn, apply, and master the DBT skills and is considered a coach rather than a problem solver or fixer. Family members must learn to do the same.

Many family members would like a list of "things to do," a script to follow, a magic recipe of methods to apply in situations so as to be able to cope and help their loved one. Unfortunately, there is no such "how-to" problem-solving list. A seemingly endless variety of difficult situations can arise with your loved one with BPD, and it would be impossible for anyone to create a list of all of these situations and their potential solutions. As Dr. Linehan says, there are 98 ways to respond to any given situation with DBT methods, so the person applying DBT methodology, be it family member or clinician, must use the techniques or strategies that are most appropriate for the situation. This requires improvisation, flexibility, a firm grasp of DBT techniques, and acceptance of its philosophy. Use the methods you are most comfortable with, the ones that suit your personality, and switch strategies when they do not seem to be effective. Be flexible but stick to the DBT principles.

DBT Assumptions

Embracing the underlying philosophy of DBT, which is an evidence-based treatment, will facilitate acceptance of loved ones with BPD and set families on a path to compassion. The following DBT assumptions encapsulate the philosophy underlying the treatment and are different for the person with the disorder and the person treating him. The first crucial step toward family relationship repair is accepting that the person is doing the best she can, right now, at this very moment.

People with BPD are doing the best they can. To implement DBT and to benefit from its wisdom, both the therapist and the person with BPD must accept the fact that "the person with BPD is doing the best he or she can in the moment." You probably believe she is manipulating you, or that she could do better if only she would try harder and apply herself. Or you may feel that your loved one is extremely willful. If you stopped to ask yourself, "Why would anyone want to put themselves into so many crisis situations? Why would anyone want to be financially dependent on others, live on social security or welfare, continuously lose jobs or relationships, or spend so much time in the emergency room?" you would realize that your loved one, in this very moment, right now, is doing the best she can. As a family member, it is crucial that you also accept this DBT assumption, as it is the first crucial step toward repairing your family relationship. This will help you decrease your own judgmental attitudes and foster acceptance of the person with BPD, as she is, in the moment.

People with BPD want to improve. Does a person with BPD want to improve his life? Of course, he does! Why doesn't he change his life? Why doesn't he work toward accomplishing his own personal goals? The problem is that he does not know how; he lacks the skills to do what others take for granted or find so easy to do.

People with BPD must learn new behaviors in all relevant contexts. DBT proposes that a person with BPD can learn new behaviors to replace the old ones that have proven to be ineffective in solving his problems or achieving a better quality of life for himself. He can learn to be effective in all the relevant situations he encounters in his life.

Families are often confused by their loved one's behavior because they see her doing what is needed in situations involving people who are not close to her—yet she cannot seem to apply the same behavior with someone she is close to emotionally. Or she may be able to assert herself strongly and refuse to do something when you ask her, yet she is unable to say no when a friend or a colleague makes a similar request. This apparent competence, as discussed in Chapter 1, demonstrates your loved one has the ability to apply appropriate behaviors in some contexts, yet is unable to do so in other situations.

People with BPD cannot fail in DBT. Psychiatry is the only area of medicine that blames the patient when the "medicine" fails to work. People with BPD are often described as "treatment resistant," and their lack of improvement in treatment is considered a failure rather than a consequence of inadequate or ineffective treatment. DBT does not consider people as having failed if DBT has not succeeded in helping them; instead, DBT looks at the clinicians and how they have administered the treatment, or at the components of the treatment itself. Based on the DBT assumption that people are doing the best they can, how can they possibly fail in DBT?

People with BPD may not have caused all their problems, but they have to solve them anyway. DBT encourages people to live in the moment, to solve problems in the moment, and not to let past painful situations determine their present lives. They need to radically accept their present reality as it is (see Chapter 7 for more on radical acceptance). They are encouraged to step away from blaming current problems on past events or on the actions of others, as this will not be effective in solving the present problem. DBT accepts that people may have had terrible things happen to them in their lives, but reality is what it is and we cannot change the past. Even if blame is justified, it does not solve the present-day problem. In the moment, those with BPD need to focus on solving their current life problems.

People with BPD need to do better, to work harder, and to be motivated to change. Whereas DBT proposes that people are doing the best they can and want to improve, it also proposes that people can push harder and do more in the next moment than they are doing in the current moment. A person with BPD needs to be motivated to change his behavior and be willing to do the work required to bring about changes in his life, such as learning and practicing DBT skills. Motivating a person with BPD to participate in DBT can be very difficult when you consider the number of times he may have sought help, the number of times the help has failed him, and the humiliating experiences he may have had in the past with therapy. It is not surprising that he may not be jumping right into DBT.

Family members often ask for the names of therapists to treat their adult loved ones. Sadly, a family member offering such a list of names to an adult with BPD often proves to be an ineffective way to help. When a person with BPD finds a clinic on her own, or makes an appointment herself, seeking treatment becomes her decision, her choice. If you provide the names of therapists, treatment is your idea, these are your therapists, and the process is seen as another effort on your part to "fix" or control her. A person can be in a room with the most qualified BPD therapist around, but that is not a guarantee that she will commit to this method of therapy or be willing to or to do the work required to bring about change.

The lives of BPD individuals are unbearable as they are currently being lived. DBT acknowledges that the person is suffering and that the pain he is experiencing in his life is unbearable at this moment.

DBT Assumptions About Therapists

The most caring thing a therapist can do is help the person change in ways that bring him closer to achieving his ultimate goals. This requires discussing and agreeing upon what the person would like to achieve in therapy and in his life, not what other people want him to do or become. These goals are broken down into small steps. The therapist can walk along beside the person, coaching him as he tries out new behaviors. The therapist can be a guide through emotional hell but cannot remove or eliminate painful experiences from the person's life or do the work of learning and practicing DBT skills for him.

Being effective when practicing DBT requires a compassionate attitude of acceptance that internalizes DBT principles. Clarity of communication on the part of the therapist is crucial to dispel the ambiguities and misinterpretations that cloud the perceptions of people with BPD and make relationships so difficult. Precise communication provides structure.

The DBT therapeutic relationship is a relationship of equals. DBT encourages self-disclosure by the therapist. This helps to equalize the relationship for the person with BPD and show her that other people have relationship difficulties as well. It also encourages the person with BPD to express her feelings about the therapist in the actual relationship so that she can learn to negotiate problem solving while practicing and reinforcing DBT skills. This gives her a model for adaptive problem solving. The principles of behavior (see Chapter 3) are universal and affect both therapist and patient—therapists can be reinforced by their clients if they do something well or if they make a mistake.

DBT therapists can fail. There can be a personality mismatch between the patient and the therapist, just as there can be a mismatch between a parent and a child. A very intense, outgoing parent may not be the best parent for a shy, introverted child. A direct and irreverent therapist may not be the best for someone who cannot deal with even a hint of what seems like sarcasm. Some people do better with a male therapist than with a female one. Some therapists may not be able to practice DBT.

DBT can fail when therapists do not. Sometimes the person may just not be ready to be in DBT therapy. He may be too young, have not yet acknowledged that he really has a problem, or be unwilling to do the work required to change his own behavior. DBT may not work because it may just not be the right treatment for this particular person. It is not a panacea. However, to date, DBT is the treatment with the most randomly controlled clinical trails showing its effectiveness in treating people with BPD.

Families report that even when the person seems to resist DBT or is forced to drop out because of therapy-interfering behavior, such as constant lateness or missing sessions, some benefits can usually still be seen in his subsequent behavior. DBT skills can also be modeled and reinforced by family members until the appropriate time arises to try DBT again.

> Families report that even when the person seems to resist DBT or is forced to drop out because of therapy-interfering behavior, such as constant lateness or missing sessions, some benefits can usually still be seen in his subsequent behavior. DBT skills can also be modeled and reinforced by family members until the appropriate time arises to try DBT again.

Therapists treating people with BPD need support. DBT is unique in that it is a team treatment rather than therapy by a single practitioner. The team is called a consultation group. It provides the therapists with support, enables their difficulties and successes to be validated, and gives them the opportunity to discuss problems and be offered alternative approaches to difficult situations by other team members. This has been shown to decrease therapist burnout and to improve the team's ability to practice DBT.

DBT Assumptions About Families

Families spend more time with the person with BPD than anyone else. They have their own needs and often are recipients of abusive behavior; moreover, they live with constant fear of the consequences of their loved one's impulsive behaviors. The unique circumstances that families of those with BPD find themselves in require a unique set of assumptions. When family members accept these DBT assumptions, anger and guilt will decrease so that compassion for their loved ones with BPD can develop.

Family members are doing the best they can. Maladaptive methods of coping often develop in families as a response to the extremely difficult situations they find themselves in, especially when they do not have the benefit of information, explanations, insight, or guidance. Many therapists cannot deal with BPD patients and limit the number they will treat in their practices. While a therapist can terminate therapy with the person with BPD because she takes up too much energy or causes too much angst, families do not have this alternative, this way out. They are in it for the long haul. They know that their loved one is suffering, and they struggle as best they can to help this person they love so very much. They are terrified at the thought of losing her, do not know what to do to help, and feel utterly powerless. Under the circumstances, they are truly doing the best they can. Their intentions are to help, even when they do not know how.

The daily stress of coping with someone you love very much who does not trust you, misconstrues and misinterprets what you say, blames you for all his problems and never lets you forget anything you ever did wrong is not exactly an optimal prescription for domestic bliss. The stress on family members is daunting and leads to medical and emotional complications. The surprise is not the number of divorces of couples dealing with BPD but the number of couples who remain together. Some parents sever relationships with children with BPD as do children with a BPD parent. They do the best they can for as long as they can.

Family members need to do better, work harder, and be motivated to change. You may be aware that sometimes you have made the situation worse. You are highly motivated to help and willing to change your behaviors, if you only knew what to do, if you had a plan to follow or guidelines on how to react more effectively. Your primary goal is usually to find a therapist or therapy that can help your loved one, to "fix" him.

Family members see that their loved ones can go into emotional anaphylactic shock in response to any wrong word they may inadvertently utter. They know they have to do things differently. They are more than ready to learn new behaviors. They desperately want to decrease the stressful interactions in their homes, to keep their loved ones safe from harm, and to ensure that their loved one enters effective treatment. As Marsha Linehan has stated, the family is an untapped resource for reinforcing DBT skills in the person's everyday environment.

Families need to change in order for things to change. Although family members are not the ones with BPD, they must change first so that things can improve. This is despite the fact that they have been the recipients of difficult BPD behaviors for years, did not cause the disorder, and cannot control it. What they have been doing up to now has not worked, including vacillating between leniency and authoritative behaviors. Contracts, boundaries, tough love, rules, punishments, and limit setting do not work. Practicing DBT methods can improve relationships. What do you have to lose by trying DBT methods?

Some family members try to solve any and all the problems for their loved one. When they do this it is as if they have dived into the "problem pool" and are swimming laps with their loved one, rather than coaching him and helping him develop a sense of his own accomplishment. Solving problems for your loved one "fragelizes" him, thereby fostering dependence and a sense of being incompetent. Family members must believe that their loved one has the capacity to get through his emotional hell. They need to tolerate their own distress and give their loved one the opportunity to master life skills. A baby will never learn to walk if he is never allowed to fall down and get up again.

Family members coping with people with BPD need support. Family members are generally isolated and under extreme stress. They have tried to educate themselves on the Internet, in chat rooms, or by reading self-help books. There are few reliable, scientifically based books available on BPD. They need appropriate information and access to coping skills that integrate their love, compassion, concern, and grief. Informed family members experiencing similar problems can be a major source of support. People in the same situation can help them through their fears and be cheerleaders, reminding them of the DBT skills to use, reminding them not to personalize when their son, daughter, husband, or wife tells them they are the worst mother, father, wife, or husband anyone ever had. DBT is a team treatment and families, too, need a team. Their team can be other family members who have attended classes like TARA's family DBT skills training class, or the DBT therapists who are working with their loved one.

Family members need to radically accept their loved one's condition. Your loved one is not her disorder; she is a person with a disorder. She is not intentionally manipulating you or avoiding responsibilities. Family members need to radically accept that their loved one's behaviors that are so difficult to cope with are symptoms of the disorder, part of the disability. They need to reframe situations and imagine their loved one as if he were a person struggling to walk with crutches. Most family members are angry, confused, overwhelmed, feeling powerless and hopeless, living in perpetual fear for their loved one's safety, and are apprehensive about the future. They must radically accept that these are their own responses to BPD behaviors.

Family members have to radically accept present reality as it is. Family members must accept responsibility for past insensitivity to their loved one's pain and develop compassion for her present pain. Trying to justify past behaviors, proving that things were not their fault, attempting to reattribute blame, or demanding apologies for past hurts are all futile behaviors. We can only live in this present moment. This is as relevant for family members as it is for people with BPD. If you can accept the principles of DBT, who was right or wrong in the past will no longer matter. Mindful synthesis of acceptance and change must become the family's primary goal.

> Family members must accept responsibility for past insensitivity to their loved one's pain and develop compassion for her present pain.

The family relationship is a relationship of equals. A person with BPD lives with a pervasive feeling of being out of control, especially when he is emotionally dysregulated. It seems as though he regulates his own feelings by trying to regulate you. Consequently, he spends a great deal of energy trying to control those around him. If you do anything that challenges this paradigm, you will probably be accused of trying to control him. Looking at the situation dialectically, most family members are fearful about the safety of their loved ones and often try to control their behaviors, going so far as putting them in residential treatment or hospitalizing them to keep them safe or making therapy appointments for them without consulting them. Although the feeling that you need to control things may be justified, you must tolerate your own feelings and not act upon them. This is another example of doing the wrong thing for the right reason. If you are over-controlling, your loved one is deprived of the opportunity to learn cause and effect. When you control him; tell him what to do; allocate money, car use, school choices, all on your terms, you are telling your loved one that he is incompetent. DBT philosophy emphasizes that the therapist and patient are in a relationship of equals because this evens the playing field, mirrors a sense of competency, and reinforces mastery. The family relationship, too, must be a relationship of equals. Let go and allow your loved one to experience the consequences of his own decisions and choices.

DBT can fail when families do not. When DBT skills training has not succeeded in helping the family, the family DBT therapist and skills group teacher should not consider the family as having failed but should consider what could have made the teaching more effective. DBT has to be taught to families, not only from the perspective of the person with BPD but from the family's own perspective. This requires understanding the disorder, the family members' experiences with the person with BPD, and a dialectic synthesis of both perspectives. Most people with BPD are not in treatment, yet families are coping with them every day. The person who walks into a DBT therapist's office saying "I want help, I want to learn DBT, I want to change my life," is generally not the person with whom the family member is coping every day. It is a lot easier to make progress and find dialectic synthesis with someone who is facing his problems than it is with a person who is denying them or who is blaming you for all his problems.

DBT Goals

Behaviors To Decrease	Behaviors To Increase
Emotional dysregulation	Emotional regulation skills
Behavioral dysregulation (impulsivity)	Distress tolerance
Interpersonal chaos	Interpersonal effectiveness skills
Cognitive dysregulation	Core mindfulness skills
Self dysregulation	Core mindfulness skills

DBT Treatment Stages and Targets

DBT is conducted in stages, with each stage having its own set of specific goals and targets to achieve before moving on to the next stage. Similar to triage, these stages help to establish a clear progression from one goal to the next. This is an important part of this very structured therapy.

Although these targets are presented in order of importance, DBT puts forward that they are all interconnected. If a person does not stay alive, he will not have the chance to receive help. If he does not stay in therapy, he will not get the help he needs to change his quality of life. DBT aims to convince people to stay alive, stay in therapy, and build a life worth living. As the person makes a commitment to life and stopping self-destructive behaviors, DBT provides him with support in learning how to create and keep a life that is sustaining.

Pretreatment Targets

When a person begins DBT, she is not in actual treatment; she is in pretreatment, where commitment to treatment is established, goals are determined, and specific behaviors are targeted for change. A great deal of time is spent orienting the person toward understanding what DBT is about, motivating her to agree to the goals of the treatment, and agreeing on what behaviors will be the initial targets of treatment. If the person is cutting herself, a primary treatment target would be to stop cutting. The therapist has to sell the person on the idea that DBT can work for her, can bring positive changes into her life. Just as a car salesman sells a car, the therapist has to sell new behavior to a person who basically does not believe that she has the ability to change, does not believe the changes will actually make a difference in her life, and who is distrustful of the therapist's ability to accomplish these goals and commitment to her. The person must feel she can trust the therapist. The therapist has to be able to use commitment strategies such as evaluating the pros and cons of continuing the same behavior or of changing the behavior, playing devil's advocate, foot-in-the-door, door-in-the-face techniques (see Chapter 10), connecting present commitment to prior commitments, examining freedom of choice and the absence of alternatives, and the shaping of behavior toward goals (see Chapter 3). Once the person with BPD has made an initial commitment, treatment begins.

DBT is unusual because it requires that the therapist define what she will do for the patient and clearly define her role. Both parties must agree on the parameters of the therapist-client relationship and be willing to work on problems together. For someone with BPD, this is a very new approach to therapy. It generally takes time for him to trust the therapist, the therapy, and himself. The therapist makes it clear that she cannot do the work for the patient. The patient may ask, "Will I get better?" The therapist might respond with something like, "I cannot promise that you will get better. I can walk along beside you, cheerlead your efforts, and walk along the path out of misery with you. I won't hold your hand in hell but I will walk beside you and guide you out."[1] Family members need to adopt the very same approach.

DBT allows time for the therapist-client relationship to develop. Based on the person's past experiences with therapists who have dismissed him, told him he was a bad patient, that he cannot be helped, is in essence hopeless, and is not experiencing any improvement in his life as a result of therapy, his caution and distrust seem to be entirely appropriate responses. DBT's structured organization helps the person define the role of each participant, removing ambiguities that can cause distress and discomfort. If family members understand how DBT is structured, they will be more able to accept the process and not have expectations that radical changes will occur in a short period of time. Family impatience and pressure for rapid progress, especially at critical times, can derail the treatment.

Family impatience and pressure for rapid progress at critical times can derail the treatment.

People must commit to stay in DBT therapy for a designated period of time, usually 1 year. This time period can be negotiated. The person agrees to attend the therapy sessions, to work at changing the targeted behaviors, to work on the problems that will come up that might interfere with progress, to participate in skills training for a specified period of time (depending on how the specific DBT program is set up), to call the therapist on the telephone for skills coaching, and to pay the required fees. The therapist agrees to make every effort

---

[1] Linehan, 1993a.

to conduct competent and effective therapy, obey standard professional guidelines, be available for weekly therapy sessions and phone consultations, provide needed therapy backup, respect the integrity and rights of the patient, maintain confidentiality, and obtain additional consultation when needed.

Stage One Treatment Targets

Keeping the patient alive by reducing or eliminating dangerous and life-threatening behaviors, such as suicide attempts, suicidal thinking, and aggression, is the primary goal and absolute priority of Stage One DBT. No one can do effective therapy if the client is dead. The risk of suicide is an ever-present danger when treating patients with BPD. DBT has been proven effective in decreasing these behaviors in people with BPD.

An important note on suicide: Among all of the personality disorders, BPD is the one most associated with suicide. BPD has a 10% suicide rate, and as many as 75% of people with BPD make at least one nonlethal suicide attempt. As the number of suicide attempts a person makes increases, the probability of completing suicide increases. Personality disorders are estimated to be present in more than 30% of people who die by suicide, in 40% who make suicide attempts, and in about 50% of psychiatric outpatients who die by suicide. Furthermore, between 60% and 80% of people with BPD self-injure, doubling their risk for suicide. Deliberate self-injury, known as *parasuicidal behavior,* is an action or behavior whose intent is to cause self-harm and results in acute injury, including tissue damage (such as cutting or burning). This behavior poses serious risk if there is no outside intervention. Self-injurious behaviors frequently occur among hospitalized people with BPD. It is very important that clinicians and family members realize that suicidal and self-injurious behaviors are not behaviors that the person can stop at will. Many people with BPD report feeling a sense of relief after they self-injure as the behavior may release endogenous opiates (see Chapter 2) and produce relief of emotional pain (analgesia), almost as if the person had taken painkillers such as morphine, Vicodin or Percodan. For others, self-injury can lead to dissociation, which also decreases their emotional suffering. Suicidal and parasuicidal behaviors usually indicate that a person is in extreme emotional pain and is experiencing intense feelings of shame. These behaviors must be taken very seriously.

Another Stage One goal is to decrease or eliminate therapy-interfering behaviors such as missing sessions, coming late, not doing homework, not practicing any of the skills, or interfering with the therapist's ability to teach DBT skills by arguing and interrupting. You cannot learn to speak French if you do not show up for French class, nor can you learn to play the piano if you never practice. Another therapy-interfering behavior that is targeted in Stage One is the use of hospitalization as a way of handling a crisis and behaviors that push others' limits, causing them to burn out and lose their motivation to help. These are the types of behaviors frequently experienced by family members.

Stage One of DBT also targets the reduction of quality of life-interfering behaviors. Quality of life–interfering problems can include any or all of the following: substance abuse and other addictive behaviors; risky sexual activity; eating disorders; extreme financial difficulties such as overspending, gambling, or bankruptcy; dropping out or failing in school; personal work-related dysfunctional behavior such as quitting jobs, not looking for jobs, difficulty keeping jobs; incarceration for drunken driving or domestic violence; housing problems or problems arising from not taking care of one's health (such as diabetes). DBT strives to increase behaviors that will enable the person to have a life worth living by teaching behavioral skills to build relationships, manage emotions, and deal effectively with life's problems.

Stage Two Treatment Targets

The goal of Stage Two DBT treatment is to reduce emotional misery and increase the capacity for normative emotional experiencing. Many of the problems people with BPD have are due to how they experience their own emotions. Enhancing the experience of positive emotions while decreasing vulnerability to emotions in general can help them overcome their fear of their intense feelings.

Many of the problems people with BPD deal with are due to how they experience their own emotions.

DBT Phone Coaching

DBT therapists are required to be available for phone coaching through all stages of therapy. People in DBT are expected and encouraged to call their therapist in the moment, when they are actually in a crisis. Phone coaching encourages people who have difficulty asking others for help to learn and practice how to ask effectively rather than demanding help abusively or avoiding asking at all. Phone coaching is encouraged for those with BPD who struggle with shame, fear, or uncertainty over whether their need is valid. During the phone call, the therapist has the opportunity to intervene in suicidal crisis behaviors, to assess the suicide risk in the situation, and to empower the person by asking questions such as, "What skills could you use in this situation?" "I can hear how much pain you are in right now; however, how does this behavior get you to your goal?" "What else do you think you could do to feel better?" The phone calls should provide coaching regarding the situation at hand, as the person is about to engage in the usual maladaptive behaviors he uses to cope when in a difficult situation. Negative consequences can be avoided if, in the moment, he is coached.

A person with BPD is attending a party. He is standing in a corner, trying to blend in with the wall, alone and extremely distressed. He feels that no one wants to talk to him because he is unattractive and a loser. He quickly jumps to the conclusion that he will never fit in, have friends or a partner. He begins to think about cutting himself. At this point he calls his therapist and describes the situation. The therapist acts like the coach at a football game, reminding him of tactics and skills he has learned, and encouraging him to apply them. The therapist may remind the person that he can do "hard things" or that he has handled similar problems skillfully in the recent past. For a person with BPD, this coaching can help build a sense of mastery. Sometimes the coaching will focus on tolerating the current distress until the next session. The therapist does not engage "what if I do this and they then do that" type discussions but stays relentlessly focused on the moment, on using skills in the present situation.

(Continued)

Eventually, over time, the person will think about calling his therapist, will imagine the conversation, and will come up with the answer to "what skills can you use in this situation?" for himself. He will no longer need to call. Over time, DBT therapists receive fewer phone calls from people with BPD than do therapists who practice other forms of therapy where accepting phone calls is not a required component of the treatment.

A person with BPD sometimes does not register what she has experienced in a therapy session until the session is over. If she can call her therapist after a session, she will have the opportunity to address issues that arose without ruminating over them until the next session. Phone coaching affords her the opportunity to repair her relationship with the therapist. This builds trust and reinforces the principle that DBT is a relationship of equals between the patient and the therapist. This process empowers the person with BPD and also builds self-mastery. Therapists need to observe their personal limits by being aware of the time spent during these phone calls and not allowing them to become a substitute for an in-person therapy session.

In Stage One of DBT, people act out but still seem to be apparently competent. In Stage Two, they seem less apparently competent. Although they may be safer, they are also "stuck." What is life like for a person with BPD who has finally achieved behavioral control, is no longer making suicide attempts or thinking about suicide as an alternative to problem solving? Is this person now "cured"? What about the person who has managed to stop drinking or has quit using drugs? How do we describe her quality of life? In Stage Two a person experiences intensely painful emotions yet seems better able to control emotion-linked actions—however, his life still seems to be characterized by pervasive unhappiness. He seems unable to initiate actions or behaviors to create changes in his life that will bring the satisfactions others seem to experience. He often avoids situations that bring forth emotional responses because they are so painful. He may remain stuck in routines where he is not challenged to take emotional risks, such as going on with dead-end romantic relationships or staying at underpaid jobs that lead nowhere, thereby avoiding major changes in his life. He seems to have given up or withdrawn from active participation in life. Relationships, jobs, family contacts, and friends are avoided as well as situations or experiences that may be related to past traumas.

In Stage Two of DBT the person often withdraws to avoid unwanted emotional experiences. If your daughter sees you as a cue for intense emotional arousal, she may actively avoid any interactions with you, disregard you, dissociate, sever the relationship, or disappear for protracted periods of time in order to cope or as a means of maintaining her own emotional control. Avoidance becomes her means of coping with what she perceives as your hurtful behavior. To decrease the pervasive avoidance of emotions, the person needs to learn that experiencing emotions need not be traumatic. Rather than avoid, she has to be willing to expose herself to painful emotions while resisting their emotionally linked behaviors, changing those behaviors by using new coping skills and tolerating the distress this may evoke. The person is exposed to what she is afraid of, or to painful emotion in small doses, in a safe, trusting environment. Trust and a sense of safety are key components to ensuring success of this exposure to her own emotions. This is sometimes called *exposure therapy* by therapists. Past painful experiences should not be dealt with until the person has achieved a measure of behavioral control and learned skills to deal with her emotional pain. Decreasing posttraumatic stress responses if the person has experienced trauma is also a goal of Stage Two DBT; but this cannot be addressed until the person has developed the ability to tolerate distress.

Stage Three Treatment Targets

The third stage of DBT focuses on solving ordinary life problems. These might include returning to school, pursuing career goals, and improving general living conditions. The person works on developing ordinary happiness rather than focusing on unhappiness. In this stage the person sets individual goals, creates a sense of self-mastery, and increases respect for himself or herself.

Stage Four Treatment Targets

In Stage Four the person aims to develop the capacity for freedom and joy. The goal is to have a meaningful life that includes relevant work, supportive and nurturing relationships, and a spiritual attachment that gives him a sense of hopefulness.

How DBT Is Practiced

DBT is not just skills training. To conform to effective implementation as supported by research, DBT is generally practiced as a comprehensive outpatient program that includes individual psychotherapy, skills training, telephone consultation (also known as phone coaching), therapist consultation team meetings, and ancillary services. This means that proper DBT treatment is done by a team, usually consisting of a primary or individual therapist, two group skills trainers, a psychopharmacologist (part of the ancillary service), a case manager (also ancillary), and a team leader. Each member of that team must have proper training in DBT. The DBT primary therapist (the individual therapist) is responsible for treatment planning, ensuring progress toward DBT targets, and management of crisis and life-threatening behaviors. This therapist also consults with the person with BPD on how to interact with other therapists. However, the primary therapist does not tell the other therapists how to interact with the person with BPD; therapists do not have to behave consistently across their team. DBT is unique in that it enhances the therapist's capacity to treat the person in the required weekly therapist consultation meetings as well as in supervision (by a master therapist) for DBT adherence and competency monitoring, and continuing education. A DBT treatment manual contains specific exercises and homework assignments that are utilized in all DBT programs. Ancillary treatments can also include inpatient psychiatric treatment, day treatment, case management, and family psychoeducation. A program or person claiming to practice DBT but offering only skills training is not doing the comprehensive type of DBT that has been shown to be effective.

Why Is It Important to See a Trained DBT Therapist?

DBT may be the most hopeful and helpful of any BPD therapies available now, but it is very rigorous. If DBT is not practiced as designed, it may not produce the same positive outcomes. When DBT

How to Know If a Therapist Practices Authentic DBT

It is very important that DBT therapists be qualified to provide DBT; otherwise, the treatment may very well fail and hopelessness will be reinforced within your loved one. This will then lead to continued distrust of DBT and all other therapies. These are the questions to ask potential DBT therapists:

- Have you completed a 10-day intensive DBT training? Are you a member of a DBT consultation team?
- Have you been supervised by an expert DBT therapist? Are you familiar with the main sets of DBT strategies (behavior therapy, validation, dialectics)?
- Do you teach skills, practice behavior analysis, review diary cards?
- Do you do phone coaching?
- How many clients have you treated using DBT?
- How many patients with BPD do you now have in your practice?
- Do you believe you have been successful in helping your patients with BPD lead better lives?

The answer to most of these questions should be yes. You have a right to check on the therapist's credentials; to know if the therapist is licensed in his or her state; to know the extent and nature of the therapist's education and training; the extent of the therapist's experience in treating clients with similar problems; and the therapist's arrangements for coverage and/or emergency contacts.

is not practiced in accordance with the model developed with research but, instead, is practiced "my way" by a therapist without adequate training, it will probably fail. The person with BPD will once again experience shame and feel hopeless, disappointed, distrustful, and reluctant to ever try treatment or DBT again. Outcomes from "knock-off" DBT will not justify additional DBT programs or trainings in your community. A useful analogy is antibiotic treatment: A person with a severe bacterial infection is prescribed an antibiotic that has been shown to be effective with this particular bacterial infection. If a different antibiotic is administered, the person will not get better. If he receives a substitute medication, he will not get better. If he takes the medication for only 2 days and then discontinues it, thereby not taking the required dose, the infection will not respond and the person will remain sick. Marsha Linehan is currently developing a method for certifying therapists who practice DBT so that people can be assured that their therapist is truly qualified to offer DBT treatment.

5

Understanding and Applying Validation

Since feelings are first, who pays any attention to the syntax of
things will never wholly kiss you.

—e.e. cummings

GETTING YOUR SIMPLEST NEEDS MET CAN BE VERY DIFFICULT WHEN
people do not understand what you are saying. Have you ever
traveled in a country where you could not speak the language?
Straightforward requests such as "Where is the . . ." or "How do
you get to . . ." or "What is the price of . . .?" become monumental
impasses when you do not share a common language. As you struggle to be understood, you probably find yourself becoming agitated,
raising your voice, feeling frustrated, misunderstood, stressed, and
isolated. Not being heard or understood is an unpleasant, aversive
experience. Can you imagine feeling this frustrated each and every
day? This is how people with borderline personality disorder describe
their daily lives. Feelings of frustration are magnified when she is
with you, the person she is closest to, the person who is supposed to
know, love, and understand her. Imagine how frustrating and disappointing it must feel when her efforts to communicate with you
persistently fail? The person with BPD must feel invisible, as if she
does not count. This is experienced as emotional pain.

In all cultures, one of the severest punishments that can be inflicted on a prisoner is solitary confinement. It is a form of torture. It takes a person with a strong sense of self to endure long-term isolation, as a sense of community and connection to others is a basic human need. People with BPD do not seem to be able to connect to others or to communicate their feelings, thoughts, and needs. Their emotional feelings of isolation can be compared to that of Helen Keller. Deaf and blind from infancy, she lived imprisoned in her own mind. Her life must have been so very painful—not being able to communicate with anyone, unable to learn even ordinary life skills, lacking the means to get even her simplest needs met. Small wonder that she had frequent violent temper tantrums. Learning sign language freed Helen from her isolation and allowed her to communicate with others, overcome her disabilities, and go on to lead a remarkably productive life. Her experience parallels the life experiences of people with BPD who often feel as though they are wandering about in a foreign country where no one speaks their language or bothers to listen to them. They are desperately searching for an emotionally safe place where their thoughts and feelings will be heard and accepted without criticism, blame, or judgment. They need others to recognize that they are in emotional pain. They must learn to identify and talk about what they are feeling, how to be emotionally honest, and how to trust others. *Validation* can be their sign language. It is an emotional language that allows you and your loved one with BPD to communicate from the heart.

Validation Defined

Validation is the art of affirming another person by actively accepting the person as he is, in the moment, and communicating that acceptance to him. It is the experiential appreciation of another person's worldview. It is the ability and willingness to fully enter into the experience of another person. By validating a person you are authenticating the individual as who he actually is, supporting, allowing, and empowering the person, and his feelings, behavior, or responses.

Validation is the art of affirming another person by actively accepting the person as he is in the moment and communicating that acceptance to him.

Validation is defined as "To attest to the truth or validity of something. A response that is valid is well grounded or justifiable, relevant and meaningful, logically correct, appropriate to the end in view. Being valid implies being supported by objective truth or generally accepted authority; compelling serious attention and acceptance; granting official sanction, giving permission to." According to Webster, validation is "A strengthening, reinforcing confirming establishing or ratifying as valid." To validate is to confirm, authenticate, corroborate, verify, substantiate, and acknowledge.

How can you get help from others if you do not know how to ask for what you need? Helen Keller had to learn how to communicate with the world around her. People with BPD, too, need to learn a way to reach others, to be heard and felt. Validation is an emotional language that resonates with some of the core elements of BPD, particularly the sense of emptiness, isolation, unworthiness, and incompetence that seems to pervade the lives of people with BPD and define their daily existence. Validation includes warmth, genuineness, and responsiveness. As people with BPD experience being validated in various situations, they begin to develop a stronger sense of who they are, decreasing their pervasive negative sense of self. It must be extremely painful to not know who you are or what you feel while simultaneously feeling incompetent and worthless. When you couple these negative feelings with an inability to tolerate distress or pain, it is not surprising to find that people with BPD engage in maladaptive behaviors just to be able to tolerate their distress, bear their painful emotions, and feel better, in the moment.

Marsha Linehan wrote, "There is nothing that an individual experiences, feels, thinks, does or says that is not himself or herself. Validation treats the person as relevant and meaningful, as compelling serious attention and acceptance. The person, in the moment, is visible and seen."[1] When you validate a person, your reaction is determined by your own response to the person, in this very moment. Your response needs to be independent of any arbitrary set of rules, roles, contracts, boundaries, any philosophical point of view, any past behaviors, or any future expectations. Validation does not employ the logical words we generally use to interpret or explain situations or to solve problems. Instead, it uses emotions as a new language.

---

[1] Linehan, 1993a.

Imagine yourself walking down a seemingly endless long hallway in a hotel, carrying a huge bunch of keys that are neither numbered nor marked. Door after door stretches out on either side. You know you have a key to open each door. Suddenly, you hear your loved one screaming for help. You run down the hall, frightened and desperate to find her room so you can help her. When you locate the room, you realize you do not know which key will open her door. Without the right key, you are unable to help, you are powerless.

Validation is the key that can open the door to relationship repair. Validation is the key that opens the door to emotional communication. It is a tool that can help to restore trust and build new and better relationships.

Validation can be used strategically when your loved one becomes emotionally aroused. Emotional arousal will often decrease when you communicate and reinforce the authenticity of her feelings and behavior; this will let her know that her thoughts, feelings, and actions make sense, and can be tolerated. As arousal decreases, your loved one can begin to solve her problem. Validation may even help you to motivate your loved one to participate in Dialectical Behavior Therapy.

By now you know that information, thoughts, emotions, and memories are each processed in specific parts of the brain. Emotions are processed primarily in the amygdala, an almond-shaped structure in the brain's limbic system. Once aroused, the amygdala reacts the way your car responds when you push the gas pedal down to the floor. The prefrontal cortex functions as the brain's brake, controlling impulses, decision making, and judgments, especially in social situations. As people with BPD tend to be supersensitive to environmental triggers, hypervigilant, exquisitely sensitive, and extremely vulnerable emotionally, it could be said that by communicating emotionally through validation you are "talking to the amygdala," "speaking in limbic language" opening the door into your loved one's universe, into her own specific reality.

Using Validation to Reduce Misinterpretation and Misattribution

Picture yourself surrounded by people you love, your family and dearest friends, all gathered around a table in anticipation of sharing a dinner that you prepared for this special occasion. Nonchalantly, you ask Carole, your daughter with BPD, to pass the butter. To you, this is a simple, innocuous request. However, Carole responds in an extremely angry tone of voice, saying, "You think I am too fat!" Or, with indignation, "Why me? I'm not your maid! Why don't you ask someone else?" Or, "Why don't you want me to eat?" The meaning of what you actually said appears to have been totally misinterpreted. How can something as benign as "pass the butter" be so misunderstood? In complete confusion, you probably defend yourself, apologize, try to clarify the situation or explain your request. This upsets Carole even more, increasing her agitation and heating up the interaction. As you struggle to avoid the emotional bullets, other family members may jump in with what they believe are helpful comments, such as, "just calm down," "you're making a mountain out of a molehill," "why don't you apologize!" or other criticisms. Tension and strife now reign over the festive table as hurtful words, accusations, and/or dishes may be hurled across the table. The dinner you worked so hard to prepare is ruined, and has degenerated into a tense combat zone. You are off and running, doing the BPD dance. Does this situation seem familiar? Just what happened here? How do you interpret this situation? Could the conflagration have been avoided? Was there a more effective way you could have responded?

From the way Carole reacted, she clearly misinterpreted what you said and did not understand the meaning of your request. Your intention was misconstrued and transposed into a personal criticism, a blaming statement, or a judgment. When your daughter misinterpreted what you said, you personalized her misinterpretation and defended yourself. She then felt even more misunderstood and frustrated. Her emotions, now dysregulated, kept escalating. You probably responded by becoming increasingly more frustrated and emotionally aroused yourself. As everyone's emotions continued rising, communication between all of you ceased. Your daughter will keep trying to make you understand why she responded as she did to what you thought was a very simple, benign, neutral request. If you continue to not "get it," her emotional response will continue to escalate. It seems as though Carole's life depends on your acknowledging how hurt she was by your saying "pass the butter." Why do people with BPD seem to misinterpret and misattribute what other people say?

When you try to understand why "pass the butter" can trigger such an intense reaction, you realize that there seems to be a major disconnect between your experience and interpretation of the family dinner, what you think happened, and your loved one's perception and interpretation of the same event. It is as though you are living in alternate realities or parallel universes. A metaphor for how multiple perspectives can be evoked by the same experience can be found in the ancient Japanese tale "Rashomon," in which one series of events is told from the point of view of four different people, resulting in four completely different stories. It is as if each of you is traveling in a different train, going to the same destination, along the same route, passing through the same countryside, and ending up at the same station—yet each person is having a completely different experience of what appears to be the same journey.

People with BPD seem to experience a disconnect between the meaning of words spoken to them and their interpretation of the words. What is said is simply not understood. Words are misinterpreted, the intention of what was said is misconstrued and often made personal, things are understood wrongly, meanings are attributed that were never intended. Thus "pass the butter" becomes an ambiguous statement interpreted as a personal criticism. It is as if those with BPD have emotional dyslexia, processing words meant to be neutral as emotional statements implying criticism, judgment, or blame. When people with BPD misinterpret the thoughts and intentions of others, they are often left feeling isolated, suspended in their own lonely, parallel universe.

Validation bypasses reason, logic, cause and effect, and "the truth of a situation," which we generally use to interpret or explain experiences or solve problems. There is no right or wrong to anyone's emotional response, no ultimate truth in any situation. Every situation elicits different emotions in different people.

Perhaps you have seen a TV commercial for a gel shoe insert that conforms to the shape of an individual's foot. Each of us has our own unique foot shape. If you substitute each person's unique footprint for each person's unique interpretation of emotional reality, you can begin to understand why we need to find a way to communicate emotionally with our loved one suffering with BPD. When you begin to validate your loved one's emotional feelings and responses to situations or experiences, they may begin to trust you enough so that you can introduce a different perspective on the situation.

For family members, validating effectively involves much more than reciting a list of rules or a preset script. Validation must be sincere to be effective. You cannot fake your feelings—they must be authentically heartfelt. This requires developing empathy for the pain your loved one experiences along with a desire to help him. This is compassion. For your validation to be credible, you must make an effort to let go of your anger, expectations, judgments, and efforts to control.

Validation is the art of generous listening. It communicates your complete acceptance of the person, as he is now. When your heart accepts the pain your loved one with BPD lives with each and every day, he will know that your efforts are authentic. To be believed, what you say needs to be imbued with compassionate understanding. If you are radically genuine, completely sincere, and can acknowledge how hard he is trying, you will be on the road to effective changes and improvements in your relationship. When these basic DBT premises are accepted, you can incorporate validation into your life.

Validation requires balancing acceptance and change; this is essential to practicing dialectic philosophy. It requires a continual process of synthesis, reconciling the opposite points of view inherent within each situation. For the person you love with BPD, the present is experienced as unremitting emotional pain. Your expectation that he should or can change in this very moment is experienced by him as nonacceptance and invalidation. It implies that you have not registered the pain he is feeling, how hard it is for him stop the behaviors he knows are harmful, and the difficulty he experiences in trying to learn and practice new behaviors. A family member or a therapist who focuses on behavioral change while ignoring the intense pain the person is feeling can precipitate extreme anger, aggressive attacks, noncompliance with treatment, or withdrawal from treatment.

Validating Essentials: Sympathy, Compassion, and Empathy

Sympathy

Sympathy is being sensitive to or affected by the feelings of another person, particularly feelings of sorrow, sadness, or pity. Sympathy is defined as emotional or intellectual accord, sharing the feelings of another, feeling loyal, as, "I am sympathetic to your cause." A person with BPD is likely to misinterpret expressions of sympathy as indicating that you feel sorry for her because she is incompetent or a loser, leading to further feelings of hopelessness. Sympathy is not the same as validation. Validation requires that you reflect back what the other person is feeling, even if you do not feel the same way or do not agree with what he is feeling.

Compassion

Compassion is the humane quality of deep awareness and understanding of the suffering of another person coupled with the wish to do something to relieve that person's suffering. It is love with action. It is motivated by genuine insight into the ultimate nature of reality and appreciation of the impermanence of all things. The more you understand the nature of what is going on around you, the less you will falsify or distort reality and the more compassion you will feel. The more powerful your compassion, the more resilient you will be in confronting hardships and the more able you will be to transform them into positive experiences. Compassion can be a source of inner strength. The more compassionate you become, the more altruistic and courageous you will become and the less prone you will be to feeling discouraged and hopeless. Hope enables people to overcome despair. Compassion develops the courage to overcome fear and the inclination to be stopped by fear from doing what should be done. When you are able to accept and recognize others, you will be more sensitive to them and more aware of their suffering, therefore your tendency to be selfish will decrease. Doubt or suspicion interfere with the cultivation of compassion as it requires faith. This may explain why compassion is a component of all religions. Compassion asks, how can I alter the circumstances so the person I love does not suffer in the future or get into this predicament?

CULTIVATING COMPASSION

Compassion is not an emotion but can be thought of as resembling a mood or a state of mind. It does not occur naturally as emotions do but needs to be cultivated through intellectual understanding and training. When compassion is first being cultivated, it can be stimulated intellectually such as by imagining the juggler tossing balls in the air, your loved one wearing the TARA tiara (Chapter 2) or carrying the stone of pain. Eventually, it must become a natural and truly spontaneous response to situations that demand it and should not be dependent on intellectual stimulation. Developing compassion is not easy nor is it automatic. It takes time, practice, and commitment. Changing your attitude takes more than lip service. Transforming the mind takes constant effort. Rituals or ceremonies can reinforce your sense of commitment or your sense of personal obligation. When you first begin to feel the suffering of others, you may have a temporary feeling of uneasiness or anxiety; however, keep going. Once you cultivate compassion, an enduring mental transformation happens that becomes a permanent part of you. Compassion usually develops first for individuals closest to you, then extends beyond to the immediate family, then on to the general community or *sangha*, to the universal.

COMPASSION AND ANGER

Anger can be aroused by compassion but it is anger without malice; there is no intention to do harm. Anger can sometimes help you act. It energizes you and can lead to forceful action that will get you through a difficult time. Angry compassion can fuel advocacy.

No living being desires unhappiness or suffering. Suffering is an emotional experience that leads to confusion and misunderstanding. People with BPD are suffering all the time and need someone to sense their pain while making a real effort to help them find a way to help themselves. Compassion for the suffering of the person with BPD is the fulcrum of both DBT and mentalization, and may account for why these treatments have such successful outcomes. The efficacy of all BPD treatments depends on compassion. If you truly want to help your loved one, you too must cultivate compassion for him. Tara is the Buddhist goddess of compassion, and compassion underlies the philosophy of TARA's family psychoeducational programs.

> "When you understand, you cannot help but love. You cannot get angry. To develop understanding, you have to practice looking . . . with eyes of compassion. When you understand, you love. And, when you love you naturally act in a way that can relieve the suffering of people."
> —Thich Nhat Hahn

Empathy

Empathy is the ability to put yourself in another person's place, to vicariously feel the other person's feelings as if you were that person, wearing his shoes, understanding his experience. It starts with the awareness of another person's mental states, emotions, and thoughts. It means that you are able to experience someone else's life and feel an emotional reaction triggered by what the other person is feeling. Empathy allows us to connect or resonate with another person, to identify emotionally with him, to know that person more completely than the person can verbalize or communicate explicitly to others. Feeling empathy for a person means that the person is understood within his own frame of reference. Empathy is derived from the Greek *pathos*, meaning feelings, emotions, or experiences. When you can be empathetic with a person with BPD, you are sharing or relating to how he feels. It tells him that what he is feeling makes enough sense to be understood, thereby diminishing his sense of isolation, of being "crazy." This experience is akin to how family members react in support groups when they realize that others share their "raised eyebrow" or *Gaslight* syndrome family experiences.

Family members often confuse validation with empathy. There is a difference between the two. Empathy is experienced from moment to moment. In a specific situation, in the moment, you may sense that a person is angry or sad. Your feelings of empathy will create a sense of safety for your loved one. Empathy can be validating but it is not enough on its own. To be effective, empathy must be balanced with reality, the reality that asks, "Is the person's response to the present situation valid? How will this response move the person along toward his ultimate goal?" A person with BPD can easily misconstrue your empathy as a message that you believe he is incompetent because he cannot change how he is feeling or the situation that causes him distress.

A waiter approaches your table in a very busy restaurant. From his body language and facial expression you can sense that he is quite stressed but you do not know why. Perhaps he had an argument with his boss, too many customers arrived all at once, the kitchen is filling his orders too slowly, or he has a personal problem. However, you feel ill and need a glass of water as quickly as possible. Empathy and validation would go like this: "I can sense that you must be very stressed right now as your face is tense and your shoulders are hunched. It must be so difficult when so many people come into the restaurant all at once. I realize how hard you are trying to take care of all your customers. I do not mean to give you extra work but I wonder if you might please bring me a glass of water when you get a chance." See his face light up; you will get your water quickly. This type of exercise is assigned to family members who do not believe that validation can possibly work.

When you can sense the waiter's feelings and sense his frustration, you are being empathic. Empathy is feeling another's feelings; validation is reflecting back to the waiter your own awareness of how hard he is trying to do a good job, and that you understand his frustration from within his frame of reference, in the context of his own experience as the waiter. If you cannot empathize with the waiter's feelings you will not know what to validate. This is why it is so important for family members to understand what their loved ones with BPD experience in their daily interactions, how isolated they feel, and how they misperceive the world around them.

*Feelings +
the empirical situation =
empathy + validation*

Empathy and validation require that family members become participants in their loved one's world while simultaneously remaining observers of that world. People who are allergic to everything and have inadequate autoimmune systems are forced to live inside "bubbles" to protect themselves from infection or allergy. Imagine that your loved one lives inside such a bubble, except her bubble is her reality based on her unique perspective of the world. It is her unique gel footprint. You know your loved one must emerge from her bubble so as to live a better life. You can help her by going inside her bubble, into her world, validating her experience, and empathizing with her feelings; but then you must help her find a way to come into your world, even if it is for only a moment. You need to balance becoming a participant in your loved one's world with remaining an observer of her world. You stay outside while simultaneously going inside. If you can succeed in getting your loved one to put just a toe into the water of the explicit reality we all share, the common denominator of everyone's experience, even for a moment, she is making a tiny little change (TLC). Every time you help her untwist a cognitive distortion or try out an alternative point of view, you will have made a TLC and will be doing the kind of shaping (see Chapter 3) that, over time, can create change.

Your daughter's boyfriend breaks their date for that evening. Empathy and validation are both needed in this situation. Empathy addresses the feelings of sadness about not seeing her boyfriend while validation addresses the facts of the relationship. "I can sense you are sad about what happened tonight with Joe. Breaking up with someone is very upsetting and is a stressful experience for anyone.

I would feel disappointed, too. However, are you sure that breaking tonight's date means Joe is breaking up with you? Is it possible that he has to be at school tonight and is planning on seeing you tomorrow? Do you remember the last time he broke a date with you? You felt the relationship was over and were feeling so rejected. The next day he came over and you two went out to a movie. What do you think you can do tonight to feel better?"

Validation looks at the emotions in the situation in context, the empirical situation, and the history. Your validation is based on the conclusion you draw from your empathetic experience. Validation is inherently analytical, of truth, of wisdom, of effectiveness. Empathy is the exploration of the feelings as well as the "facts" of the case. You need to understand the experience and the context of the experience specifically for the other person, not for yourself. To empathize you need to perceive the internal frame of reference of the other person. You can then explore the situation together. When you empathize you do not lose the sense of "as if" you were the other person, but you keep in mind that you are not the other person.

DEVELOPING EMPATHY

Picture the word *pain* written on your loved one's forehead when you observe him becoming dysregulated so as to remind yourself to empathize with the emotional pain he feels all the time. A TARA mother imagined tears running down her daughter's face and was able to become more empathetic in the moment. Or, imagine your loved one wearing the TARA tiara (see Chapter 2) to remind yourself of the biological underpinnings of BPD. Each ball bouncing on the tiara represents a neural network in dysregulation. How would you handle daily stresses, difficult emotional situations, and intense, out-of-control feelings if you could not count on your own good judgment and the ability to control your own impulses? Your loved one is doing the most or the best he can right now.

Validation as Unconditional Acceptance

Everyone is familiar with the concept of unconditional love; it goes with the "being a parent" territory and plays a major part in sibling, partner, and spousal relationships. Dr. Linehan states that

"Unconditional love requires blind faith and a lot of denial. It requires that you look into the eye of reality and not be afraid of whatever you might see there."[2] It is what the "for better or worse" part of the marriage vow is all about. Although you may think you love someone unconditionally, your love does not always include unconditional acceptance. A Broadway play is called *I Love You, You're Perfect, Now Change*. In actuality, we generally offer *conditional* love—we love our child or partner when he does the "right" things. He is only loved and respected when he behaves in a certain manner that is acceptable to us. The Dalai Lama tells us that Tibetan children are loved not because parents feel that "my child is good" but rather because "this is my child." Love increases if the child improves and cultivates good qualities.

Unconditional acceptance communicates that you accept your loved one as he is, for now, in the present moment, without judging or evaluating his feelings or his responses. You must be able to unconditionally validate what he feels or how he responds to his experiences, both verbally and nonverbally. Unconditional validation provides your loved one with a sense of safety and communicates acceptance that encourages trust. This is not easy to do because it means giving up all your efforts to control the other person or to impose your values, expectations or opinions on him. For most of us, it is harder to unconditionally validate someone we love than it is for us to love him unconditionally. It is counterintuitive. To communicate unconditional acceptance, you need to make an active effort to listen and observe what is said and how it is said, felt, or done in a nonjudgmental manner so that you can understand what is actually being said and be able to unconditionally validate the person.

People with BPD desperately need to feel unconditionally accepted. Love is not enough, especially if you claim to be offering your loved one unconditional love, telling him you are always there for him, yet at the same time are continuously trying to change him. This renders your love meaningless and confusing. How can he make any sense out of your unconditional love when you do not accept him as he is? You are sending a confusing message. How can you be there for her when you are not accepting her as she is? This simultaneously

---

[2] Linehan, 1993a.

How can he make any sense out of your unconditional love when you do not accept him as he is? invalidates her. She was trying to communicate with you but you failed to hear or feel her or to read her subtitles. She now feels isolated, alone, and probably embarrassed about whatever it was she was trying to tell you. Is it any wonder that it is so difficult for her to trust you?

Does it seem unfair to you that it is you who has to learn a new form of communication when it is your loved one who has the problems? Would you build ramps in your home if your son was injured and confined to a wheelchair? Would you continue to cook a particular food item if you knew your daughter was allergic to it? In the same spirit, your environment must be modified to accommodate the needs of the person you love with BPD. This, too, is unconditional acceptance.

Families coping with a loved one with BPD are well aware that the behavior of their loved one needs to change so that she can have a better life. In an effort to bring about behavioral changes, well-meaning family members may tell their loved one what to do, give her instruction as to how to do it, or actually do it for her. Or they might give her ultimatums, impose rules and regulations, or write contracts. With encouragement from well-meaning but uninformed therapists or other family members, they may impose boundaries or set limits. Many 12-step programs and self-help books echo this advice. The problem underlying your efforts to make the person you love with BPD change her behavior is that she interprets this as your saying, "You are unacceptable as you are now, in this very moment."

People with BPD often interpret their families' efforts to be helpful as punishment, or as an attempt to control them. There is actually a grain of truth here! Families may also be asking their loved ones to do something that they are not capable of doing for now, such as getting a job when they have no skills, calming down when they lack the ability to control their emotions, or entering a DBT program requiring sobriety for a certain period of time when they do not have the distress tolerance skills to be able to accomplish this. They interpret their inability to fulfill these demands as proof that they are "losers" or "bad," and feel shame. When their painful feelings are not accepted by the people closest to them, the situation often backfires, leading to abusive or impulsive behaviors, rage attacks, episodes of cutting, or suicide attempts.

Charlotte expects Jenny, her 17-year-old daughter, to be home by 11 P.M. When Jenny has not returned on time, Charlotte, worried, frightened, and concerned for her safety, went looking for Jenny in the place where she said she was going to be. Jenny was not there. By the time Charlotte returned, Jenny was already at home and was visibly upset. Charlotte immediately demanded that Jenny return the car keys because she had broken the "curfew contract" they had arranged with her therapist. Jenny began crying hysterically. Charlotte's response was, "I cannot talk to you when you are this upset. When you calm down, we can talk." Jenny insisted that they talk right then. Charlotte refused, saying they were both too upset at the moment to talk and could talk tomorrow after they had both calmed down. Jenny then went into the kitchen and proceeded to swallow every pill she could find. The police were called and Jenny was hospitalized for her "suicide attempt."

What actually happened here? Was this a suicide attempt, or is there another way to interpret this situation? Charlotte was so frightened for her daughter's safety that she failed to observe and respond to Jenny's emotional state, to validate her daughter's feelings and distress, and to empathize with her. She never asked Jenny the simple question, "What happened?" Jenny was clearly very upset, could not seem to cope with her own painful feelings, and did not know how to ask for the help she needed. Charlotte's response to Jenny's lateness was based on an arbitrary set of predetermined rules. For Jenny, in her moment of emotional distress, the curfew contract no longer existed. Charlotte did not hear Jenny, completely ignored her feelings, and did not give her a chance to explain. Demanding that a person in acute emotional distress wait until the next day to discuss the problem is simply not reasonable. Jenny did the only thing she could think of doing to decrease her emotional pain in the moment; she swallowed every pill she could find. Was she manipulating her mother or was she trying to stop her painful feelings? Did she want to die or did she want immediate relief from her pain?

To help someone with BPD, you must be able to respond in the moment. Jenny clearly was upset, apparently triggered by something that had happened to her before she came home. Additionally, Charlotte's insensitivity to her emotional state and invalidation of her feelings surely added a sense of isolation to the burden of Jenny's emotional distress. Is Charlotte a noncaring mother? Absolutely not! She is a mother who was terrified that some harm had come to her young daughter. Once she realized that Jenny was safe, her fear seemed to turn to anger. Charlotte was following the inappropriate advice to make a contract with her daughter that included arbitrary rules that Jenny could not follow. Charlotte did not have the opportunity to show her love and concern for her daughter in an empathetic way, to validate her daughter's distress, or to help her decrease her arousal so that they could get to a place where the problem could be discussed. This mother was doing the best she could at the moment; however, her way of helping was inappropriate and ineffective for this particular situation. She did the wrong thing for the right reasons.

When we validate another person, we are neither discounting nor trivializing his responses but are taking him and his behavior seriously. When a 3-year-old boy is afraid of the dark, his behavior is valid for a boy of 3 with his life experience. Would it be helpful to trivialize the child's fears by saying, "It is stupid to be afraid of the dark," or "Don't be silly, snap out of it"? To be helpful, you must search for, recognize, and reflect the validity inherent in a person's unique response to an event, amplify that response, and then reinforce it.

> *When we validate another person, we are neither discounting nor trivializing his responses but are taking him and his behavior seriously.*

Modes of Validation

There are five different levels or modes of validating. They are paying attention, accurate reflection, intuitive understanding, validating the past, and validating the present. Each addresses a different aspect of a person's emotional experience in any particular situation and incorporates different skills and strategies. There is no set order for using these methods of validation. You can use them one at a time, in any combination of the five modes, or all five modes at once, depending on the situation. Whatever level of validation you use, it requires being fully present in the moment, totally focused on listening to the other person.

Paying Attention:
Taking Your Loved One's Emotional Temperature

Paying attention is actively listening to your loved one with your eyes, your ears, your mind, your body, and your heart. It is telling the other person that you have received the nonverbal message she is sending you and have read the subtitles of what she is feeling. By listening to and observing another person in a nonjudgmental manner, you communicate clearly that you are really interested in what she is thinking and feeling. You "get it," you are accepting what she is saying without agreeing with, criticizing, or judging her.

Paying attention begins with observing. Carefully paying attention gives you the opportunity to observe your loved one's nuances of voice tone, body language, gestures, facial expression, feelings, and verbal and nonverbal efforts to communicate with you; simultaneously, you are demonstrating that you are paying serious attention, actually accepting the person in the moment. You must be fully present in the moment, totally focused on listening, to take your loved one's "emotional temperature." When you first begin a conversation with your loved one, in person or on the phone, listen and pay close attention to his voice tone and body language (if face to face) before you react, before you do or say anything. If you are multitasking, you will not be able to get an accurate reading of your loved one's emotional temperature. Slicing vegetables, cooking dinner, sorting laundry, paying bills, text messaging on your BlackBerry, or engaging in other activities is distracting to you and to the other person.

Contemporary lives are stressful and full of distractions. We do not take the time to really see what is happening in front of us. We have to learn how to observe. Imagine that you are a British Guard in front of Buckingham Palace, wearing a big black furry hat, taunted by the tourists. You carefully observe but you never, ever respond. You need to learn to observe without responding, just like the British Guards. Observing provides you with the clues to what your loved one is feeling. As your ability to observe improves, your sensitivity and awareness of your loved one's feelings and reactions will become keener. This ability improves with practice. You will also know when you have inadvertently invalidated your loved one or when you have succeeded in validating his responses and averted an escalation.

When you validate while paying attention you are communicating *unconditional acceptance* in the moment. There is no right or wrong in validation because whatever a person feels is what they feel. No one can tell anyone else what to feel in any situation. Our feelings are our own response to how we experience each moment of our lives.

Describing What You Observe

Describing what you observe in the course of your interaction with your loved one helps you to prevent judgments and possible overtones of criticism from seeping into your understanding of a situation

---

Checklist: Helpful Hints for Paying Attention

- Stop what you are doing, pay active attention
- Focus on what he is saying or seems to be feeling
- Make eye contact
- Notice body language: is your loved one tense, relaxed, have his arms folded?
- Is he fidgeting, foot tapping, or agitated?
- Notice facial expressions: Is he frowning, smiling, surprised, neutral?
- Notice mood: Is he sad, bored, happy, sleepy, angry?
- Notice level and tone of voice. Is he speaking in a normal tone, a low, sad tone, an agitated, angry or excited tone?
- Notice nonverbal communication; read his emotional subtitles by being aware
- Ask yourself: What do you think his body language is trying to tell you?
- Notice if this is the right time to talk or to bring up painful subjects. Back off if the person is not ready and willing to discuss difficult matters. If he tells you he is not ready, stop!
- Communicate with warmth and be supportive
- Listen without bias and preconceived ideas
- No judging, criticizing, interpreting, offering advice, jumping to conclusions, et cetera.

or event. Describing can be done both internally ("She appears upset") and externally ("It seems that you are upset"). Describing helps to clarify communication because it dispenses with wrong assumptions and inferences. When Detective Friday on *Dragnet*, a TV detective program, interviewed witnesses who went on and on recounting the saga of their experiences of a crime with endless details, he would interrupt with, "Just the facts, Ma'am, just the facts." To describe a situation you must state "just the facts" without offering inferences, predetermined ideas, theories, or judgments about the situation.

Describe in detail (either to yourself, silently, or to your loved one) only the behavior you have actually observed. Omit extraneous details that have no relevance to the emotions generated by the situation. Label each experience as what it is. Call a thought a thought: "I can see that you thought he betrayed you last night when he did not call." Describe an emotion as an emotion: "I can sense that you are feeling disappointed and hurt about what happened with your boyfriend." Describe specific behaviors, physical reactions, urges, and any other changes you observe. Clarify what you have observed to be sure that your understanding of the situation is accurate. It is okay to ask questions. "Have I got it right? Have I understood the situation?" When you are not sure, ask, "What happened?" Or say, "Can you help me out? I really want to understand what happened here." Acknowledge the situation and your loved one's opinions and/or feelings. Do not hesitate to ask if the other person actually feels validated. Avoid going on and on as if you were reciting the preamble to the Constitution before you get to the point. Keep it simple and succinct. Remember, just the facts. Keep your opinions, judgments, moral values, or codes of behavior out of your observations. Describing is not about you.

Accurate Reflection: Being a Mirror

Once you have described a situation accurately and without judgment, you can reflect back to someone. Reflecting is not done within yourself but is a method of interactive communication with your loved one. By reflecting, by being her mirror, you are simply identifying and communicating in a clear way just what you sense, hear, observe, and understand about the situation in the present moment. Reflecting helps your loved one feel heard. Identify what her thoughts, assumptions, and emotional responses seem to be to a given situation and reflect her feelings back to her. Use simple, uncomplicated language.

Reflect feelings. Demonstrate that you sense the emotions someone with BPD is feeling, that you recognize his emotional state and acknowledge that his emotions and feelings are unique expressions of his very own self. To reflect feelings you can say, "I can sense that you are very sad about losing your job." Reflect back what your loved one expresses he is feeling, thinking, wanting, or needing. Legitimize his emotional responses. "I can only imagine how embarrassing it must have been to miss that appointment," and what he seems to be feeling, as in, "I sense that you are really very angry about this."

Reflect meanings. Reflect back the meaning of what your loved one is saying by legitimizing the "facts" of his responses. "Are you saying that you dislike traveling on trains? In that case, I can only imagine how frustrating the train ride must have been for you." To be sure you understand, ask questions to clarify what you think he is saying, thinking or feeling.

Reflect nonverbally. Reflect back in a manner that shows your loved one you are taking her seriously by the way you listen, not just by the words you say. You can nod your head, say "wow," "yes," "I see," or "uh huh," "I see, of course," or just shake your head to show her that you are paying close attention. Be aware of your body language. Try to put your body in the same position as your loved one, lean forward if she is leaning forward, cross your legs if she is crossing hers. Keep facial expressions and eye contact natural, respectful, and focused on the person. When it is your turn to listen, listen mindfully without thinking about what to say next. Try to take turns speaking and do not interrupt.

Matching Voice Tones

As people with BPD often feel invisible and unheard by their loved ones, reflecting in this way helps them to feel heard. When you validate by reflecting back, pay special attention to your loved one's tone of voice. Determine what you think it is and then moderate your voice tone so as to match and mirror the emotion in your loved one's voice, in the moment. Convey emotion with your own voice and facial expression. If she is screaming, raise your voice so that it is a just a little bit lower than her voice and a little bit less intense. If you respond with a cold, calm voice to someone with BPD who is raging, she will escalate even more because it will seem to her that you have not registered her distress. Conversely, if she is sad, use a lower tone, but do not use a tone as low as the one she is using. To be effective, exaggerate your voice tone in either direction so that it is slightly lower or higher than the tone the other person is using at the moment. When validating, use clear and simple words to describe emotions.

Define and clarify the various nuances of emotion such as the differences between annoyed, bothered, angry, and furious. Be sure your voice conveys warmth and acceptance and is not sarcastic.

Be sure your voice conveys warmth and acceptance and is not sarcastic.

Phyllis's daughter Mary Lou called her, screaming and crying hysterically because she was stuck in the middle lane of a highway. Her car had broken down. She was yelling, "I told you this car was junk, no one would listen to me, I told you, I told you!" She was zooming into the stratosphere. Phyllis was at work and caught off guard. She was scared because Mary Lou was in a very dangerous situation. She tried pacifying her in the usual way, telling her to call the police and to calm down. This did not help. Mary Lou was getting more and more out of control. Then, miraculously, Phyllis remembered her DBT skills. Even though she was at her desk in the dignified financial office where she worked, she started yelling into the phone, "Oh my, Mary Lou, this is just so terrible, you must be so scared! If this happened to me, I would be frightened, too. What can you do now?" Mary Lou calmed down somewhat and began to quietly sob. As Phyllis continued to validate her daughter's fear and frustration, she slowly decreased the intensity of emotion in her voice, lowering the tone of her voice a little more with each sentence. She kept asking Mary Lou what she thought she could do about the situation, reminding her of other difficult situations in the past where she had managed to deal with problems successfully, on her own. Then, with her nose all stuffed up from crying, Mary Lou said, in a halfway normal tone of voice, "Let me go, Mom, the cops are here."

Phyllis describes how she does this. "First, reflect back to them—as if you were a mirror in front of their face—the emotional state they are expressing in words and then what they are feeling in their heart. That might sound like the same thing, but it is not. Their emotion might be rage, or happiness, or sadness, but they can't seem to identify their own emotions. You have to demonstrate it for them so they can identify their own emotion. Reflect back so that they can hear themselves. Mimic their voice, whether it is way up or down low."

"When Mary Lou calls me up, the first thing I do is listen to the tone of her voice. She'll start the conversation in a very low voice: 'Ma . . .' As soon as I hear that *Ma* I bring my voice down real low, too. Immediately her voice comes up a bit. By hearing my response to her, she can hear herself and somehow this seems to perk her up. When she calls crying hysterically, my voice gets higher pitched and I try to make it convey more emotion. Whatever emotion people with BPD experience, they seem to go to extremes. I remind myself that she cannot help this."

Generally, in emotional situations, we tend to raise our voices, escalating from frustration to anger as we try harder and harder to be heard. When someone with BPD hears her tone of voice echoed back, she feels the other person has actually heard her. Have you ever noticed how infuriating it is when you are upset, or in a crisis situation, and someone answers you in a dismissive "tra-la-la" voice? Imagine you are frantically trying to get help because your house is burning. A neighbor responds in a low, calm voice saying, "Don't worry dear, just calm down, everything will be just fine." You feel as if he has not heard a word you have said, is not taking you seriously, and has not registered the urgency you are trying to convey. Or perhaps you are feeling very sad because your dog has died. A friend says, "Snap out of it, it's only a dog! You can get another one at the ASPCA!" His response trivialized your feelings and made you feel as if he was not hearing, understanding, or caring about you. You now feel even more frustrated, isolated, and sad. This is how people with BPD feel most of the time. For them, daily life is like crossing a minefield of invalidation.

Above all, do not respond to emotionally charged situations with a neutral voice or facial expression. Remember the research of Nelson Donegan discussed in Chapter 2. Neutral responses are confusing to your loved one. They are usually interpreted as anger or hostility and will trigger negative responses.

Putting Reflection into Action

Twenty-one-year-old Jessica was hospitalized after making a suicide attempt. Her mother was terrified and in shock. At a subsequent family therapy session Jessica revealed how angry she was at her mother because she did not show any emotion when she was hospitalized. Her mother replied, "I may have had a blank expression on my face, but inside of me I was feeling anxious and terrified by the experience and was so frightened for your safety. I did not know what to do or how to react. You, my beloved daughter, were in a hospital, describing how you felt when you tried to kill yourself. I feel powerless to help you and was devastated. I guess I just froze." Jessica said that she interpreted her mother's reaction as proof that she did not want to visit her any more at the hospital, and that she was ashamed of her. Jessica's interpretation of her mother's not showing any emotion in response to what she was saying meant that her mother didn't care about her.

You receive a telephone call from the school informing you that your teenage daughter, Ann, had a fight in the cafeteria and threw another girl's lunch tray onto the floor. When Ann comes home you can see that she is very upset. Validate her by saying, "I can sense you are very stressed. What happened?" Listen to the story Ann has to tell and then try to reflect it back to her: "So, if I understand what you are telling me, you finally had a seat next to Mary at the lunch table and Jenny moved your lunch tray one seat over without your permission so that you were no longer sitting next to Mary. Is that right? Have I understood the situation correctly? That must have been so disappointing. Did that make you feel as though you did not count, as if Jenny did not want you to be her friend? Is that what got you so mad?"

To reflect accurately you need to look at what happened and at your loved one's response from her perspective, regardless of what you personally think about the situation, why it happened, or how she responded. Allow your loved one to correct you and add to your summary. Come to a shared understanding of the situation. Ask, "Is that right? Have I understood?" Perhaps Ann has difficulty making friends and finally had a seat next to someone she admired in school, someone she would like to have as a friend. This probably meant a great deal to her. When Jenny moved her lunch tray, Ann might have interpreted this action as a personal rejection—whether or not the action was intended this way. You might offer an alternate or neutral explanation for what happened: "Maybe the table was crowded and Jenny moved your tray to make room so that another girl could join the group. Is that a possibility?" Empathy and validation in this situation would go like this: "I can see how upset you were when Jenny moved your tray. It must have been so disappointing for you to lose your place next to Mary. If I couldn't sit next to my friend, I would have been disappointed and frustrated, too. Anyone would be disappointed. However, how did throwing Jenny's lunch tray on the floor solve the problem? Was there something else you could have done to solve the problem? What was your goal in this situation? Was it to be Mary's friend? Was it just to sit next to Mary at the table? How will you handle this situation if it comes up again? How can you make amends with Jenny and Mary?"

Remember to be nonjudgmental, both verbally and nonverbally. If you make a validating statement with a scornful, angry look on your face or in a sarcastic tone of voice, you may do more harm than good, and you certainly will not be believed. Conversely, a too-sympathetic voice tone may be interpreted as patronizing. By reflecting back with a nonjudgmental tone you are respecting the other person's emotions, desires, reactions, and goals. You are not required to approve of behavior, nor should you judge the effectiveness of reactions. If you say "Throwing Jenny's lunch tray on the floor was wrong and made the situation worse," you will induce more shame and be ineffective in helping your loved one learn how to handle this situation if it arises again. Remember, empathy is always part of observing, describing, and reflecting.

Here is another example, two versions of the same situation encountered by a mother and daughter.

DAUGHTER: (*angrily, slamming fists on the table*) That's it! I'm quitting that job!

MOTHER: Oh no. Not again. You can't afford to quit another job. How will it look on your resume? You need to work! What are you going to do for money if you quit this job?

DAUGHTER: Oh great, I'm being abused at work and now you're abusing me. With a response like that from you, I think I'll quit life.

MOTHER: I'm not abusing you, I'm trying to help you. You can't afford to lose another job. And I won't stand for being accused of abusing you when I'm simply trying to point out how you are harming yourself . . . . You never want to hear the truth. You're always trying to manipulate me by trying to make things my fault and make me feel guilty.

DAUGHTER: You're incapable of guilt . . . . You're a cold-hearted bitch and you've never been there for me, ever, especially when I've needed you the most. Why did I think you'd be there for me this time? I don't know why I even bother talking to you at all. I give up!

How could the mother have applied validation in this scenario and interacted more constructively?

DAUGHTER: (*angrily, slamming fists on the table*) That's it! I'm quitting that job!
MOTHER: Wow! I can see you're really upset. What happened? (*Said with intensity, matching and reflecting daughter's voice tone.*)
DAUGHTER: I'm being abused by my boss and I'm not going to put up with it. I quit.
MOTHER: No wonder you're so upset. If I felt my boss was abusing me, I would be upset, too. What did he do? (*Said with intensity.*)
DAUGHTER: I found out that he asked my assistant to do something he should have asked me to do. When I confronted him, he told me it's easier to go to her for certain things when he sees I'm in a kind of a "bad" mood. I told him to go to hell and stormed out. How dare he treat me like that?
MOTHER: I can see that you're furious! I can imagine that his asking your assistant to do your work must have made you feel incompetent. Are you frightened about losing your job? Are you worried that he might promote your assistant?
DAUGHTER: (*lowers her voice*) Yes, but it is hard for me to think straight when I'm this upset.
MOTHER: How about sitting down with me and having a cup of tea so we can talk.
DAUGHTER: Yeah, I guess so. Thanks.

In the first scenario, when the mother jumped to conclusions, judged her daughter, and personalized her response, she shut the door to any meaningful discussion or effective exploration of the situation. She made matters worse by making her daughter feel even more misunderstood, and both of their emotions escalated. In the second scenario, the mother validated her daughter's response and asked what happened, opening the door to exploration with validation so that the situation could be discussed in a trusting atmosphere and alternative solutions explored.

Reflecting back or restating what your loved one is feeling, thinking, wanting, or needing legitimizes his emotional responses.

Reflecting back or restating what your loved one is feeling, thinking, wanting, or needing legitimizes his emotional responses. People who are accustomed to having their feelings invalidated or who doubt the accuracy of their responses usually think that what they are feeling does not make any sense or is inappropriate.

Find the Nugget of Truth

Dr. Linehan states that there is "a kernel of truth" in everything that those with BPD say. It is your job to find that nugget of truth in your loved one's feelings and/or response to a situation and to reflect it back to him, to validate it. Sometimes you may feel like you are searching for a lost ring in the sand at the beach, or a contact lens in an airport restroom. You may need a magnifying glass to find that nugget of truth, but do not give up. Somewhere, based on who he is, not on who you are, there is a valid basis for whatever it is your loved one is thinking or feeling. For people with BPD, being taken seriously is a significant experience that reinforces their own sense of what they are feeling. Finding this nugget of truth and validating it is an essential component of the dialectical reconciliation of opposites that will ultimately repair your relationship.

People with BPD have an uncanny ability to observe things in the environment that others do not see. When their astute observations are ignored or ridiculed, they must feel even more isolated. How can they develop decision-making skills or the ability to evaluate situations if they doubt their perceptions and cannot validate themselves? You can play a role in changing how they perceive themselves. If you look hard enough, there will always be some validity in your loved one's response to any situation. Take a leap of faith and acknowledge the situation as she sees it by assuming there is validity in what she is thinking or feeling. Search for the nugget of truth in what she is saying, find what might be valid or make sense in her situation within the context of her sense of reality, and reflect it back to her. Finding the nugget of truth in your loved one's response is an absolutely essential component of validation and of the dialectical reconciliation of opposites that can ultimately repair your relationship. You are on a tightrope. Your loved one does not always make sense; she may exaggerate or minimize situations, may think in extremes, devalue what is valuable, idealize what is ordinary, and make dysfunctional decisions. However, that is her experience, her reality; it belongs to her. Do not prejudge her opinions, thoughts, and decisions.

Intuitive Understanding

When you have the ability to imagine how your loved one might perceive a situation given his neurobiological makeup, his typical patterns of responding, and his life experience, you are validating with intuitive understanding. You try to link the behavior you are observing with a possible trigger, even though you have not been given specific information about the trigger and may not know what actually occurred.

Do not assume that your loved one will respond to any experience the way you would. How would you react if you were supersensitive, hypervigilant, and biased toward negative thinking? Picture all the systems within your loved one that are dysregulated during a stressful moment and imagine how hard it would be for you to make good decisions and control your impulses if you felt this way. Be aware of how intense his emotional reactions usually are and how hard he is trying to control them. Research demonstrates that people with BPD are shame prone and rejection prone, so you can usually count on shame as your loved one's most likely emotional response to most experiences. Try to imagine what it was about what just happened that might have led to feelings of shame, incompetence, fright, anxiety, or loss. In the moment, while trying to imagine the emotions possibly evoked by the situation, remind yourself that you really do know how this person reacts, what he generally does when he feels stressed or dysregulated. Maybe he uses drugs, has rage attacks, blames you for all his problems, cuts himself, or gets drunk. It is not hard to understand why someone who is rejection-sensitive would think that she was being rejected if someone moved her lunch tray, rather than adapting a benign interpretation, such as the table is crowded. Ask yourself, *If I were my son/daughter, how would I perceive this situation, how would I respond?*

The technique of intuitively understanding or "emotionally guessing" can be referred to as "mind-reading." It is the ability to read situations astutely so that you can predict how your loved one might feel in most situations. You will have to learn to think on your feet, like a detective. You examine all the clues and try to piece them together to determine what might have precipitated the reaction. What was the trigger? Try to summarize or reorganize what she is telling you into a more coherent explanation by clarifying or reframing her story. When you mind-read, you are telling your loved one that you understand her experiences and responses to events even though she has not told you all about them directly. By becoming sensitive enough to read her reactions and communicate what she may be wishing for or thinking about, you will become more effective at validating your loved one. Hone in on your own intuitions, have the courage to act on them, then validate her nonverbal communication. Choose a response that is appropriate for the situation, in the moment. This will help her identify what she is feeling, know herself better, and feel more secure about identifying her own feelings in the future.

Unfortunately, a list of appropriate intuitive responses to all situations simply does not exist. Each scenario is unique, requiring awareness, understanding of your loved one's past experiences and reactions, interpretation of the situation in the present moment, patience and the courage to improvise. If Karen breaks up with her boyfriend, she may act very cavalier and tell you that the breakup does not bother her at all. Or she may tell you, "I don't want to talk about it." At the same time, your intuition, observations, and emotional temperature-taking tell you another story. You do not need to be a rocket scientist to deduce that she would probably feel sad, rejected, unworthy, unattractive, and humiliated. You can articulate these emotions to Karen even though she has not told you that this is how she feels, because it is a safe bet that anyone would feel sad or rejected in this situation. Take a risk; verbalize what your intuition tells you Karen is feeling, even if she is afraid to admit or reveal her feelings. Because you know her so well—probably better than any therapist does—and know her history, you are in the best position to read her unarticulated responses. Ask yourself what the "common denominator" response that most people would have to a similar situation would be and integrate this with the typical way she responds based on her BPD dysregulations and her life experiences. Tell her that anyone would feel "that way" in this situation. Let your loved one know that you sense her responses to an event, even though she has not told you directly, by validating what you think she might be feeling. It might be said like this, "Wow, it must have been so humiliating to hear Jim say he wants to break up with you," even though Karen never said she was humiliated. "Anyone would feel like that if her boyfriend broke up with her." This is a good time to ask, "What happened?"

Gwen, a woman with BPD, talks about her inability to decipher the world around her. "On the day I was born, all the newborn babies got on a line to meet God and to get their *How to Act in All Situations Throughout Life* book. When it was my turn, God had run out of the book. Ever since that day, I have been looking over other people's shoulders so that I could read their book and know how to act."

Many people with BPD, like Gwen, do not know how to identify their own emotions and therefore do not know how to respond to what they are feeling, or even whether their feelings are appropriate for the situation. Validating their nonverbal communication by intuitively understanding their feelings, or mind-reading, helps them identify what they are feeling so that they can then validate themselves. Remember that your mind-reading, validation statement, is only an intuitive "guess." If your loved one says, "No, that's not how I feel," accept that your hypothesis was incorrect. Do not force your mind-reading interpretation onto the other person. Ask another question and move on to another guess.

In order for you to help your loved one, you must be able to see the world through his eyes, radically accepting that his reality is different from your reality. You will have to learn how to speak his emotional language, to translate what he is feeling into words, to develop a mutual emotional language both of you can understand. You read the subtitles when you view a foreign film so you can understand what is happening on the screen. When you talk with your loved one, try to imagine that there are subtitles flashing beneath him. Imagine that he only speaks Chinese and cannot learn English. Wouldn't you do everything you could to learn Chinese so that you would be able to communicate with him? Ask yourself, what would another person's response be in a similar situation? Integrate this knowledge with the typical response of your loved one (her modus operandi) based on her BPD dysregulations, patterns of responding, and life experiences.

Validating the Past

All behavior, in some way, is valid in terms of past experiences and past learning. The present makes more sense if we understand the past. All of us incorporate our past experiences into our present behavior as well as our responses and interpretations of present experiences. A woman who had been raped in an alley at night is now afraid of alleys and refuses to walk through them. This can be seen as a valid or wise adaptation to her past experience. However, because she was raped in an alley does not mean that all alleys are dangerous. Although her feelings are justified based on her past experience, the present situation does not support her fear. You could say, "I can certainly see why you would be afraid of alleys and would not like to go through them because of your past experience. However, it is daylight now, this is a different alley, you are not alone, I am here with you and not all alleys have rapists hiding in them. I can see why you are reluctant to walk through an alley, but going through this alley is the shortest way to get to our destination. What do you think we can do about getting to our appointment, as we are very late?" Change can occur when you repeatedly validate past experiences while reevaluating these experiences in the light of current reality.

Change can occur when you repeatedly validate past experiences while reevaluating these experiences in the light of current reality.

The suitableness of any behavior depends on the circumstances in which the behavior is occurring. Behavior can be appropriate for the short term but not for the long term. Responses learned in the past that were appropriate to the past may no longer be needed or appropriate in the present, such as the fear of alleys in the example above. Feelings, thoughts, and actions may make perfect sense in the context of a person's present experience, physical and emotional state, and life to date, but not according to his past. If you were always thin it is understandable that you would be accustomed to eating anything you like without worrying about your weight. However, you are much older now and your body chemistry has changed. Your teenage eating habits are not suitable to sedentary adult life. If each time you went to a therapist you were told that you cannot be helped, not wanting to go to a new therapist would be valid in terms of your past experience. If you have lost all your prior jobs, you would probably view getting a new job as an adverse experience and feel negatively about it.

Behavior that would make a person a good mental patient, such as passively obeying rules and regulations, is not the same kind of behavior that will make the person successful in everyday life. Behavior may be valid in terms of your loved one's private experience of reality but is not valid in terms of how the behavior is viewed by others. When Ann threw Jenny's lunch tray onto the floor, her action was valid based on her private experience, but it was not valid for Jenny and the other girls at the table. Privately, you may feel frightened because you did not study hard enough for an exam but publicly you seem relaxed. Privately you are very anxious about giving a speech but publicly you appear calm. Behavior can be effective at attaining desired goals or ends. Some behavior can be effective for short-term goals but not for long-term goals. Dropping out of school may relieve the immediate distress of going to school but does not get you to the long-term goal of getting your college degree. What you know about your loved one's life can help you understand what she is attempting to communicate or accomplish. You can make use of this knowledge by asking, "How does this behavior get you to your goal of saving up to buy a car?" Evaluating your own perspective of what happened and her version of the same event can also help you to determine what is valid for your loved one in the present moment so that you will be able to validate more effectively.

Although validation of the past can help a person accept how or why something happened in the past, blaming present problems on past events prevents a person from taking action in the present and moving forward. By validating past experiences, acknowledging past pain in the context of the present, you can help your loved one let go of past pain, move on, and begin to live in the present.

Validation also addresses the "should" and "should not" thinking that so characterizes people with BPD. "Given a situation like X, how could Y be otherwise?" If anyone refuses to accept a given reality, he cannot act to overcome or change that reality. If everything is everyone else's fault, if he is waiting for the other person or situation to change, the person with BPD will never learn new behaviors. Dr. Linehan wisely states, "Wishing reality were different does not change reality. Believing reality is what one wants it to be does not make it what one wants it to be. Saying reality 'should not be' a certain way is also tantamount to denying reality."[3] These are core cognitive distortions (see Chapter 3) that characterize the thinking of many people with BPD. Change occurs when you repeatedly validate past experiences while reevaluating these experiences in the light of current reality. Remember, neither wishing nor denying reality can change reality.

Validating Memories

People with BPD seem to have a tape loop perpetually playing a pain mantra in their heads, repeating all the hurts they have ever experienced in their lives. This litany of suffering is waiting waits in the wings for its cue, the slightest reminder that might trigger a past memory or act as kindling for the next upset. Once triggered, the past hurt takes center stage and dominates the scene. Your loved one will begin by becoming upset about an incident that just occurred and will then relate it to a past incident that, to you, seems completely unrelated to what upset her in the first place. From a logical perspective, you do not see any connections, emotionally or otherwise, between the past situation and the present event. You do not realize how the present pain triggered the past pain, how the present anger triggered the past anger. Unpleasant memories rear their ugly heads, and once again you are doing the BPD dance. How do you deal with an event that happened 20 years ago that you may not even remember? Or one that you and your loved one remember completely differently? You will usually respond by defending yourself, explaining the situation, arguing about the "truth" of the event, or debating who was right or wrong based on the "objective" facts. Your response will have the same effect as throwing gasoline on a fire. Your loved one will probably erupt, and you will not know how to put out the emotional conflagration. Do not try to correct the "facts" or the "logic" of the memory; instead, validate the emotion of the memory, whether or

---

[3] Linehan, 1993b.

not you agree with your loved one's recollection. If your loved one says, "You were never there for me when I was growing up!" you could say, "It must be awful to feel that I was never there for you. But that was then and this is now. What are we going to do about this situation we are in *right now?"*

Do not try to correct the "facts" or the "logic" of the memory; instead, validate the emotion of the memory, whether or not you agree with your loved one's recollection.

Accept That Your Own Past Learning May Have Led to Ineffective Behaviors

Part of validating the past is acknowledging that you may have made mistakes in the past. You may have been advised to hospitalize your loved one or place him in residential treatment if he cut himself or exhibited impulsive behaviors. You might have been encouraged to implement limits and boundaries. You were desperate about his safety and did not know what else to do. A well-known Internet site advises family members to imagine "duct tape" on their own mouths to remind them not to respond to their loved with BPD. This level of invalidation could escalate anyone's emotions. For you, as a family member, learning new, effective methods to help your loved one can be a very painful experience because you must take responsibility for all the "wrong" things you may have done for the "right" reasons, often with the guidance and support of professionals.

Phyllis eloquently validated the past. "How do you make them understand that you actually accept how they are feeling in their hearts? Don't say things like, 'Oh don't feel that way,' or 'That didn't happen,' or 'Why do you keep bringing that up for 30 years?' That makes them get sadder, angrier, or rage even more. Maybe it is because they think you don't hear or understand them that they get louder and angrier. It seems as though they will go on throwing the same thing in your face, for another 30 years. Somehow, you have to make them understand that you do believe them, you do hear them, and you feel their pain. You might not really feel like doing this because your loved one is screaming at you, while telling you about something from the past for the hundredth time that they have totally misconstrued or was never true in the first place. Year after year you continue to argue, over and over again, wasting your breath, saying things like 'That's not the way it happened,' or 'Oh, please stop bringing that up, it's ridiculous for you to keep talking about that.'

"For 35 years, my husband Jack brought up an incident that happened when I was 18. I had just met Jack when I began dating Billy. After 2 months, I dropped Billy, kept dating Jack, and eventually married him. Over the course of our marriage, Jack threw my dates with Billy in my face over and over again. He blamed our broken marriage on Billy and used him to justify cheating on me. I would respond by saying, 'Will you stop bringing that up already, it was nothing. Stop blaming how you acted all through our married life on Billy.' But nothing got through to him. We have been separated for 9 years and Jack still calls me to remind me about Billy.

"Once I learned how to validate, I decided to try it, even though it killed me to do it. How dare Jack use such nonsense as an excuse for a lifetime of betrayal and mental and physical abuse? The next time he brought up Billy, with as sincere emotion as I could get into my voice, I began, 'Oh, I realize that my going out with Billy while I was going out with you must have been so embarrassing. No wonder you have been so angry at me all these years! I am so sorry.' Well, he stopped in his tracks, stared at me and was actually speechless! Then he said, 'How come it took you so many years to finally understand?' It's been over a year now, and he has not brought up Billy again. Validation helped me more than it helped Jack because I no longer have to hear about what I did with Billy when I was 18. I guess it helped him, too, because he must have really been in pain about this for all these years."

Validating the Present: Normalizing

A person's response to a situation can be justifiable, reasonable, well-grounded, or meaningful in light of his current experience or ultimate life goals. Facts about a person's environment can justify how he is feeling and can reflect the wisdom or the validity of his response to the present situation. *Normalizing* is validation that communicates to your loved one that his response is understandable, or his behavior is understandable given the present circumstances, so much so that "anyone would feel that way." Normalizing validates or justifies behavior in relation to the present circumstances. When you validate a person's feelings it does not mean you are validating his behavior, the action he engaged in as a response to how he felt about a situation. This important difference is a core example of dialectical thinking. Feelings may be justified but the behavior is not. "Given a situation like X, anyone would feel angry, sad, disappointed" et cetera. Yet, everyone would not "act" in the same way as did your loved one with BPD. Even though your loved one's feelings may be justified, he could have responded in a different way. You can identify the inherent accuracy, appropriateness, or reasonableness of the feelings elicited by the situation, yet comment on the inherent ineffectiveness of the behavior and ask what else he could have done in that situation.

Feelings may be justified but the behavior is not.

Tom and John were having lunch at school when Tom insulted John's mother. John got very angry and, while fighting with Tom, threw a chair through the cafeteria window. Although John's anger was a valid response to the insults to his mother, the way he chose to deal with his anger was not valid. He not only failed to solve the problem effectively but also created a severe consequence for himself as he is now in trouble at school. A school counselor might say the following, "I can only imagine how angry you were at Tom for saying mean things about your mother. Anyone would get angry if someone insulted his mother. However, throwing a chair through the window was not the most effective way to solve the problem. What else do you think you could have done to deal with your anger and the disrespectful way Tom was speaking? What do you think you can do now to make amends?" John's feelings (anger) are validated but his behavior (throwing the chair) is not, and is shown to be inappropriate. If the *reason* for John's anger had not been validated, he would probably have felt that no one understood what had happened and would see himself as a victim. He would either shut down or continue to escalate until he got himself into even more trouble.

People with BPD realize that the way they experience interpersonal situations is unique; other people do not respond emotionally the way they do. However, they have not developed the ability to identify their own feelings and lack the emotional vocabulary to describe them. They do not realize that the emotions they are feeling may be normal and appropriate responses to the given situation. Their difficulty empathizing with the feelings of others makes them generally unaware that others, too, experience doubts, fear, anger, rejection, and disappointment. Their acute sensitivity is like an emotional sonar system that makes them extremely vulnerable to the nuances of other people's feelings or mood shifts. Although they are keen observers, they have great difficulty interpreting the information they receive from what they have observed.

When someone else, especially someone who matters to them, acknowledges their private emotional responses to a situation in a nonjudgmental way, people with BPD realize that their own seemingly unacceptable and painful responses are, in fact, valid. Given the contexts of an experience or interaction, their responses are normal, predictable, and justifiable. When you reveal similar experiences of your own, and your responses to those situations, you are teaching your loved one that you might have reacted in a similar way and that you, too, can be vulnerable. This helps your loved one to be less afraid of her emotional responses and able to accept them as normal and natural. When you say to your loved one, "Anyone would feel disappointed if her hair cut didn't turn out well, especially before the prom!" you are describing how you or others would react, letting her know that it is okay to feel what she is feeling in this situation, giving her permission to feel her own feelings by giving her insight into how other people feel. This helps her to realize that all of us experience painful emotions in response to certain situations.

Colette was getting married in 2 weeks. Wedding invitations had been sent out to family and friends, all the details had been arranged, her wedding dress was perfect, the flowers were ordered, and the wedding banquet was all planned when, out of the blue, her fiancé announced that he no longer wanted to get married. Colette went into a rage, threw him out of their apartment, and tossed his clothes and possessions out of the window. Her reactions were so extreme that she was hospitalized and then diagnosed with BPD. Months later, when discussing what happened, a friend said, "It must have been so embarrassing for you to have to cancel your wedding. How humiliating it must have been when everyone found out your fiancé had changed his mind. If that happened to me I would have felt so ashamed. Anyone would have been humiliated. No wonder you were so angry with him that you threw everything out of the window." "Wow," she said, "I never realized I was ashamed or angry!" Colette went on to finish her medical training and is now a doctor.

People with BPD have difficulty tolerating their own painful, negative emotions, such as shame, fear, guilt, humiliation, loss, or sadness and will usually try to avoid observing, recognizing, or experiencing them. Just as very young children think grownups can read their minds, people with BPD think other people know what they are feeling. If you do not acknowledge their negative feelings you send them the message that negative emotions, such as anger, jealousy, or disappointment, are unacceptable. Your loved one interprets this as, "If I feel an unacceptable emotion it means that I am unacceptable." Or she may interpret this as a message that you do not care enough about her or are not interested enough in her to figure out what is upsetting her. Have you ever seen a child playing dress-up with adults' clothing? Imagine the person you love with BPD as a child dressed in adults clothes, pretending to be a grownup. Keeping this image in mind can help you reframe her responses and remind you to be compassionate.

People with BPD are responding to situations in the best way they can. We usually focus on their dysregulated or apparently "crazy" behaviors and ignore how hard they are trying to cope or control their behavior. As Charlotte's teenage daughter waited for her mother to come home, she tried very hard to control her behavior and cope with the feelings that had been triggered by something that had happened to her that evening. When Charlotte would not listen to Jenny, Jenny could no longer cope with her feelings and swallowed pills. The person who avoids the dark alley is also trying to cope. Try to focus on the positive aspects of your loved one's behavior. You must learn to find the "nugget of truth" in their responses to various situations.

What to Validate

Now that you understand how validation allows you to communicate through emotions and why this is vital for interacting with your loved one with BPD, here are some suggestions for specific behaviors or responses that are important to validate.

Feelings or emotions that you can recognize. "I can sense how stressed you are right now! Are you angry? What happened?" Or, "Getting a B in that class seems to have made you feel so happy. I realize how much this grade means to you."

Legitimacy in wanting something. Validate that what the person wants is reasonable to want, given his life or his present circumstances. "I can only imagine how much you want a car! If I were in your situation, I would want a car, too. Anyone living so far away from the nearest town would want a car. What do you think you can do to get a car?"

Beliefs, opinions, or thoughts about something. People are entitled to think what they think. You are not the thought police. An effective way to help your loved one is to validate whatever he believes or thinks. This does not mean that you approve of or agree with him. "I can certainly see why you want to come home as late as you want, however, . . ." or "I can sense that you feel cleaning up the kitchen is a waste of time, yet . . ."

True values about something. Everyone has a right to his beliefs, moral values, or creative ideas even if you do not agree or approve of them. "I realize that you're the kind of person who . . ."

How difficult a task is. Acknowledge the difficulty. "I can sense how hard it was for you to call her." "I can only imagine how stressful it is for you to come to Thanksgiving dinner. However, how does not attending family functions get you to your goal of a having a better relationship with your family? How about coming over just for appetizers or dessert and coffee as a first step toward improving that relationship?" This is validation combined with a change strategy.

How hard a person is trying to accomplish a goal. Always validate effort, even if it does not meet with success. Acknowledge what she is trying to accomplish and how hard it is to change. "I can see how hard you are trying to work on this relationship. I really appreciate the effort you are making." "I realize how much this job means to you and I see how hard you are trying to get there on time every morning."

Things people do that are effective for themselves. "It must have made you so proud of yourself to have painted your apartment." "It must have felt so good when you didn't get angry at Jenny for moving your lunch tray. I realize how hard you were trying to control your anger. You can do hard things."

Things one person does for another. Validate consideration shown toward others, or efforts made to help others. "I could see how much you cared about your friend when you gave her your lunch."

Validating the emotions of your loved one does not invalidate your own feelings. "I can sense how hard it would be to call me to say you will be late. However, when you don't call, I really worry."

Misconceptions About Validation

Validation is not an easy concept to master. It will take a commitment on your part to keep trying and practicing. Be prepared to accept your own mistakes. Everyone makes mistakes, especially when they begin to change how they interact with their loved one with BPD. Mistakes can be an opportunity to learn.

The single biggest problem with communication is the illusion that it has taken place
– George Bernard Shaw

Validation Is Not the Same as Understanding

Understanding is not a prerequisite for validating. Do not ask "why" someone feels what she feels. It is not necessary to know why she is feeling what she feels because validation is not about logical explanations. You can validate things you do not understand. This is counterintuitive for most of us because we believe that by understanding what caused a problem we can solve the problem. Validating another person suggests that you see and know her, but it does not require that you understand her. It requires only that you accept whatever she is feeling, in this moment. What she feels is what she is feeling—"why" does not matter.

Validating another person suggests that you see and know her, but it does not require that you understand her. It requires only that you accept whatever she is feeling, in this moment.

In fact, you probably have great difficulty understanding what she is feeling because it is so different from the way you perceive or interpret situations or appraise your own experiences. You would not react to or interpret situations in the same way she does, or get as angry or as hurt. We often tell people that we "understand" when we actually do not. "I understand" is a platitude, like an atheist saying "God bless you" when someone sneezes. Telling your loved one that you understand when she can sense that you do not is extremely invalidating. She will probably get angry, feel patronized, and distrust you even more.

Validating Is Not the Same as Loving Someone

Validating a person is not the same as loving him; they are not equivalent. No matter how much you love someone, if you do not validate his feelings, he will not feel loved. If someone doesn't feel heard, how can he feel loved? If he feels isolated, invisible, or as if he does not count, how can he feel loved? Sometimes the way we love those with BPD can be harmful to them, such as when we try to solve all their problems. This is not helpful.

Validation Is Not a Synonym for Praise

Praise can be perceived as a judgment because it can be interpreted as you bestowing approval on what someone else has done. He has done what he was expected to do, his behavior has met with your approval. Validation is always about the other person. Praise is often only about you. It is important that you make this distinction. Instead of saying, "Your dinner tonight was excellent," you could say, "It must feel so good to have prepared such a delicious meal. I could see how hard you worked."

Validation Is Not the Same as Being Proud of Someone

A person with BPD can feel that what he has done does not count unless it results in your being proud of him. Like praise, he may interpret your pride in what he has done as his meeting with your approval. You may feel you are complimenting him, whereas he may feel you are judging him. It is far more important and effective for a person to feel proud of himself and of what he has accomplished.

Barbara tells her son, "I am so proud of you for getting an A in math." What he hears is, "If you did not get an A in math you would be unacceptable to me and I would consider you a failure. Nothing you ever do is good enough." A better way to express this might be, "I can see how hard you worked in this class. I realize what an effort you have made. I'll bet you feel really proud to have gotten an A and to have your hard work recognized."

Validation Does Not Mean That You Approve or Disapprove of the Person's Feelings

It is important to accept that a person's feelings belong to him and it is not up to you to approve of or disapprove of, or agree with or dis-agree with, those feelings. Whatever someone feels is what he feels. There is no right or wrong way to feel. Feelings do not have to be socially desirable or acceptable to be valid. You cannot dictate another person's feelings. By balancing acceptance with change, you can validate another person's feelings even if you do not agree with them—however, do not validate inappropriate behavior. If someone gets so angry that he is smashing dishes, validate his anger but not his breaking of the dishes.

Validation "Do Nots"

While there are many different ways to validate effectively, there are also validation mistakes that can lead you to being ineffective, and even to causing harm. Here are some common pitfalls.

Do Not Criticize, Judge, or Blame

An aim of nonjudgmental validation is to decrease the misinterpretations that trigger emotional eruptions. Reflect back what the person feels without judging, blaming, or criticizing. Imagine how you would feel if you were allergic to bee stings and were walking through a flowering meadow. Instead of enjoying the colors and scents of the flowers, you would be in fear of being stung by a bee. Likewise, imagine that your loved one is so severely allergic to any sort of criticism, blame, or judgment that any exposure is the equivalent of being stung by a bee and going into immediate emotional anaphylactic shock. When you observe an instant mood change, a sudden rage attack, or a complete withdrawal or dissociation, you are recognizing emotional anaphylactic shock. Although this may not have been your intention, you need to be superaware of how easily your loved one misinterprets your behavior or responses, feels invalidated, and consequently reacts emotionally. Be extra sensitive and aware so as to detect when the nuances of what you say or do are interpreted as criticism, blame, or judgment.

Do Not Be Distracted—Focus

Learning to pay close attention is the first step you can take to improve your ability to observe. Multitasking, distracting, answering the phone, or changing the subject while your loved one is talking to you interferes with your ability to observe and will probably trigger negative responses.

Nora is a busy executive who manages her complicated family and business life by referring to her ever-present BlackBerry. Her son, James, interprets her constant attention to her BlackBerry as a personal rejection and responds with insults and abusive anger. Trivializing what is said, cutting conversations short, interrupting, not responding to disclosures, and pursuing discussions when it is clearly not the appropriate time to do so are also likely to trigger emotional dysregulations.

Do Not Pick the Wrong Time to Have a Sensitive Discussion

Determine if it is the appropriate time before you bring up an important, sensitive topic. If it is not a good time to talk, you can say, "I can see how stressed that phone conversation was for you. I realize that you are angry. It is hard to talk about anything when you are upset. Can you let me know when you feel like talking?"

Do Not Be Willful and Controlling

Do not tell your loved one what she "should" feel, want, think, or do, or how to act, or to be different in some way. This is very invalidating. If she could do things differently, she would. She does not want to feel as bad, isolated, or incompetent as she does. She is already experiencing feelings of shame because she failed to do what she thinks she "should" have done. How does creating more negative feelings for her get you to your goal of improving your relationship? Give up being willful. Do not try to get your way regardless of her wishes. By trying to control your loved one, you will make her feel even more incompetent and probably cause her to feel even more dysregulated.

Do Not Try to Fix or Solve Your Loved One's Problems

Do not solve his problems for him, such as finding him a doctor, paying his rent, making his phone calls, or bailing him out of trouble. This sends him the message that he is incompetent and incapable of solving his own problems, leading to the passive dependency so characteristic of people with BPD. The least effective way to help the person you love with BPD is to do the very things for him that he should be doing for himself. When you get upset because your loved one is not doing something he needs to do for himself, remind yourself that you may have deprived

The least effective way to help the person you love with BPD is to do the very things for him that he should be doing for himself.

him of the opportunities to learn how to solve his own problems and deal with the natural consequences of his own decisions.

Do Not Jump into the Problem Pool

If you want to pull someone out of a deep hole, do you jump in after her? Now that you are in the hole with her, you will not be able to help her out. When you observe that your loved one has a problem, and you jump into it, flounder in the problem pool, and swim laps with her, you are engaging in an exercise in futility that will not help either of you. You need to balance becoming a participant in your loved one's world with being an observer of her world, staying outside while going inside. This is not easy. Many family members go down the enabling, appeasing, disabling, or problem-solving road rather than becoming successful validators and change agents. You need to encourage your loved one to help herself. This is called "creating mastery."[4] If someone feels incompetent, she is not likely to solve her own problems or risk trying new behaviors. If you do not create mastery, you foster hopelessness and dependency that may masquerade as depression. Sensitive, empathetic validation and encouragement can go a long way.

Do Not Respond with Logic

Give up searching for logical meanings or interpretations of situations. Your perceptions occur in the logic processing part of your brain, in the prefrontal cortex. Your loved one lacks the skills needed to respond logically to situations that trigger strong emotional responses

---

[4] Linehan, 1993a.

because he is probably processing the situation in the emotion area of his brain, the amygdala. He likely interprets most things self-referentially, as being all about him. Trying to be logical with someone with BPD can lead to never-ending, middle-of-the-night discussions about the "truth," interminable debates about who is responsible for an event, or endless defending of your own behavior. If you are engaged in these kinds of arguments, you have succumbed to BPD and have dived into the pool of your loved one's misinterpretations and cognitive distortions (see Chapter 3). Too much logic on your part can result in nonemotional validation, which will not be effective. Many family members are so far from intimate terms with their feelings that they have to take a taxi to reach their emotions.

A father wrote this letter to his daughter with the best of intentions. How do you think someone with BPD might interpret it?

> I am really proud of the growth you have demonstrated in school, but remain concerned about your cigarette smoking. I know that you often feel high levels of stress and find smoking reduces those feelings. I recognize how uncomfortable the feelings of stress must make you feel. As a one-time smoker I am also well aware of the relaxing effect that smoking can provide the smoker. But, as you know, smoking is considered offensive by many people and there is clear medical evidence that it is harmful to your health. I began smoking at age eighteen and chose to stop "cold turkey" at age twenty-three. I decided that the quality and duration of my life would be improved by stopping. As a substitute I chewed a lot of gum to satisfy my oral need, and I began an active exercise program to reduce my feelings of stress. After a few weeks of discomfort, I began to feel better.
>
> I am sharing my thoughts on smoking with you not because I am in any way upset that you are a smoker, but rather because I love you and hope that my experience in stopping smoking might be helpful to you. I know how difficult it is to break a habit like smoking, but encourage you to give it a try. I expect that if you substitute regular exercise for smoking you will feel less stressed and more energetic. What can I do to further assist you in stopping smoking? I'm here to help you.

This father is clearly concerned about his daughter and trying to help her, yet his letter lacks warmth or any words that convey emotions, and it has a very judgmental and businesslike tone. His letter would probably be acceptable to a daughter without BPD, but, for someone with the disorder, it would probably ignite an explosion. His daughter will probably interpret "smoking is offensive to some people" as meaning that he thinks she is offensive. He is giving advice while telling his daughter that he disapproves of her behavior and decisions. He would probably meet with more success if he reprioritized his goals and accepted his daughter as she is, in the moment, instead of comparing his own accomplishments to her failures. He would benefit from learning to feel his own feelings and being less judgmental. A more successful approach might be, "I can see how distressed you are about your final exams. I realize how hard you are working at school and how much effort you are putting into getting good grades. It must make you feel so good about yourself to be doing so well in school. I realize smoking cigarettes helps you cope with your stress. I was a smoker and felt the same way. At the same time, when you smoke, I worry about your health. Do you think there is another way of relieving your distress besides smoking? I love you."

Do Not Respond with Anger

Most family members have been the recipients of abusive or difficult BPD behaviors, many for a long period of time. As detailed in Chapter 1, families have generally not had the benefits of valid information or psychoeducation, have had little or no support from other family members or friends, and consequently may feel burned out and hopeless. Anger would certainly be an appropriate response if you believe your loved one with BPD is manipulating you, is lazy and willful, or hurting you intentionally—especially if you thought he could just "snap out of it." If you have given up looking for solutions, your ensuing despair would probably transpose into anger. Stigma toward BPD may fuel your anger by describing your loved one as a "bad" or treatment-resistant patient. The way you are coping with your own grief, pain, anger, and disappointment may lead you to be disrespectful, sarcastic, patronizing, condescending, or contemptuous. Unfortunately, anger interferes with compassion and the ability to validate effectively. To help you cope with your own anger, imagine your loved one wearing the TARA tiara while he is exploding at you.

This will help to remind you that neurological dysregulations underlie the difficulties he has in controlling his behavior.

Do Not Personalize

A few typical response to your efforts to validate might be your loved one saying, "stop the psychobabble," "don't use what you learned in that class or in that book on me," or attacking you personally. Do not be discouraged. These attacks indicate that your loved one realizes that your responses are very different from your usual responses and does not trust that they are authentically genuine. You can respond with, "it must be so frustrating to think your mother is using psychobabble to talk to you. No wonder you are upset; however I sense that you are very stressed. I really want to help. What happened?" Try to keep your own emotions out of your response. Be relentlessly persistent. Remind yourself that you are with someone who feels isolated and unheard, and is desperately trying to get help. The tirades are not really about you, they are about the intensity of the pain she is feeling and her inability to find a way to tolerate it. It is pointless to respond by personalizing, defending yourself, arguing, or debating the issues. Try saying something like "It must be so awful to feel that way." Right or wrong, this is how she is feeling, at the moment.

Verbal diatribes and abuse are characteristic of temper tantrums during the "terrible two's." Do you take it personally if your two year-old screams, "I hate you. Go away." Do you go away and justify leaving because a two year-old says to go away, or do you stay and help solve the problem? When you are told "You are the worst mother in the world," try responding with, "It must feel awful to feel that you have the worst mother in the world!" This is very hard to do. Just keep reminding yourself that the behavior is caused by her pain, frustration, lack of coping skills, or the inability to distract herself from her pain. Let compassion in. These harangues are left-handed compliments that indicate that your loved one trusts you enough to express her emotions and to be vulnerable in front of you.

Do Not Focus on Being "Right"

To be effective, ask yourself, "Would I rather be right or be effective?" Give up trying to control every situation and be right all the time. Instead of being right, lose the battle voluntarily and without bitterness, but win the war. Develop the ability to act wholeheartedly, without reservation. Be ready to respond as needed and to participate with spontaneity. Let go of ego. BPD misery is not about you. It is an illness, an invisible disability.

Do Not Validate the Invalid

Many families find it very difficult to deal with the out-of-control, maladaptive and dangerous BPD behaviors. This is understandable. You may be mortified because someone you love is behaving in such socially unacceptable ways, and are probably ashamed to acknowledge these problems to yourself or to others. To avoid calling a "spade a spade" family members often minimize the seriousness of these behaviors, acting as if they are perfectly acceptable. This happens most often in conflict aversive families. It is as though they are appeasing their loved ones, normalizing pathology, or validating the invalid, thereby avoiding experiencing their own feelings. Some might call this denial. Their responses are not genuine as, underneath, they are usually outraged, seething with anger, and deeply ashamed. A large elephant is sitting at the dinner table and everyone is pretending not to see it. Remember the story of the emperor's new clothes? How can you ignore a naked king or an elephant at the dinner table? Your loved one is aware that his behavior is unacceptable and, when he is no longer emotionally dysregulated, will usually feels a great deal of shame. When you validate behaviors he knows are unacceptable, your acceptance of his inappropriate behavior is interpreted as an indication that he is so undesirable and unworthy that his maladaptive and harmful behaviors are not even worth noticing. Validating the invalid is the antithesis of validation.

Jane, age 20, uses sex to cope with her painful feelings. Her promiscuity and unsafe sex put her at a high risk for contracting sexually transmitted diseases. When Jane is emotionally dysregulated, her decision making and judgments are far from optimal. She copes by meeting men in bars and bringing them home to party. Her roommate goes to work early in the morning and is fed up with the parade of strange men passing through their apartment in the middle of the night. She cannot sleep. She demands that Jane move out immediately. Jane's father, Drew, is extremely judgmental of Jane, deeply ashamed, and even mortified by her "appalling" behavior. In spite of his feelings, he believes he is validating Jane when he says, "It must feel terrible to be thrown out of your apartment. If that happened to me, I would feel bad, too. I can see that your roommate was jealous because you had so many dates and she didn't." This is validating the invalid. He could have said "I can see you are unhappy because your roommate didn't want you in the apartment, but what did you think would happen when you brought men home every night and made so much noise? Is there some other way you could have coped with your painful feelings?" When Drew did not express his concern for his daughter's safety, nor even mention how dangerous her behavior was, he took up residence in his daughter's bubble without making any effort to bring her into the real world. How can Jane learn the consequences of her behavior if her father seems to approve of her outrageous behavior with his validation of her invalid, maladaptive behaviors?

Meanwhile, one night, Jane had too much to drink, was sick in her date's car, and was ill the next day. Her mother, Rose, responded by writing a letter to Jane.

> I can only imagine how embarrassed you were when you threw up in that guy's car. I would have felt the same way if I drank too much, and got sick. Anybody would. I can see how hard it is for you to hang out with people who drink a lot if you don't keep up with them. However, I remember you telling me about times when you refused to drink and it was not a problem for your friends. You felt so good about it. So, the next time you're in that situation, remind yourself how good you felt when you decided not to drink. Remember, you can do hard things.

At first glance, this letter Rose wrote to Jane reads well. Rose seems to be trying very hard. However, when she read it aloud to her daughter, her sarcastic and nasty tone of voice and body language did not correspond with her words. Her tone of voice conveyed anger, judgment, and shock at her daughter's "immoral" behavior. The lack of sincerity in Rose's voice conveyed her mother's disdain, which added shame to Jane's confusion and distress. It did not help her learn the skills she needed to negotiate the world

Harry's 19-year-old son, Ben, spent 2 years in a residential treatment center for mentally ill adolescents. Ben believed there was never anything wrong with him in the first place and blamed all his problems on his parents' divorce and his placement in the residential treatment facility. He was furious with his father for placing him in this program, launching into frequent insulting tirades of verbal abuse. Harry responded, "I can see how angry you are with me because I placed you in residential treatment where the treatment you received was not helpful. If my father had put me in such a place, I would be mad, too." Because Harry felt guilty, he accepted full responsibility without ever reminding his son that it was his own out-of-control behavior that led to his hospitalization. How could Ben ever learn to accept responsibility for his life and his illness if blaming his father for his problems was validated by his father? Although there was a nugget of truth in what Ben was saying, his abusive behavior toward his father was not acceptable. By failing to address the reasons for Ben's initial hospitalization and his abusive behavior, Harry validated the invalid. A more appropriate and effective response might have been, "I can see you are angry about your experience in the residence and I regret that the residence I picked for you was not the best. Your anger is justifiable. However, what do you think we could have done differently when you were having frequent explosive outbursts, were out of control and behaving in ways that were dangerous to yourself and to others? How does being rude to me now change that?"

Why Is Validation So Difficult?

It is counterintuitive. We are accustomed to interpreting experiences and solving problems with logic. Western culture does not encourage validating someone's emotional responses, as emotional awareness of daily interactions is counterintuitive to how we normally react. In today's fast-paced society we often do not take the time to notice or acknowledge people's feelings or the efforts they are making to do their jobs. We tend to notice these things even less with the people who are closest to us. Don't you feel good when someone notices how you feel and appreciates the efforts you are making? If you are a parent, it was probably not necessary for you to use validation techniques to communicate emotionally with your children who do not have BPD. Their adjustment to life attests to your good parenting. Why do you now have to learn a new way of responding to this child with BPD? Why do you have to change your own behavior when it is the other person who has the problem? If constant validation is what your loved one needs to make his life easier and to improve your relationship, are you willing to make this sacrifice and learn a new way of communicating?

It involves intense feelings. Your loved one's intense feelings probably frighten you and make you feel uncomfortable and anxious because you do not assess interactions or experiences in the same way and you would not get as upset as he does in comparable situations. His intense responses and assessments of situations confuse you. Because you are unaware of what triggered his emotional response in the first place, you will probably find it very hard to understand his extreme feelings or reactions. His emotional intensity is alien to your way of behaving or being, especially if you are conflict aversive. You certainly would not get as angry if someone did not make your latte correctly, as frustrated if you could not get into a movie, or as disappointed if a friend did not call. You may have a friend whose company you really enjoy and find it difficult to see why your loved one experiences this same person as hostile and aggressive. Your loved one's reactions are so quixotic that it feels as if he is walking about holding a match while carrying a stick of dynamite or a grenade with the pin pulled. You, on the other hand, feel like you are walking through a minefield.

It will take vigilance, patience, and a lot of energy to learn to validate, the same kind of vigilance and energy you used when you taught your children to dress themselves, to eat with a fork and spoon, or when you toilet trained your toddler. This is how change happens, one baby step at a time.

Practicing Validation

At the onset it seems very difficult; however, with practice, validation gets easier and easier until you find yourself doing it automatically with everyone. If you find it difficult to validate your loved one, if you feel you are not quite ready to try or fear the consequences of making a mistake, try practicing with people you are not emotionally involved with or with strangers such as waiters, taxi drivers, or salespeople. Practice several validations every day. After practicing many times with strangers, you will be ready for the big time, validating your loved one.

If you find it difficult to validate your loved one, if you feel you are not quite ready to try or fear the consequences of making a mistake, try practicing with people with whom you are not emotionally involved.

There is no set rule for how or what to validate. Start by slowing down and really looking at the person. Try to observe and then describe to yourself what you are seeing. Notice body language, tone of voice, facial expression, rhythm of movements, and the other person's eyes. Reflect back what you think the person is feeling, remembering to match voice tones. Consider the job she is doing. Imagine how you would feel if you were doing her job and how you feel when someone really notices you. You will know when you get it right by the way the person responds to you.

Talking to a waiter in a restaurant when it is very busy. "I can see how hard you are trying to do a good job at servicing your customers. It must be so stressful when everyone arrives all at once. I can imagine how frustrating it must feel when people do not realize how hard you are trying." It is important to note that if you take too much of the waiter's time to validate how really busy he is, you could actually be invalidating him.

Talking to a waiter in a restaurant when it is slow. "I can only imagine how frustrating it must be to come to work, ready to work hard and to do a good job, and then not have any customers at all. If I were in your place I would be so disappointed."

Talking to a taxi driver. "It seems like it would be very hard to remember all the streets in the city. I can only imagine how difficult it was to learn the names of all the streets. I can see how much effort you have put into doing your job well."

Talking to a salesperson. "It must be so frustrating to hang up clothing all day and rearrange stock because people are looking at the merchandise, trying things on and do not put them back in place. I admire your patience. Thank you for helping me."

Talking to a friend at dinner. "I can sense how hungry you are. I appreciate how considerate you are, waiting for me before you ordered. I realize you had a busy day and didn't have time to eat." Or, "This is a really nice restaurant and the food is so good. I appreciate how much effort you put into picking such a pleasant place for us to meet. Thank you."

Talking to a secretary, office assistant, or co-worker. "It must be so stressful to have three people giving you tasks to do all day and constantly changing your schedule. I admire your flexibility."

Acceptance-Acknowledgement Declaration

Now that you have practiced with people you do not know, or who you are not as connected to as your loved one with BPD, it is time to validate her. If you can truly accept these essential DBT principles, that your loved one is in pain, is doing the best she can, and wants to do better, you are ready to acknowledge that you may have inadvertently said or done things in the past to contribute to her pain. All of us inadvertently hurt each other's feelings, or overlook opportunities to say or do the right thing. This Acceptance-Acknowledgment Declaration is a helpful way to cut through the years of frustration and isolation that your loved one with BPD has experienced and to begin to repair your relationship. It is a way for you to apologize and accept responsibility for the harm you may have done in the past. It can be thought of as your very first baby step toward reestablishing trust. Although it is not necessary to use these exact words, your goal should be to communicate their meaning. To achieve success, please do not try this speech until your heart understands and accepts the meaning of the words, the pain someone with BPD lives with each and every day and how hard she is trying to control her behavior. When you accept this, your loved one will know that your efforts to be helpful are authentic. Use the script below as a guide for saying what your loved one has been waiting to hear. Keep it brief and repeat it as often as needed.

Acceptance-Acknowledgement Declaration

I never knew how much pain you were in or how much you were suffering. I never understood how sensitive a person you are or how stressful some situations could be for you. I must have said and done so many things that hurt you because I did not understand. It was never my intention to cause you pain. I am so sorry! What can we do now to improve our relationship? What do you need from me now to make things better?

The Acceptance-Acknowledgement Declaration can provide you with a starting point for validating in specific situations. It can be thought of as your very first baby step toward reestablishing trust between you and your loved one. You will probably have to try it more than one time and may have to vary the form to fit your personality or unique style. There is no harm in repeating this declaration, especially if you see that it is being accepted, is helping to improve communication, and that you are making TLCs—tiny little changes. You may be taking three steps forward and then two steps back—but at least you are no longer making things worse. DBT philosophy does not aim to prevent mistakes but rather to learn how to deal with them effectively and repair them. However, it does not require you to grovel, cringe, or fawn. Sometimes you may need a magnifying glass to see your own and your loved one's TLCs more clearly, but it is still important to notice, reflect, authenticate, and support the efforts being made.

Accepting and acknowledging in this way does not mean you should spend time feeling guilty or blaming yourself for not doing what you did not know how to do and what no one taught you to do, or for following the advice of experts who told you to do things that might have harmed your loved one. Remember the child who did not flourish when given milk? Would you have given milk to your child if you knew she was lactose intolerant? Of course not! You did the best you could at the time. If you did do the wrong thing, it was for the right reasons.

Validating the emotional responses of others is hard to do and may seem impossible to master when you first begin. When you are first learning a new language, you will surely make mistakes, mispronouncing words and making errors in grammar until the new language becomes a natural part of your everyday life. When your efforts to validate are sincere, a mistake in wording can be easily overlooked. If what you say comes from your heart as well as your mind, if you have compassion and the humility to admit mistakes, your relationship

When you integrate validation into your daily interactions with the person you love with BPD, you become a therapeutic parent, partner, friend, or sibling, preventing potentially volatile situations from escalating and are on the road to repairing relationships.

will improve. Progress will occur in proportion to the trust that develops. When you integrate validation into your daily interactions with the person you love with BPD, you become a therapeutic parent, partner, friend, or sibling, preventing potentially volatile situations from escalating and are on the road to repairing relationships.

Writing a Letter of Validation

As people with BPD are so sensitive to facial expressions, body language, and voice tones, sometimes writing a letter can help you to bypass possible triggers so that you can get your message across. Reading your words instead of hearing your voice or actually seeing you gives your loved one a chance to focus on your message rather than just the emotions that may accompany your personal interaction.

Validate one small event at a time. Pick something small to validate, such as an emotion you realized he was feeling, something he did well, something he did for himself or for you (like cleaning the dinner dishes, running an errand, calling when he was going to be late), or the effort he made to do something. Validate only one situation at a time. Do not use this letter as an opportunity to validate someone's lifetime achievements or failures, or your own. Keep it simple and stay in the present.

Do not begin sentences with "you." A person with BPD generally interprets the word "you" as the finger of judgment pointing at her. Whenever possible, begin sentences with "it," as in, "It must be difficult, stressful, embarrassing." "You" sentences can also be interpreted as your efforts to control her by telling her what to do or accusing her of failing to do something. When you start sentences with the word "you," you are on a slippery slope heading toward emotional escalation.

Keep the focus on the other person, not on yourself. This letter is absolutely not about you. Everything you write should be about your loved one's feelings and his reactions, not yours. Beginning sentences with "I" as in "I am proud of you" is not effective because it is about how you feel and think, signifying that the other person has met your expectations or done what you think is acceptable. It is much more important that the person feel good about what he has done for himself, with or without your approval. However, you can use "I" in some instances, as in "I can only imagine how proud you must be feeling about yourself." This statement is still about your loved one, and you are reinforcing self-validation.

Do not give advice. Do not use a validation letter as a forum for telling your loved one what he should do, ought to do, needs to do, what you would do, or how to solve a problem. People with BPD have no confidence in their own abilities and believe that they are incapable of solving their own problems. When you give advice, the implicit nonverbal message you are sending is that you believe your loved one cannot solve a problem on his own. This fragelizes him and reinforces his sense of incompetence and his inability to deal with his own life. Even if his history has been characterized by poor decisions and judgments, be mindful, stay in the present and have faith that he can learn, change, and develop mastery of his own life. You can also ask your loved one for advice as in, "How do you think you can solve this problem?" "What can you do to avoid this situation in the future?" "How do you think you can repair your relationship with your friend?" By asking your loved one what he thinks, you are implicitly saying that you believe he has the capacity to solve the problem. If he is ever to improve the quality of his life, you must encourage him to make decisions for himself in every possible situation. Your goal is to create a "sense of mastery."

Do not use this letter as your personal soapbox. A validation letter is your attempt to validate your loved one's feelings or reactions pertaining to only one incident or event that has recently occurred. It is not about the status of your entire life or hers. This letter is not a forum to explain what you did right or wrong throughout your life, to defend the choices you made or why you made them, to defend your personal point of view or justify your actions. It is neither an apology letter nor a demand for apologies. Do not revisit past slights or bring up your past mistakes or hers. Do not look into a crystal ball to predict future behaviors. Stay mindfully focused on the present situation.

Self-disclose to normalize behavior or situations. Avoid turning the agenda onto yourself. Only refer to yourself when you are normalizing such as, "I would feel the same way if that happened to me," or "When I was dating and someone I liked didn't like me, I felt really hurt." Keep the "talking about yourself" to a minimum. Do not be afraid to be vulnerable. Being warm and sincere will help to establish acceptance.

Have realistic expectations. Do not expect to be forgiven as a response to your letter. This letter serves to tell your loved that you are finally seeing and hearing her. It is just your first small effort toward repairing your relationship and ending the isolation your loved one has endured. If you expect this particular relationship to yield true reciprocity, for now, you will be disappointed. You will have to find reciprocal relationships with other people. End your letter on an upbeat, positive note with a mastery-creating sentence such as, "What do you think you can do to solve this problem?"

Sample Validation Letters

Phil is 30 minutes late to pick up Ava, his 23-year-old stepdaughter, after her DBT session. He nonchalantly says, "Sorry I'm late; I was picking up the new grill that Mom bought me for my birthday." Ava, in an exasperated tone, says, "I'm the last one here, and you made my therapist stay late, that's not fair. And I'm hungry. Can we stop for dinner?" Ava is obviously embarrassed because her therapist had to wait with her, and anxious because she feared Phil had forgotten to pick her up. Besides feeling angry, she is distressed, dysregulated, and hungry. In short, she is a lit stick of dynamite. Phil, oblivious to her feelings, says dispassionately in a low, calm voice; "'No, we have dinner at home. We're going to use the new grill.'" Ava screams, "Why are you being so f—ing invalidating to me?" Phil responds calmly, "You sound very angry." Ava, escalating, screams, "That's not how you f—ing do it, read the f—ing DBT book!" Ava's screaming disturbs Phil and he does not know what to do. Hoping to calm her down, Phil turns on the radio. Ava interprets this as "Phil is trying to ignore me." She turns off the radio. Phil grabs her arm and says "Don't f— with me!" By now, he, too, is angry. They continue arguing, exchanging insults back and forth. By now Phil is furious and Ava's anger is soaring up and up into the stratosphere of dysregulation. Additionally, her hunger is escalating her dysregulation. Phil finds her behavior outrageous and disrespectful. Both of them are now dancing the BPD bolero. Ava, enraged, says, "I can have you put away in jail for abusing me, I have all the power in this relationship, don't you know that? I have cuts on my arms and you just grabbed my arm and hurt me, I could have you put in f—ing jail!" Ava repeats this about 10 times.

Phil has succeeded in invalidating Ava at every possible turn. He realizes they are both out of control but does not have a clue what to do to bring down her emotions. Her behavior escalates in step with each invalidation. As they make their way home, Ava continues to scream at Phil while he goes on responding in a low monotone, "Ava, you are screaming like an animal, and you must stop." All hell breaks loose when Phil receives a business call and calmly says, "I can't talk now; I'm trying to get my daughter home for dinner." Ava screams, "'I'm not your f—ing daughter I'm your f—ing stepdaughter and don't you ever f—ing forget that! I don't know why my mother ever f—ing married you. I f—ing hate you!" By now they are at home. Ava turns to Phil, spits in his face, gets out of the car, and slams the door.

In retrospect, Phil realized he did virtually everything wrong and missed every opportunity to see the situation from Ava's point of view. He is sure the results would have been very different had he been able to see her point of view. In an effort to repair their relationship after attending a TARA workshop, Phil writes Ava this letter of validation

Dear Ava:

I've been thinking about what happened. I realize now it must have been so awful to be you that night, you must have been frustrated by having to wait for 30 minutes, not knowing if I was going to pick you up at all or what was going on. You must have been very angry and felt like you didn't count when I finally arrived and I acted so flippant, as if I didn't care at all that you had to wait, were upset and hungry. It must have seemed like my birthday grill was more important to me than picking you up on time, getting you home or your being hungry. I can see how you got more and more infuriated when I said we couldn't go out to eat because we were using the new grill at home. Turning on the radio must have made you feel like I was trying to ignore you. No wonder you were so angry. I would have been angry, too, if that had happened to me. I will try to be more aware from now on. I didn't know how much pain you were in and how utterly devastating it must have been for you that night, and how infuriating it must have been to watch me invalidate you without knowing what I was doing, especially since you were really tired and very hungry. I realize the only way you knew how to let me know how you felt was to spit in my face. I'm really sorry, Ava. However, is there another way you could have let me know how angry you were with me besides spitting at me? I will try to see things from your point of view from now on. What do you think we can do to work on our relationship? I love you.

Phyllis's letter of validation is in a different style. Here the skills used are noted in parentheses.

Dear Mary Lou:

I heard the state of despair you were in when you called. My goodness, it must have been so awful for you to have had an anxiety attack during your final exam, to have to leave school and go home. Pre-calculus is a very hard class to take and I would have been nervous too (*validating and normalizing anxiety feelings about exam*). All your classes are very difficult. I can see how stressful it must be to do so much work in school and realize how hard you are trying. How painful it must be to think of yourself as being "too dumb for college and a loser." Mary Lou, what is a loser (*untwisting a cognitive distortion*)? Remember back in 1996, when you graduated high school with honors, received the President's Medal of Achievement (*being her daughter's memory*)? And in 1998, when you got your associate degree in Computer Information Systems? Just look at your accomplishments; doesn't this prove to yourself that you are quite a capable and competent woman (*serves as her daughter's memory, reminds her of past accomplishments*)? I'm right there beside you (*does not jump into the problem pool with Mary Lou*) if you need me; however, I know that you will figure out some way to get through this class (*creating mastery, not trying to solve her daughter's problems for her, stating her belief in her daughter's competence and ability to solve the problem*). Your tutor is helping you, and I have great faith that you will eventually get the B+ that you want. You have passed difficult math classes before, and you'll do it again (*reminds her that she can do hard things*).

Love, Mom

Key Validation Concepts to Keep in Mind

You will become effective only when your loved one can trust you. For years, your loved one with BPD has felt emotionally isolated and misunderstood. How can he trust someone he feels has never heard him? He will begin trusting you when he senses you are truly listening to him, actually hearing what he says, and really trying to communicate with him. Having the humility to acknowledge your own mistakes will help you begin to repair the damage brought about by years of miscommunication. This will be a very slow process but, over time, you can do it.

Having the humility to acknowledge your own mistakes will help you begin to repair the damage brought about by years of miscommunication.

Here is a summary of key validation principles that should help get you started and keep you on course toward better communication with your loved one:

- Listen with full attention.
- Match voice tones.
- Listen to feelings, not the content of what is said—listen to the music, not the words.
- Validate first, then remind the other person of her goals and that she can do hard things.
- Cultivate compassion. Walk in your loved one's shoes.
- Remember that no one *wants* to feel the way someone with BPD feels.
- Remind yourself that this is someone you love, who did not choose to have this disability.
- Be flexible and improvise.
- Find the nugget of truth.

With the implementation of validation techniques and pivotal acceptance strategies, family members of people with BPD can improve and repair their relationships. Validation strengthens and reinforces progress by balancing change with acceptance. It can act as feedback for the person with BPD and will promote her ability to validate herself. Above all, validation builds trust because the person with BPD finally begins to feel she is being heard and understood.

Although there are no miracle cures for this disorder, people with BPD can do better and can change, even if it is in baby steps. Learning and applying these skills will help.

Don't Forget to Validate Yourself!

Anyone coping with a loved one with BPD needs access to a community for moral support. This is what Buddhists call a *sangha*. Coping with BPD alone is like being adrift in a raft at sea without a compass or a map. Seek out support from others dealing with the same problems; this is crucial to relieving your own isolation and despair.

Remember to validate yourself. You have done the best you could with an extremely difficult, exhausting, and emotionally draining problem. You deserve validation for your heroic efforts and dedication to your loved one. You must also remember to take care of yourself, to take time out to do the things you like to do, to "inhale oxygen" before you try to help anyone else.

6

Mindfulness

MINDFULNESS INVOLVES FOCUSING YOUR MIND ON THE PRESENT moment, paying attention to your immediate experience, just one moment at a time. To be mindful you must slow down and be fully aware of what is going on inside and outside of your own being, awake and aware of your own life. Being mindful creates a state of openness where new thoughts, feelings, and behaviors can be experienced. Learning how to focus your mind in the moment helps you develop your natural ability to pay attention.

You may have already observed that your loved one with borderline personality disorder generally has difficulty focusing his mind, so much so that he may have been thought to have attention-deficit hyperactivity disorder, or ADHD. Being mindful and experiencing just one moment at a time helps people with BPD develop the ability to regulate their attention and control of their runaway emotions. Learning the practice of mindfulness makes those with BPD more aware of what is happening in the moment so that their thinking becomes less distorted by their emotions and more reality based. It also helps them decrease their tendency to personalize and thereby become more effective at problem solving. Mindfulness helps people develop distance between a stimulus and their response to that stimulus, so that they have the space to choose how they will react. It creates room for something else to occur, for some other behavior to emerge. This is helpful for both you and the person with BPD.

Contemporary life is characterized by fast-paced, overstimulating environments. Information and experiences come at us simultaneously from many directions. We are capable of selecting what we pay attention to so as not to feel overwhelmed. Although all of us face these challenges in our daily lives, people with BPD seem to have greater difficulty blocking out stimuli from their environments so as to avoid feeling so overwhelmed. They seem to lack a rheostat for adjusting their attention. This is why mindfulness is such an important skill for people with BPD to learn.

Mindfulness practice is derived from Eastern spiritual traditions. It is a key component of Zen Buddhism and meditation; it is also an essential "core" component of Dialectical Behavior Therapy. Although it is taught as a separate DBT skill, it is incorporated into all the other DBT skills as well. Imagine DBT as a tapestry. A unique golden thread runs through it, from the top to the bottom of the border, as part of the flowers in the design and as part of the tapestry background. In the same way, the principles of mindfulness weave through all of the DBT skills, making DBT a compound treatment, the goal of which is greater than the sum of its parts. Mindfulness describes three primary states of mind: emotion mind, logical mind, and integrated mind.

> *Mindfulness describes three primary states of mind: emotional mind, logical mind, and integrated mind.*

States of Mind

Sometimes you can be in a purely emotional state of mind, a totally logical state of mind, or in a third state of mind that integrates emotions and logic. These mind states are components of the mindfulness module of DBT as developed by Marsha Linehan. At different times all of us experience these distinct states of mind. Mindfulness in DBT requires awareness of these three different states of mind. A primary goal of DBT is to be in an integrated state of mind as often as possible.

Emotion Mind

Emotion mind is "hot," mood dependent, and emotion focused. It is usually very intense and can lead to the kinds of ruminations we might call "middle-of-the-night thinking." Emotion mind may feel as if an experiential tape loop is playing over and over again in your head, reigniting and escalating your emotional responses to an experience. Imagine driving a car without any brakes, with your foot pressed down on the gas pedal, going full speed ahead, without stopping for lights or observing speed limits. This is emotion mind. Anyone who is very upset is in emotion mind. It is very difficult to think reasonably and logically in this state because we are responding to our emotions without any brakes. Emotion mind occurs in the amygdala, which, as described in Chapter 2, is the part of the brain's limbic system where emotions are processed.

The lives of people with BPD seem to be controlled by their emotions; consequently, they are frequently in emotion mind. They do not seem to know how to suppress or comprehensively distance themselves from their own emotions or how not to become their emotions. They need to learn how to experience their own emotions without knee-jerk responses, to be able to choose how they react to their emotions. When they feel angry, they need to learn to notice the feeling and experience the feeling, but be able to respond without expressing anger. At the moment a person with BPD is in the emotional mind of anger, thinking and behaving angrily, it will be very difficult for him to examine logical alternatives or do effective problem solving. He will be unable to think logically until his emotional state deescalates. The actions a person takes when in an emotional mind state, such as anger, usually result in responses that have unwanted consequences, like fighting with someone or becoming involved with the police. It is not necessary to get into a fight with someone because you feel angry; aggressive behavior does not have to be a knee-jerk response to anger. By practicing mindfulness, people with BPD can learn to slow themselves down and have more control over how they will respond.

Logical Mind

Logical mind is "doing mind" or "reasonable mind." Logical mind is cold, rational, goal oriented, problem solving, and discrepancy processing. It monitors and evaluates the present in relation to past problems and progress toward goals. When a person is in logical mind, his thoughts and feelings are seen as valid reflections of reality. Logical mind is governed by the prefrontal cortex (PFC), which is the area of the brain that controls decision making, judgments, and impulses. The PFC can be thought of as the brain's brake. When a person is in logical mind, he is thinking coolly, rationally, in a focused manner, considering facts and empirical evidence, and solving problems intellectually. Emotion does not control logical mind. In fact, logical mind can operate without emotion.

Integrated Mind

DBT defines an integrated state of mind, known as *wise mind*, as a synthesis or dialectic integration of both emotion mind and logical mind. This integrated state of mind is not controlled by either emotion or reason. It is "being mind," the direct, immediate, experience of thoughts and feelings as sensations. It allows and accepts. To be in integrated mind is to be totally in the present with all of your senses, responding to the complexity of the unique patterns represented in each moment. Getting to integrated mind takes practice, yet the effort needs to feel effortless. It can sometimes seem very difficult to get there. When you are first learning something new, it may seem as though it will be impossible for you to accomplish your goal. Many new activities take practice until they can be done skillfully and effortlessly, such as speaking a foreign language, riding a bicycle, cooking, or driving a stick-shift car. Wise mind is about reality—not getting out of it, but staying in it. Being in wise or integrated mind can feel as if one part of yourself is talking to another part of yourself, as if you have developed a "self-observing ego." Integrated mind is neither an absence of emotion nor an absence of reason, nor is it the presence of emotion or of reason. It is a synthesis. Whenever you are feeling extreme emotion, you are probably not in an integrated state of mind.

> "Like Archers: if they start out competing, they'll never achieve good marksmanship. It is after long practice without thought of winning or losing that they can hit the target . . . if even a single thought abides in the heart you will be chained by winning and losing." –Ying-An

What Practicing Mindfulness Means for Families

When your loved one tries to communicate with you when he is in emotion mind, his emotional gas pedal is usually pushed down to the floor. You, on the other hand, are responding from logical mind, have put brakes on your own emotional responses, and are probably offering logical solutions to the problems at hand in a rigid manner. Or you too may be in emotion mind because you are probably feeling frightened, angry, out of control, or powerless. Either way, communication and problem solving are not happening between you. It is no surprise that everyone feels upset! When you are frustrated or distressed it is infuriating to interact with a person who does not understand your feelings, who gives you logical reasons for why you should not feel what you are feeling or who tells you why your feelings do not matter. The person with BPD is struggling to move from emotion mind to integrated mind, while her family member is usually having an equally difficult struggle going in the reverse direction, from logical mind to integrated mind.

Our society discourages showing emotions. From early on, we are taught to mask our feelings. "Boys don't cry," and "don't be a cry baby" are common admonishments. Showing emotion is equated with losing control. Our societal definition of maturity censors drama queens who put on emotional displays of anger, joy, disappointment, jealousy, shame, or fear. Adult functioning is evaluated by our ability to be cool and rational, solve problems logically, and not show emotions. As adults, many of us overlook or have forgotten how to interpret the nuances of emotions. All of us, from time to time, have difficulty identifying the emotions we or others are feeling, or actually acknowledging or feeling our own emotions.

Jim has great difficulty expressing his own emotions as well as identifying the emotions of others. For their wedding anniversary, Jim's wife Julie arranged a very special celebration. She selected a restaurant that served his favorite foods, invited their best friends, and gave Jim a wonderful gift. Jim responded dispassionately by telling Julie how well-cooked the meal was and how impeccably it was served. Jim was actually delighted with the evening, glad to see his friends, and appreciative of what Julie had done for him. However, he did not know how to tell her so. His unarticulated and emotionally barren response left Julie feeling unappreciated and emotionally isolated. Jim was so far from his own feelings that he needed to take a taxi to get to his emotions.

Wise Mind as Emotional Communication

Learning how to come to a dialectic, mindful, or integrated synthesis of emotion and reason will help to improve your communication with your loved one. Your loved one may not be accustomed to emotional response from you, to being heard on this level. When you first begin responding in a more emotional than logical state of mind, she will not trust the change in you and may tell you to stop the "psychobabble." She does not believe that your responses are authentic, sincere, and radically genuine. At these times it is important to keep going, to be persistent. It will become easier with practice. People who excel at logical work such as engineers, computer experts, lawyers, and CEOs quickly come to recognize the "logic" of integrating emotions when communicating with a loved one with BPD. This chapter will show you how to practice staying mindful.

Frank is the owner of a successful family business that has had the same operational system in place for many years. Traditionally, Frank takes inventory by physically counting each piece of merchandise. Frank's sons are encouraging him to get up to date, to "modernize" by installing a computer-based tracking system. Frank believes "if it ain't broken, don't fix it!" Although he knows the computerized system might save him time, improve his business, and increase his profits, he resists because he does not trust a machine to do what he has done by himself for so many years. It will take Frank a long time before he trusts that what the computer is telling him is actually true. In a similar spirit, family members resist practicing mindfulness because they do not see its obvious connection to the actual problems they face. They find it difficult to understand how slowing down, focusing, and applying these techniques can actually make a difference in their stormy relationship with their loved one with BPD. Sometimes you just have to trust and try something new. It really does work!

You have probably tried to help your loved one in many ways that have not worked or have even made the situations worse. If all the experts you have consulted have not helped, why should you trust that this new way will be effective? Why do you have to be the one to change the way you think and act? Change is not easy for anyone! Why should you have to learn an anti-intuitive way of behaving that is so different from your regular way of responding? After all, you are not the one who has BPD. Believing that what you are doing will work will help motivate you to work at changing your own behavior.

Mindfulness Skills

To practice mindfulness you need to learn two sets of skills, *what to do* to be mindful and *how to do it*. The "what to do to be mindful skills" include *observing* or *perceiving behavior*, *portraying* or *describing* what you see, then *participating* or *taking part* in the moment. Your goal in practicing mindfulness is to perceive nonjudgmentally, portray one-mindfully, and participate in an effective manner.

Perceive

Perceiving, or observing, begins with slowing down, being aware of what you are actually doing, what you are experiencing, and just noticing what you are feeling. Learning to observe what is going on around you, moment by moment, requires that you remove inferences and judgments from your observations. Observing means you are just seeing, hearing, experiencing what is, in the moment, without determining why it is happening, what it means, or what the outcome or consequences will be. Observing is experiential and provides you with information, much of which may be derived from your sensory awareness. Observing is not about you; it is not personal. It is about the experience in the moment. How can you solve a problem if you do not know what the problem is? Observing will give you answers as well as new directions to explore.

You cannot solve a problem if you cannot observe the problem.

Practice observing in neutral situations with people you do not. Try writing down your perceptions of a waiter, people in a restaurant, a train conductor, or a salesclerk in a store. Notice body language, facial expressions, tone of voice, who they are with, how they are dressed. You will be surprised at how many conclusions you have jumped to, how many inferences and judgments have crept into your observations, and the justifications and explanations you have offered yourself to explain what you have observed. Once you have gotten the knack of observing this way, try writing down your observations of someone close to you. If you catch yourself saying, "she is doing that because . . ." then you are not observing. You need to become a detective and get "just the facts." Be like the British Guards in their high black hats who just observe the crowd of tourists around them without responding.

Observing requires maintaining and controlling your attention, particularly your emotional attention, noticing what you are feeling without being confined to language or intellectual constructs. Observing does not require any action or response from the observer. It is the process of watching your mind in action, feeling your own body, separating your thoughts from your sensations. One of the principal purposes of your brain is to think; thoughts indicate that your mind is working. Thoughts are not facts and do not require you to act upon them. Meditation teaches us how to push aside thoughts and return, over and over again, to what we are focused on observing, such as our breath, the sounds in the room, or sensations in our bodies. When our mind strays, goes off in all different directions, we must bring it back, over and over again, to what we are observing.

Observing acutely will free you from your preconceived ideas of "what is" that can often lead to ineffective responses. Observing and perceiving allow you to see what is, so that you can respond to behavioral and emotional nuances that you might otherwise have missed or overlooked. You can clarify what is actually happening around you, see relationships more clearly, understand what triggered events and determine what the problem at hand really is so you will be better able to respond effectively. It is easier to solve a problem when you can see the actual contingencies around it than when you are jumping to erroneous conclusions.

OBSTACLES TO PERCEIVING

It is very difficult for family members to simply observe because they are so accustomed to fixing or controlling any situation or problem that arises. Although this may be acceptable for parents of very young children, it is neither acceptable nor effective when dealing with anyone, especially an adolescent or adult with BPD. When you fix or control situations or solve problems, you are fostering your loved one's dependency on you and sending the message that you believe the person lacks the ability to solve her own problems. It is a clear vote of no confidence that negates the abilities of the person with BPD by fragelizing her while simultaneously complaining that she does not take charge of her life. How can anyone become independent and capable when she is constantly getting the message that you believe she is incompetent?

As a family member, you have probably experienced BPD in an informational void without any guidance or support. In this environment, infused with fear for your loved one's safety, it is no surprise that you find it hard to develop the rationale for simply observing behavior without jumping in to fix things. This is further complicated by the confusing, erroneous information and preconceived ideas you already have about BPD. If you believe people with BPD manipulate, you will infer that what you are observing is an example of manipulation, and you will respond to that perception. A belief is more than just an idea; it can shift the way you actually experience yourself and your life. We all have perceptual biases. Practice asking yourself, "What have I observed to make this inference?"[1] Try to avoid finding the "meaning of events" or interpreting behaviors and emotional responses to behaviors, such as, "He did that because he was adopted," "She was rude because she was tired," "He bought that because he knows I hate it."

Portray

Portraying, or describing, is verbalizing what you have observed, perceived, or experienced without interpretations, labels, or judgments. When you describe, you are answering the questions: Who? What? When? Where? Notice that "why" is not included in the questions to ask yourself as it will only lead you onto the path of inference, supposition, and conclusion jumping. Portraying will simply provide you with the facts of a situation. You can only describe what you have actually observed. You cannot describe someone's intentions, thoughts, objectives, or motivations. Remember, the way you think determines the way you feel, and the way you feel determines the way you act. Inferences in place of observations and preconceived ideas instead of facts lead to erroneous conclusions, emotional responses, and perceptions of situations and other people that are replete with distortions. This can be a barrier to reaching your goals or shaping new behaviors.

---

[1] Linehan, 1993a.

Label a thought as a thought, a feeling as a feeling, an event as an event, an emotion as an emotion. You are not depicting causes; you are just describing what *is*. When you learn to observe and describe, you will be able to make the connections between triggers, cues, and behaviors, between cause and effect, thereby rendering your relationship with your loved one with BPD less baffling. You will have started on the path toward responding more effectively.

You can only describe what you have actually observed.

Portraying, or describing, will help you determine what is actually happening around you and help you avoid responding to erroneous interpretations of behaviors or situations. This ability will provide you with the opportunity to prevent explosive episodes by honing in on the subtle behavioral and emotional changes that may be early warning signs of emotional triggers or the onset of mood changes. This awareness, coupled with acceptance strategies such as validation and DBT change strategies, can reduce stressful family interactions. There will be fewer surprises and more opportunities for prophylactic responses. Both you and your loved one with BPD need to make the distinction between an actual observed event, your perceptions, thoughts, or evaluations of the event, and your emotional response to the event.

Participate

Participation is practicing what you are learning, actually working at making changes. Participating is trying the dance at a dance class rather than watching from the sidelines, getting into the swimming pool when you want to learn how to swim, speaking Italian in Italy even though you might make a mistake. Many activities that seemed impossible to do at first with much participation and practice can be done skillfully and effortlessly. Think about how much participation it took for you to master reading and writing!

People with BPD are usually burdened with strong feelings of worthlessness and shame that are not necessarily supported by the facts of actual situations. Stephanie, a young woman with BPD, is invited to a party. She is reluctant to go, thinking no one likes her and she is not as attractive as the other girls. At the party, a good-looking man asks her to dance. She notices that her heart is racing and her face feels flushed, and she begins to perspire. She has automatic thoughts such as, "I am a loser, why would he want to dance with me? If I dance with him, everyone will see that I do not know how to dance and I will make a fool of myself! I am wearing such an ugly dress and all the other girls look so perfect. My fingernail is broken and I have a run in my stocking. He will see that I am not good enough."

Stephanie was unable to accept the young man's invitation to dance. She could not let go of focusing on herself so as to participate in the moment. Participation asks you to forget yourself, to get involved, to enter fully into your experience in the moment. Fully participating requires becoming one with an activity, being spontaneous and letting go of control. It means doing something while being fully aware that you are doing it. A person who is shy or anxious must overcome enormous fears to do this, and it can be very difficult. He will have to work very hard to "act opposite"[2] of how he might be feeling so as to practice these new behaviors and truly participate in his own life.

People with BPD frequently complain that a job or activity is "boring." If you are not participating in the activity, you will feel bored and isolated. Watching other people dance is not as much fun as dancing. If you play on a baseball or football team, you will not feel isolated. Participating helps a person feel less excluded and more a part of the world around him. It encourages acting from intuition and doing what is needed in the moment, thereby creating a sense of mastery. Playing tennis, for instance, requires full participation in the moment.

Practicing Mindfulness

The path to mindfulness involves changing how you view the world around you, how you focus your own attention, your ability to be persistent, your willingness to cede control and be effective. It means evaluating and examining how you think, feel, and react in your

---

[2] Linehan, 1993a.

interpersonal relationships. You need to give up judging yourself and others, experience each moment as it comes, and focus on being effective.

A Feeling Is Not a Fact

Your emotional response to a situation can be reasonable according to your assessment or beliefs about the situation even though your beliefs may not be justified by the actual facts. Although your feelings may be valid, explanations of why you are feeling what you feel may not be valid. You can experience fear although you are not actually in danger. Panicking in a life-threatening situation, such as when seeing a snake, may be a reasonable response but it is not a reasonable response if, in actual fact, the snake is merely a stick—you are not threatened and are safe and sound.

Just because you are feeling jealous is not proof that you have a real reason to feel jealous. If you assess that you were rejected by a friend and you feel rejected, it does not mean you were actually rejected. Whether you were or were not rejected does not matter if that is how you feel. We must validate a person's feelings without criticism or judgment and then address her assessment or belief about the situation versus the actual facts of the situation, as *you* might see them. Stating judgments as if they are facts ("You're cheating on me!") can be perceived as a way of trying to control someone else's behavior.

Carla's boyfriend Miguel was a tango dancer who often felt jealous and was convinced that Carla was cheating on him. When he felt this way he would search their apartment for proof of her lover's existence. Even though he never found proof of anything that might possibly substantiate his suspicions, he acted on his feelings. The more Carla denied having an affair, the more he escalated, becoming so violent that she had to call the police. For Miguel, his feeling was so absolutely a fact it was as if they were etched in stone.

Be Nonjudgmental

Judging is shorthand for deciding whether a person, place, thing, situation, or behavior is good or bad, worthwhile or worthless. A judgment is not a fact but is a quick way to label or evaluate something or to describe the consequences of behavior. If you tell a friend that Joe's restaurant is "bad," your judgment is based on your comparison of Joe's to your personal standards of what makes a restaurant bad or good, what you believe a restaurant experience "should" be like, or on what happened to you on the particular day when you ate there. It may mean you thought the food at Joe's was bad, the place was dirty, the prices were high, the décor unattractive, or that your waiter was nasty. Your judgment is not a statement of fact but is a shortcut for stating your personal preferences. Over time, judgments can be taken as statements of fact. If someone speaks with a particular accent, you may judge her as uneducated and less valuable as a person. An accent is therefore your shorthand way of judging a person as unworthy or inadequate. Is your judgment a "fact"? The person with the accent may have a doctorate in nuclear physics while you may be a high school graduate. Sometimes judging is actually helpful, as in deciding what restaurant you like best or hiring a new employee. Judging can be feedback on performance, a way to evaluate or choose, or serve as a comparison as in good, better, best. People with BPD judge themselves harshly all the time and find judgments lurking around the corner of every raised eyebrow, sneeze, yawn, or shoulder shrug. You must be acutely aware of how your responses can be misconstrued as judgments.

People with BPD judge themselves harshly all the time and find judgments lurking around the corner of every raised eyebrow, sneeze, yawn, or shoulder shrug. You must be acutely aware of how your responses can be misconstrued as judgments.

How you use a word can make it a judgment; for example, describing someone as "voluptuous" could be interpreted either as sexy or as overweight. Statements of facts, opinions, or preferences are not judgments or reflections of reality. Three friends were at a nail salon. Arlene and Carol both selected dark red polish. Lucy remarked that she did not like dark polish. Arlene decided to try the dark color for a week to see if she wanted to keep it or change it. She then dropped the subject. Carol, on the other hand, became angry, declaring that Lucy was "abusive" because she had criticized her choice of nail polish. Lucy had merely stated her color preference and was not judging one color "bad" or the other color "good." Arlene was able to make this distinction but Carol could not. Lucy does not like red nail polish; Carol does, and Arlene does not care one way or another. We all need to accept that everyone sees things differently and has different preferences. Lucy learned to be very careful when stating her preferences around Carol. Whenever your preference is interpreted as a judgment by your loved one, you must take the time to explain that it is not a judgment. This may seem simple to you, but it can be very complicated for someone with BPD.

People with BPD tend to judge themselves and others in extreme ways. They will often use excessively positive terms, idealizing or glorifying, or excessively negative terms, demonizing or devaluing themselves or others. They look at themselves with harsh and critical negative self-judgments that increase their sense of shame. Studies have shown that people with BPD experience shame more often and more intensely than do those without the disorder. They have a tendency to interpret situations self-referentially, meaning they perceive most interactions as being about them. For instance, a simple comment such as "pass the butter" may be interpreted as a comment about your loved one's weight. If your loved one is constantly judging herself negatively, how can she reduce her sense of shame? If she is burdened down with negative judgments that are not facts, how can she examine the evidence pertaining to her interactions with others?

People with BPD are so supersensitive that they could be described as allergic to actual or imagined judgment, criticism, or blame. Reducing negative emotions requires reducing judgments. This is very hard to do because any comment a family member makes can be interpreted as a judgment. Your goal must be to give up judging altogether and allow what "is" to simply "be." Being nonjudgmental is a component of the Buddhist attitude of acceptance.

Clinicians often display judgmental and negative attitudes toward people with BPD, as do many popular self-help books, the media, television, and movies such as *Fatal Attraction*. Their volatile and abusive behaviors perpetuate this attitude. As a consequence of the continuous stress and painful experiences you may have had in coping with BPD, you too may view your loved one as your "enemy," and you may have developed a judgmental attitude so as to justify her behaviors to yourself. You need to remind yourself, over and over again, that the person with BPD is doing the best she can in this moment. Try to see reality as "what is," in the moment, without evaluating it as good or bad or right or wrong. Acknowledge what is helpful or harmful without judging either.

Peter's wife Christine is a compulsive shopper. She has no regard for the money she is spending. Peter believes Christine is manipulating him. It is extremely difficult for Peter to change his view even when presented with research findings from neuroscience or the latest DBT studies that discredit his hypothesis that Christine is purposefully overspending his money. He continues to see Christine's behavior through the lens of manipulation. He believes she is spending money just to spite him or because she disrespects him. In reality, she may actually be shopping to help herself tolerate her emotional pain.

Although Christine may really love her husband, she may be having affairs with other men because this provides her with instant relief from her emotional pain. Meanwhile, Peter feels betrayed and inadequate. Any husband would feel the same way. Christine's affairs or her excessive shopping are behaviors that are only about herself. Though they hurt Peter, the behaviors have little to do with how she truly feels about him.

Understanding how or why something happened (for instance, if Peter were to accept that Christine's shopping was her way of relieving emotional pain) does not mean that you approve of what has happened. Although Peter does not like or approve of Christine's behavior, he can accept that it is what she needs to do for herself, for now. He will have to depersonalize the situation and then decide whether he can accept her for what she is, right now, and forgive her maladaptive behavior. If Peter can possibly tolerate the situation and if Christine participates in evidence-based treatment such as DBT, their marriage may survive.

A father feels his son is just lazy and does not want to work. It will be very difficult for him to accept an alternative explanation, even if we demonstrate that his opinions are based on misinterpretations of his son's motives. Changing your ideas means taking responsibility for your own thoughts, behaviors, and attitudes.

It is important that family members not judge themselves and accept that they, too, are doing the best they can. You may have inadvertently harmed your loved one, may have done the wrong thing, even though that was not your intention. Try to unglue your opinions and be flexible. Prioritizing your goals will help you to see things nonjudgmentally. Ask yourself, "Would I rather my daughter have a clean room, or that she stop cutting herself?" What is your priority?

Prioritize

Prioritizing is like triage in a hospital emergency room. It does not mean that you do not want to see both a cleaner room and no cutting; the question is, which do you focus on first? If you give up judging behavior it does not mean you are approving of the behavior. If a husband tells his wife she is a bad wife because she is spending too much money, she will feel guilt and shame, get dysregulated, and will probably spend more money so as to feel better at that moment. He would probably have more success if he could say, "I can see you are in a great deal of pain; however, when you spend so much money, I feel very bad, worry about our budget, and feel like I cannot make you happy. What do you think we can do to solve this problem?" Judging behavior is not the same as pointing out the potential negative consequences that behavior may bring. State the consequences of behavior rather than judging the behavior. Accept that the behavior is not about you, or happening because of you. By not personalizing the difficult behavior in question, you will be more effective in helping your loved one and yourself. This requires humility, courage, and persistence.

Being nonjudgmental is difficult. It requires you to stop adding judgmental evaluations onto what you perceive, such as "that is good" or "that is bad." If a student did not do his homework, is he a bad person? Is he lazy? Or is he doing the best he can? All you can observe is that this particular assignment was not done. When you say that a person is "bad" because the assignment was not done, you are jumping to a conclusion that may not be based on the actual qualities of the person or the facts of the situation, and have come to a conclusion that is based only on your own thoughts and interpretations—not on facts. Judging the student as bad for not doing the assignment does not help to get the assignment done, nor does it change the behavior that interfered with completing the assignment in the first place. It might be more effective to simply ask the student, "What happened to your homework?" before you draw any conclusions.

Focus on One Problem at a Time

When you do one thing at a time, with your full attention and concentration, totally in the present, you are being mindful. By focusing on each moment as it is, you will have the clearest, sharpest, most unbiased perceptions of a situation as it is now, in the present moment. Because people with BPD have such great difficulty staying focused in the moment, as you try to solve one problem they will invariably throw more problems into the mix, diverting your attention until you feel confused, overwhelmed, and dysregulated yourself. How can anyone solve 10 problems at once? Do not allow yourself to be distracted. Ignore efforts to divert you; stay on the same agenda like a train on a track, diligently sticking to the subject. This persistent focus, returning over and over again to the problem at hand, is what we mean by "focusing one-mindfully." It is a good strategy for you to implement when trying to deal with a problem.

Margo called the TARA helpline for a referral to a DBT clinician in her area. June, the volunteer answering the phone, asked Margo for her name, address, and telephone number. Margo refused to provide the information. June asked again and stated that without this information she would not be able to help Margo. Margo insisted on a referral without providing the information. This went back and forth several times. Margo's voice tone escalated and she complained that June was too businesslike and that no one could get help on a helpline from someone as rigid and mean as June. June validated Margo by saying, "I can only imagine how frustrating it must be to ask for help from someone who sounds so businesslike; however, I cannot help you unless you provide the required information." Margo continued to refuse. Finally, June said, "I am sorry; I cannot help you," and hung up. Margo immediately called back and was abusive. June replied, "I can hear how upset you are. How does telling me how awful I am help you to get a referral? How else do you think you can get what you want?" Again, they went back and forth. June never deviated from her focus. Finally Margo lowered her voice and provided the required information. June then went on to help her find a therapist in her community.

Focus on the Present

People with BPD spend a great deal of their emotional energy worrying about past pain or potential future problems. "If I do that, this will happen." Dwelling on the past or the future prevents you from focusing on the present. Family members, as well, tend to focus on either the future or the past. To be mindful, practice focusing on the moment you are living in, right now. The present problem or pain is difficult enough without worrying in advance about what will become of your son if he does not graduate from college. If he is now 17 years old and struggling to pass high school math, using drugs, having trouble managing relationships, and cutting himself, how does worrying about getting a college degree help him? By mindfully focusing on the present moment, your loved one will not feel as overwhelmed and will realize that this one problem is solvable. Emotions can begin to deescalate, increasing the possibility of negotiating solutions to the problem.

How can you get to your future if your past is your present?

How to Be Mindful Effectively

Do what works, what is needed in the situation, and let go of what does not work, even if you feel it was the "right" thing to do. Ask yourself the question, "Would I rather be right or be effective?" To help your loved one with BPD you must let go of being right. Focusing on what is right is like imposing your culture on a country you are visiting. What is effective in one culture may not work in another. Would you keep your shoes on when visiting the home of a friend in Japan? Think of your loved one as living in a different culture. Get to know his culture, learn to speak his language. Because you are probably terrified that your loved one may harm himself or engage in dangerous behaviors, you try to control him. Unfortunately all you will usually accomplish is alienating your loved one. In the long run, you will have to learn to tolerate your own painful feelings such as fear, loss, anger, failure, insecurity, and powerlessness. Being effective means you have to let what is be what it is and allow the person to experience the natural consequences of his own behavior. This is not tough love. Sometimes you must be totally honest with yourself and ask yourself, "Who does the behavior you are asking for most benefits, you or your loved one?". Who benefits by your being right? Who is really bothered by a messy room, you or your daughter?

To be effective in avoiding emotional eruptions, you must develop the ability to perceive and portray your interactions while simultaneously suppressing your own urge to "fix" or control what you are observing. Open the doors and windows of your mind's emotional rooms so that you can be in the moment without worrying about what might happen tomorrow or how the situation came to pass. This is what is going on and this is what is, right now. If your daughter, who was arrested last week for drunk driving, asks to use the car again tonight, and you say no, you must acknowledge the elephant in the room and explain to her that this is a consequence of her earlier behavior. Denying "what is," that your daughter had been arrested, is also an impediment to being effective.

Maintaining a Relationship

It is very hard to accept what has happened to your loved one and your family because of BPD. This painful mental illness is not fair, but saying it is not fair does not change anything. Thinking that you should not have to work so hard to get through everyday life with someone with BPD does not change the fact that this is what you need to do. When millionaires marry they have prenuptial agreements in place to facilitate divorce. They have every advantage money can buy and this may make their divorces a lot easier than the average person's divorce. At the same time, when it comes to the day-to-day stuff of relationships, they need to work as hard as everyone else to make their marriages work and will feel just as bad as anyone else if their relationship ends. If Donald Trump forgets his wife's birthday or does not call to say he will be late for dinner, his wife will be just as angry as your wife. There is no shortcut to the work required to make a relationship thrive. The subtleties of everyday life need constant attention.

If you have ever ridden horses or studied dressage you know that you can never relax when you are in the saddle. The reins in your hands are your connection to the horse and how he responds to you and to your surroundings. If a bird suddenly jumps out of the bushes and frightens the horse, you must react immediately without judging, thinking, or inferring. Good horseback riding happens when you are in wise mind and have synthesized your riding skills, your intuitions of the moment, and your observation of what is going on around you. If you do not notice how a horse is responding, you may wind up walking! When you are dancing the tango, you respond to your partner, he responds to you, and you both respond to the music. When a jazz musician plays in a group, he responds to the other players and they respond to him, spontaneously and in the moment. If we miss the cues others send out, we will never become good horseback riders, tango dancers, or jazz musicians.

For family members, being fully in the moment means focusing your full attention on your interaction with your loved one with BPD so that you can see the emotional nuances of her feelings or reactions. Doing one thing at a time with your full attention, totally in the present moment, accepting each moment as it is, involves intense emotional concentration. If you do not focus, your loved one will feel that you are ignoring or rejecting her, or see this as proof that she is not worth talking to or does not count. Simply focusing, paying complete attention, will improve your relationship. Multitasking will not work. If you are cooking dinner, driving, washing the dishes, checking your BlackBerry or your e-mail while you are talking to your loved one, you are not being mindful.

What Interferes with Families Being Mindful?

Emotionality. When facing the maladaptive, dangerous behaviors so characteristic of BPD, you will probably feel out of control and powerless. You will be desperate to help, save, fix, or rescue your loved one, feel frightened and even angry. Anyone who is worried about the safety and well-being of someone she cares about would respond in a similar manner. As your loved one's out-of-control behavior escalates,

---

Tips for Being Mindful

- Focus on what works
- Keep an eye on your goals and values
- Give up opinions and judgments in favor of facts
- Give up expectations of reciprocity in the moment
- Stop wanting
- Instead of being right, lose the battle but win the war[1]

---

[1] Linehan, 1993

so will your efforts to control the situation and keep your loved one safe. These strong emotional responses on your part will interfere with your ability to observe, describe, and participate in a focused, nonjudgmental manner

Willfulness. Your emotions can heighten your desire to control to the point that your controlling attitude or behavior can be described as willful. Willfulness is a major factor that stands in the way of practicing mindfulness so as to effectively help your loved one and yourself. Characterized by very rigid thinking, willfulness means that the ideas or opinions of others, what they want or are working toward, or anything that contradicts your own assumptions, even scientific research findings, are dismissed in your efforts to prove that you are right and to get your way. Willfulness is the state of mind in which you are trying to control, direct, or manipulate life, particularly someone else's life. It is an indication that you are denying reality or trying to change it, or that you have not accepted what is happening around you. Willfulness is refusing to take actions that will work and, instead, imposing your desires and decisions on the other person or situation. It means you think you can fix everything, you know the best solution, and you must have your way. Willfulness prevents you from truly observing another person's pain because you are too busy working at trying to stop it or discounting it. Willfulness also fragelizes the other person, so that they feel incompetent and dependent. You may do all of this with the best of intentions, with great love and concern and the belief that you are actually helping. Willful family members often pay for apartments, traffic tickets, and lawyers; replace wrecked cars; and encourage avoidant behaviors such as sleeping all day, quitting jobs, or dropping out of school. They make appointments, make excuses, and solve problems that in the end help their loved ones to avoid experiencing the natural consequences of their behaviors.

Willfully responding with "No" or "Yes" prevents you from merging your goals with another person's and rules out any possibility of negotiation. Family members court disaster when they respond with "yes, but . . ." or resolutely do things their way, despite any evidence that their way will be effective. Dismissing the evidence that your loved one's behavior is due to an overactive amygdala and an underactive prefrontal cortex and insisting that he do things he is unable to do, such as abiding by behavioral contracts, will surely trigger explosive and destructive episodes. Getting past your own willfulness must be a priority goal for family members. Willfulness creates an impenetrable barrier to communication. It is both relationship-interfering and reinforcement-interfering behavior. Willfulness is not a situation-specific behavior but an underlying life attitude. For the fragile borderline sufferer, involvement with a willful person can smother any chance he has to develop a sense of himself as a functioning adult person capable of making his own decisions. If you are willful, your loved one will drown in your ego.

Family members of people with BPD are understandably willful given their past experience and present situations. Gary is a bombastic man who is used to being right, unquestionably. He adores his 24-year-old daughter Edith, who has BPD. Edith has difficulty keeping jobs. Gary solved this problem by having her work at his office. Edith has her own car, but she needs new tires. She informs Gary that she has saved money for tires and plans to buy them at Sears. She will put the money she saves on the tires toward a convertible that she really wants to buy. Gary sees himself as a car expert and ridicules his daughter's decision, telling her that the tires she wants are not safe. He refuses to allow her to buy them, stating, "I will not allow my daughter to drive a car with cheap tires." He will pay for a set of the best tires because he has decided that is what Edith should have. She protests at first, then capitulates, becomes depressed, and cuts herself. Gary feels he is a caring, concerned father and that his daughter is unreasonable. Sadly, Gary did not recognize that his willful behavior undermined his daughter's decision-making ability—in essence, wiping it out, creating more dependency, and preventing Edith from experiencing the self-validating pleasure of her own ability to make effective decisions in her life. After all, Gary felt he was only trying to protect her. Edith felt ashamed for having made such a "stupid" decision. Gary may have been right about the tires but was ineffective in helping his daughter. His willful behavior prevented him from being mindful.

People who are willful are generally extremely uncomfortable whenever they feel they are not in control. They probably find it difficult to even be in a car if they are not driving. Willfulness often disguises feelings of fear or inadequacy. It is important to find the courage to face your fears and discuss the emotions you are feeling in a skillful way rather than avoiding them. Giving up willfulness is crucial for repairing relationships and creating a sense of competency in the person with BPD. Allow yourself to be vulnerable and to trust that whatever happens can be dealt with when it happens. You must accept that life is not perfect, problems will always arise, and problems can be solved or accepted. The key to turning willfulness into *willingness* is having the courage to take a risk and feeling you are in a safe place for expressing your feelings. Willfulness creates an impenetrable barrier to communication.

Willfulness creates an impenetrable barrier to communication.

What Reinforces Families Being Mindful?

Willingness. Willingness is the opposite of willfulness. To be willing you must accept the situation you are in, in the moment, in wise mind, and commit to participating in that situation without reservation. Willingness is giving up trying to control behaviors or outcomes. By giving up control you can do what is needed in any situation. Willingness is wholehearted, spontaneous participation, responding to situations as needed, without resentment or preconceived ideas of what has to be done, how to do it, or when to do it. Willingness is a state of mind that gives you the ability to go with the flow, no matter where the flow may lead. To be willing you must be able to consider the other person's needs as well as the common good. Willingness means you respect and have faith in life, and accept universal emotional responses to living without concern for your own "ego." If you are focusing on your own needs, you are not being willing. Have the courage to face life as it comes, moment by moment, without a script, with the confidence that you are alive, a part of the universe, and that you are doing the best you can. Trust yourself, be vulnerable, and give up ego. Be willing to feel your feelings and to practice new ways to see the world.

You may not be happy if your loved one is using drugs, cutting herself, or driving with "cheap" tires, but that is what is happening at the moment. That is her choice, for now. Ultimately willingness requires that you act in spite of your fear, your disappointment, or the lack of reciprocity you may feel in the moment. By opening your arms to life, opening your hands, palms up, in a gesture we describe as willing hands, you can work at letting go of control. Practicing willingness cultivates compassion.

Humility. Practicing mindfulness requires humbly accepting that we may have made mistakes. Sometimes what you always thought to be true turns out not to be true; what you learned before is wrong. Beliefs you held for a very long time are suddenly challenged and you know deep inside yourself that there is some truth to this new information. Willfulness at these times can be very destructive. Facts do not cease to exist because we choose to ignore them. Sometimes this happens to family members as they begin to understand the dynamics underlying BPD behaviors. When you realize that your loved one was not manipulating you but simply could not control her impulses, it means you may have made mistakes, caused your loved one pain, or sent her to places that were not helpful, such as wilderness camps, residential treatment centers, or boarding schools. Or you may have practiced tough love and tried not to show any emotion while she was raging. This knowledge can certainly make you feel guilty and provoke anger or hostility. You cannot hold yourself up to impossible standards. Remind yourself, with humility, that we all make mistakes and we all do the best we can. You did not receive reliable information, you were not informed of what you needed to know to make effective decisions, and probably had no support. In the best of possible worlds our loved ones should have received accurate diagnoses from the onset along with evidence-based treatment such as DBT. Unfortunately, this probably did not happen. Accept that mistakes were made and move on.

Let Go of Ego

Borderline personality disorder is not about you. You will be most effective when you can mindfully observe situations and interactions with compassion and without personalizing. Sometimes you will have to abandon your ideas of how to help, cede control, and face confrontations so as be able to change your own behavior and become more effective. Remind yourself that your loved one is someone who has dysregulated neurological systems that do not provide him with accurate information about the world around him. His inner state of mind usually leads him to feel out of control, believing that a feeling is a fact or feeling that he is always doing the wrong thing. He will experience shame in situations that seem so trivial to you that they do not even register as possible triggers. When you observe your loved one from this perspective, you cannot help but feel compassion. Although he may not offer you the emotional reciprocity you want or deserve, you have the ability to obtain it from others. He does not. Opening your hands in willingness, opening your heart with compassion, and giving up ego is the key to being mindful.

7

Grieving and Radical Acceptance

THIS CHAPTER DEALS WITH TWO VERY DIFFICULT TOPICS, GRIEVING and radical acceptance. Acknowledging and accepting the existence of a mental disorder in someone you love is excruciatingly difficult. Understanding the neurobiology of the disorder (Chapter 2) and learning skills for improving your relationship (Chapters 3, 4, 5, and 6) can help those who love someone with BPD to reach a point where acceptance and a more harmonious relationship with their loved one is possible.

The onset of mental illness precipitates a "lifetime of losses." People with borderline personality disorder and their loved ones live lives of chronic sorrow. Your life no longer has a sense of safety or security; nothing is turning out the way you thought it would. The dreams you had for yourself, for your family and your loved one, the life you imagined, the future you planned—they all seem lost. The person you love and thought you knew so well seems to have disappeared. Your dreams for a happy future have been usurped by constant feelings of fear, anxiety, hopelessness, and failure. Whatever efforts you make to fix things or to improve situations seem to fail. You feel as if you are standing on the prow of a boat, helplessly watching your loved one drowning in the sea. You scream for help but no one responds to your cries. You have no life preserver to throw out to him, no means to save this person you love so dearly. Painful feelings

It can be very confusing to have to come to terms with your grief for a child, a spouse, a partner, a parent, a sibling, or a friend who is actually alive.

of loss, insecurity, and powerlessness have overtaken your life—along with grief for the losses you, your loved one, and your family have probably not yet even identified or recognized. It can be very confusing to have to come to terms with your feelings of grief for a child, a spouse, a partner, a parent, a sibling, or a friend who is actually alive.

The presence of a mental disorder in a loved one brings about profound changes in every aspect of family life. It is a unique family tragedy wherein all members suffer from a profound sense of loss. Families often struggle with accepting the existence of a mental disorder in their loved one—no matter what disorder is diagnosed. A loved one's mental disorder can bring enormous emotional pain, fear, dread, shame, and, sometimes, social disgrace to the family. To make matters worse, families are often blamed for causing the disorders, the brunt of the blame usually falling upon mothers. For years the psychiatric community blamed schizophrenia on "schizophrenogenic" mothers. Autism was blamed on "ice box" or "refrigerator" mothers, described as cold and withholding. Although science has resolutely disproved these theories, the blame game lingers on.

A family member's ability to accept and acknowledge borderline personality disorder is especially confounded by the behavioral inconsistencies that characterize the disorder, as described throughout this book. The person you love is "apparently competent" sometimes, and impossible to deal with at other times. He may be a charismatic, charming, and amiable person one moment and a rigid, recalcitrant, angry stranger the next. The positive characteristics you love seem to be elusive and capricious. What causes the switch in moods? How do you bring back the person you love and get him to stay around? While BPD may be apparent to those closest to him, others may not be aware that something is not as it should be. Friends and other family members see the person with BPD as highly intelligent, artistically gifted, extremely sensitive, and often quite charming; others may have never witnessed the distressful behaviors you describe. Your observations and concerns are not deemed credible, resulting in the "raised eyebrow" response of disbelief. You are therefore isolated and without support, making coping with this painful situation even more difficult. Grief seems to be an appropriate emotional response to this sad and frustrating family experience.

When a person has BPD, both that person and his family lose something precious. Many of the family's responses to the situation are expressions of normal grieving, but the psychiatric world generally does not acknowledge the grief that family members feel when coping with a loved one with BPD. This omission is seriously disabling to both families and their loved ones with BPD and interferes significantly with the family's ability to move forward emotionally. Professional failure to openly discuss this loss heightens the family's sense of confusion, powerlessness, and isolation, and leaves them feeling profoundly sad.

Further complicating this problem, mental health professionals often meet family members for the first time in the emergency room as a consequence of a suicide attempt, self-injurious act, or aggressive behavior. In the midst of a hospital admission, an episode of substance abuse, or an encounter with the police, the family will probably seem as dysregulated as the person with BPD. When therapists actually ask to meet family members under nonemergency conditions, it is often in an attempt to understand the family's allegedly "negative" effect on the patient—to observe the family for pathology.

Unfortunately, clinicians generally offer little or no helpful educational information on BPD to families. This silence may be due to the medical community's commitment to "confidentiality." Family members, however, equate this refusal to offer information, consolation, or any sort of validation as proof that they are being blamed for causing the disorder. As family members are usually already replete with guilt, feeling they "caused" this mental disorder in their loved one, they may interpret being ignored by the clinician as evidence that they do not deserve better treatment from clinicians, heightening their sense of guilt. They are left in limbo, without a clue as to how to ameliorate the family crisis.

Grief and Invalidated Grief

Grief is the normal and natural reaction to loss of any kind, an inherent response or reaction to separation or loss that traverses all societies, cultures, and social classes. It is the conflicting feelings caused by the end of or change in a familiar pattern of behavior. The word is derived from *grave*, as in a heavy weight that presses on persons who are burdened by loss. While feelings of loss or grief are normal and natural, they are not always acknowledged by society. For instance, grief may follow events that are unrelated to death, such as separation or divorce from a partner or spouse, relocation to a new home, a change of job or school, the closing of a business, or filing for bankruptcy. Giving a child up for adoption or foster care, losing custody of a child, or aborting a fetus are traumatic losses. A loved one going to prison or going off to military service can also be experienced as a severe loss for a family. The "empty nest syndrome," when children leave home to go off to college, is a popular aphorism for sadness and loss. Loss of a pet, property, or possessions are situations that give rise to feelings of loss and grief, yet these responses often seem to have no place in society's notion of grieving. People who left New Orleans because of Hurricane Katrina, never to see their homes again, are surely grieving the loss of home, possessions, neighbors and neighborhood, jobs, status, and position—of all things familiar. Terrorism, civil wars, and natural disasters such as earthquakes and tsunamis lead to traumatic grief. We can even grieve the loss of our health, our youth, our energy, our dreams, our opportunities, but we are socialized to feel that these feelings of grief are abnormal and unnatural. Both the griever and those around him often ignore, neglect, or misunderstand the experience of grief. When societies fail to recognize or acknowledge these losses, people experience disenfranchised or invalidated grief.

Families of people with BPD experience invalidated grief because their profound sense of loss is generally not recognized or acknowledged by others. Roberta has two daughters, one of whom has BPD. She has lived in the same suburban town for many years, knows many people in her neighborhood, and has been involved in many community activities. At a neighbor's party, people asked about her younger daughter, Susan. "How is Susan getting along? What college is she going to? What is her major?" Roberta's older daughter, Jackie, was never mentioned. It was as though she did not exist, even though all the neighbors had watched both girls grow up and knew Jackie as well as they knew Susan. Everyone knew that Jackie had "problems," had BPD, but chose to simply ignore her existence. How did this make Roberta feel? The grief she felt was not publicly validated by her neighbors, nor was it acknowledged by others in her social circle or by society at large. As a result, Roberta felt that she did not have the right to grieve—after all, how could she justify grieving for her daughter, who was biologically alive? Roberta learned to hide her feelings, keeping her grief hidden in her emotional closet.

Disenfranchised grief is grief that is not acknowledged or validated by society. The loss and the person grieving are not recognized, legitimated, or supported. The importance of the loss is dismissed or minimized. This invalidates the loss, increases the burden, and intensifies the griever's emotional reactions to her own experience. For instance, "You'll find another boyfriend. He wasn't so great!" "So what if you lost your mother's ring, you can always get a new one." "Oh, you gained 20 pounds, but you don't look fat!" "You aren't old, you look so good for 60." "Oh, that job wasn't so good, anyway! What are you worrying about? You'll get another job." These are all examples of comments that invalidate the grief or loss a person is experiencing.

Society's failure to react to what a person has lost is equivalent to saying that the person or thing lost is not valued, or that there is something wrong with the griever for dwelling on a loss that no one else seems to notice or acknowledge. The griever will often feel shame because she is experiencing feelings of loss when everyone around her implies that her feelings are inappropriate. The person grieving, the person experiencing loss, experiences her grief in private, in isolation, and without needed social support. The griever's reactions may be harshly rejected or met with disapproval. "I do not want to hear another word about Joe; he is a loser and you are wasting your time even thinking about him."

Stigma

Family members dealing with a loved one with BPD often receive a nonverbal message from their social milieu that it is not okay to talk openly about their painful experiences and feelings with BPD. Sometimes family and friends tire of hearing about one crisis after another. Married couples often socialize with other couples, go on vacations together, and entertain each other in their homes. If one couple in the group divorces, the single partners are often shunned by the other couples as potential threats to the stability of the group.

Unfortunately friends may ostracize a family dealing with a mental disorder as if the disorder were as contagious as the flu, tuberculosis, or leprosy.

In the same way, a child with a mental disorder, whose parents are part of such a social group, may be seen as equally threatening. Unfortunately friends may ostracize a family dealing with a mental disorder as if the disorder were as contagious as the flu, tuberculosis, or leprosy.

This is stigma. Mental illness is generally viewed by society as a blemish or a mark of imperfection, a flaw in character or a moral shortcoming; in almost all cultures, mental disorders are highly stigmatized. A mentally ill person may be viewed as someone evil and to be feared, or as someone to be hidden away from others and never discussed. It is as though the person now wears a scarlet "C" on their chest—for "Crazy."

In an article published in the *Journal of the American Medical Association* in 2001, Myrna Weissman, a professor in the department of psychiatry at Columbia University, compared the ways mental health professionals viewed a mother's interactions with her son with a mental disorder versus with a physical disorder. The mental health professionals implied that the mother's response to her son's mental disorder was an indication that she was over-involved, too focused on him, enmeshed, and unable to control him, and that she had no structure in her home. The clinicians advised her to "get a life." However, the very same behavior when the woman's son developed leukemia was lauded by the medical professionals treating him as an indication of her good mothering and solid family support for her sick child.

Suicide is a taboo act that is also highly stigmatized in our society. If a person attempts suicide, the family generally does not receive sympathy or support. Families are not given compensation, such as time off from work during or after a loved one's suicide attempt or subsequent hospitalization—yet time off is given for maternity leave, physical illnesses, and the death of a close family member. Relatives may be no better; they may pontificate that the suicide attempt was merely a ploy to gain attention or to manipulate others. No matter what may have motivated a suicide attempt, the family has just experienced the terrifying possibility that their loved one might have died. Trivializing a suicide attempt invalidates a family's grief and despair. They may bury their feelings of grief and loss inside themselves or may convert their feelings into secondary emotions such as anger or fear. A family member may be told, "Your wife has *suicidal ideation*." This phrase elicits fear and dread in the hearts of family members, yet they are not provided with a definition of this term, explanations of the behavior, or validation of their fears. This insensitivity is iatrogenic—harm causing—and adds to the family's pain. For family members, "suicidal ideation" is frightening.

Gary's son Steve lives in a city 2,000 miles away. His son calls him at work and says, "It is easier if I die. My life is so difficult for me that I have no other choice left but to die." Gary proceeds to ask his beloved son relevant suicide protocol questions: "Where are you now? Is anyone with you? Do you have a plan? Have you the means? What are your plans for today? What happened before you began to have these feelings? What else could you do to feel better right now?" How did Gary feel while he was asking his son these questions? For a family member, this experience is terrifying, and needs to be acknowledged and validated. While a family member in this situation is grieving, he or she is not allowed the diminished social responsibility offered to people who are grieving for more socially acceptable loses. When Gary ended his phone call with his son, probably saving his life, he had to resume his workday as if nothing had happened. How could his co-workers possibly understand this situation?

Society is replete with rules and rituals. There are behavioral norms for all kinds of situations, such as writing thank you notes after receiving a gift, bringing wine or flowers when invited to dinner, taking turns picking up restaurant checks, celebrating success with friends and family, paying tolls, and observing speed limits. As Arlie Russell Hochschild, a sociologist at the University of California, Berkeley, states, we have "feeling rules" that tell us how we are supposed to feel in certain situations, and "thinking rules" that tell us how to think in certain situations. "I have a right to be angry." "What he did was not fair." These universal rules help us to normalize behavior. Unfortunately, society does not condone grieving for a son who is alive but is threatening to kill himself. How can you mourn for your wife with BPD when she prepares your dinner every night? How can you grieve for your daughter who has BPD yet gets an A in chemistry? You know that significant changes have occurred; she is no longer the individual she once was; her personality is significantly altered. She is still physically alive but somehow it feels as though she is no longer there. The qualities and personality of the person you love may no longer be present, as if the person has left her body, leaving behind her physical shell.

Only those close to the person may notice these changes. By sharing these thoughts and observations with your friends or relations, you run the risk of being seen as abnormal or eccentric at the least—or at most as if something is wrong with you. Your feelings may be viewed as outside the realm of what is socially acceptable. A person with Alzheimer's disease is alive in body but has lost his personality, his awareness of the present, and possibly his memories of his own life. His family can no longer communicate with him; though he is still physically alive he is no longer available psychologically to himself or others. Caring for a loved one with Alzheimer's is recognized as devastating and debilitating for families, and this recognition has spawned a vitally needed system of caretaker support. Living with or caring for a person with BPD can be equally exhausting and debilitating. These caretakers need respite and support too. They are grieving and their grief must be acknowledged.

Parental Grief

Parents of children with BPD are part of an exclusive club that all its members wish they had never joined. Most parents are profoundly devoted to their children, and those whose children have BPD are no different. This can be observed at family classes held by TARA, the organization that developed the family psychoeducation program upon which this book is based. BPD has significantly changed the child that the parents love and their entire family, creating an enormous dissonance in their lives. They are experiencing an unnatural loss, a psychosocial death. This robs parents of their ability to carry out their functional role and leaves them with an oppressive sense of failure. Parental identity is ripped asunder when they feel they have failed to provide basic parental functions, problem solving, and protection of their children. Some parents grieve their inability to communicate with their children with BPD and the loss of the opportunity to reconcile or repair their relationship. Sometimes there is an involuntary severing of the relationship. No matter who makes this choice, it creates debilitating pain for parent and child. This sense of loss stays with the parents each and every day. It is ongoing, as there is no closure. This grief is compounded because the loss of the relationship is not recognized or acknowledged. How can a parent grieve for a person who is devalued by society for being a drug addict, an alcoholic, a sex addict, a bulimic, a shopaholic, a gambler, a liar, or a loser? The tiny bud the parents nurtured does not seem to have bloomed into the magnificent flower they expected. Parents feel as if they have been cheated or robbed; their family seems irretrievably lost to them. There are also intangible, secondary losses that can evoke intense grief, such as a parent's loss of reputation and standing in the community. If there is a death by suicide, it brings additional stigma, judgment, and blame. Suicide may also bring an ambivalent relief that leads to even more guilt. As the bereaved parents search for meaning in their invalidated loss, they may also experience a loss of faith in God and in their essential philosophy of life.

A job description for a parent might read, "Wanted: Person to be all loving, all-good, all-concerned, totally selfless, totally available and motivated only by the needs of the child and concern for his welfare." Our society places unrealistic expectations on parents that can only be fulfilled if you happen to be "perfect" according to standards few can realistically attain. These criteria are not applied to other relationships, like friendship or marriage. It is no wonder that parents feel so much guilt when their children are suffering. They measure themselves against impossible standards and unachievable ideals that do not allow for the normal feelings of frustration, ambivalence, and anger that are part of any close relationship.

You probably believe that you are supposed to be able to fix things so that they will work out to your children's advantage and protect them from all pain and frustration. You want to make their lives better than your own while correcting all the inequities that occurred in your own life. You want them to benefit from every opportunity and advantage that you can possibly provide. Parental love is universal, crossing all cultures and socioeconomic classes. Being a parent can also be a rather thankless job. There is no hall of fame for parents, no Parent of the Year Award.

Raising a child is an enormous responsibility. The reality of the child's presence requires a host of accommodations and profound changes. You change your priorities, make different decisions, do different things with your time. As you watch your children grow and develop, you redefine your own sense of self, your own role, your own reality. The memories of your child that you accumulate over time remain within you, perpetually rekindling your love for the child, regardless of their age. Perhaps that is why so many photos of various stages of a child's life are usually displayed around a family home. These photos of childhood cue memories that are woven into the tapestry of the parent-child connection and serve to cement the unparalleled closeness that characterizes this relationship. Psychiatry calls this *attachment* (see Chapter 9). Memories of each stage and event of your child's development are integrated into the person as you see her now, in her present life, even though she may now be an adult.

Having a child is your ticket into the next generation, your stake in the future, the continuity of your genetic line, and your immortality. The child may represent the union of you and your significant other, both biologically and psychologically. Making sure that your child is safe seems to be a primordial drive. As you are raising a child you have the opportunity to see your own childhood from a new perspective. All of this contributes to the incredible emotional bonding that takes place between parent and child. The intimate closeness and physical and mental interdependence of the relationship between the parent and the child has no equal anywhere. The child becomes an integral part of the parents' lives, an extension of themselves, internalizing their feelings, thoughts, behaviors, and attitudes. This close identification, under optimal conditions, breeds a type of empathy in which the parent is able to feel what the child feels and understand him in ways that do not require words. Even in adulthood, some children continue to see their parents as omnipotent. By the time they have reached adulthood it is hoped that they are aware of their parent's actual limitations and can see them as fallible people.

Sadly, there are parents who violate their responsibility to their children and do them harm. Though unpleasant and unpalatable as this is to consider, it is a tragic fact. Rather than the safety and security children need to grow up healthy and happy, they encounter abuse in the sanctity of their homes. The media have done a good job of calling our attention to these situations. When a child with a biological predisposition toward BPD grows up in an abusive environment, it is a surefire guarantee for developing severe BPD symptoms. For many years, experts believed that abuse was the cause of BPD, but this is not the case. Many people with BPD were not abused or mistreated as children, yet they have the same symptoms and maladaptive behaviors as children who have endured sexual, physical, and emotional abuse and neglect. Abuse of any kind is unacceptable; however, it is simplistic to attribute development of BPD to abuse. In families with multiple children, one child may develop BPD while the others turn into well-adjusted adults without any BPD symptoms. This disparity suggests that there is a genetic basis for BPD just as there is for other mental illnesses, such as depression, where genes have been shown to play a significant role in whether a person develops depression due to life stresses.

For many years, experts believed that abuse was the cause of BPD, but this is not the case.

When a child has a mental disorder such as BPD, both parents will experience grief and loss, but they may not be able to lean on one another for support as each may be grieving in different ways. The support they usually provide for one another, that they count on, may no longer be available. The closeness of the relationship can exacerbate the loss experienced because of BPD, as each partner is vulnerable to the other's feelings. While struggling with his own grief, a person must also cope with the grief of his partner or spouse. The grief and pain on his partner's face is a constant reminder of his family's difficulties. There is no psychological or physical respite from their grief. This is loss upon loss.

Partners may make irrational demands that their spouses take away their pain and "fix" the problem, and are disappointed and angry when they cannot do this. Sometimes feelings of blame and anger are directed toward the other person. Guilt abounds. They may feel resentful and doubt they can ever recover from this loss. The partner may no longer have time, interest, energy, or the desire to relate on any level or care about her significant other, as her own emotional resources are now in short supply. Partners may feel ashamed because they failed to protect their child and their family, cannot deal with the situation themselves, or have run out of the strength and resilience the situation requires. Misunderstandings and feelings of helplessness overwhelm them. This atmosphere is not conducive to maintaining a good relationship—especially if one partner's idea about how to solve their problem is the polar opposite of the solutions favored by the other. One may have a laissez-faire, avoidant approach while the other advocates for a disciplined, tough love stance with contracts and rules. Tension builds between them and often culminates in explosive arguments. Partners may need a break from each other. It is little wonder that having a child with BPD often results in divorce.

Spousal and Partner Grief

How would the job description for a perfect partner read? "Wanted: person to love whom I can trust completely, who cares about me, and who will not hurt me. Must be reliable and honest, a person who will be safe for me to love. Must become my best friend, my confidant, my partner. Must reciprocate my feelings. Must have mutual interests, shared goals and values."

For real intimacy to occur, each partner must be able to feel vulnerable with the other. Vulnerability is at the core of intimacy. To sustain the trust crucial for any good relationship, feelings need to be reciprocated. A partner usually becomes a best friend, the person who listens, with whom we feel safest, who will not judge us, who will accept and love us despite our imperfections. Optimally, the relationship becomes a safe harbor, a place of solace to return to after dealing with life's daily stresses, a place where burdens are shared and physical, psychological, and spiritual support is found. An intimate relationship can relieve the sense of isolation and aloneness many people feel in today's busy, often alienated, world.

Couples usually learn how to negotiate and compromise with each other. As time passes, roles, responsibilities, and needs may change, especially when a child or children become part of the relationship. Illness, death, failures, and successes are experienced. To survive life's stressors, the ability to change is essential. Have you known couples who struggled to achieve a specific goal, such as attaining a certain position at work, buying their dream house, succeeding as an artist, or producing a film—yet when the goal was achieved and the situation changed, one partner was unable to accept the changes? His original role in the relationship defined him and he could not adapt to change. Given this description of a relationship and in consideration of the day-to-day stressors couples of any culture must deal with, how does one partner having BPD affect the delicate balance required to maintain a successful partnership and a good quality of life?

People with BPD often thrive in relationships in which their dependency is encouraged, as they find it difficult to make decisions and deal with stressful situations. Some people whose partners have BPD derive a sense of control and identify themselves as "fixers" and "solvers of all problems." They feel this is how they fulfill their role in their families' lives until they realize they are no longer partners but have become caretakers, ultimately responsible for every single decision, with no respite. While some enjoy this role, many spouses over time become dissatisfied with an unreciprocal relationship. Sometimes, because children are involved, they feel they cannot leave. These partners are grieving.

BPD attacks the core of a relationship, undermines trust, and operates in a world devoid of logical cause and effect. Because people with BPD often believe that "a feeling is a fact," they may become convinced that the other person is not faithful. Partners spend time and energy defending themselves against their loved one's misinterpretations and misunderstandings. As a partner, it is necessary to remind yourself of the biology underlying BPD. The person with BPD can be flooded by self-doubt and shame or be unable to handle daily responsibilities. Sexual relationships can be intense or nonexistent. The intimacy required for a healthy sexual relationship may be too stressful for the partner with BPD, who may blame her partner for these problems. This severely undermines the partners' sense of self. When partners of people with BPD trust their loved one with intimate details of their lives, they may find emotionally sensitive information used against them, and consequently, they feel betrayed. In an intimate moment a woman with BPD may ask her 50-year-old partner, "Have you ever cheated on a girlfriend?" He may respond, "Yes, when I was 16 and in high school. I was thrilled that two girls liked me." She will use this confession as justification for distrusting him. "You cheated on your girlfriend when you were in high school so I know you will cheat on me." These partners grieve the loss of their hopes and dreams for a fulfilling, reciprocal relationship.

As all family members struggle to cope with BPD, they experience grief in various forms and degrees that will metamorphose over time into other feelings, such as denial, anger, and guilt.

Denial

Although family members may realize that something is seriously wrong with their loved one, they often will deny this realization. They cannot accept that BPD has so profoundly affected their loved one and themselves, despite having been recipients of maladaptive

BPD behaviors for a very long time. After a while, they become so accustomed to these abusive and dangerous behaviors that they begin to consider them as "normal." This is called *normalizing pathology*. It is an unconscious way of making it easier to deny a loved one's actual psychiatric disorder. Thus, they walk a tightrope, vacillating between the pain of denying the disorder and the pain of facing and accepting it. Somehow, if families believe the person is being obstinate, willful, difficult, mean, controlling, or manipulating to get attention, the situation can seem less painful. "If she could just 'snap out of it' and got a job, everything would be better." The excuses family members can come up with to account for their loved one's difficult behaviors would rival even Scheherazade's fantastic tales. Given the terrible stigma attached to any mental disorder, it is not surprising that family members might choose to deny its existence rather than acknowledge and accept it.

Nancy suspected that her husband met criteria for BPD. She would listen intently in TARA's family class as other people described their experiences, muttering to herself, "Oh, my husband isn't that bad." This is a typical family response. Family members can be quite confused by the many different guises of BPD behaviors. "She is just a bit more extreme than the average teenager." "He'll grow out of it." "This is just a stage." Disbelief is a typical response to BPD. A great deal of time is spent questioning whether the presence or absence of a particular symptom indicates that the person "really" has BPD. If a person does not self-injure or attempt suicide, the family struggles even more with acceptance of the disorder. When families are finally able to understand the thinking and emotional processing deficits of BPD, they can start to accept the disorder.

Denial can sometimes be therapeutic. It gives a person time to face the reality of a difficult situation, serving as a buffer between the actual painful event and the ensuing feelings and consequences. Unfortunately, the very nature of BPD facilitates denial of its existence. Much family confusion can be attributed to the high-functioning abilities of the person with BPD, to her apparent competence, especially with people she does not know. How can someone be "crazy" yet graduate from college with excellent grades? How can a gifted painter, musician, doctor, lawyer, or CEO have BPD? How can a person be an opera singer performing on stage or have works of art on exhibition at a prestigious gallery, yet still have BPD? Families and partners are dealing with someone in an invisible wheelchair, someone with an unrecognized allergy to his environment, someone with a hidden artificial limb who is trying to run a marathon.

Although intellectually you may deny what is happening with your family member, your body will often react to the stress of the situation. Constant stress can cause physical health symptoms such as sleeplessness, migraine headaches, digestive problems, auto-immune disorders and high blood pressure, as well as emotional effects such as memory problems, unpredictable emotional swings, or depression. Your worry and concern may lead to your feeling anxious, frantic, confused, bewildered, even numb and disoriented. Your response can range from mechanical behaviors to panic attacks. Or, you may just shut down, withdraw, or dissociate. Some respond with robotic stoicism. Although we know that BPD has genetic components, for families it seems to be contagious—parents worry that they too "are going crazy" and feel they may not survive this experience. No longer is anything in life assumed to be "safe."

Unable to comprehend what is happening, it may seem easier to completely deny the situation. Unfortunately, as Marsha Linehan has said, denying reality does not change reality nor does wishing reality were different change reality.[1] Admitting that a loved one has BPD means accepting that this person you love is flawed, may be unable to achieve what you had hoped for him, may be unable to care for himself in the future, and may be dependent upon you for years or for life. This is an excruciatingly painful realization to face, and justifies feelings of grief.

> As Marsha Linehan has said, denying reality does not change reality nor does wishing reality were different change reality.

Anger

The crushing of your hopes and expectations coupled with the unnaturalness of your loss may lead you to feel anger or angry sadness. "Why me? Why my loved one? This is not fair." You may feel as if

---

[1] Linehan, 1993a.

you have lost control of your life. Family members may become bitter, easily hurt, oversensitive to slights, and difficult to be around. These new reactions, often very different from your usual feelings, heighten fear and anxiety, leaving you feeling as if you are losing your mind. Without intending to, you may displace your anger onto others.

For some, admitting that your loved one has BPD is tantamount to admitting that you failed to provide effective help, and therefore failed as an effective parent or partner. This sense of failure can be experienced as anger—in this case a secondary emotion in response to your sense of shame, fear, frustration, and failure. A great deal of energy is expended maintaining this anger, eventually impinging upon your ability to enjoy other areas of your life and increasing your sense of helplessness. At the first meeting of every new TARA DBT family workshop, the anger in the room is palpable. Although each family's "saga of the disorder" is different, the experiences enormously varied, and the cultural backgrounds diverse, anger is usually the common denominator of the feelings that are expressed. Unfortunately, the person you love with BPD probably senses your anger and personalizes, interpreting it as a judgment or criticism. This exacerbates the situation and escalates into the familiar themes and variations of the BPD dance. Some people convert anger and sadness into numbness and depersonalized feelings.

Guilt

Guilt is another response to loss. For parents, guilt is exaggerated by their heightened sense of responsibility for the well-being of their child. They hold themselves responsible for BPD because they feel they failed to keep their loved one safe, to love her enough, or to love her "correctly," and have fallen short of the unrealistic standards by which they judge themselves. Filled with self-reproach, they blame themselves for the problem and obsessively dwell on "if only's," "I should have's," and "why didn't I's." Because they feel they should have been able to prevent the disorder, they end up feeling incompetent and helpless. Feelings of ambivalence are a normal part of every relationship ("I get really angry with you when you forget to put gas in the car!"), but loving someone with BPD makes family members feel guilty for having negative reactions to something their loved one has done. All of these conflicted feelings lead to even more guilt. No matter how many positive things there may have been in their lives, parents will search their memories for any negative experiences that may have contributed to the illness. They are filled with guilt and a sense of unworthiness. Guilt exacerbates grief and interferes with the development of compassion for their loved one. By acknowledging and grieving their loss, family members can free themselves from the emotional quicksand that surrounds them.

Grieving Rituals

A ritual is a highly symbolic event that confers significance and meaning onto particular life experiences of a person or group of people. Rituals are rites of passage that allow us to cross the threshold from one status to another and serve to "mobilize the power of community for healing."[2] Rituals are powerful vehicles that allow the community to come together to witness or interpret an event, and offer the opportunity to contain or express emotion. Marriages, graduations, bar mitzvahs, communions, confirmations, baptisms, even funerals are societal rituals. Rituals that indicate loss are critical to grieving as they serve to sanction the expression of grief.

Grief needs to be recognized, not pathologized. When someone's grief is not acknowledged, or is inhibited and invalidated, neither the actual loss nor the griever is recognized. Mourning is the outward, public expression of grief, the process of acknowledging death or loss. People who mourn are trying to learn to live with their losses so that they can go forward with their lives. Mourning is a response to loss according to the rules of society. It is a social communication of the emotional state of the person who is grieving so that others can respond with care and concern. Family members of people with BPD can be said to be in perpetual mourning because their invalidated loss repeats itself continuously. It has no finite parameters. Just when it seems as if progress is being made, another crisis may occur.

---

[2] Remen, 1996.

Family members trying to cope with these daily crises can be said to be people with "persistent traumatic stress disorder."

Society has developed culturally prescribed rituals for the public expression of grief that allow others to respond to the distress of the person grieving. When a family is grieving, the normal rules of behavior in society are temporarily suspended. Special religious services are held. The griever may wear clothing that distinguishes him from others. Friends and other family members may prepare food or assume some household responsibilities. Every culture and society has unique rituals for grieving. Hindus wear white, Catholics wear black. Jews cover their mirrors and sit on small wooden stools for a week, Christians hold wakes. Rules for mourning tell grievers what to wear, how to act, what to eat, and how long each stage of mourning should last. Indonesian tribesmen from the island of Sulawesi and Sumba are known for their very special rituals for grieving their ancestors. Funerals in Bali are expensive family affairs including unique percussion orchestras called gamelan bands. The more bands you hire, the more you have honored your loved one. Marching bands play at funerals in New Orleans. Funerals can occur years after the death while families accumulate the funds needed to honor their loved one. In most countries, in the case of death, there are laws governing legal rights such as who has control of the deceased's remains, who makes the funeral arrangements, or who signs the death certificate. In some cultures and societies, family members alone are allowed to mourn, while others such as friends, lovers, or co-workers, may not be included in the process—despite strong emotional attachments and feelings of loss that may be just as or even more profound than those of the family.

Family members in TARA's DBT family workshops exhibit profound grief and need to be given an opportunity to acknowledge these feelings for themselves and for the person with BPD. They need the grief they have experienced throughout their long struggles to cope with BPD to be validated. A frank and open discussion of conflicting feelings is needed so that they can acknowledge their feelings to themselves and to each other. For many family members, TARA's family classes present the very first setting in which they can publicly express their grief for someone who is not physically dead. They need to reveal these hidden feelings in a *sangha*, a safe place among fellow sufferers. *Sangha* is the Buddhist term for community. After this emotional discussion, a ritual, a rite of passage, is needed to acknowledge families' pain and isolation and transpose these feelings into a sense of hope and community.

TARA's Grieving Ritual

Elisabeth Kübler-Ross stated that "the response to loss is problematic only when emotional responses are distorted thus difficult or impossible to experience fully."[3] This surely describes the emotional state of the families in TARA's DBT classes who have been denied the means of expressing their grief for the losses brought about by the presence of BPD in their lives. TARA's grieving ritual allows family members a socially accepted and shared means of expressing the emotions associated with their grief. It gives their grief structure and gives them an opportunity to offer meaningful support to one another.

The hope is that you will find your own community with whom to share your feelings and who will participate in this grief ritual with you, and whose members you can support in return. If you do not have your own community or support group with which to share this grieving ritual, try conducting it with members of your family. Clinicians might consider including some variation of TARA's grief ritual into their own practices.

The Ceremony

The TARA grieving ceremony has the following elements:

1. The group sits in a circle, placing photos of their loved ones in front of them, and discusses the differences and similarities between a mental disorder and a physical disorder, the concept of grief, and inhibited and invalidated grief. Although it is extremely painful to talk about grieving for someone who is alive, these topics resonate with family members. It is as though a taboo has been lifted and they can finally speak the unspeakable, they can finally go where angels fear to tread.

---

[3] Kübler-Ross 1982.

2. Each participant is given a candle and two smooth black stones about 2.5 to 3 inches in diameter. They are asked to examine their stones while they mindfully think about what their loved one has lost due to BPD. They then are asked to think about what they have personally lost as a result of their loved one's BPD. After a few moments of mindful silence, each participant takes a turn telling the group what they and their loved one have lost because of this illness. After they describe their loss, participants drop their stones into a large glass bowl. Slowly, the bowl is passed around the room as all the participants share their losses with one another. Each falling stone makes a distinctive sound as it joins the other stones at the bottom of the bowl. People invariably cry. This ritual seems to be especially meaningful to the fathers and husbands in the group, as this is often the first time they have ever allowed themselves to acknowledge or to express these painful feelings of grief to themselves or to anyone else, even their own spouses. Hearing others acknowledge how profoundly they have been affected by this disorder is incredibly moving to the participants. They realize that they are sharing this experience with others; they are not alone. Each black grieving stone has become both a visual symbol and an aural testament to their loss. As the clear bowl fills with black stones, the individuals' stones can no longer be identified.

> Hearing others acknowledge how profoundly they have been affected by BPD is incredibly moving.

Each person's loss has now merged with the collective community of grieving stones and has become a part of the communal loss, the *sangha* of loss.

3. After family members drop their stones into the bowl, they light a small candle. The twinkling candles around the table are symbolic representations of the loved one. As participants publicly grieve their losses, the candles shine in front of them.

4. The group stands in a circle and each is given a branch of Chinese evergreen. The bowl of grieving stones is filled with water and placed in the center of the circle. Participants mindfully think about their green branches and tell the group their hopes for themselves and their loved one. They then place their branch into the bowl. The bowl of stones, symbolizing loss and sorrow, is transposed into a nurturing habitat for flourishing evergreen. Thus the ritual has transposed pain

and sorrow into a representation of hope. We have transposed our lemons into lemonade.

5. Group members join hands in a circle for mindful meditation on community and hope. They perform a guided meditation, breathing in hope and breathing out pain. They focus on sharing the experience of pain, their connection to the group, the skills learned to affect change, and the existence of evidence-based, effective treatments for BPD. The participants have created a path out of suffering. As they continue their breathing, holding hands, an electric current seems to pass through the family members.

This shared experience gives participants a sense of trust and solidarity with one another. They are no longer strangers, but instead, a community, a *sangha*. The intimate ritual creates a unique bond, and the group undergoes a perceptible change when it is over.

Class evaluations indicate that this grieving ritual is particularly meaningful to participants. It is an excellent therapeutic tool for dealing with invalidated, unacknowledged, and inhibited grief. It offers a structure that helps participants express their grief and adjust to their loss. Hearing others experiencing the same feelings as they feel as part of the ritual confirms the reality of what they are feeling and allows for spiritual catharsis. The ritual gives grievers concrete actions to take: They light a candle, drop a stone into a collective bowl, plant a branch, and say a prayer. This provides social support while allowing the bereaved participants to join a larger community of grievers, the *sangha*, thereby validating the loss and reaffirming hope through the strength of the group. It is a rite of affirmation and a rite of passage that helps the family members onto the road to acceptance. Participants seem to regain confidence, as if a painful pressure has been relieved. Their grief needs to be processed after the ritual is completed. They are now ready to radically accept BPD and are motivated to work harder to help create changes.

Radical Acceptance

Radical acceptance is a key concept of DBT derived from meditation and Eastern philosophies, particularly Zen Buddhism. Acceptance is acknowledgment, from deep within you, of what *is*, in the moment, and also tolerating what is. Fundamental to this concept is the word "radical," as it is the wholeness and completeness of acceptance within you that differentiates this kind of acceptance. Radical acceptance requires being open to fully experiencing your own life, as it is, without wishing it were not so and without pretending it is different. Acceptance is entering into the reality of this moment, without judgment. Radical acceptance is the fulcrum that balances validation and change. It is pivotal to the application of DBT skills in the everyday environment as well as for the practice of the philosophy of DBT. Radical acceptance is a choice that we must make about each facet of our lives. For instance, your spouse may not be the perfect partner. You can either maintain the status quo by continuing to complain about his inadequacies, get a divorce, or radically accept him as he is and try to find strategies to help change the things about him that most bother you.

"Not everything that can be faced can be changed, but nothing can be changed until it is faced." –James Baldwin

What are the alternatives to radical acceptance with regard to your loved one with BPD? You could maintain the status quo. Your loved one has BPD; you cave into his demands or argue over control, over who is right or wrong. Or you can keep calling the police when his aggression leads to violence, or hospitalize him for his suicide attempts. You can keep going from crisis to crisis. Although what you are doing has never worked before, you can continue to do it. A prominent 12-step mantra is that "insanity is doing the same thing over and over again and expecting different results."

Or you could abandon ship. You cannot tolerate the constant sense of impotence you feel when coping with BPD. You decide to give up, to stop participating in the relationship. You did the best you could for as long as you could, until you could not do it any more. Enough is enough. You can tell yourself that she is hopeless, will never get better, will never change, or does not want to change. You can cut off all communication. For spouses this may mean divorce. You observe your personal limits and realize that you can no longer tolerate never-ending crises and pain. If this is what you choose to do, remember that this decision can be made *for now*, but it does not have to be forever. At another time you may change your mind and choose to continue working on the relationship.

Or you can radically accept the situation. You can accept that your life is what it is right now and your loved one's life is what it is right now. You can accept that you and your loved one are both doing the best you can, for now. You meet him where he is in the present moment. You accept your grief; you accept that life has turned out differently from what you hoped it would be. It is what it is. You play the cards you were given.

Steve Wynn is a very successful entrepreneur and owner of the W hotel chain, the Bellaggio Hotel, and the Steve Wynn Hotel in Las Vegas. He is a man who places a very high value on esthetics. Despite suffering since childhood from a genetic disease of the eye, a degenerative disorder of retinal tissue, Wynn has exemplary taste and has a prestigious art collection. Wynn is a man who radically accepts his life. In 2005 he was interviewed by Charlie Rose. These are some of his comments: "Life is what you make it. All of us are going to die sooner or later. This is a piece of information that we do not like, over which we have no recourse and we cannot make it go away. We are all going to die; we are here on term limits." This extraordinarily accomplished man has been unable to see in the dark since he was a child. His eyes do not adjust to the darkness. He asks himself, "So what! What frightens me the most and makes me the most uncomfortable is self-pity. I have no place in my life for self-pity. I am not going to live forever. I've got diminished vision but I focus on what I can see and I can remember what I see. I do not feel sorry for myself; I am doing the best I can. You need to concentrate on what you can do and turn a handicap into an inconvenience rather than a tragedy in your life." He considers his eye disorder a "factoid," merely a part of him. He is not the only one with this problem. He doesn't let this factoid "blot out the sun" of the many good things in his life.

For family members, radical acceptance means accepting that your loved one lives in constant emotional pain and is doing the best she can, for now. If you cannot accept this reality, you will exhaust yourself with efforts to deny, fix, or control your loved one's life or your own life; you will make very little progress in applying the acceptance and change philosophies and strategies needed to help your loved one toward a less stressful, happier, more fulfilling life. You can wish life were different, you can hope that life changes, you can wish it were not as it is. Believing reality is what you want it to be does not make it what you want it to be. If you refuse to accept a given reality,

"One must pick and choose one's battles in life or risk living in many emotional foxholes."
–Donald S. Neviaser

you cannot overcome or change that reality. Radical acceptance means you open all the windows and all the doors in your mind and in your heart, and allow whatever is to be. As Donald Neviaser points out, "One must pick and choose one's battles in life or risk living in many emotional foxholes," so that nonacceptance, in the long run, will harm you.

Radical acceptance is the fully open experience of what is, just as it is. It is unrivaled entering into reality, at this moment. It rests on letting go of the illusion of control and depends on courage and trust. It is a willingness to notice and accept things just as they are, right now, without judging mistakes, succumbing to impatience, or expressing disappointment or anger. Although radical acceptance might make you feel powerless, it is neither a passive approach to life nor an approval of behaviors or situations that are inherently unacceptable. Radical acceptance is neither resignation nor defeat; nor is it adverse to change. We must radically accept that we do the best we can and that we can only do what we can do. We are not and cannot be perfect; we all make mistakes. We must accept our humanity and place ourselves in the global scheme of all of life. Saying something "shouldn't be" is tantamount to denying its existence. Radical acceptance means that whatever "is" is just what was meant to be. Once you have accepted this premise, you can work toward change.

Radical acceptance of your loved one with BPD means giving up the illusion of control and the desire to establish control in every situation. This is very hard to do, especially when you fear for the safety of your loved one. So many family members, faced with the impulsive, self-destructive behaviors of people with BPD, persist in trying to control their loved one's behavior by making rules and regulations, or by imposing contracts, boundaries, or limits. However, such rules and regulations often make the person with BPD feel as though he is fighting to survive and may result in his becoming even more rigid and inflexible. The energy you save when you accept reality will serve as fuel for the courage and persistence you need to change reality.

When you love someone who is suffering and harming herself, it is natural to try to help to minimize or protect her from her pain or the consequences of her behavior. Radical acceptance requires that you give up these efforts, letting go and allowing whatever is going to happen to happen so that natural consequences can occur. You must get past the litany of "what if's" going on in your head and accept by allowing whatever is to be, to be. At first, you will find this frightening. It means taking a risk and working at tolerating the distress this may bring you.

For example, if your loved one seems to be headed for failure in school, you may want to intervene, perhaps by coaching him, by nagging, or hiring a tutor. Naturally, you will be disappointed. You can express your disappointment but you must also radically accept the situation and allow the natural consequences to occur.

Acceptance means acknowledging that BPD is a chronic condition, that it can be fatal. Over and over family members ask, "Will he get better?" "Will she recover?" Do we constantly ask if a diabetic will recover or get better? Do we try to "fix" her? Or do we accept that the person has diabetes, help her to take responsibility for her disorder, and learn to live with it? Can a person have a decent quality of life in spite of having diabetes? If you are diabetic and insist on eating a pint of ice cream every night and do not take your insulin, chances are your life will be rather miserable. However, if you accept diabetes and choose to do what you have to do live healthfully with it, you can have a decent quality of life. The choice is yours. When a person with BPD does get better it generally means that he or she has made the commitment to change and to work at changing. When you do not radically accept BPD and do not allow the person to experience the natural consequences of her own behaviors or her own choices, you become an impediment to her motivation to change her own behavior.

Many people feel that if they understand something, or understand why it happened, that this is equivalent to acceptance, but this is not the case. Understanding how or why something happened does not equal acceptance of what happened. You may understand why someone dropped out of school, but that does not mean that you accept his actions. Understanding of something and acceptance of it are different; you need not accept to understand, and you need not understand to accept. Just because you understand BPD does not mean that you accept it; you must learn to see the difference between understanding and acceptance.

The energy you save when you accept reality will serve as fuel for the courage and persistence you need to change reality.

Likewise, acceptance is not the same as approval. You may accept that your son painted his bedroom walls black, but this is not the same as approving of his choice.

In all of our lives, many things happen that we did not plan for and did not choose, yet we have no alternative but to accept them. There are many situations that are not good that we must accept, such as death, loss, or mental illness. You will never be 18 again, you will never enjoy your first taste of ice cream again, you will never again have the experience of first love nor experience sex for the first time. You cannot stop aging and no one lives forever. Although the choices you must make are not always optimal, accepting these choices does not mean that you judge them as good. If a man returns from war without legs and confined to a wheelchair, how do we view this situation? Do you think, he is not dead, therefore the outcome is positive? Or, he is handicapped, therefore the outcome is not good. What choices do you have? Can you change this situation? No. How do you cope?

Turning the Mind

The first step toward radical acceptance is turning your mind. This is consciously working to look at things differently. You must actively work toward accepting, even if you do not like what you have to accept. It is often frightening and painful to try to accept something, in the moment, that may be against your nature to accept, especially when you realize the potential danger of a situation—such as your child being arrested. You must practice tolerating your own fear. Review your life and think about the consequences that resulted for you and for your loved one whenever you reacted to your fears and jumped into the "fixing" pool with him instead of accepting what was happening. You may have gotten short-term relief but the end result was long-term pain

Imagine walking down a road and coming to a fork. On one side a sign is posted that reads Acceptance Road; on the other side a sign reads Deny Reality Road. Which road do you choose? Acceptance is an active choice that must be made again and again, in varying situations. Turning the mind is the act of choosing to accept, of making a commitment to accept over and over and over again. Making a commitment to accept does not mean you have actually accomplished accepting. At most, it means you are trying, you are walking in the direction of acceptance. Acceptance requires repeated commitment, an enormous amount of persistence on your part as well as faith. On some days it may be easier to accept than on others. Many factors can influence your ability to accept, such as your health in the moment, environmental circumstances, or the very nature of the thing you must accept.

Balancing Radical Acceptance with Change

Only after you are able to radically accept the situation at hand can you begin to introduce change to that situation. Families are usually terrified that the person with BPD will make a scene, rage, become violent, cut himself, completely withdraw, or actually kill himself; therefore, they accept whatever he is doing at that moment. These appeasing responses are a blueprint for failure, reinforce the person's harmful behaviors, and will not be effective in bringing about any positive changes toward development of self-reliance or problem solving. An all-accepting attitude prevents the person from experiencing the natural consequences of his behavior and impedes experiential learning. Accepting any type of behavior because you are afraid of confrontation or change, or are conflict aversive yourself, may bring you immediate relief—but it will not solve long-term problems.

Some families, alternatively, insist on change and accept no compromises. They dominate their loved one with rules, regulations, and ultimatums. The person may rebel or feel totally dependent, incapable of acting without some kind of external control.

Balancing acceptance with change is the most effective way to cope with BPD behaviors. DBT teaches change techniques, discussed in Chapter 4 and 8, that will be effective only if you have accepted your loved one as she is, and accept that she is doing the best she can in the moment.

Radically accepting something is not the same as resigning yourself to whatever has happened. If you refuse to accept a given reality, how can you possibly overcome or change that reality? Christopher Reeve, the handsome, successful actor who played Superman, fell from a horse and was paralyzed. He radically accepted his paralysis and then did everything he could, personally and politically, to change his situation. By doing so, he helped other paralyzed people. Could he have accomplished so much if he had denied he was paralyzed or spent his time feeling sorry for himself? Reeve did not passively withdraw from life and was certainly not defeated. He was not averse to change but was vibrantly open to the future. His accomplishments are a tribute to the power of radical acceptance. When Dana Reeve married her husband, she expected to be married to a handsome, sexy Hollywood star. She did not plan on being married to someone confined to a wheelchair. Her expectations for her marriage and her actual experience were miles apart. We cannot edit life. Dana and Christopher Reeve were dealt a bad hand but they played it very well. In the midst of their pain, they made remarkable advancements and helped many other people.

Accepting Pain

"We must embrace pain and use it as fuel for our journey."
—Miyazawa Kenji

Pain is a part of life. It comes and goes. At some time or other, everyone experiences pain. We stub our toes, fall down, and lose things or people that we love. No matter how hard you try you can never totally protect another person from pain, get rid of pain, or get through life without pain. Pain comes and goes, and it can never be totally avoided. When you first learn any sport, you will feel pain as your body adapts to using your muscles in new ways. "No pain, no gain!" Ballet dancers experience pain whenever they dance. Giving birth is extremely painful. Being aware brings pain. Making a mistake is painful. Is there anyone who has never made a mistake? Sooner or later, all of us fail at something. Failure is painful. No one bats a thousand all the time. One cannot live a life without pain. Denial is trying to suppress pain. Denying pain makes it worse, magnifies and intensifies it, and leads to fighting or rejecting reality. "Pain creates suffering only when you refuse to accept the pain."[4] DBT teaches that suffering is fighting pain, is not accepting pain. Avoidance leads to worse suffering. Suffering can be relieved but cannot be eliminated.

---

[4] Linehan, 1993.

Kenji reminds us that "We must embrace pain and use it as fuel for our journey."

Welcome to Holland

Emily Kingsley is the mother of a boy with Down's syndrome. In her essay, "Welcome to Holland," she compares the planning for and anticipation of having a baby to the planning one might do for a fabulous vacation to Italy. You dream about what it will be like to be in Italy. Excited and eager, you do research, plan your itinerary, study Italian, anticipate the sights you will see, the foods you will eat, the shopping you will do and friends you will visit. You have many friends who are also going to Italy.

You set out on your journey but, unexpectedly, there is a change in plans. A mistake occurs and you do not get to Italy. Instead, you wind up in Holland. You have no choice in the matter and must stay in Holland. There is no way you can get to Italy. You are shocked and disappointed. "I signed up for Italy! I'm supposed to be in Italy. All my life I've dreamed of going to Italy."

What do you have to gain by not accepting that you are in Holland? Is Holland so awful, or is it just a different place, a place you had not planned on going? Can you radically accept that you are in this different place for good? You will have to learn about all the wonderful things there are to see and do in Holland. You will have to learn a whole new language so as to communicate with people you would never have met if you were not in Holland. You will discover that these people may be different from Italian people, but they are still wonderful people. Everyone you know is raving about Italy but you are in Holland. "And for the rest of your life, you will say, 'Yes, that's where I was supposed to go. That's what I had planned.'"[5]

You dreamed of one life and are now living another. No one plans to have a child with BPD, to love someone with BPD, or to marry someone with BPD. If you spend your life grieving because you did not go to Italy, you will never enjoy the good things in Holland. Your original plans changed; your dream did not materialize. You are entitled to be disappointed, because the loss of your dream is a significant loss.

---

[5] Kingsley, 1987.

The pain of that loss is legitimate, and it will never, ever totally go away. Now you need to radically accept your pain and loss so that you can go on and enjoy what you did get. By radically accepting you will be free to change the situation, to enjoy the tulips, windmills, and Van Goghs of Holland.

To balance radical acceptance with change, you must first radically accept that your loved one is in an emotional wheelchair, will never play football, will not be a ballroom dancer. Then you must build ramps around your house, get a special car so that he can drive and collaborate with the physical therapist. You must change your expectations, reframe your problems, accept what he can actually do and stop grieving for what she cannot do. The energy you save by accepting reality will fuel the courage and persistence you will need to foster change. Sometimes we are confronted with very challenging life situations. What appears to be a catastrophe can be a challenge to overcome. We need to mobilize our full strength and the strength of our families to meet this challenge. In the process, we grow and reach depths within ourselves we did not know were there. We need to learn to live well despite challenging situations. BPD is not hopeless. People do get better. You can help. He might not be what you thought he would be but his good qualities deserve recognition. Remember, Holland, too, is a wonderful place.

8

Dialectical Behavior Therapy Skills for Behavior Change

Interpersonal Relationships, Emotion Regulation, and Distress Tolerance

Attitudes and emotional tone are what we hear, not just words. Communication does not depend on syntax, eloquence, or rhetoric. Insight won't motivate people unmotivated to change. Words lose their power when you use them to overpower.

—Anais Nin

A PPLYING DIALECTIC PRINCIPLES TO THE THINKING OR PHILOSOPHY that guides your daily life will inevitably lead you to search for the middle road between opposing points of view, such as when balancing acceptance and change. If your idea of how to make sure your loved one is safe and not in any pain is to solve all his problems for him and to put out any potential BPD fires, you are creating dependency in your loved one while appeasing or "enabling" him. Although you may have solved the immediate problem in the short run, no long-term skills that will help your loved one learn to solve problems on his own have been mastered. You may have actually "disabled" him.

You must work toward a synthesis between acceptance of your loved one and the recognition that he needs to change. When applying DBT techniques, validation (see Chapter 5) is a principal acceptance strategy. However, if you implement validation alone, without modeling and supporting other important techniques for behavior change, you will not be effective. A validating statement is only half of a sentence. To be dialectic, validations must be balanced with the use of change strategies like those taught in DBT. You will improve your relationship with your loved one if you validate and then *model, teach, and reinforce* effective change techniques.

Dialectical Behavior Therapy skills, taught in four separate modules, teach people with BPD comprehensive strategies to bring about behavioral changes in specific areas. The skill modules are called Mindfulness, Interpersonal Relationship Skills, Emotion Regulation Skills, and Distress Tolerance Skills. Mindfulness is discussed at length in Chapter 6. This chapter deals with the other three modules. These DBT skills target changing the rigid, black-white, all-or-nothing thinking and behavior patterns that prevent so many people with BPD from reaching their potential and living a more fulfilling life. Through the learning, repetition, and practice of these DBT skills, new neuronal pathways can develop in brain regions that correlate with the areas affected by BPD neurological deficits so that behaviors can change and difficulties can be overcome. This process is called *neurogenesis.*

DBT encompasses life skills and techniques that can be beneficial to all people, not only those with BPD. It would probably be helpful if children were taught these skills in school. When a family member is learning DBT skills so as to help and support a loved one, it is imperative that a distinction be made between the life skills of the family member and the person with BPD. Family members do not generally have the same lack of skills as do their loved ones with BPD. They generally have successful relationships, jobs, and interests; can manage their lives; and have various means of tolerating distress. While latest research indicates that there is a large genetic component to BPD, the primary goal of TARA's DBT family

> *As a family member, you can model, reinforce, teach, or cheerlead the use of these more effective means of solving problems or getting to goals, thereby becoming a therapeutic parent, partner, or loved one.*

workshops (and of this chapter) is not to teach you the DBT skills for your own use but, instead, to teach you to recognize the lack of skills in your loved one, and how to help guide him into utilizing DBT methods for solving problems and changing his behavior. As a family member, you can model, reinforce, teach, or cheerlead the use of these more effective means of solving problems or getting to goals, thereby becoming a therapeutic parent, partner, or loved one.

This point of view is not generally shared by the clinical DBT community, which believes family members themselves should be taught DBT skills. This implies that family members do not know how to tolerate their own distress, regulate their own emotions, or have successful interpersonal relationships. They are generally taught these DBT skills in multifamily groups where they participate along with their loved one with BPD. It can be very difficult for family members who have been recipients of abusive behavior or who have fretted over the safety of their loved one to participate authentically in a group like this without fully understanding how BPD influences their loved one's behaviors and responses or why the clinician is stressing emotional responses rather that "right" responses. Understanding affords family members the opportunity to cultivate compassion for their loved one's suffering.

Change Is the Only Constant

People with BPD find it extremely difficult to cope with even the subtlest changes in themselves and others. They usually view any external effort to change them as an attempt to control them or as an outright criticism of their behavior. This inability to deal with change interferes with the development of collaborative, flexible relationships. DBT recognizes that the person is doing the best he can in the moment (this is the acceptance half of the dialectic), but also that he needs to change and to try harder if his life is to change.

We all need to accept that change is the only constant. Change is like the ocean, a constant that, from moment to moment, is never the same. The ocean is changed by tides, winds, currents, storms, the seasons, and environmental events. Although a person may seem to be the same person all the time, she is constantly changing, always in flux. We vary in how we feel physically, going from hungry to full, energetic to tired. Our moods change all the time. You may feel like talking sometimes and want to be alone at other times. You may be preoccupied with your own problems right now and, at other times, be interested in the world around you. Time changes people. Children's needs differ from those of adults. As you get older, you want and need different things. Relationships are never static because the changes you undergo within yourself every day are paralleled by the daily changes other people experience. Recognizing the constancy of change, and that it can be a positive force in a person's life, is a core component of DBT.

As a family member of someone with BPD, you cannot force your loved one to change with rules, contracts, or ultimatums, or by instructing him on what to do. Instead, you must ask your loved one what he could do differently to solve a problem, and remind him of other times he has successfully solved similar problems. In this way you can help guide him toward more effective responses that he can eventually incorporate into his behavioral repertoire. Instead of viewing this as *changing*, you can reframe this for both of you as *learning*.

Interpersonal Effectiveness Skills

While we have all experienced interpersonal conflict at various times in our lives, people with BPD experience problems of this type almost all of the time. Interpersonal effectiveness skills teach a person with BPD how to be effective in getting what he wants, how to say "no" to what he does not want, and how to deal with disagreements or conflicts. These skills may seem basic and simple to you, but for people with BPD they are extremely difficult. When you yourself model DBT interpersonal effectiveness skills for your loved one, you help him to clarify and define relationships, and improve communication while decreasing the misunderstandings that usually lead to emotional explosions.

The ability to get along with other people is a vital component of any successful, fulfilling life. For people with BPD, relationships are the places in their lives where they experience the most frustration, failure, and shame, a treacherous jungle fraught with murky pools of quicksand. Because relationships are so important, it makes sense that

DBT would focus on teaching people specific skills for how to improve their relationships. If you know what you feel, and what you want and do not want, and are able to tell the difference, if you are able to understand what others are feeling, saying, asking for, or needing in the moment, are able to respond appropriately and communicate clearly, you will be more skillful at negotiating your relationships.

Interpersonal effectiveness skills require the ability to process verbal information (language) and interpret nonverbal emotional information (tone of voice, facial expressions, gestures, and body language), as well as awareness of what is actually happening in specific situations. If you distort what you hear, personalize neutral statements, are unable to control your emotional responses, cannot focus on the moment, and are easily distracted, it is no surprise that relationships become your personal minefield. Relationships are even more difficult if your amygdala works overtime and even a neutral facial expression or benign comment can set you off. As people with BPD get older, sustaining relationships seems to become even more difficult. Many give up interacting with other people altogether, avoiding them to the point of becoming reclusive.

Oddly, people with BPD are often able to cope quite well with peripheral relationships but seem to run into major difficulties when dealing with close or intimate relationships. The more emotionally involved they are with the other person, the more that person can trigger their reactions. The degree of closeness an individual feels toward the person she is interacting with will affect her ability to handle the situation, rather than the details of the actual situation. You can consider your daughter declaring, "You are the worst mother in the world," as a left-handed compliment because it is an indication that you really matter to her, that she trusts you enough to risk expressing herself and exposing her feelings.

No relationship is without disagreements. No marriage is perfect, and friends are not available all the time. We all make mistakes, but people with BPD often think they need to be perfect. To maintain relationships, at some time or other, everyone has to deal with conflict or discord so that we do not "throw out the baby with the bath water." We can all benefit from improving our relationship skills. DBT provides structured skills that clarify what is reasonable to want or not want, while teaching how to respond effectively in various situations.

When you can recognize the difficulty your loved one is having with relationships and can identify the skill deficits he is struggling with, you can help him find solutions. What follows are skills you need to learn so that you can become more effective at "heading problems off at the pass" and turning situations around so that you are not the constant recipient of abuse. You become part of the solution rather than part of the problem. Key components of DBT interpersonal relationship skills are *defining goals, nurturing relationships, developing assertiveness, building self-respect, understanding cause and effect, accepting mistakes, balancing priorities and demands, balancing wants and "should," building mastery,* and *asking for what you want.*

Defining Goals

Successful relationships depend heavily on defining your goals, on knowing what you actually want and need. First we determine what our goal is at any given moment (Getting into college? Making friends with your roommate? Getting an A in a course?). Defining one's goals will then determine behavior and will drive how we respond to a situation.

Situations that demand decision making often bring on aversive feelings in people with BPD. These aversive feelings (anxiety, anger, et cetera) can then interfere or prevent the person from deciding what it is they want. As a result, it is important that people with BPD learn to focus on what they really want or do not want. This can be especially difficult when what they want is not the same as what the other person wants; misunderstanding and conflict can result. As a family member, you must hone in on what your loved one wants, become attuned to him. Be attentive and try to discern what your loved one's goal is at that very moment, while also keeping your own goal or perspective in mind. Help your loved one to think about his goals by asking him specifically what his goal is in this situation.

Here again you must recognize that something that is simple and automatic for you, like deciding what you want, can be very difficult for someone with BPD. How can you possibly get what you want if you cannot even ask yourself the right questions to figure out what it is you actually want, cannot determine what you want to change or accomplish, and are unable to define your goals? This becomes even more difficult if you have a hard time identifying your emotions. Saying no to things you might not want to do or do not want can be equally difficult for your loved one, especially if she is afraid that people will not like her or will reject her if she says no, resulting in her feeling worthless and full of shame.

Many people with BPD find it exceedingly difficult to assert themselves. They back down, cave in, and capitulate to the desires or demands of others. An important goal for them to work towards might be to learn how to resist a change that someone else is trying to make, and to learn to believe that they have a right to want what they want. They have to ask themselves, "Do I want to be liked, or do I want to be effective at getting what I want?" Remember how Gary disapproved of his daughter's choice of tires? She was unable to stand up to her father's demands, capitulated to his willfulness, and bought the tires he chose. Afterward, she felt incompetent and ashamed.

There may be no secret to success, but the key to failure is surely trying to please everyone

At the same time, some people with BPD tend to sacrifice their own needs and wants because they believe relationships will go more smoothly if they try to please everyone. They believe they will get approval and avoid problems if they acquiesce to what others want. They cave in to the priorities of others and give up on their own objectives, sometimes not knowing whether or not it is "okay" to have their own objectives. Unfortunately, this creates resentment, which will smolder until they either run away from the relationship or blow up. Many young women with BPD have indiscriminate sex or put themselves into abusive situations, believing this is how to get men to like and accept them.

When you are faced with out-of-control BPD behaviors, you may often respond in a similar manner. When you are afraid of the adverse consequences of saying no or refusing a demand, which may evoke rage attacks, self-injurious behaviors, increased drug use, or a suicide attempt, you might allow dangerous behaviors to continue. Thus you are normalizing pathological behaviors, or reinforcing maladaptive behaviors. You are allowing yourself to be emotionally blackmailed, ceding to unreasonable demands, giving more money than you can afford or should give under the circumstances, standing aside while the person engages in dangerous behaviors, and going along with explanations that you know are not true. You are buying the CoCo Puffs (Chapter 3). Both of you will end up feeling misunderstood and will resent one another. One of you may max out on stress and eventually explode or leave the relationship. Your loved one will probably not understand what happened, as she is so accustomed to your acquiescing or appeasing her behavior.

For all of these reasons, improving interpersonal relationship skills must begin with defining goals. Ask your loved one, "What do you want? What don't you want?" Ask yourself the same questions. Your loved one is not accustomed to answering these questions for herself, therefore this kind of language must become a regular part of the family vocabulary. You can help by asking, over and over again, "How does this behavior get you to your goal?" The goal can be something as simple as ordering lunch at a restaurant, or a more involved goal such as choosing a major at college. Once you have defined a goal, you can then figure out the best way to get to that goal.

Nurturing Relationships

Most people take relationships for granted, assuming that when someone loves them they no longer have to do any work to maintain the relationship. This is even more pronounced with people who have BPD, who often do not understand that relationships are always in flux and require constant awareness and sensitivity—regardless of the degree of closeness. For two people to be attuned to each other, their relationship will require constant attention and work, surely necessitating making changes.

In response to the question, "What do you look for in a good relationship?" a wise therapist answered, "Someone who is capable of growth and change." Being skillful at maintaining relationships requires flexibility, courage, humility, and spontaneity. You must know what you want, ask for what you need, have the ability to say yes to what you do want and resist pressure and say no to what you do not want.

A person with BPD generally becomes emotionally dysregulated faster and more intensely than other people and has no idea how to prevent situations from escalating into eruptions, nor how to repair a relationship by finding balanced solutions to stressful, conflict-laden situations. Whatever ability they have to control their own emotional

responses is lost when they are emotionally triggered and dysregulated. They also have difficulty tolerating unpleasant feelings such as
fear, anxiety, rejection, and frustration. Their responses will often be
out of sync with the responses of the people with whom they are interacting. Communication difficulties increase as the ability of either party
to resolve the problem decreases. Everyone's vulnerability to emotions
increases when they are stressed. Avoidance is a coping strategy so that
ending a conversation or relationship becomes easier than dealing with
feelings of stress or frustration. However, avoidance does not get
anyone what they want and will usually create even more stress.

You may have observed that your loved one with BPD has difficulty dealing with subtle changes in people. Even momentary changes
such as micro facial expressions can trigger responses. They usually
misinterpret any change as a consequence of something they said,
did, or did not do or as having been caused by something that relates
to them. Many experiences are interpreted as self-referential (see
Chapter 2). Their responses to most changes are heightened when
they involve the people closest to them. If you come home in a bad
mood, this must mean that you are angry with her, do not love her
anymore, or that you know that she has done something awful. She
rarely considers that your boss may have given you an extra assignment that needs to be done that evening, or that you had a very difficult day at work, do not feel well, or were just in a car accident. In these
situations, you will need to validate and calmly explain your specific
feelings in detail so as to remove potential misperceptions.

Carl gets up daily at 4 A.M. to work at his restaurant. He returns
home at 6 P.M., is usually extremely tired, and sinks into his favorite
chair to relax before dinner. Nancy, his daughter, sees him and asks,
"Dad, are you mad at me?" Annoyed by her question, he usually
snaps back with "Don't be ridiculous! Why are you asking me that?"
Nancy gets upset by his response and they are off doing the BPD
dance. After Carl learned about BPD, his response to Nancy changed.
He now nurtures his relationship with his daughter, carefully explaining his feelings by saying, "It must feel really bad to think your dad
is angry with you; at the same time, I am just tired after a long day.
If I sit here for a few minutes I will revive and maybe we can play
Scrabble after dinner."

It is very important for all of us, and especially people with BPD,
to remember that their relationships require constant attention

"The ability to repair a relationship is much more important than the ability to prevent it from rupturing in the first place" –Marsha Linehan

and nurturing. Do not take your relationship for granted; be attentive and validate your loved one by noticing how hard she is trying and the efforts she is making. In this way you are modeling how to nurture a relationship, the benefits of doing so, and how important it is.

Developing Assertiveness

People with BPD must learn to be assertive without getting angry. They generally do not know how to assert themselves in calm, rational ways that do not damage a relationship. Their only possible alternatives seems to be becoming abusive or becoming a doormat. They cannot seem to ask for what they want without getting angry— there is no middle ground. It seems to be easier for them to understand extremes, as nuances and subtlety are very difficult for them to interpret.

When someone with BPD experiences very intense angry feelings, he may become confrontational, avoid the situation and/or the person altogether, or vacillate between avoidance and confrontation. Confrontation and avoidance are both based on the emotional state of the moment and are inappropriate responses, as neither succeeds in solving the relationship or objective problem or in getting the person what he wants. Some people feel so uncomfortable when they get angry that they have learned to inhibit or overcontrol both the feelings and expressions of anger. They can be described as *conflict aversive*. This leads to developing passive, helpless behaviors that appear to be the opposite of assertive behavior. Shame and self-criticism are often by-products. However, a situation that triggers a passive response can also spark a very intense, angry, confrontational response. When a person with BPD interprets your behavior as being aggressive toward him, he may respond with retaliatory and insulting remarks. Even a benign remark like "pass the butter" can provoke a response such as, "Why me? I'm not the maid!"

Although it may seem counterintuitive, a person with BPD who may seem to be outwardly confrontational and hostile may actually find it very difficult to express her opinions and assert herself. In spite of the intense emotion she may be exhibiting, she is not addressing what she actually wants; therefore, she is not taken seriously, will not get what she wants, and will become even more emotionally escalated. Feeling unheard leads to feeling invisible, invalidated, humiliated, and ashamed. She may even end up losing relationships because her behavior is neither interpersonally skillful nor effective.

People with BPD need to learn how to assert themselves in relationships and handle situations so that they do not lose the relationship and get to their goal while maintaining their own self-respect. As a family member, you must learn not to react to your loved one's anger, and instead look for the underlying source of the problem at hand, listen to the words, not the music. You must find the humility and compassion to see situations from the other's point of view and try not to personalize or defend yourself.

Building Self-Respect

When two people are engaged in a conflict and have become rigid and polarized over the issue, they are less able to compromise or negotiate a solution. Each person is probably in "emotion mind" (see Chapter 6), clinging to his own position, focusing on being right rather than being effective. When this happens, "winning" the argument becomes a matter of self-respect. It is difficult to maintain self-respect while agreeing to another person's demands and giving up your own priorities.

We all need to practice negotiating solutions to problems so that each person keeps his self-respect. You must find the humility and compassion to see situations from the other's point of view and try not to personalize or defend yourself. By giving up on what may be the logically "correct" solution or being right in every situation, in favor of modeling "gray" solutions rather than either/or thinking, compromises can be reached. People with BPD will often say, "If I cannot solve this problem, I guess I have to die."[1] When you understand the skill deficits that lead to this polarized thinking or black-white, opposite alternatives, you can challenge these statements and cheerlead alternatives toward more effective problem solving.

---

[1] Linehan, 1993a.

Applying effective means helps to maximize the possibility that goals will be met.

Situations that have the potential to cause emotional eruptions or the severing of relationships are opportunities to teach coping skills, particularly if you, yourself, model the skills. Sometimes restating the problem in a more focused manner can help the person really see the issue that is causing the problem, challenge his faulty beliefs, and begin repair of the relationship.

Mara has just lost her job. Lucy, her mother, returns from work to find the kitchen counter strewn with food and dishes. Lucy wants to start the family dinner but there are pots, dishes, and glasses in the sink. She asks Mara to help clean up the kitchen. Mara responds by screaming, "I am not your maid. Do it yourself!" Her mom replies, "Gee, Mara, I can see you are really upset about losing your job. Anyone would feel bad about getting fired. That must have been so humiliating. I would have felt awful, too. However, how does yelling at me solve the problem? Perhaps after dinner we can have a cup of tea together and talk about what happened. What do you think? Would that be helpful?" Mara agrees. "What do you think we can do to get dinner started now?" A volatile eruption was avoided by applying skillful means, and each person was able to accept the other person's priorities and demands in the moment.

Understanding Cause and Effect

People with BPD have difficulty understanding that their behavior affects other people and realizing that other people's thoughts and feelings may differ from theirs. They do not understand cause and effect, and therefore have a hard time learning from their mistakes. By pointing out the consequences of your loved one's actions in a validating, nonjudgmental, and compassionate way, you can help her learn to consider the consequences of her actions in the moment.

We have all seen how people with BPD can provide friends with excellent problem-solving strategies, evaluate cause and effect, and see how a situation got from point A to point B. They are often quite able to help other people sort out interpersonal issues and conflicts, but when faced with similar situations in their own lives they are unable to come up with the very same solutions. Understanding any problem demands the understanding that when you do A, B happens, that there are consequences to all actions. *If I borrow a book from a friend and do not return it, he will not lend me another book. If I call someone 10 times a day, he will be annoyed with me and stop taking my calls.*

As obvious as cause and effect may be to you, the obvious is not obvious for people with BPD. You have to explicitly and nonjudgmentally explain, "When you do not show up on time, I get anxious and worry about what might have happened to you. I feel as though I do not matter enough to you for you to call and tell me what is going on. Then, I get angry and do not want to be with you. What do you think you can do so that we avoid this kind of situation?" If one does not see the role of cause and effect in situations, one can justify not taking responsibility for one's own actions. Cause and effect have nothing to do with whether behavior is "bad" or "good."

Accepting Mistakes

We all make mistakes. Living your life by trying to avoid making mistakes is an impossible goal. If you are so scrupulously afraid of doing wrong, you may not try doing anything at all. When people with BPD make a mistake, they judge themselves harshly because of their perfectionism and polarized thinking. They need to accept that everyone makes mistakes, and that mistakes are reparable. Repairing mistakes develops compassion for oneself and can reduce feelings of shame.

"Mistakes obviously show us what needs improving. Without mistakes, how would we know what we had to work on?"
—Peter McWilliams

Repairing mistakes is one way of nurturing relationships. The Chinese say that crisis is an opportunity. DBT sees failure as an opportunity to start over again, only this time you will do a better job because you know more.

If, in the heat of the moment, you do not handle a situation skillfully, the way you repair the mistake can be a model for your loved one with BPD. For example, "When you called me yesterday, I was so involved with my work that I did not realize how upset you were about missing your class. It must have been so frustrating when I did not 'get it.' I am really sorry." You are modeling behavior that demonstrates that everyone makes mistakes and demonstrating how you apologize when you make a mistake. You are also showing the person that you care and are really trying. Being humble while validating someone's feelings shows the person that a mistake is not fatal and can help develop the trust needed for successful relationship repair. Reggie Jackson once remarked that home run hitters also strike out a lot. Do not apologize for everything you do or take responsibility for everything that goes wrong. Remember, everyone makes mistakes, they are a part of life.

Balancing Priorities and Demands

In DBT terminology, the ability to balance what you want to do with what is being asked of you by others is called balancing priorities and demands.[2] Priorities are things that you want to do and that are really important to you. Demands are things other people want you to do, things that often create pressure and stress. People with BPD have difficulty distinguishing between priorities and demands. Because of his difficulty in saying no, your loved one may overcommit, trying to meet others' demands until he reaches the point of being overwhelmed. Feeling overwhelmed can result in feeling stressed and dysregulated, which can lead to acting impulsively to put an end to or escape from aversive feelings.

It is very difficult for people with BPD to decipher priorities in situations, to decide what has to be done, and to distinguish between what they really must do, what they want to do, and what is less important for them to do. As a result they often do too much. If your loved one gives a dinner party for 12, cooks the entire meal, and stays up all night baking bread, will the success of the dinner party depend on the bread? Working through the night will leave her so exhausted, stressed, and overwhelmed that she will probably end up feeling emotionally vulnerable, overwhelming, arguing with her friends, going over the edge, and not enjoying her own party. Of course, she is comparing herself with a friend who baked his own bread for his dinner party, thinking she "should" be able to do as well as he did and feeling inadequate because she did not. You can remind her that her friend is a professional caterer whose staff helped him prepare the dinner.

---

[2] Linehan, 1993a.

You can help your loved one by pointing out the priorities and demands in situations as they arise. People have to be able to say no when it is necessary, and know that doing so is okay. You can point this out to your loved one with BPD by modeling how to say no assertively, without anger. A friend might be angry or disappointed with you if you cannot take care of her cat, babysit, or lend her money. It is important to practice tolerating that disappointment and recognizing that, if she is a good friend, she will understand. Your example shows your loved one that it is possible to tolerate the negative consequences that may result.

For a person with BPD, the alternative to overcommitting can be doing nothing at all, having no structure whatsoever to the degree that he will stay in bed all day or isolate himself. The dilemma is how to achieve a balance between too many priorities and no priorities at all, between overcommitment and no commitment. Dialectics asks us to find the synthesis or balance between opposites—in this case, saying yes to every demand and saying no to every demand. Effectiveness in a relationship depends on finding a point of equilibrium between your and the other person's priorities and demands. Whereas most adults can compromise and negotiate, people with BPD do not have this proficiency. Remember, what is obvious to you is not obvious to someone with BPD.

Conflict arises when one person's priorities do not coincide with the other's. Each person must decide what is most or least important to him and to the person he cares about. People with BPD find it very difficult to understand why you are making a demand or how something can be a priority for you when it is not important for them. Equally, they do not understand why you do not see the importance of their demand. If you ask him to call you when he is out because you are concerned about his safety, he will feel you are trying to control him or do not trust him. When you make a demand of your own or do not comply with his demand, he personalizes your refusal or lack of understanding of his demand and interprets your behavior as an indication that you have not heard him, are rejecting him, and do not love or care about him. If you are not skillful, you will find yourself off and running into a war of wills.

Jane and her mother are preparing for a family party beginning at 7 P.M. They have a great deal of work to do before the party. Jane promised to make the hors d'oeuvres. At 5:30, her boyfriend Frank calls and asks Jane to drive him to work. Jane cannot say no, and wants to drop everything so she can drive Frank to work. She seems to have completely forgotten about her promise to help prepare for the party and insists that her mother lend her the family car. Her mother's priority is to have the hors d'oeuvres ready when the guests arrive. How do you resolve this dilemma? Whose priority is more important? If her mother says no to the use of the car and demands that Jane finish the hors d'oeuvres before she drives Frank to work, or presumes that Jane understands the importance of her priorities, she is on the road to a major confrontation. Jane is unable to say no to Frank's request for fear that he will break up with her if she does. Although her mother may not interpret the situation this way, this is how Jane views it. Jane is now emotionally dysregulated.

Jane's mother would be wise to accept and validate that Jane's priority has changed and that Jane feels she must meet Frank's demand. She then needs to explain her own priority in a nonthreatening, noncritical, nonjudgmental, and compassionate manner. A negotiation has to occur so that each participant can achieve her goal and "save face." To achieve a balance between priorities and demands, her mother could say, "Wow, I can see that you don't want to disappoint Frank and how much it means to you to drive him to work right now. At the same time the dishes aren't done and the hors d'oeuvres need to be prepared before the guests arrive. How do you think we can solve this problem?" Jane can only think of solving the problem by running out the door; however, she needs her mother's car. Jane is in an emotional state, taken over by the urgency of her impulse to do what Frank asked, and she cannot comprehend her mother's demand. If her mother refuses to give her the car, Jane would interpret this as a sign that her mother does not care about her and is trying to control her.

As long as Jane's mother does not personalize and get dysregulated herself, this situation can become an opportunity for her to teach Jane how to compromise, to practice willingness, and to negotiate agreements that reflect inclusion of each person's point of view. Because Jane does not know how to solve the problem, her mother suggests a compromise. If Jane puts the dishes in the dishwasher before she leaves, her mother will clean up and start the hors d'oeuvres. She asks Jane to be back by 6:30 so as to finish the hors d'oeuvres. She then asks Jane to do the cleaning up after the party in return for her mother doing the extra work before the party begins. Jane agrees to this compromise and is grateful that her mother understands. Although her mother did not get 100% of what she wanted, she asked for 50%, settled for 25%, and averted a scene. Her nonjudgmental acceptance of the situation gave her the opportunity to model negotiation of priorities and demands.

Begin clarifying the differences between your priorities and your loved one's, your demands and her's, by discussing and defining goals. You can ask, "What are your priorities in this situation? How does doing ___ get you to your goal?" Repeat this statement as often as necessary. If this message sounds like a broken record to you, you are correct. Repetition is an effective technique for teaching and reinforcing new behaviors. How often do you play a piece of music on the piano before it sounds like what the composer had in mind? How often did you hold a cup for your baby before she was able to drink on her own?

DEFINING YOUR OWN PRIORITIES

Balancing priorities and demands means you yourself also need to be acutely aware of your own priorities and demands. Ask yourself, "Are the behaviors I am concerned with life-threatening, therapy-interfering, relationship-interfering, or family-interfering behaviors?" Are you focusing on issues that are about control, that matter to *you* and that will make *you* feel less anxious—and that are not really about her? Are these issues equally important to her? Does she have the actual capability or skills to do what you are asking, or to make the changes you would like her to make right now? Who is bothered by laundry that is not folded, you or your loved one? For her, it is hard to figure out why what you are demanding is so important to you when it is so unimportant to her. Are you more concerned with being right than being effective? Is it more important that she come home at the time you set or that she not engage in dangerous behaviors while she is out? What is your priority

> Ask yourself, "Are the behaviors I am concerned with life-threatening, therapy-interfering, relationship-interfering, or family-interfering behaviors?" Are you focusing on issues that are about control, that matter to you and that will make you feel less anxious—and that are not really about her?

in each situation? What is more important, limiting the time spent on the computer or recognizing that she has no friends and spends all her time alone? What is your priority in these situations? How will redefining your own priorities change your behavior?

Communicate your priorities and demands clearly in a gentle way while validating and respecting your loved one's priorities. Explaining your priorities and demands, and discussing those of your loved one, will help bring structure to your environment and eliminate chaos. Your relationship will improve.

DEVELOPING REALISTIC EXPECTATIONS

It is also important to have realistic expectations of what your loved one can do, expectations that are based on her abilities and not your own priorities or preferences. This means you will probably have to change your own priorities with respect to your loved one. You must learn to accept what she is capable of doing, and not be disappointed when she does not meet with your idea of "success." Instead of being disappointed that she is dating a pizza delivery man, be happy that someone is interested in her.

Like the ocean, people are always changing. People interpret experiences differently and do not respond the same way all the time; however, your loved one with BPD is generally inflexible and has the unrealistic expectation that you will respond the same way all of the time—the way he wants—and will get upset when you do not. He has difficulty picking up cues from others that might help him anticipate responses, and has a naïve view of what others can and cannot do. Often he overestimates or underestimates people and frequently ends up feeling disappointed or rejected. When you are overestimating the abilities of others, you are apt to underestimate your own abilities.

It is a mistake to demand too much change too quickly. Remember, change occurs in baby steps. We crawl before we learn to walk, we walk before we can run. Time is required for the tiny changes that go into shaping new behavior so that change can occur. This is a process. Do not target behavior for change that is too big or too all-encompassing; make sure your expectations are realistic. Change should not be thought of as major life decisions such as returning to school or getting a job, but can be simple things such as putting socks in the hamper when you want the room cleaned, writing a resume as a start to searching for a job, taking one course when you want to return to school. Change is being sure you have filled the gas tank instead of running out of gas on the road. Change is paying a bill, returning a call, or showing up for an appointment on time. Conversely, if you place too few demands on a person with BPD, it can be interpreted as a sign that you think he is incompetent. If you do not ask for any change or up the ante, what will motivate your loved one to change?

Balancing Wants and Shoulds

"Wants" are things we do because we want to do them. They give us pleasure, we feel like doing them. "Shoulds" are things we do because we ought to do them or we have to do them. Your loved one will feel out of balance, unhappy, angry, and resentful if she never does anything she really wants to do and is always doing things she should do. Conversely, if all she ever does is what she wants to do, and she is never doing what she should do, she is living without a sense of responsibility or accomplishment. For harmony, a balance must be attained between wants and shoulds.

Your loved one also has trouble distinguishing between wants and shoulds. You can help make this distinction by consistently pointing out the difference between wants and shoulds in a nonjudgmental way. "I know Cindy invited you to go to the movies; at the same time you said earlier that you had no clean clothes to wear to your job interview tomorrow. If you go to the movies tonight instead of doing laundry, how will that help you to have clean clothes tomorrow?" Be persistent. Repeat questions like these over and over again.

Building Mastery

It is very difficult to go through life when your core belief about yourself is that you are incompetent and do not count. When you have no sense of your own value, you are like a leaf in the wind, dependent on what others think of you to know who you are. In order to attain a better quality of life, it is imperative that your loved one develop a sense of mastery, competency, and respect for himself.

Beth asks her mother the very same question every day, "Am I a good person?" Needing to ask someone else every day if you are a good person and being unable to answer this question for yourself is a very sad commentary on how Beth sees herself. Her daily question speaks to the essential lack of self-worth that characterizes so many people with BPD. How does Beth's mother feel when her daughter asks her this question? A good response would be to validate the difficulty of the question and to cheerlead by reminding Beth of past accomplishments. Beth's mother responds by saying, "It must feel so bad to wonder if you are a good person. Remember when you volunteered at the animal shelter? Doesn't that seem like something a good person does?" "I'll never pass that test. I'm a loser." "That must feel awful. However, didn't you win the math prize last semester? You can do hard things."

Asking for What You Want

Being effective in relationships encompasses getting what you want or changing what you do not want. Keeping and improving your relationships is important, but it is equally important to do so while still respecting and liking yourself, and getting your needs met. Because this is such a quagmire for people with BPD, DBT teaches a skill in mnemonic form that details how to ask for what you want while maintaining self-respect and keeping the relationship. This is DEAR MAN (see below), an Interpersonal Effectiveness skill developed by Gordon Bower and Marsha Linehan.

Families, too, will benefit from a structured way of asking for what they want. DEAR CCC (which stands for Describe, Express, Assert, Reinforce, Concentrate, have Confidence, Compromise) is a mnemonic exercise used in TARA's DBT family skills workshops to describe and define family goals and to get what you, as a family member, want. When family members can communicate clearly what they are actually asking for and help the other person understand what they want in a nonjudgmental way, people with BPD will be better able to handle difficult situations, improve communication, and decrease confusion, misinterpretation, and ambiguity.

DEAR CCC will help your loved one to seriously consider what you are asking for. When you and your loved one are both familiar with DEAR CCC, you can simply say, "I am stressed about this situation and would like to do a DEAR CCC with you." If your loved one is in DBT, she will refer to this as DEAR MAN (Mindful, Appear confident, Negotiate). Either way, you have a clearly defined strategy that allows both of you to know what to expect from the discussion. The structure of the technique allows both people to feel safe when they try to explain themselves, instead of smoldering with hidden resentments that are often expressed as sarcasm, anger, or willfulness. Most important, DEAR CCC levels the playing field. This exercise allows you to prepare what you are going to say in advance; you can even write it out, like a script. You can practice making your request and have the opportunity to have a contingency plan waiting in the wings as you think of the possible ways your loved one might respond, especially how you will respond if she says no or disagrees. Mastery of DEAR CCC decreases stressful episodes by helping avoid potential emotional triggers; it will guide you toward removing potential judgment, blame, and criticism from whatever you are trying to say. DEAR CCC gives both parties the opportunity to practice compromising and finding solutions to problems by negotiation, thereby learning to give to get. It models how to shift from an inflexible, rigid position to a more fluid position without "losing face."

Mastery of DEAR CCC decreases stressful episodes by helping avoid potential emotional triggers; it will guide you toward removing potential judgment, blame, and criticism from whatever you are trying to say.

This technique can be used in myriad situations and relationships. TARA families have worked through many relationship dilemmas successfully with DEAR CCC, so much so that they have incorporated this skill into their day-to-day family vocabulary. Implementing DEAR CCC is part of weaving your own DBT tapestry, and can be done verbally or in written form.

Describe
Express
Assert
Reinforce
Concentrate
Confidence
Compromise

Describe. First, describe the situation as if you were a detective writing a police report. State the facts as you see them. Try to be as objective as you can. Do not make judgments or give opinions, explanations, or interpretations. Be brief and specific without explaining everything in minute detail. The more you talk about the situation, the greater the chances that you will go off track. Avoid comparative statements such as "this was the worst, the best, the ugliest, the coolest." Because your loved one cannot read your mind, explain exactly what you are reacting to in the current situation without embellishment, without blaming anyone for anything, without apologizing, bringing up the past, or anticipating the future. Stick to the specific facts of the present situation. The Describe skill is a very effective way to teach your loved one how to move away from his tendency to personalize experiences, use hyperbolic language or dramatic emotional descriptions.

> MOTHER to DAUGHTER: When I came home from work there were dirty dishes on the counter.
> EMPLOYEE to BOSS: I have been working in this position for over a year and have learned all aspects of the job.
> CUSTOMER to WAITER: My steak is not properly cooked.

Express. Whereas Describe sticks to the facts, Express conveys what you feel and believe about a situation. Since most people are not adept at mind reading, you can safely assume that your feelings are not self-evident. By clearly communicating what you are feeling to your loved one, you decrease the potential ambiguity arising from misinterpretations. To Express, give a brief explanation of what you feel or believe about the situation. Use phrases such as I want, or I don't want. Avoid using the following words or phrases as they will decrease the likelihood that you will get what you want, "You should," as this tends to make others feel guilty or as though you are telling them what to do; "I need," which can be interpreted as demanding rather than as expressing; and "I can't," which can be interpreted as a demand that others do something for you. Try not to use these expressions.

> MOTHER to DAUGHTER: When there are dirty dishes in the sink and on the counter, I feel frustrated and disrespected. It makes me feel that my cooking dinner is not appreciated.

EMPLOYEE to BOSS: I enjoy working here and feel frustrated because I am not advancing or being challenged to accomplish more, or to learn new aspects of the job.

CUSTOMER to WAITER: I really like this restaurant and look forward to coming here. I want to enjoy my meal here. I am disappointed that I cannot eat this dinner because of the way this steak has been prepared.

Assert. This is where you ask for what you want clearly and specifically. Say no so that there is no doubt whatsoever that you mean no. This does not mean that you have to be nasty. Unless you spell out exactly what you do or do not want, it will not be evident to the other person. Be direct. Just as you cannot read someone else's mind, understand that others cannot read your mind. It can be hard to express what you want in a clear and direct manner. While someone is struggling to communicate with you, he is not taking into account that it is just as hard for you to ask for what you want. When you are reluctant to ask directly for what you want, an ambivalent undertone seeps into your request. Your loved one senses your double or mixed message and will misattribute it as due to something he did or did not do.

MOTHER to DAUGHTER: I want the kitchen cleaned up before I get home so I can start dinner.

EMPLOYEE to BOSS: I would like a salary increase and a promotion to the next level.

CUSTOMER to WAITER: I would like you to bring me another steak, cooked the way I originally ordered it.

Reinforce. Give your loved one a good reason for giving you what you want. Tell her the benefits she will receive and positive consequences that will result from your getting what you want or need. Help her to feel good in advance for doing or accepting what you want. Reward her afterward. You can also discuss how unpleasant it will be if you do not get what you want or need (demonstrating negative consequences). Pay attention to your voice tone. Keep it calm. You do not have to be angry or sarcastic to assert yourself or reinforce what you want. You have a right to ask for what you want or to say no to what you do not want. Saying no or denying a request does not make you a bad parent or a bad spouse.

MOTHER to DAUGHTER: If the kitchen is clean when I get home, I can get dinner ready earlier and we can have more time to spend talking and planning what we will do at the mall tomorrow.

EMPLOYEE to BOSS: From my job history you can see that I am a fast learner and a hard worker. If you give me a raise and a promotion, I will work even harder for the company. Since I already am familiar with so many aspects of the job, I can learn the new job quickly and save you money. I would like an increase in salary and a promotion to the next level.

CUSTOMER to WAITER: I have had good food and service many times at this restaurant. If I continue to be a satisfied customer, I will look forward to returning and will bring my friends.

Concentrate. Stay on track. Do not allow yourself to be distracted from your objective by how the other person responds. Ignore attempts to divert you from your request. Become a "broken record." Repeat your request as many times as you have to until the other person realizes you are serious. Express your opinion over and over and over again. Ignore attacks, diversions, and distractions. Think of attempts to divert you as if they were a smoke screen, a fog, or a scrim placed across a stage set to obscure your sight. Your objective is beyond the smoke, fog, or scrim. You can only get to your objective by ignoring her responses and continuing on, staying focused, and concentrating on your objective. If you respond to attacks, succumb to threats, allow yourself to be distracted or the subject to be changed, you will have taken a detour from your objective and will not get to your goal. Stay on the main highway, avoid being forced onto the service road. Be relentless, like a train on a track. Keep making your point in a gentle, kindly, nonjudgmental manner without anger or aggression.

MOTHER to DAUGHTER: I realize you got home late from school; however, I cannot cook dinner unless the kitchen is clean.

EMPLOYEE to BOSS: I know business is slow but I would like to stay at this job and am asking you to consider my request.

CUSTOMER to WAITER: I can see that you are very rushed and the kitchen is busy; even so, I cannot eat the steak this way. I want a new dinner.

Confidence. Try to appear effective and confident, even if you have to fake it until you make it. You are practicing a new behavior and probably are not used to communicating this way. Do not capitulate to your loved one's demands or priorities. Above all, do not whine, whisper, or whinge. Apologizing for what you are asking for, hemming and hawing, faltering or groveling are all ineffective. Being sarcastic, attacking, or yelling at the other person, blaming or criticizing him will only get you to a dead-end. Pay attention to your voice tone, look him in the eye, and speak in a determined voice. It is not necessary to yell. Practice in front of a mirror or with a friend. Try to tolerate your own distress and fear and then go full steam ahead. By acting in a nonthreatening and validating manner you can make the other person feel good about giving you what you want.

Compromise. Be flexible. When you sense you are not getting what you want, come up with alternative suggestions for solving the problem (consider preparing these ahead of time so you have them ready, just in case). Be creative. Ask yourself, would you rather be right or effective? Is winning the important thing or is it getting as close as possible to your goal? Demonstrate that you are not trying to control the situation. Allow the other person to save face by asking him for his ideas and alternative solutions he would be comfortable with to solve the problem. Do not demand total capitulation. Be willing to give to get.[3] Compromising means you will settle for less than you originally requested. Maintain "no" but offer something else or some other way to solve the problem. Focus on what will work. The goal of the Olympic competitors is to win a gold medal, but this is not the Olympics. The goal of family members implementing these skills at home is to arrive at "gray" solutions that are a synthesis of your request and the other person's ability to meet your request. You will have achieved a greater victory in the long run by negotiating a solution than by winning in the short run. Throw the ball to your loved one by getting him to participate in the problem solving. Try, "I cannot agree and you seem to really want me to; what can we do about this? How do you think we can solve this problem? What should we do?"

> You will have achieved a greater victory in the long run by negotiating a solution than by winning in the short run.

---

[3] Linehan, 1993b.

MOTHER to DAUGHTER: While you are studying for finals,
I am willing to clean up the kitchen. However, once finals
are over, I want the kitchen cleaned up by the time
I get home.
EMPLOYEE to BOSS: I am willing to wait for a raise for
6 weeks if you give me a promotion. This will give you
the opportunity to see how well I do in the new position.
CUSTOMER to WAITER: If you cannot give me a new steak,
I would like a reduction on my bill.

Compromise, or negotiation, is an important part of any relationship. We do not always want the same things. This skill needs to be learned by people with BPD and their family members so that normal negotiations are not seen as power struggles. Negotiation does not have to be a competition, or a war of the wills; however, if your loved one does not accept this, it will be impossible to get through the next 5 minutes.

Implementing DEAR CCC gives a person with BPD the opportunity to focus on what is being asked of him without letting his intense emotions divert him from the situation at hand. While your loved one needs to learn how to be more rational and logical in his thinking, family members in general need to be less cold, clinical, judgmental, reductive, rational, analytical, logical, deductive, rule-oriented, and rigid when they ask for what they want. In simply describing a situation, there is a dialectic dilemma of opposite points of view that need to be synthesized to achieve balance. Add an emotional perspective to your description such as, "When this happens, I feel . . ." while still being objective. This will put you on the road toward wise mind (see Chapter 6) and improve your relationship. By looking at a situation from your loved one's emotional perspective and trying to intuit her emotional message, by reading the subtitles, you will become more effective

Here is an example of a DEAR CCC in action.

Ben worked for a small music company owned by three young men. He was one of their original employees. His responsibilities had increased over the years, as had his salary. However, Ben was also a musician and found he had less and less time to work on his own music because of the time and stress involved with doing his job. He knew he had to change something but found it daunting to approach all three of his bosses at once. He decided to do a DEAR CCC. His goal was to get a day off each week so that he could work on his own music. Here is script for his DEAR CCC.

Describe: I have been working here for 3 years. I work 5 days a week, from 10 A.M. to 6 P.M. or later. When I get home I am so tired and stressed that I cannot work on my own music.

Express: I really am dedicated to the growth of this company and support all of your efforts. However, I have been studying music since I was 4 years old. I went to music schools and studied the piano and flute. Creating music is the most important thing in my life; it is my gift. I am a musician. If I do not create music, I am not happy. If I have no time to work on my music, I am unhappy and frustrated and therefore my performance at work suffers.

Assert: I am asking you for Fridays off because I need time to do my own music.

Reinforce: If I have some time to do my own music I will do a better job at work, be more efficient and nicer to the customers. If I am happier, if I am not stressed, I will be a more effective employee. Having some time to work on my own music will make me happier. I am asking you for Fridays off.

Concentrate: I realize this idea may seem out of the ordinary. However, I know that Fridays are the least busy day of the week. I will be a happier employee if I have some time to make my music and that will benefit the company.

Confident: I know I can get my work done in the four days and I will be available to come in to work if we are very busy on a Friday. I will make sure that this will not affect how orders are filled.

Compromise: I can see that you are concerned that I will not get all my work done. I realize that this may create difficulties for the company so I am willing to put in extra hours on the four days I do work to make up for the hours I am off on Friday. Or, I can work one half-day every other Friday. We can try this out for one month and then reevaluate the plan. What do you think?

Ben used a pleasant voice tone and was not sarcastic. He did not beg or get angry, and surprised himself by accomplishing his goal. He got Fridays off!

How you ask for what you want will often determine whether or not you succeed. Validate the other person before you make your request. Try to be kind, interested, and considerate of the other person. If you attack, demand, or generally make someone feel uncomfortable, why would he want to do anything for you? If you ask for something while gritting your teeth, hunching up your shoulders, clenching your fists, scowling or grimacing, by being verbally abusive and overly aggressive, or by employing physically menacing gestures like pointing fingers or raising your hands, you will not get what you want. Conversely, stand up for yourself. Do not apologize for things out of your control. Do not cower or grovel. Be forthright in expressing anger. "I get angry when you erase or read my e-mail messages. I am asking you not to do that again." Do not censure anger but express it directly in a calm, nonjudgmental manner. Do not threaten ("If you do not do this, you will be sorry"). Do not blackmail the person to get what you want ("If you do not do this I will never give you money to go to school"). Do not use manipulative statements ("If you were a good person, you would do this"). Do not make unrealistic promises, especially ones you cannot keep. Do not judge. Do not use "should" or "should not." Smile. Try a little humor. It is okay to be funny.

Imagine in advance how you might feel if this request were made of you. Before you do a DEAR CCC, anticipate reactions to your request, practice your responses, and rehearse what you will say if you ask for something and think the answer might not be what you want. Prepare yourself for success or disappointment. Even if the discussion gets painful, try not to avoid, capitulate, or personalize. Above all, keep focused. If your body is tense and you feel really upset, you can say, "I cannot keep talking about this now. How about continuing this discussion later on?" Be compassionate toward yourself and the other person. Allow time for trust to develop and face to be saved. Be patient.

Emotion Regulation Skills

Most stabile and competent adults can generally control their emotions. People with BPD cannot. Wherever they go, they carry the invisible stone of their emotional pain. They are exquisitely sensitive, hypervigilant, and intensely reactive. Their emotions take a long while to settle down. Not knowing how to regulate their own painful, aversive feelings, such as shame and anger, makes people with BPD walking powder kegs. Because of their deficits, they tend to regulate emotional pain with actions that bring quick, short-term relief, such as cutting themselves (parasuicidal acts) using drugs or alcohol, shopping or overspending, binge eating, anorexia, gambling, or engaging in unsafe sex. The consequence of these behaviors is usually more emotional pain. Alternatively, they may cope by avoiding or dissociating from the trigger or the actual emotion they are feeling. Some people with BPD may have developed too much control of their emotional responses. They may be described as emotionally over-controlled or emotionally constipated.

How do you regulate your own emotional responses? You probably do not have the same difficulty with emotional control or with identifying your own and others' emotions as your loved one does. In the past this may have caused you to become impatient, judgmental, intolerant, and disapproving of her inability to do what seems so easy for you. Remember, you do not have the same underlying neurobiology as your loved one; you have a biological advantage. Her emotional control is impaired by her neurobiological makeup, so that the two of you are not on a level playing field. Neutral situations are interpreted negatively by those with BPD, and ambiguous situations are so confusing that daily life is like walking through a minefield of potential emotional triggers. The Emotion Regulation Skills of DBT teach people how to cope with and regulate their intense emotional responses. Although this is difficult to accomplish, it can be done.

> Remember, you do not have the same underlying neurobiology as your loved one; you have a biological advantage.

Each of us expresses our emotions in our own way, so there may often be a mismatch between the way two people express their emotions and react to the same situation. You may not be aware of how you express your own emotions or the effect this has on your loved one. You may be the kind of person who remains calm, rarely raises your voice, and has a face that may not reflect the emotion you are feeling. You may have so much emotional control that you are almost emotionally inexpressive maybe you are one of those people who has to take a taxi to his emotions in order to be more expressive. Your loved one, on the other hand, may respond with emotional intensity and may not be able to control his emotional responses. Or maybe you are an overly expressive family member. If so, you must temper your reactions so as to be more in harmony with the level of your loved one's reactional style.

How can you find a synthesis of your opposite reaction styles, mirroring your loved one's style? Family members must learn to be constantly aware of their loved one's emotional state and when it is becoming dysregulated. You cannot change your loved one's emotional reactions; instead, you can help him to be more aware of when a dysregulation has occurred. Point it out: "Wow, you seem upset. What happened?" This will help him identify his own emotions. You must always pay attention to the reaction of the other person. Observe him, being particularly aware of any sign that he may feel unheard. The emotional volatility is almost certainly less about the actual incident than it is about not being heard. Your job is not to regulate your loved one's emotions for him but to promote his awareness of his own emotional states.

For people with BPD, emotions seem to be a mysterious part of life that just happens to them, something over which they have very little control. They are also not always aware of their own bodies' reactions to what is happening to them, and how this in turn impacts their emotional states. They are unaware that physical cues can give them information about their feelings. Somehow, they have not made the connection between the emotions they are feeling and their own body sensations, such as muscle tension, racing heartbeat, shortness of breath, sweating, chills, or stomach tightness; or, more positively, feeling calm and relaxed.

Physical or environmental stressors can also make people more vulnerable to their emotions. You and your loved one must both learn to connect the effect of illnesses and bodily changes, such as a cold, an infection, a toothache, menstrual cycles or menopause, to the ability to cope with stress. You must also learn the effects of mood-altering drugs or alcohol on your coping ability, and try not to use them. By paying attention to your body, making sure you get enough sleep, eating a balanced diet, avoiding nicotine and too much caffeine and sugar, including exercise in your daily life, avoiding overscheduling and overdoing activities, you can reduce your physical stressors. Practicing these skills builds mastery over emotional responses. These are the goals to work toward in all your interactions with your loved one.

Avoid Potentially Triggering Situations

You have probably observed that your loved one puts himself in stressful situations that trigger intense emotional responses. Avoiding situations or people that cue these negative emotional responses can be a way to help control emotions until more skillful methods of handling the situation are developed. The downside of avoiding cues or triggers is that it may reinforce already avoidant tendencies, or lead to trying to control people and situations that might set off emotional reactions. You can help your loved one find a balance between avoidance of potentially triggering situations and acceptance that some situations will always be challenging with phrases and questions such as, "How do you feel when you are around Susie? Does that happen all the time when you are with her? What do you think you can do about it?"

Cede Control

If your loved one interprets what you say or do as a demand, or if what you have said is perceived as your telling her what to do, you are sure to get a response ranging from a simple negative to a volatile eruption. The phrase, "You're trying to control me," is probably something you have heard countless times. If you could not regulate your own emotions, or never knew what you were feeling or when your feelings might change, you too might feel out of control. Arbitrary rules and boundaries are generally ineffective with people with BPD because they are also perceived as your efforts to control her. Little wonder that control issues are a major component of BPD relationships. Any demand you make will probably be resisted because she interprets capitulating to your "demands" as the equivalent to ceding control of herself and being engulfed by you. This becomes further proof of her incompetence. To underscore your respect for her need of a sense of control in every situation, be sure that any request or suggestion you make includes some variety of the phrase, "it is your choice."

Regroup with Mini-Respites

Sometimes, in the moment, you or your loved one may be too stressed to find a creative solution to a problem or too worn-out to implement a solution. This may be a good time for a mini-respite, a planned timeout to regroup. A quick change of scene or removal from the center stage of a crisis can give you a new perspective and increase your ability to cope with your own or your loved one's emotions. A mini-respite can mean doing something pleasurable for yourself, such as going to your favorite café for a special coffee or buying yourself flowers, a scented candle, or a fragrant bar of soap. It can be visiting a museum exhibition, going to a ballgame, or taking time out to watch the sunset. What qualifies these actions as mini-respites is that you are choosing to take this break and have planned the activity specifically to soothe yourself. It is important that you not avoid situations or run away from crises by calling it a mini-respite. A mini-respite is your choice. You are taking a break, a DBT vacation, and you are the one in charge or in control of your break.

Anticipating a pleasurable event that you brought about yourself as the result of changes you made in your own life is reinforcing and can be a motivator for more positive changes. If you are under siege as a consequence of the behaviors of your loved one with BPD, try to find something pleasurable, even if it is only a small thing, to do for yourself each day. By having compassion for yourself and being mindfully aware of yourself, you will achieve more balance and stress relief than you would by going to an expensive spa for a weekend while ruminating about negative events.

People with BPD do not realize that it can sometimes be more effective to wait before reacting to a situation. Making a statement such as "I am really upset right now and would like to take a break and continue this conversation later on or tomorrow" is not in their conversational repertoire. Describe to him how you sometimes take mini-respites to feel better when you are having a difficult day, when you are presented with a problem you cannot solve in the moment, or when you just feel flooded and stressed. Although taking these mini breaks may seem obvious to you, remind yourself that the obvious is not always obvious to your loved one. By modeling how you regulate your emotions in your daily life, you are teaching your loved one a more effective way to regulate his own emotions. However, his tendency to use avoidance as a coping strategy means you must be wary that suggestions to take a DBT vacation does not become a new way to skip facing problems, or that he interprets a DBT vacation as your approval of avoidance as a mean of solving problems.

Do the Opposite

Acting opposite[4] is a DBT skill in the emotion regulation module that teaches a person to do things that are contrary to what he feels in the moment. The purpose of "opposite actions" is not to avoid what you are feeling but to expose yourself to the feelings you are afraid of and to practice doing what you are afraid of doing. Instead of running away when they feel frightened, people with BPD are taught to approach their fear (unless there is imminent danger). If they are feeling guilty or ashamed and the emotion is justified, instead of avoiding, they are taught to try to repair the relationship by making amends and apologizing. If your daughter failed to show up for an appointment, she needs to call the person herself, explain, and apologize—rather than avoiding the person. The longer she waits, the more difficult the situation becomes.

> "Courage is doing what you're afraid to do. There can be no courage unless you are scared."
> —Eddie Rickenbacker

Having the courage to act opposite of how she is feeling will diminish the time your loved one spends ruminating and beating herself up with "if only's" and "what if's." If you are depressed and sad, try to do something active, such as going for a run, working out at the gym, riding a bike, or cleaning your house. The hardest opposite action to do is acting opposite to feeling angry.[5] This is very hard to do because it is counterintuitive. Angry feelings can lead to confronting, approaching, or fighting. If your loved one is angry at someone, she would usually try to stay away from that person and to resist ruminating over him or the situation. Instead, when you are angry, try to allow yourself to feel compassion for the person you are angry, act opposite to what you are feeling, with by putting yourself in his place, seeing the situation from his point of view, and imagining how it must feel to be him.

Your facial expressions can trigger emotions. If you put an angry scowl on your face, you will soon feel angry. Model this skill for your family member. Try a half smile instead of a frown so that you

---

[4] Linehan, 1993a, b; Dalai Lama and Daniel Goleman, 2003.
[5] Linehan, 1993b.

allow compassion to show on your face. Practicing opposite actions is as useful for family members as it is for a person with BPD as it can decrease intense emotional reactions and give budding relationships a chance to bloom. The Emotion Regulation skills taught to people with BPD can be equally effective when adopted by family members who are having difficulty coping with the BPD emotional roller coaster ride they are living on.

Learn to Respect Negative Emotions

Negative emotions are not pleasant, of course, but this does not mean that we should always try to cover them up, reverse them, or deny them. Do not focus on changing negative emotions by trying to make your loved one feel better immediately. Negative emotions are a part of life and your loved one must learn to tolerate them. People with BPD need to accept that they can survive painful emotions. Remind your love one to be a DBT surfer by "riding the wave" of painful feelings.[6]

Try not to ignore or disregard negative emotions by telling your loved one that "She need not feel that way." Telling someone that she does not feel what she is feeling is extremely invalidating. When someone feels something, that is what she is feeling; it has nothing to do with you or your feelings. Likewise, do not encourage your loved one to deny or avoid her pain. The more a person tries to deny or avoid pain, the more pain and suffering she will experience

For a highly reactive and sensitive person, the ability to cope effectively with daily problems and responses does not depend on willpower. Solving problems and tolerating distress requires skill power, knowledge of skillful means to solve problems. Willpower is a revved up car engine, running and ready to go. However, it takes the skill power of the steering wheel to get you where you want to go.

"It's not that some people have willpower and some don't, it's that some people are ready to change and others are not."
—James Gordon, MD

Negative emotions are a part of life. They need to be felt, tolerated, and overcome. They cannot be wished away, ordered away, ignored, denied, trivialized, or changed in an instant.

---

[6] Linehan, 1993b.

Encourage your loved one to feel his emotion, even if they are negative. How can he cope with his feelings if he does not know what he is feeling and is too scared to find out?

Distress Tolerance Skills

The Distress Tolerance skills of DBT teach a person how to survive or do well in a difficult situation without making it worse. Sometimes you have no choice but to tolerate and accept unpleasant situations, as they are, in the moment. They cannot always be changed. Even if a person has mastered all the emotion regulation skills, there will still be times when he will experience some type of emotional or physical distress. Sooner or later, we will all experience loss, death, rejection, or failure. Everyone has a bad day, an unpleasant experience, a frustrating time at work, a disagreement with a friend, or an argument with a partner. If you want to run for public office, you have to accept the possibility of losing. If you want to have a baby, you will have to accept the pain of childbirth. The Brady Bunch is a fictional family—nobody's life is that perfect. The best we can do, in the moment, is to try to bear the pain skillfully. What do you do when you miss your train, cannot get a ticket to a performance you want to see, are jilted by your boyfriend, lose money in the stock market, or learn your building is being demolished and you have to move?

It is not what happens to you that matters most; it is how you deal with it.

Maturity is realizing that certain situations are very painful and that there is no alternative but to bear that pain. Most people have probably figured out ways to tolerate daily stresses, as the ability to cope with distress or distract themselves is most likely intuitive for them. Unfortunately, this ability is often lacking in people with BPD so that they will often respond to stress in ways that make matters worse. Temper tantrums and demanding behaviors are not effective means of dealing with a difficult situation. The theater is full, the money is lost, the building will be torn down, and the boyfriend is gone. A suicide attempt may get him back temporarily but, in the long run, this strategy will fail. All she has managed to do is to harm herself.

Change can be painful at first, and the pain must be tolerated if we are to accomplish long-term progress. TARA family class participants are asked to wear their watches on their opposite wrists for the duration of the class (see Chapter 3). This simple act demonstrates how difficult it is for most people to tolerate the distress of change. Without the ability to do so, a person with BPD cannot do better. DBT teaches skills for distress tolerance.

What do you do to relax, to cope with your problems, or to feel better when you are stressed? This question may seem simplistic to you until you realize that your loved one cannot answer this question in quite the same way that you do. Family members describe a broad range of activities they engage in to feel better, ranging from going for a walk, swimming, riding a bicycle or going to the gym, reading, listening to music, lying down in a darkened room with a scented candle, getting a massage, or going to yoga class. Others may call a friend. People with BPD do not have an internal repertoire of activities to pursue when they are stressed, therefore they will usually do something impulsive or destructive instead. They choose behaviors that bring short-term relief but that are often accompanied by long-term, negative consequences. This should not come as a surprise to you based on your experience interacting with your loved one and your understanding of the underlying biology of BPD. You certainly know he lacks distress tolerance skills. Although family members generally have highly evolved strategies for coping with distress, over time, constant fear, anguish, and perpetual concern seems to diminish the families' capacity to tolerate distress. The daily strain of coping with a loved one with BPD seems to burn out their resilience in the face of stress.

Learning DBT skills teaches you to accept that your loved one lacks the essential ability to tolerate distress, which is integral to accepting life, as it is, in the moment and being able to endure and survive life's crises. Recognizing this skill deficit in your loved one will help you to guide your loved one in new ways to cope with distress and painful emotions. These skills will also help you to cope with the distress you yourself experience when you are faced with another crisis or emotional outburst. Distress tolerance skills are not meant to be a "cure," rather they are meant to help your loved one get through a difficult moment.

Find a Distraction

You may not always know what triggered an emotional response, but you can probably tell when a person's emotions have changed. How can you help change a response so that the emotional cascade that disrupts family harmony is reduced or avoided? First, validate the emotion you sense, then try distracting your loved one by trying to focus her attention on something else without trivializing her response. Distracting is a means of counteracting highly charged negative emotions by substituting different thoughts, images, and sensations. This can decrease negative emotions.

When you are trying to distract your loved one, be sure to do so nonjudgmentally while validating his feelings, or you will risk eliciting responses as "You are not paying any attention to me, you are ignoring me." Distract him by asking him to focus on something else for a moment. "I can only imagine how very sad you must feel about not being invited to Jane's party. I would feel the same way if a friend had not invited me to her party. I really want to talk to you about what happened; however, I have to cut these vegetables for dinner. Perhaps you can help me and then we can have a cup of tea and talk." Or, "I really want to focus on your problem but I have to cook dinner now. Perhaps if you read me the recipe I can get dinner cooked faster and then we will be able talk." By doing something else, changing activities, you are activating a different part of your loved one's brain, and the emotional response may begin to subside. Try statements like, "Can you help me slice the onion? Fix the television? Thread a needle? Clean the kitchen?" Or "Come to the mall with me," and so on. When you invalidate what your loved one is feeling in the moment saying, "It's not that bad, it's not as though Jane is your *best* friend," you will escalate his dysregulated emotions, provoking even more intense negative reactions.

Find a Soothing Activity

When you see your loved one in emotional distress, you can remind her of things she can do to feel better by encouraging activities that are self-soothing, such as listening to music, lighting a scented candle, making herself something special to eat, or going to a particularly favorite place, such as a lakeside or a park. The high sensitivity of people with BPD can make it difficult for them to soothe themselves. Often they could not be soothed as infants. They need to learn how to recruit their senses for self-soothing, to be kind and nurturing to themselves. When you see your loved one in pain, you may remind her of things she likes to do or can do for herself that involve her senses, such as taking a scented bath. Validate her distress and talk about what you do when you are stressed while gently suggesting soothing alternatives. She may or may not take your suggestion to try to soothe herself. Above all, do not tell her directly what to do.

Improve the Moment

Your loved one calls you, quite upset because someone may have criticized him at work, his ex-girlfriend appeared at an event with a new boyfriend, a friend rejected him, he was embarrassed because he was dressed inappropriately for a party, he had an argument with someone he is close to, or he has been fired from a job he really liked. How do you respond so that you can help him tolerate his negative emotions? If you can improve the moment so as to make the distress more tolerable, you may be able to avoid the usual meltdown. Validate the emotions you can identify. You can start by saying, "Wow," the mnemonic for *Wait, Observe, Wing it*, to gain a scintilla of time to collect yourself and think of what to say next. Then try the following strategies for improving the moment.

"The only pain one has to survive is 'just this moment.'"
—Marsha Linehan

Delay. Remind your loved one that, when he is very angry or distressed, it is okay to say, "I am too upset to discuss this situation right now," or "I am going to leave the room and take a walk. I need a break." It is probably difficult for you to realize that this is not an innate response for people with BPD, but something they need to learn to do. You are modeling that it is okay to leave the "war zone." Leaving the situation can decrease the negative emotional cues.

Ice. Intense physiological stimuli can change the emotional response a person is feeling the same way the body reacts to being doused in cold water or taking a cold shower. This is an example of what is known as the mammalian diving reflex. Whales, seals, and dolphins dive deeply into the ocean where the water is extremely cold. The icy water triggers their autonomic nervous systems, slowing down their hearts and breathing rates so that they can stay underwater for a longer time. In humans, the cold water serves to slow the heart and breathing rate and can distract and divert attention from whatever is being felt at that moment. Putting ice on your wrists or on the back of your neck, or putting your face into a bowl of ice is painful and distracting; however it decreases the emotions you are experiencing in the moment, thereby avoiding the need to turn to cutting or other harmful behaviors as a means of distress tolerance. This is almost counterintuitive, since you might expect your heart rate to go up from the shock of the cold water.

Calming breaths. The body and the mind are one, the body houses our stress. By changing how you physically respond to stress, you change how you feel. By relaxing your body, negative emotional responses decrease. Breathing deeply for a few minutes can bring down emotions and help focus and regulate them. This is why yoga classes and meditation, which make use of calming breathing techniques, can help people with BPD develop relaxation skills. Suggest taking a yoga or meditation class with your loved one.

Focusing on the present. A negative emotion evokes memories of similar negative feelings, ratcheting up the intensity of the current emotional response. Ruminating on past suffering or worrying about future suffering can sabotage your loved one's own good feelings in the present with "what if" laments and "if I do this, he will do that" dirges. If she has a boyfriend, she will worry about when he will leave rather than enjoying the time she has with him. She may feel that she does not deserve her wonderful job, and bring about getting herself fired. She cannot always see things as they are, in the moment. Be a positive reflection, help her focus on the positives in her life. Be a magnifying glass and show her all her competent and positive accomplishments. If your daughter thinks her boyfriend is going to leave her because he did not call, remind her of times when he did not call because he was sick, yet came by the next day with flowers. You can help your loved one by focusing on the present moment, encouraging her to breathe through her pain.

Marie called her mother, sobbing, after her boyfriend, Jim, broke their date for the evening. How can her mother help her to tolerate her distress and regulate her emotions?

MARIE: Jim broke our date for tonight. The same thing happened last year when Peter broke up with me. I will never have a boyfriend, I am a loser!

MOM: Wow, I can see you are feeling really stressed and upset. What happened between you?

MARIE: I can't keep a boyfriend, I'm just unlovable and a loser. Remember when Peter broke a date with me and then dumped me?

MOM: I can sense how hurt and scared you are because it might seem as if the same thing is happening again because Jim couldn't make tonight's date. However, Jim is not Peter. What happened with Peter was over a year ago. That was then, this is now. How about taking a few deep breaths with me and then telling me all about it.

MARIE (crying softly): Jim broke tonight's date.

MOM: Let's breathe together the way we did in yoga class. That always helps me to think more clearly. What do you think? (They take several deep cleansing breaths together.) Now, why did Jim break the date? What happened?

MARIE: His boss got a rush job and he has to work late tonight and then he has to study for his exams.

MOM: So, looks like he isn't like Peter at all. How can you find a way to get through tonight's disappointment? What can you do to feel better? How are you progressing with your college application essay?

MARIE: Thanks for reminding me. I guess I can finish my essay tonight. I'll call Jim back to see how his work is going and what time he is picking me up tomorrow.

Crisis averted.

Why Are DBT Skills So Difficult?

All of these techniques can be derailed—they are not always easy to implement. Here are some common reasons that efforts to solve problems, manage relationships, regulate emotions, and tolerate distress may fail.

Lack of skill. One of the principal reasons for being ineffective in solving relationship problems is not knowing what to do or not knowing how to solve the problems. This is an indication of skill deficits. If your loved one could not ice skate or drive a car, what would you do? The answer is the same when it comes to relationship problems—you must teach the appropriate skills. Your success in teaching these skills by modeling them for your loved one will depend on your ability to acknowledge what the problem is without attributing motives, blame, or interpretations to the behavior, and also on how sincere you can be.

Worry thoughts. Faulty beliefs and distortions can interfere with your loved one's capacity to solve problems and be effective. Being ineffective is saying, "I can't do it, I am stupid." Or, "it's all your fault." You can help counter worry thoughts and anxiety by untwisting the cognitive distortions, examining the evidence, offering alternative solutions to the problems, and asking for ideas on how to solve the problem.

Excessive emotions. People with BPD seem to be allergic to even a hint of perceived blame, criticism, and/or judgment; this will often trigger emotional dysregulation and lead to getting angry, anxious, frustrated, frightened, ashamed, or guilty. They seem to be conditioned to either blame themselves whenever they feel they are ineffective or blame those closest to them, resulting in intense emotional reactions. They will often attack you for voicing even a hint of what they feel is criticism. They need to learn to tolerate aversive feelings and radically accept that, moment by moment, we do not always get what we want.

Indecision about priorities. Your loved one does not know how to determine what the priority is in many situations. She can learn to determine how to decide on priorities by implementing decision-making techniques, such as pros and cons, wants and shoulds, cost-benefit analysis, and short-term advantages versus short-term disadvantages. You can help by saying, "What are the pros and cons for making this choice?" Many people with BPD try to avoid making decisions by doing nothing, but even that is a choice. The inability to make decisions or to determine priorities is a component of BPD and is not willful behavior designed to annoy you.

Environment. If you break your leg, you cannot run the marathon. If you have no place to live, it will be more difficult for you to get a job. If you live in the suburbs and do not have a car, you will have a hard time getting to therapy in the city. If it is raining, you cannot have a garden party. All of us are limited by the problems posed by our environments. No matter how skilful you may be, situations in the environment can interfere with your ability to solve problems. Sometimes the environment is simply impervious to even the most skilled person, such as the expert climber trying to reach the summit of Mount Everest during a blizzard. Michelle Kwan had to give up her chance at winning the Olympic gold medal for ice skating because she sustained an injury and could no longer compete.

When to intervene to change a situation within your loved one's environment and when not to is a very confusing issue for families. They usually fear that helping means enabling, or that they should be implementing "tough love." Should you pay for school, buy the car, or pay the rent? Unfortunately, there is no hard and fast rule to help you decide. You too can benefit from making a pros and cons list. Ask yourself, is the person trying to help herself? What are the consequences that will ensue if you do not help? Does she have the skills to accomplish this goal now, without your help? How does not helping her get her to her goal? Is she is really trying to change, is this an environmental problem, or is this the same old situation? Above all, be flexible and compassionate when you make your decision.

9

Mentalization

Understanding Misunderstandings

M ENTALIZATION-BASED THERAPY (MBT) IS A RELATIVELY NEW evidence-based treatment for borderline personality disorder developed in England by Anthony Bateman and Peter Fonagy. It incorporates elements of cognitive and psychodynamic therapy. It differs from Dialectical Behavior Therapy in that DBT focuses on how the person with BPD can learn to control her emotions and change her own behavior, while MBT focuses on understanding the misunderstandings that occur within relationships by changing how a person perceives interpersonal situations and experiences. MBT does this by fostering an understanding of what is going on in one's own mind and simultaneously in the mind of another person, in the moment, within the interaction. When you have the ability to understand how you are seen in the mind of another person you are *mentalizing*. Mentalizing is an interpersonal way of seeing daily life that requires awareness and acknowledgment of your response to the other person as well as how that person may be thinking, feeling, or reacting to you. When you are mentalizing you are exploring alternate interpretations and intentions from your point of view and the other person's point of view. When you are mentalizing, the past, the present, and the future are all connected.

Learning to mentalize gives families a new perspective on how people with BPD think, insightful methods of communicating that will develop and enhance trust, increase empathy and compassion, and tools for improving and repairing relationships, both in the immediate moment and in the long run. For family members, practicing mentalization techniques along with a DBT-based attitude of acceptance and change can improve relationships. These techniques can be prophylactic, so that you become more proactive and effective. Understanding mentalization and application of MBT techniques will help you to avoid the stressful interactions that have become the common denominator of your daily life and bring down highly volatile, emotional responses in the moment. As family members are generally on "BPD duty" 24 hours a day, applying MBT skills can make a major difference in improving family dynamics.

Making Sense of Ourselves and Others

The ability to make sense of or understand other people can be thought of as social intelligence. The evolution of man's emotional brain has given us the ability to interpret social cues and facial expressions, which has helped to ensure our survival as it allows us to collaborate and cooperate with others. Understanding how others react allows us to live and work together as a society.

At the same time, this ability does not necessarily come easily. One of the most complex problems all of us face is how to make sense of or understand other people as well as ourselves. People are quixotic and mercurial; their thoughts and feelings shift from moment to moment. What someone is saying out loud is not always what he may really want to say or a reflection of what he is actually thinking or feeling. People can hide what they feel and they can also lie. The better you are at reading people and yourself, the better your chances are at having successful relationships, and the greater your chances are of having a fulfilling life. Learning how to mentalize can help you because maintaining good relationships depends on successfully communicating with others.

You are mentalizing when you can imagine the mental states of another person, when you have a sense of shared understanding, a meeting of the minds. This vital component of communicating with others requires the ability to see the other person's perspective, to realize how another person may interpret a situation or experience while simultaneously being aware of your own perspective and interpretation of the same event. This is mentalizing.

"Mentalization is seeing and understanding yourself from the outside, as others see you, while simultaneously seeing and understanding others from the inside."
—Jeremy Holmes

When a person is mentalizing, he is seeing people and situations from alternate perspectives. There is no right or wrong—only different points of views or alternate perspectives on every situation. Because mentalizing embraces alternative views of or reactions to situations, it is nonjudgmental and enhances mutual understanding. Rather than focusing on insights into the patterns of relationships, contents or outcomes of situations, or the history of altercations, mentalization focuses on the process involved in being able to maintain thinking about one's self, another person, and the relationship, in the moment.

When you call your girlfriend, she is curt and cool to you. Your gut tells you that she is very angry with you; your relationship is on the rocks and seems to be falling apart. Slow down, reflect upon the situation, and mentalize by trying to imagine what your girlfriend is thinking and feeling. You realize that you failed to acknowledge her birthday. You were too busy to plan a special celebration for her, and birthdays do not matter to you. However, because you know your girlfriend so very well, you know birthdays are really important to her. Once you realize you have forgotten her birthday, you can use mentalization to understand how she feels and why she is being curt with you. You can apologize with sincerity and make amends.

The ability to mentalize other people and yourself can make misunderstandings much less mysterious and guide you toward knowing what has to be done to repair relationships. When you are able to use mentalization with your boss, for instance, you can intuit how he is thinking, and you will know the right time to ask for a raise and the strategy to use to effectively influence his decision. Likewise, when you can interpret your own feelings, explaining yourself to yourself, you will be able to convey this information to your partner and improve your chances of getting what you need from him or her. The ability to mentalize gives you intuitive insight into what is happening inside someone else. It is the process of making your own mind visible to yourself and to someone else while seeing and responding to what is going on in his mind.

Mentalization requires flexibility. Flexibility is needed to be spontaneous and to adapt to adversity or change, to be open to new experiences, to tolerate ambiguity and face life's challenges and stresses with courage. Flexibility develops when you can safely change your perceptions or mental representations of yourself and other people, which is a key attribute of mentalization.

Mentalizing is a process, a mental action that requires feeling and thinking about feeling, thinking about thinking, and having your mind and the mind of the other person in mind at the same time. Mentalization is a two-person psychology that helps people to decipher the social world around them. It can help demystify your own personal world and will help you understand what is happening when you connect to others.

Besides having an intellectual grasp of ourselves and others, we also have noncognitive, intuitive, and empathetic responses to social situations. We feel *and* we think. Mentalization augments our ability to define (for ourselves) and communicate (to others) what we feel. You are mentalizing when you ask yourself, "Why did I say that?" "Did I hurt her feelings when I did that?" "Why did I forget to call?" "What was I thinking when I said that?" "Why did I order pasta when I am on a diet?" "Why did I get so angry at her?" You are trying to explain what is going on in your own mind, to interpret your own actions and behaviors and theirs, and to understand yourself, others, and your relationships.

When you are mentalizing, you are attributing intentions and meaning to behavior and interactions based on mental states. Mental states include feelings, emotions, desires, needs, beliefs, ideas, thoughts, intentions, and reasons. They are the foundation of interpersonal behavior. Mental states are changeable, unstable, suffused with emotion, and hard to control.

Mental states are also uniquely our own. Each of us has our own separate mind, our individual mental model of reality. Although we may seem to be sharing an experience with someone else, every experience is actually unique and different for each person. You may experience your roast chicken as missing salt. Someone else may believe the chicken tastes just right, while a third person may think the chicken is too salty. No one is right or wrong. You may not be able to identify a flower by its odor, taste the difference between one wine and another, or know when a friend is angry. For someone else, these things may be easily done—yet he may not be able to hear the difference between Beethoven and Bach, Paul Simon and James Taylor, or a cello and a guitar, the way you can. What is perceived as the color red by one person may appear to be a completely different color to someone else, and yet be totally unrecognizable to another person who is color-blind. An art teacher asked his students to mix paint to match the color red used in Coca-Cola ads. No two students mixed the same red, and not one of the students mixed a red that matched the red in the ads.

Perceptions are also uniquely our own. We communicate through a mutual acceptance of the common denominators of our experiences—however, to do this successfully, we must be able to intuit the mental states and reactions of others. This is mentalization.

Have you noticed that you get tense when you spend time with certain people while you find yourself in a good mood when you are with others? Studies in social neuroscience show us that we have biological systems in our brain that attune us to and are influenced by other people. Social interactions result in a transfer of feelings. Emotions pass from person to person, from outside to inside. We have an impact on other people and they have an impact on us. People can change your mood or your mind, can make you feel better or feel worse, and you can change the way they feel. When you are feeling connected to someone, feeling that your minds are meeting, you are feeling her emotions. The closer a person is to you, the more significant the relationship is to you, the stronger the emotions you may feel and the more influence the person will have on your brain and your neural circuitry, so that emotions seem to be contagious. This is why mentalization can be so effective—mentalizing develops awareness of what is going on in another person's mind so that you can begin to respond to his or her feelings accordingly. When you are interacting with someone with BPD, this can result in helping her diminish her emotional dysregulation and improve your communication and your relationship.

Just as it is important to use mentalization skills to communicate with another person, it is equally important to use them to connect to your own feelings. Your feelings are your gut-level indications of what is happening around you. They are your thermometer for evaluating situations and relationships. To get your needs met you need to be aware of your own feelings, to be able to identify what you are feeling, to notice conflicting emotions, and to be able to attribute meaning to your feelings. You need to be able to ask yourself, "What happened that got me to this state?" and then modulate how you express your emotion, both outwardly and inwardly. Your emotions may present themselves as nonconscious cognitive appraisals, as physiological responses such as sweating or tightness in the chest, or as motor behavior such as knee shaking or finger tapping.

Mentalizing is a form of emotional knowing. *Affective mentalizing* is mentalizing about feelings, whereas *cognitive mentalizing* is concerned with thoughts, ideas, or beliefs. You can mentalize in different time frames, such as in your present mental state ("I have a headache and must be treating everyone so badly. No wonder I am getting dirty looks from my co-workers"), in hindsight with regard to your past mental states ("I was really hurt when he broke our date yesterday"), or by anticipating future mental states ("I am really scared about giving that talk tomorrow. What if I forget what to say?").

Mentalization aims to develop stronger connections and deeper understanding between people, be they friends, families, or lovers. Enlarging your understanding of yourself and others, and recognizing your own and others' needs and feelings, enables you to sustain greater mental and emotional closeness, to share a fuller range of feelings, and to give and receive support. Feeling connected to other people can improve the quality of your everyday life. Additionally, when we feel that other people sense us, and experience us as separate mental entities, we develop a greater sense of ourselves. When a person feels known, heard, validated, and acknowledged, painful existential feelings of aloneness, so prevalent in our society, decrease.

The ability to mentalize requires feeling empathy for the other person while simultaneously feeling empathy for yourself.

The ability to mentalize requires feeling empathy for the other person while simultaneously feeling empathy for yourself. Empathy is the ability to feel another person, to mentally walk in someone else's shoes. When you are mentalizing, you are able to see situations and experiences from another person's perspective while maintaining a sense of yourself, in the moment. While you are empathizing with the other person you remain aware of what you, yourself, are feeling, of your own state of mind. The ability to empathize with yourself is as important as the ability to empathize with others. It calls for observing and describing your own emotions, the emotions of others, and the flexibility to adjust your read on the situation, yourself, the other person, and the relationship—mindfully, in the moment. While you are feeling compassion for someone else, you also need to be able to validate yourself by being protective, encouraging, reassuring, compassionate, and approving of yourself. This is what is meant by observing your own limits, knowing what you feel and what you are comfortable handling in the moment when you are interacting with another person.

Most of us do this naturally. When you are talking to someone you will pause, make eye contact, allow her to finish her sentences without interrupting. If she yawns while you are talking to her, you sense you may be boring her and may become more animated or end the discussion. If someone seems to become angry with you, you may back down, change the subject, or avoid the interaction. You can usually sense when someone is sad and needs a hug or a reassuring smile.

Everyone wants to trust someone, to feel she is heard, to sense empathy from others. The ability to mentalize develops a person's capacity to trust, to connect to others and to herself. A strong sense of who you are along with a sense of security and safety is needed if you are to allow yourself to be vulnerable and trust other people. When we mentalize we help a person feel this sense of security.

The sense of "the meeting of minds" that is essential to mentalizing is at the core of intimacy, is the reciprocity that sustains relationships. It is the passport needed for entry into the interpersonal world. The ability to mentalize fosters skillful managing of conflicts, understanding of misunderstandings, and the ability to mend rifts in relationships. The very attributes of successful mentalization are the deficits generally found in people with BPD. Research has shown that the quality of life of people with BPD improves as their ability to mentalize improves with mentalization-based therapy.

Mentalizing Yourself

Imagine yourself at an outdoor café on a beautiful day. You are admiring the view, lost in your own thoughts. A waiter interrupts you for your order. At that moment, two mental processes are occurring simultaneously within you. You are thinking your own thoughts inwardly, feeling your own feelings. Meanwhile, outwardly, you are also responding to the waiter. At this moment, based on your awareness of your own mental state, you realize you are hungry. You have translated what your body is telling you into organized images, ideas, and words that you then communicate to the waiter by ordering lunch.

The mental state you present to the waiter may not be the same as the mental state you are feeling. You may be sad or depressed about the death of a loved one, preoccupied about your job, or nervously anticipating the arrival of a friend. All the waiter knows about you is that you are polite, apparently hungry, and have placed an order. What you have said may not have been all you were thinking or feeling. Only you knew that you were hungry. You have an intimate relationship with yourself because you notice what you are feeling and can think about your own feelings. When you ordered your lunch you were interpreting your own behaviors, feeling in control of yourself, aware of both your outward responses and your inner feelings. This is mentalizing what you, yourself, are thinking and feeling.

You have a sense of stability and continuity because you know how you will react in varied situations and across different emotional states. You can tell yourself, "I am the kind of person who . . .," "I am uncomfortable when . . .," "I do not like it when someone does . . .," "I enjoy . . .," and so on, all of which define who you are to yourself. When you can explain things to yourself, interpret your own feelings, you are mentalizing yourself. "Why am I so edgy today?" "I didn't get enough sleep last night so I don't feel well." "I am sad because my friend died." "Maybe I don't like him because he reminds me of my former boss." The way you explain things to yourself determines how you react to your own experiences and to the behavior of others.

Mentalizing helps you make sense of what is going on around you, to explain things to yourself, to define who you are and affirm your sense of self. Sometimes you may not realize that you are upset, frustrated, or angry, or may not know why you are feeling this way. There are times when all of us have denied what we are feeling, especially painful feelings. You may not always know how your mind is working. Sometimes others, especially those closest to you, can see what you are not seeing. Talking to someone you trust can help you clarify what you are thinking or feeling. If you have negative feelings about someone and do not know why, your best friend telling you that she, too, dislikes this person can help you understand your own emotional response to him. You trust your friend's interpretation of you and of your relationship.

Mentalizing Others

While you are waiting for your lunch, your friend arrives. He sits down and folds his arms stiffly across his chest. You notice his clenched jaw. You sense he is tense, frustrated, and angry. You wonder if he is angry with you. You greet him by validating his apparent mental state and saying, "It seems to me that you are stressed. Is that what you are feeling? What's going on?" He tells you that nothing is wrong. You sense a discrepancy between what he is saying about himself and what you are observing and feeling from him. While you are making your evaluation of the situation, you are thinking your own thoughts but saying what is socially acceptable. You are aware of your friend's conscious and unconscious mental states. You are mentalizing another person.

Never assume that other people think or feel the same way you do. When mentalizing, it is usually necessary to ask, "Did I get that right, have I understood?" Mentalizing others requires the humility to ask these questions so as to find out what the other person is actually thinking or feeling, how he interpreted what you said or did or whether you understood his implicit or explicit communication. This helps you see the other person's point of view so that you can reevaluate your own perspective. The more you know another person, the more accurately you can mentalize his mental state. However, there is a dilemma here as it is often most difficult to mentalize the people who are the closest to you. The more you know about how people with BPD think, the more accurately you can mentalize how they are perceiving a situation.

Mentalizing Relationships

Your friend has just come from a meeting with his girlfriend. Your intuition tells you that they may have had an argument. You know from past experience that their relationship is quite volatile. You feel uncomfortable because you can sense how tense he is and you are at a loss as to what to say to him to ease the situation. You are feeling helpless. *Mentalizing a relationship* is the capacity to simultaneously be aware of and understand your own mental state and the mental state of another person and how this is affecting your relationship in the moment.

To mentalize a relationship, you are simultaneously balancing the understanding of what is going in your mind and the other person's mind within the relationship, within the situation, in the moment. As you are understanding another person's point of view, you are explaining your own point of view to yourself, mindfully observing and describing your own thoughts and feelings, just as you do when you practice the mindfulness component of DBT. However, you are also mindfully observing and describing the thoughts and feelings of the other person. This is an interpersonal skill unique to MBT. Its mastery requires mental effort, attention, concentration, and a safe and secure environment. You will improve with consistent practice. Relationships improve when the other person senses you are trying to understand her. Mentalization also helps people with BPD to regulate their own emotions, minimizing and preventing potentially volcanic emotional eruptions.

Interacting with another person via mentalization can be thought of as involving four perspectives or points of view: your inner and outer mental states and the inner and outer mental states of the other person. You respond to another based on your intuition of what may be going on underneath his behavior, what he may be thinking or feeling based on your past experiences with him, and clues you get from his present behavior. We all do this, to some degree, spontaneously, naturally, and intuitively. Every interaction has an emotional subtext. You need to learn how to read the emotional subtitles of your daily dramas, especially with your loved one who has BPD.

Mentalizing can be thought of as successful and correct mind reading. Some of us are better at this than others. We may call these people "naturally intuitive," or may go so far as to describe them as "psychic."

Implicit Mentalization

You are mentalizing *implicitly* when you have intuitive, rapid, automatic, and emotional "gut" reactions to socials cues or situations. Implicit mentalization occurs primarily in the amygdala, the brain's "low road," where emotions are processed and emotional memories are stored. The amygdala is like the brain's radar, scanning the environment for threats, danger, or emotionally salient events, and readying you for fight or flight. The amygdala operates at immense speed, automatically and effortlessly, finding emotional meaning in nonverbal messages without conscious control. This processing is fast, may be inaccurate and impulsive, and can lead to snap decisions. We are not seeing; instead, we are feeling. You are mentalizing implicitly when mirroring someone's facial expression, or when responding to a baby's cry. There are times when you react implicitly, too, without thinking of the other person's perspective, as when you nod your head or take turns in conversation, or when you respond to a smile. Mentalizing, both thinking explicitly and feeling implicitly, is the basis of identity and self-awareness.

Mentalizing, both thinking explicitly and feeling implicitly, is the basis of identity and self-awareness.

Mentalizing implicitly does not come naturally to everyone. It is harder for some people than for others. For some, trying to figure out what someone else is thinking or feeling is like deciphering hieroglyphics or speaking in tongues.

The ability to excel at mentalizing implicitly, or "reading minds," can be an enormous asset to people in various professions, such as lawyers, judges, police officers, clinicians, or salespeople. However, even these professionals make mistakes. It is essential that you recognize the limits of your own ability to read minds in this way. When you buy a gift for someone and try to find something she would like based on what you know about her, you are mentalizing implicitly. An expensive box of chocolates is a lovely gift, but not when you know the recipient is allergic to chocolate. If you get it wrong, the other person will probably feel confused, misunderstood, or invalidated—all highly aversive feelings. A person with BPD is usually unsure of what he is feeling in the first place, so feeling misinterpreted, misunderstood, or invalidated reinforces his essential uncertainty about himself and what he is actually feeling or thinking. These *Gaslight*-type situations can erode his fragile sense of self and trigger feelings of shame and isolation.

Be curious; have the humility to ask authentic and effective questions to clarify meaning and improve understanding. "This is what I thought just happened. Is that how you saw it?" Implicit mentalizing explains how emotions can be contagious, how you can "catch" a feeling from someone even though you are not consciously aware of how the emotion spreads.

Explicit Mentalization

When you use your intellect to figure out what another person is thinking or to put feelings into words, you are mentalizing explicitly. Explicit mentalization takes place when you choose words carefully to explain or express what you are feeling to someone else, when you ask yourself questions to make sense of yourself in your own mind, or when you think deliberately about reasons for your own actions. You are mentalizing explicitly when you try to make what was less conscious more conscious, when you try to understand what is in front of you, sense that you have been misunderstood, or feel that there is an obstacle in your relationship. This is a complex cognitive process wherein you are thinking about something, planning, organizing thoughts, and looking at alternative perspectives.

"Man is not a rational animal but a rationalizing one."
—Robert Heinlein

Explicit mentalization tells us what we think about what we feel. It occurs in the prefrontal cortex, the executive center of the brain, the place where we make decisions, use logic, think about what is happening, and control our behavior. In the prefrontal cortex, the brain's "high road," responses are slower, more accurate, wary, and observant. Explicit mentalization allows you to create a story involving thoughts and feelings to account for your own actions, a narrative to make your own and others' actions intelligible.

Impaired Mentalization

Not everyone can mentalize. Autism is a disorder characterized, among other things, by the inability to mentalize. Autistic people have difficulty recognizing emotions in faces. Functional MRI (fMRI) studies reveal that people with autism do not process facial expressions in the same area of the brain as do people without autism; therefore, they have trouble making sense of what other people are thinking or feeling. They lack the ability to put themselves in another person's shoes, to experience empathy, to mentalize themselves or others. This has devastating implications on the quality of their lives.

Some people do not seem to know how to acknowledge or connect to other people and may be described as socially autistic. If you have difficulty mentalizing, if you cannot picture another person's mind or see things from her perspective, you will be oblivious to her needs and feelings and be unable to empathize with her. When others misinterpret your actions or intentions, you feel unheard and misunderstood, resulting in relationship problems such as volatile arguments or passive-aggressive behaviors. When under stress, all of us have difficulty mentalizing; however, having a relationship with someone who has difficulty mentalizing can be exasperating.

People with BPD can mentalize. They can be highly empathic. Sometimes they are quite adept at connecting to others; yet at other times, when they are emotionally dysregulated, they seem to be completely unable to mentalize. Empathy for other people seems to disappear from their sight lines. You will feel as if you just "don't count." When a person with BPD is emotionally dysregulated, his thinking will become rigid and inflexible, and he will be unable to see situations from any other perspective but his own, provoking the relationship difficulties so characteristic of BPD. The ability to mentalize can return when his emotions regulate. Family members find it extremely confusing and frustrating to make sense of their loved one's intermittent or "come and go" ability to mentalize. For someone with BPD, it seems that the stronger his emotional connection is to someone, the more that person can trigger intense emotional responses.

Attachment and Mentalization

The relationships we have with the people we care the most about, those we feel the most connected to and trust the most, such as our parents and partners, are described as our attachment relationships. These relationships, components of the attachment system, originate in infancy and seem to develop as a result of an infant's ability to connect to and internalize the caring and sense of safety from a parent or close caregiver. This ability to attach to or bond with another person in infancy seems to be the basis for the development of a secure sense of self in life and the ability to trust other people. Attachment relationships help create self-awareness; we begin to generate a sense of ourselves when we sense that another person senses us. A securely attached person will have the capacity to remember or internalize his attachment person so that he has a mental representation of the people he is attached to, usually his family or caretakers, and will be able to remember these secure attachment experiences. He will have a mental reservoir that sustains and nurtures him and gives him a sense of who he is, despite whatever may be happening to him in the moment. A person who feels securely attached will be less vulnerable to feelings of isolation and loneliness. If a child's development goes awry and secure attachments do not form, behavioral problems usually arise. Mentalization-based therapy is based on attachment theory.

Babies begin to gain self-awareness as they learn to differentiate between themselves and other people, to experience themselves in the mind of another person, and to know that they are separate entities. At about 3 years of age, as their prefrontal cortexes develop, young children can begin to use language and naturally learn to mentalize. This may depend on the child's ability to form attachment relationships, so that impaired attachment seems to lead to impaired mentalization that in turn results in impaired social cognition and difficulty regulating both affect (mood) and emotions, and the ability to self-sooth. Cutting-edge research has shown that *oxytocin*, a hormone released when a woman gives birth, and also related to sexual intimacy, seems to be a biological component of the process of attachment and development of trust.

An inability or failure to mentalize seems to be at the core of BPD relationship problems. When your loved one calls you 20 times a day, it may be because he needs to hear your voice in order to feel safe, or to remind himself that you still exist. The sense of abandonment that is used to describe BPD may be an indication that the person does not feel securely attached.

The ability to mentalize seems to fall apart when those with BPD interact with certain people or in particular situations. Parents, partners, and close relatives—those with whom she has an attachment relationship—seem to be particularly able to disrupt her ability to mentalize. If a stranger says something hurtful, such as, "That dress is ugly," or "I think you are stupid," you might get moderately angry. But you will probably get much angrier if someone close to you makes the same remark. This may explain why a person with BPD may act so differently with strangers or people to whom she is not "attached" than with those with whom she is intimately connected.

Conflict with or criticism from someone to whom your loved one with BPD is attached seems to bring on a flood of rapidly escalating emotions and a deluge of emotional memories. He becomes so overwhelmed by his own emotions that he may feel as if he is drowning. Mentalization has stopped; the amygdala seems to take over from the more rational, dispassionate prefrontal cortex, and he is no longer thinking or being logical. At these times he is dominated by aversive, implicit feelings he cannot control, such as panic, anxiety, shame, helplessness, and inadequacy. He has been betrayed by his biological hyperactivity and supersensitivity. His hypervigilance and extreme sensitivity make him much more vulnerable to attachment system stressors. His sense of who he is gets shaky or is temporarily lost. He attempts to cope through various impulsive and dangerous behaviors.

> *Conflict with or criticism from someone to whom your loved one with BPD is attached seems to bring on a flood of rapidly escalating emotions and a deluge of emotional memories.*

A drowning person is only concerned with saving himself, not with how he is relating to others. When people with BPD are so dysregulated that mentalization has failed them, they cannot see your point of view nor your feelings, and they cannot seem to accept you fully as a person. They lose the capacity for flexible thinking; become rigidly fixed on their own often distorted perceptions; and arrive at assumptions, inferences, and inappropriate interpretations of your responses that generally confuse you (remember "Pass the butter"?). They feel out of control and deal with their aversive feelings by willfully trying to impose their point of view on you. They do not seem to know what they are feeling, have great difficulty communicating what they want or need, and expect those closest to them to be able to read their minds. Conflicts, antagonism, and resentment result. At these times, they seem to be oblivious of the effect their own behavior has on others; relationships become volatile and difficult. Given all of this, it should come as no surprise that interpersonal relationships are the Achilles heel of people with BPD.

Prementalizing

Your loved one is most vulnerable to losing the ability to mentalize when she has a sense of distrust or betrayal or feels threatened—such as when she feels a disconnect from an attachment figure. The person she is closest to has the strongest valence to trigger these reactions. When problems or misunderstandings arise that cause emotional arousal, she may retreat to childlike responses that predate the development of her ability to mentalize. This is known as *prementalizing.* Her limited capacity to mind-read and her tendency to misinterpret intentions, her own and others', lead to confusion, increased stress, dysregulation, and the emotional cascade that makes daily life so difficult. In this prementalizing state, she seems to regress to thinking like a 2- or 3-year-old child. You will know if this happens because extremely rigid and inflexible thinking takes over. Prementalizing can manifest in varied ways, or in *modes*, from situation to situation, and depends on the particular person with whom your loved one is interacting in the moment. Being hypervigilant for signs of mentalization failures and learning to recognize distinct forms of prementalizing, such as *psychic equivalence, pretend thinking, teleological thinking, pseudo-mentalizing, concrete thinking,* and *misuse of mentalization* can guide you so that you know what to do to avoid the behavioral cascade that might otherwise follow.

Psychic Equivalence—Reality Is Too Real

When a person with BPD regresses to prementalizing in psychic equivalence mode, he accepts his feelings as absolute, non-negotiable facts. Whatever he is thinking or feeling is experienced as being absolutely real. Fantasies are felt to be reality. When in psychic equivalence mode, people with BPD are convinced that they are absolutely right and are intolerant of any alternate perspectives. "I know what caused this and you can't tell me otherwise." "You just don't want me to have any fun" (said after wrecking the family car). A frightening thought, such as, "It is not safe here," could be terrifying. "I think you hate me" means you absolutely hate him. "I feel jealous" means you must be cheating on him. In psychic equivalence mode, people with BPD do not engage in any reality testing and can seem to be paranoid.

At these times, debates about who is right or wrong or what is true or false are pointless. Do not even try to defend your position. Anything you might possibly do will not be as upsetting to your loved one as your not doing what he wants you to do. At the same time, if you just agree with him, you risk validating the invalid and reinforcing the likelihood that the behavior will recur.

Pretend Thinking—Reality Does Not Count

In pretend mode, reality does not seem to matter. She is thinking like a 2- or 3-year-old; her thoughts and feelings, her inner world, do not seem to be connected with outer reality. Feelings do not accompany thoughts. Experience is not grounded in reality. She feels empty and may dissociate. People with BPD who are in pretend mode can remain in therapy for years and years, talking endlessly and becoming adept at using all the appropriate psychobabble jargon. As they are generally rationalizing intellectually without connecting their thoughts with their feelings, they make no progress. Because they are not addressing what they feel, they can seem dissociated from what they are talking about and sound as though they are reciting lines from a textbook. Although she may say what she thinks you want to hear, she is pretending. She sees the world through rose-colored glasses; everything is wonderful. The stories she tells you about herself and her experiences do not seem real and do not jive with what you know actually happened. You may work very hard trying to connect when your loved one is in pretend mode, but she may continue to defy your own sense of reality, leaving you feeling excluded.

People who are prementalizing in pretend mode are adept at what is referred to as "bullshitting"—which is not the same as lying. When a person is lying, he knows what the truth is; he wants to make you think something he knows is false. He is well aware of what you know and adapts what he is saying so that you will believe him. Lying uses the high road, the prefrontal cortex, and requires the ability to mentalize. A person who is "bullshitting" is not concerned with the truth in a given situation but with "changing the subject." He will say anything to get you off his back. He is not deceiving you, as his intention is neither to report nor hide the truth. If your loved one has engaged in "bullshitting" with you and you have not recognized it for what it is, you may come away convinced you have made a connection or came to an agreement; however, there will be no follow-up. You will feel disappointed when no progress is made. Treatment contracts or agreements made regarding family rules and regulations are examples of "bullshitting". The person is not trying to deceive you about the facts but only about his intentions relating to the facts. Bullshitting is impulsive. It goes by the low road, the amygdala. A bullshitter is not lying; he just wants to save face, to avoid embarrassment in the moment and to put an end to his immediate stress. He is not thinking of the consequences of his actions. It can help families tremendously in accepting their loved one if they can understand that he is not lying—just saying whatever he can in order to feel better in the moment.

Teleological Thinking—Only What Can Be Seen Is Real

When a person regresses to prementalizing in teleological mode, only an overt physical act can be accepted as a true indication of your feelings and intentions. Needs and emotions are expressed with actions rather than with thoughts or words because actions and their tangible effects speak louder than words. A tangible or physical act is needed to verify implicit feelings or prove your intent. Affection in public is needed to prove that you love him. Paying her rent tells her that you really care about her. "If you really loved me you would buy me a car." In this mode, feelings are understood in terms of actual physical outcomes. Cutting means she is in pain. "Because the door lock is on the outside of the door, you intended to lock me in."

Pseudomentalizing

When a person is pseudomentalizing, he is absolutely certain of what he is thinking but does not connect his thoughts to actual reality. He bases what he says on very little actual evidence, yet states it with absolute certainty. He makes inaccurate statements with apparent confidence. Reality testing does not happen. Although there may be a nugget of truth in what he perceives in the present moment, he extends it from the specific to the general. If you do not like what he made for dinner last night, you never like what he makes for dinner. He is sure he knows what you think. If you ask, "How do you know?" the answer will be, "I just know," without any offer of evidence or proof. If you try to prove what you feel, he will deny your feelings and your reality, and make accusations that can become abusive.

Concrete Thinking—Failure of Symbolization

When a person takes what you say at face value and does not register the emotional quality of a situation or experience, she is thinking concretely. The person is thinking explicitly and is not in touch with her own or the other person's feelings. She does not grasp the relationship of thoughts to feelings and actions. She is not processing her own implicit feelings or the information available implicitly from another person. Concrete thinking limits a person's ability to cope with reality as it limits her appraisal of reality. She does not recognize the impact of her thoughts and feelings on other people. She interprets behavior (her own or others') in terms of the influence of situational or physical constraints rather than feelings and thoughts. A person who is thinking concretely speaks in absolute terms, such as "he always forgets his responsibilities, he never comes home on time," "she is just mean," "he should get a job." She does not see cause and effect and is convinced that her feelings or the feelings of others cannot change and will always be as they are now.

Family members in TARA groups, particularly fathers, seem to exhibit a preponderance of concrete thinking styles. It is very difficult for these parents to develop empathy for themselves and their loved ones, as they cannot see the implicit feelings under concrete statements. Family members who think concretely report what their loved one says as though it were written in stone. "But he said he wouldn't go" is taken as an absolute "truth," without any doubt or any sense of the person's underlying meaning. Concrete thinkers do not read the subtitles and do not try to negotiate. They quit before they are fired. Whatever the other person tells them is repeated like a mantra.

Concrete thinking is an inability to think in abstract terms; It is thinking of objects or ideas as specific items without being able to see them as abstract representations of a larger, more general concept. A chair or table is seen as an individually useful item and not as part of a general class of furniture. The person cannot look beyond the actual words to realize what they mean, cannot move from the specific to the general. Concrete thinking often focuses on excessive details or external social factors, such as mental or physical illness, grievances, taking revenge for slights, lack of forgiveness ("It is his fault, so he deserves all he gets," or "I will never forget what he said to me"). Concrete thinking leads to blaming outside factors for problems: "It is the neighbor's fault," "the car made me late," "my teacher hates me," and so on.

When someone with BPD tells her story, she is usually over-elaborate or dismissive, or may report a poorly fleshed-out account. Although her story is usually rigidly described, it is often not corroborated by other family members. She may be overwhelmed by her own experience or unable to find a narrative strong enough to describe her pain. The stories people with BPD tell themselves are often biased and based on their skewed perspectives. Adrianna attended private schools and, by the age of 17, had traveled to Europe a dozen times as well as to Asia, South America, and Mexico. The story she tells herself is that she was raised in poverty. Noreen, raised in a luxurious home with a large swimming pool and every creature comfort, cost her affluent parents over half a million dollars for BPD and substance abuse treatments. The story Noreen tells herself is that she is poor. Although your loved one's story may not jive with your perceptions, it is important to mentalize how she came to her story about herself. If a person does not feel loved, he or she may end up feeling emotionally impoverished.

Misuse of Mentalization

When a person misuses mentalization, his understanding of the mental state of others is not directly impaired, yet the way in which he uses this understanding is harmful. He has thought about and understands the other person's mind; however, he has done so with an intent to hurt, manipulate, control, or undermine the other person. Although his intention may not be to hurt, manipulate, control, or undermine, to you it will seem to be motivated and purposeful. The person distorts another person's feelings and empathetic understanding toward accomplishing his own agenda. Because misuse of mentalization involves a realistic risk of harm to the person or to his partner, it can be appear to be almost sociopathic.

Recognizing Failures to Mentalize

Recognizing when your loved one has stopped mentalizing is like going into emergency response mode, hearing a fire alarm, and sliding down the firehouse pole. Communication between you and your loved one has stopped, minds are no longer meeting, the connection has been broken. Something has triggered your loved one, and the sooner you recalibrate mentalization the less the damage will be to your relationship in the moment, and the less the situation will escalate.

When you recognize a mentalization lapse, remember not to personalize or defend yourself. If you do, you will have capitulated to BPD behaviors and increased the likelihood that emotional dysregulation will lead to an explosive argument.

Your loved one's failure to mentalize can be intermittent, episodic, or content specific. If her sense of safety and security can be restored, arousal decreases and her ability to mentalize will return. When you can learn how to prevent mentalization from going off line in the first place, daily life for both of you can become more stable. Reflect back what she may be feeling by validating, in the moment. Ask questions so that she feels heard and understood. These can be your first baby step toward restoring mentalization. The following sections will guide you as to what to do when mentalization fails.

Maintaining Mentalization

Attachment relationships often trigger intense emotional reactions in people with BPD so that they seem to go off what we might describe as the "social script" of "normal" responses and instead resort to coercive, defensive, and rigid behaviors that are unnerving and exasperating to you. One person's problem mentalizing creates distress for the other person, evoking nonmentalizing in them, so that a failure to mentalize seems to be contagious. Under conditions of stress, for all of us, the ability to mentalize is impaired. When you are coping with a person with BPD you are often caught in this vicious cycle of contagion. It is very important for you to be aware of your own failure to stay attuned to your loved one and to be acutely aware when you sense that mentalizing between the two of you has begun to fail.

When you can sense that he is no longer mentalizing, you know you have missed something, have not been attuned to him, have somehow not read his subtitles. At these times it is highly unlikely that you will be able to repair relationships or find solutions to problems as, in response to his behavior, you will probably be having your own problems mentalizing. How do you return to mentalizing, restore your loved one's ability to think, get his prefrontal cortex back on line? While you want to reduce emotional triggers and improve and repair your relationships in the present, you also want to ensure that your loved one has a real chance for happiness and an independent, satisfying, productive life in the future. To achieve this balance, heal family relationships, and restore trust, you will benefit from integrating mentalizing techniques into your daily life.

Mentalization begins in the heart. It is an interactive process that involves how each person's thoughts relate to their feelings and affect the relationship. It is about feeling, not thinking. It is an attitude, philosophy, or style that you need to inculcate into your daily life and practice all the time. Mentalizing is an interactive process that occurs between two people in the moment. Recall that it differs from DBT, which focuses on an individual's feelings and behaviors and how the individual can control and tolerate his own emotional reactions and choose different ways to react.

Here are techniques you can use to foster, maintain, and recalibrate mentalizing during everyday interactions. They can help you shift from nonmentalizing to mentalizing, to stay in sync and maintain connections to your loved one. When you realize mentalization has gone off track, you can use this checklist of techniques to help you decrease the effects of possible triggers or cues and begin to have a more reciprocal relationship.

Be Supportive, Empathic, and Compassionate

Have empathy for the pain, distress, and frustration your loved one is feeling. Respond to her with compassion, with concerned, heartfelt caring, with a sharp clarity of recognition of her needs and pain and a sustained and practical determination to do whatever is possible and necessary to alleviate suffering. Communicate your understanding of what the other person is feeling, how she is struggling. Acknowledge how hard she is trying while simultaneously giving up your own self-serving expectations, judgments, and criticisms. To help you do this, picture your loved one wearing the TARA tiara (see Chapter 2) and imagine how it must feel to be a person who cannot rely on what she thinks or feels, and consequently always feels precariously out of control. Try to sense how she sees herself; imagine her internal world. Have empathy also for yourself; when you mentalize you are actively engaged in relieving the other person's suffering while also acknowledging, caring for, and forgiving yourself

You cannot fake empathy. It must be sincerely felt. You will not be mentalizing if you simply learn facts or repeat a memorized lesson as if you were reciting a poem you do not understand, or parroting lines from a play in a foreign language you do not speak. When you and your loved one are able to describe feelings, express doubts, see alternative perspectives, and admit fears to one another, you are mentalizing. If your loved one can trust you enough to have an emotional conversation with you, feels secure enough to be vulnerable, to capitulate emotionally, you are successfully mentalizing. If you respond with empathy and communicate with compassion, trust will develop and minds can meet. This is the goal of mentalizing.

Ask Questions—Become a Columbo Parent or Partner

Columbo was an apparently naïve TV detective played by Peter Falk who, despite seeming to be blundering about, always managed to solve his cases. He would ask his suspects simplistic question after question about the smallest details. By adapting Columbo's bumbling style of questioning, you can determine what your loved one is feeling, where he was, who else was there, how he felt physically (hungry, tired, tense, etc.), what happened before the event or after, and so on. In this way you can find out what actually occurred. With humility, ask lots of sincere, simple, and nonjudgmental questions. The devil is in the details; ferret out information like a friendly spy so that you can explore those details. The more questions you ask, the more you are engaging your loved one's prefrontal cortex. Ask questions such as "I don't understand; can you explain? Tell me more! What were you thinking at that point? What then?" Explore and elaborate on feelings rather than on behavior or content. Avoid psychobabble phrases such as "he did that because he is jealous, insecure, has low self-esteem." Asking questions actively demonstrates your desire to

It is as important to ask the right questions as it is important to have the right answers.

understand. It is as important to ask the right questions as it is important to have the right answers. Ask questions in a nonthreatening, noncontrolling, supportive, and empathetic way.

These questions are important because you can never be sure of what is going on in someone else's mind, what another person may be thinking or feeling. Thoughts are often ambiguous, obscure, hidden, or murky. None of us excels at getting inside another person's head. If you try, chances are you might guess wrong, make assumptions that are not valid, and probably "put your foot in your mouth." If you make inferences or interpretations, or jump to conclusions, you run the risk of being absolutely incorrect. Inferences such as "He is sad today because he is graduating," "She didn't go to the party because she was raped at 14," "She cuts herself because we got a divorce," "He didn't finish college because he has low self-esteem," put you at greater risk for misunderstanding.

Be curious, inquisitive, and ask questions so that you can begin to find out what the other person is thinking or feeling. Be like Socrates; adopt a "not knowing" attitude. This will help both of you, in the moment, to figure out what is happening and to avoid triggering the strong emotions and feelings that result in her feeling invalidated and isolated. This can prevent the emotional storms.

When you sense a rift in an interaction, when you feel you have hit a speed bump, that mentalization is failing, ask yourself, "What is happening now? What is the context of the problem that can be inhibiting or breaking down mentalization? How does it relate to what is going on right now?" "Is this really about the car, the laundry, what time he came home, where we go to dinner, the money she spent at the mall?" "Why is he saying this, why is she acting like this, why am I feeling this way now? What has happened between us that justifies the current state?" Consider whether the context refers to the past, the present, or the future. What have you missed? Try to ask yourself what she is feeling outwardly or explicitly. As you know her so well, what do you think she is feeling implicitly? How do you think she is interpreting your reaction? Be curious about her motivations. Question her about the motives or intentions of other people. Ask her what she thinks the motivation is for your own behavior or attitude in the moment. Often her behavior is her attempt to stabilize herself, to save face, or to regain a sense of control and coherence in the moment. To begin the process of understanding cause and effect, ask yourself and her what function this particular behavior or response serves.

These are examples of active questions you can ask your loved one that can help to maintain, attune, or recalibrate mentalization:

- What's going on? It seems to me that I've said something that got you upset.
- I seem to have gotten the wrong impression. Can you help me out and clarify the situation?
- Help me out here, please. I am trying to understand what happened. At first you seemed to be excited, and then you seemed to become angry. What happened that changed your feelings and when did it happen?
- What did I say or do that made you think I was not interested in what you were saying?
- Did I get the picture of what you were feeling?
- How did you come to think that I did not want to go to the movies tonight?
- I am really confused. What did I say that gave you that impression that I didn't like Mary?
- What was so intolerable to you that I said or did that you couldn't manage? Why would I say that?
- As I understand it, what you have been saying is___. Does that sound right? Am I getting it right? Have I understood the situation and how you felt?
- Did you understand? Have I explained myself?
- What did he say that made you think he was leaving?
- What happened that made you decide she was angry at you?
- How does thinking he does not like you help you in your current state or in your life?
- I am a little confused and wonder if you could help me out here. Can you tell me a little more about what happened because I really want to understand? Have I missed something obvious?

Listen, Observe, Validate

Really listen to her responses and opinions, even if they differ from yours. Validate to ensure that she feels heard and understood. By questioning and validating, you can continue exploring. While you are asking how she came to her evaluation of a situation, be sure to explain what you were thinking or feeling and how you came to your perspective. The *explicit* process of explaining yourself in detail will help clarify what you both may have been thinking or feeling *implicitly*—and which you did not precisely verbalize—just as Carl had to explain to his daughter that he was not angry with her, just tired after a long day's work (see Chapter 8). Your asking questions and admitting that you do not know all the answers will help her feel more secure and more willing to hear a different perspective on the situation—that is, yours.

Try phrases such as, "Wow, I really got that wrong. It must be so frustrating when I don't get it. Thank you for explaining your feelings. I really appreciate your clarifying this matter. I had such a different impression of the event. Now I understand your point of view. I can see how it differs from mine. What happened next?" Using language this way shows your loved one that it is okay to change one's mind, admit mistakes, and be vulnerable. You are also demonstrating that you are open to being surprised by her responses, that you want to learn what is going on in her mind, and that you are willing to change your own mind. While maintaining mentalization you are also modeling nonrigid behavior and effective interpersonal skills, such as negotiation and compromise.

During any interaction, try to observe emotional states, read your loved one's emotional subtitles, and decipher emotional language. Changes in facial expressions, voice tones that become higher or lower, gestures employed, shifts in physical states such as the bodily changes that happen when someone becomes tense, uncomfortably stressed, or begins to relax, changes in micro facial expressions—all these are clues to underlying mental states. (You can learn more about how to recognize facial expressions with greater accuracy by reading about the work of Dr. Paul Ekman, whose Micro Expression Training Tool is designed to help people better identify micro facial expressions.)

Notice your loved one's reaction to you. Notice also her reaction to her environment—be it a noisy restaurant, a party, or a crowded shopping mall. Pay attention to explicit clues. Use your loved one's outward behavior to help you tune into her inward feelings and thoughts, her implicit state.

If you notice these kinds of changes, you can say, "I think that I may be doing something that is making you nervous/stressed/angry/sad."

"What is it I have done or said, or what is it you feel I have done or said, that has changed how you are feeling? Have I missed the boat?" "Did I do something that made you feel ___? Can you tell me what it is? It was not my intention to do anything of the sort. I am really sorry."

Be Humble

A person who is humble has an unassuming, modest attitude, is respectful, and shows deference toward other people. It takes humility to ask questions, to admit you have misunderstood, that you do not know what to do or how to solve a problem. Willingness to listen to someone else's opinion or ideas, asking your loved one for clarification or help in understanding, tolerating uncertainty, enduring ambiguity and being wrong, accepting criticism—this all takes humility. When, with humility, you admit that you do not have all the answers and ask the other person to explain, you are implicitly saying that you respect him and see your relationship as one between equals. Do not be the expert; instead, find solutions together, side by side. You have ceded control and are open to listening to his answers. When your responses are accompanied by support, empathy, and compassion, they will be experienced as authentic. Your humility allows for the open communication that is needed for successful mentalizing.

What you say is not as important as how you say it.

Take Responsibility, Apologize

When you have reached an impasse and you can sense that your and your loved one's minds are no longer meeting, or that the other person has escalated, accept that you have probably said or done something that was misinterpreted or that triggered an attachment or emotional response. Mentalizing has gone off track, in this moment. Show your loved one that you are trying to "understand the misunderstanding" by admitting you failed to get it right, failed to respond appropriately to what he was feeling. Admit your mistakes, your own role in the rupture of your relationship. Take responsibility for upsetting or triggering him. Mistakes provide you with the chance to revisit situations and repair them. They give you the opportunity to discuss your intentions and to compare them with his interpretation of your intentions within the interaction. When you have acknowledged your contribution to the problem and apologized, you can then talk about how the other person also contributed to the problem, opening the door to compromise and negotiation. Be vulnerable.

If you do not know what you said or did, simply stop and ask:

- Was it something I said or did that made you angry? I am truly sorry. It was never my intention to make you angry.
- It seems to me that I upset you. What did I say or do that might have made you feel that way? I did not realize that what I said would upset you. It certainly was not my intention. I am so sorry.
- Have I put my foot in my mouth and misunderstood what you were saying?
- I believe that I was wrong. What I can't understand is how I came to say that?
- Can you help me go back to what was happening between us before things went wrong?

You can also apply the Acceptance-Acknowledgment Declaration (AAD; see Chapters 5 and 10) as a template for acknowledging responsibility and apologizing by adding references to intention, both yours and your loved one's. You are not apologizing for a specific event but for past attitudes and oversights in understanding feelings. The AAD can be tailored to any situation and can help maintain and restore a mentalizing connection. Many families have reported successful breakthroughs in repairing ruptures with their loved ones by humbly acknowledging responsibility, clarifying intentions, and apologizing.

Be Consistent—Do Not Get Sidetracked

Consistently pay acute attention to what is going on in your loved one's mind and in your own mind, moment by moment. Do not get derailed by problem solving or long-term goals; instead, persistently and mindfully focus on feelings and on your relationship in the moment. It is more important to consistently focus on your loved one's feelings and on your own, on *how* she is thinking, feeling, and relating to others, than on *what* she is thinking, saying, or doing. The process is more important than the content.

Imagine a shaken snow globe. The fluttering snow or glitter prevents you from seeing the scene at the base of the globe. You have to wait for the particles to settle before you can see the scene. If you get involved with the content of what he is saying, you are focusing on the snow and are missing the scene below; you will not be able to sustain mentalizing. You will end up personalizing, defending yourself, or focusing on your own ego.

Likewise, how you repair a rift and reconnect is far more important than who was right or wrong. Arguing about the content of the situation, the "truth," what did or did not happen, what is or is not morally correct, or who is the "winner or loser" in the situation is pointless. Do not get sidetracked by journeys into the past, fortune-telling of the future, or attempts at finding insights into behavior. You do not have a crystal ball, so stop guessing, assuming, and interpreting. Certainly do not entertain the possibility that you "know it all." Instead, focus on how each of you came to your point of view, on the details of what you are each feeling. Tell her specifically what you are thinking and how you came to think it so that she can correct both of your assumptions. If she becomes emotionally flooded and stops mentalizing, you and your feelings will no longer matter to her; you will no longer be in a reciprocal relationship. Both of you are now focused on one person—the person with BPD. Distress tolerance skills (Chapter 8) can help you to be persistent in these difficult situations and break the grip of her nonmentalizing.

To get mentalizing back on track, try consistently refocusing the discussion as follows:

- Bear with me; I think we need to figure out what just happened before we talk about using the car. It seems I upset you. I am really confused. What I cannot understand is how I came to upset you.
- Can you help me out here and tell me what you felt I did? I never meant to create tension between us.
- Before we talk more about using the car, I'd really like to explore what went wrong between us.

Keep It Simple

When he is feeling fragile, when mentalization seems to be lost, do not complicate the issue with lengthy explanations fraught with psychobabble terminology or psychological insights to explain or interpret behavior. Keep your language very simple. Stay in the present, be mindful, and do not interpret behavior unless you have facts to support your perceptions. Focus on the change in feelings in the moment, not on what was said or done. This is not about childhood experiences, divorces, whether you worked when your children were growing up, or how much you love them. Validate the feelings you sense. Get into the details of the incident, explore what happened, calibrate your own emotional intensity just as you would match voice tones. If he is emotionally hot, your response should be a little cooler; a little hotter if he is very cold. If you are not mentalizing his emotions, he will interpret this as you do not feel that his experiences are meaningful or merit attention. When he is overwhelmed with emotion, be supportive and empathic. While you are actively engaging with him, adjust your responses to his mentalizing capacity in the moment while being aware of your own mentalizing capacity.

If the interaction becomes too painful or confrontational, he will probably shut down, dissociate, or avoid. Accept that you have to stop for the time being. Do not assume that he can do more than what he is doing in the moment, especially when you can sense that he has stopped mentalizing and is struggling to make sense of what he is feeling.

Language: Labeling with Qualifications

The language people use can be both the cause of and the cure for misunderstandings. Language is insidious, like a virus. Language used in the course of an interaction can improve mentalization in the moment or cause it to go off line, reframing situations for better or for worse. The words we use have a profound impact on how we experience the world and define our realities. Saying, "He dumped me," or "We broke up," or "It didn't work out!" can make all the difference in how you feel, interpret an experience, or react—for instance, "I was expelled from therapy" versus "I can't go back to DBT for 1 month because I missed three sessions." The choice between these two

phrases will change how you view an
experience and, ultimately, how you see
yourself. It is very easy to misinterpret
syntax. When interacting with your
loved one with BPD, use indefinite words such as *guess, wonder, sup-
pose, surmise, realize, get the idea, presume, infer, sense, imagine.*
Some examples:

"Language is a virus."
—William Burroughs

- I wonder if . . . It occurs to me that . . . I guess that . . .
- Have you considered the possibility that . . .?
- I am wondering if he may have thought that you were angry
  with him; has that occurred to you?

Do not tell your loved one what to feel or how to think with
phrases like, "What you mean is . . . What you are really telling me
is . . . I'm sure you were feeling . . ." This cuts off mentalization
and reinforces your loved one's sense of incompetence, isolation,
and feelings of shame. Furthermore, using the word *just*, as in "Just
get a job, just get married, just finish school, just be responsible,"
oversimplifies the effort it takes to accomplish a goal or control an
emotion. This is invalidating. If instead you say, "I started to feel that
you were getting annoyed with me, did I get that right?" your loved
one has to pause and explore your mental state, think about what you
meant, and consider a different perspective. This can restart the process of mentalization by down-regulating the emotions, decreasing
your loved one's amygdala response, and reengaging the prefrontal
cortex.

Identify trite explanations or cliché responses, such as "that's
cute," or "cool," used to describe everything and anything. These are
meaningless responses that do not give you information or any sense
of what your loved one is actually thinking or feeling. Ask Columbo
questions to define words: "Is it as cute as that dress you wore to the
prom? As cute as the toy you bought the baby?" Or "This is a catastrophe!" Ask what he means, get the details. Establish criteria for
evaluation, as in, "On a scale of 1 to 10, how angry are you?"

Try to avoid using the word "you," as it can be perceived as judging, blaming, or criticizing, or as your telling your loved one what
she "should" do, think, or feel. "I" statements, such as "I feel . . .
sense . . . imagine . . ." can be more effective than sentences beginning
with "you." "We," referring to the ideas, opinions, approval,

or understanding of two or more people, such as mom and dad, can be overwhelming for someone with BPD. At all times, avoid "we."

Label Feelings

When people with BPD experience intense feelings that can interfere with their ability to mentalize, they usually have great difficulty identifying these feelings. It can be helpful for you to explore feelings together by saying, "How did that situation make you feel?" or "If that happened to me, I would have been angry and I am wondering why you didn't feel angry." By using yourself as an example you are clarifying that it is okay to feel certain ways in situations and to express your feelings. It is also helpful to talk about having mixed feelings: "I would have felt angry, too, but I would have had a hard time expressing it to her because she has been so helpful in other situations and I really appreciate her efforts. Does having mixed feelings about a friend make it hard to respond for you, too?" You can also make inquiries about what kind of response from others would help her feel differently, or how she would like others to think about her in order for her to feel differently.

Alternative Perspectives

If you sense mentalizing is precarious in the moment, that it may be slipping away, offer alternative perspectives of the situation at hand. She may not be taking into account what other people are thinking or feeling, or she may have no idea how to interpret your behavior. At these times you can ask questions that offer alternative explanations or demonstrate that every situation can be seen from multiple perspectives. Discuss the intentions of behavior, yours and his. Ask questions such as these:

- What was it in what just happened between us that led you to say that? Do you think there is another way to interpret what just happened?
- Why do you think he did that? What did he accomplish by doing that? Why would anyone do something that did not get them any benefits but created more problems?
- Why did I forget that? Did you think it was my intention to forget? Where did that idea come from? Why would I do that?

- I just do not understand where we went off track. Did I say something that got you angry? If I did, it was never my intention to do so.
- It just occurred to me that when I yawned you thought I wasn't listening. Is that how you interpreted the situation?
- How did you come to that perception of the situation?
- You seem puzzled! Have I explained my perspective?
- What was it I said that led you to believe I was disappointed? Help me out please; I really want to understand your perspective.
- I can see that you see it like this; however, I see it like that. How do you think we came to see it so differently?

As your loved one answers your questions, you will have the opportunity to clarify, reframe, or reappraise your own perspective for her. Compare and contrast your point of view of the relationship or the present situation with hers. Identify the differences and explain with honesty and humility what you thought or felt. Ask her if she thinks all people make sense all of the time. "How did you come to the conclusion that I was disappointed with you when what I was actually thinking was how much I admired your perseverance and courage?" "If I were in that situation I do not know if I could have gone back in and asked for my money back." "How did you come to think I was disappointed with you when I wasn't?" "What was it I said or did that gave you your perspective of the situation?" "I really want to understand what you are feeling. Are you perceiving or are you interpreting?"

With empathy and humility, challenge his assumption about what you or others are thinking or feeling, what he believes about your point of view, or assumptions he has made that cannot be substantiated. Collaborate in developing a new perspective of the situation rather than discussing or defending what you said or did. Truth is found by eliminating what one knows to be false. Follow your line of enquiry to the contradictory interpretations and explore them.

Mary invited Judy to a party. Judy is anxious about attending. When she gets to the party, she sees Mary across the room and waves hello. Mary does not acknowledge her. Judy interprets this as a rejection, triggering a "fight or flight" amygdala response. Mentalization stops and her emotions escalate. Judy interprets Mary's not waving back as a sign that her friend no longer likes her and does not want to be seen with her. She feels inadequate and ashamed, tells herself she is not dressed right, is too fat, is a loser, and will never have a social life. Judy calls her mother to ask her to come pick her up. Her mother realizes she has just gotten to the party and senses Judy is upset. She validates Judy's tone of voice and asks questions, beginning with "what happened?"

> JUDY: Mary didn't talk to me! I don't know why she invited me. I want to go home.
>
> MOTHER: Wow, I can only imagine how embarrassing that must feel. If my friend didn't talk to me at a party, I would feel rejected. Is that how you are feeling? I can see how you would feel that way. What I can't understand is why she would invite you if she didn't want you to be there. Do you think that was her intention? Help me to understand the situation. Where was Mary when you saw her? What was she doing when you waved hello? Was Mary wearing her glasses? Are you sure she saw you? Was the party very crowded?
>
> JUDY: She was talking to a really cute guy at the bar. No, she wasn't wearing her glasses.
>
> MOTHER: Have you considered that she was not wearing her glasses and might have had a few drinks? Is it possible that she actually didn't see you? It occurs to me that she might have been flirting with the cute guy and didn't see you. What do you think? Is this possible?
>
> JUDY: I never thought of that. I think I'll go and find her now and say hello. I'll call you back.

Demonstrate with compassion that different viewpoints and perspectives on any situation are acceptable. There are also times when, for the moment, two people may have incompatible perspectives. It is okay to identify irresolvable differences or ruptures in the relationship as irresolvable differences, for now.

Be Vulnerable

We all allow ourselves to be vulnerable with the people we trust. BPD can be described as a failure to trust; therefore, any situation that evokes a sense of vulnerability is equated to feeling unsafe or in danger. These are highly aversive feelings and can lead to a breakdown in mentalization. Trust is needed to develop and maintain a relationship and to repair it when there is a rift. Radically accepting your loved one (see Chapter 7) will help her to trust you. Show her that it is okay to be vulnerable by allowing yourself to be vulnerable with her. By being vulnerable yourself you are demonstrating that it is safe to express your feelings or to state what you want or do not want. You can ask, "What do you think it would feel like to be vulnerable with me and to tell me how you would feel in that situation?"

Show her that it is okay to be vulnerable by allowing yourself to be vulnerable with her.

Be Radically Honest and Authentic

To mentalize you must be authentic, radically genuine, and ruthlessly honest with yourself and others. If you do not explain yourself, how can she possibly understand your reaction? Getting the elephants out of the room creates clarity and lessens ambivalence and ambiguity. By being honest and radically genuine you avoid validating the invalid. Do not be afraid to admit what you are feeling. Explain how her perspective or what she is saying or doing makes you feel, even if she has said something that hurt you. Have courage—making omelets requires breaking eggs. Try sentences like, "When you do X, I feel Y . . ." This will help her understand how what she does affects you. These baby steps can explain cause and effect and help her develop empathy for others. The key is to articulate your own thoughts, feelings, and intentions honestly, with sincerity, compassion, and humility.

When you are not authentically feeling what you say you are feeling, your micro facial expressions will give you away. When you are not genuine you are probably intellectualizing what you think you "should" be feeling, or hiding your negative feelings, such as anger or disappointment. This double message creates confusion and erodes the trust needed to foster a meeting of the minds in the moment. This is as effective in repairing relationship ruptures as trying to put out a fire by throwing gasoline on it. When you try to intellectualize emotions without feeling them, or hide your responses, your loved one will sense that you are inauthentic and know that something is radically missing. His response will often be something like, "Stop the psychobabble you learned in that class," or "that you read in that book."

Applying Mentalization Techniques in the Heat of the Moment

What makes a person stop mentalizing? What state is he in when mentalization ceases? Is his response mild, moderate, or extreme? When you see the shift, what do you do? How do you get him to connect with you again? When you sense you and your loved one are no longer mentalizing, these techniques may help you to restore mentalization.

You will know a break in mentalizing has occurred when you notice a shift in mood or a change in facial expression or voice tone during an interaction with your loved one. If she becomes overtly hostile, sullen, or irreverent, or actively evasive (such as by yawning or distracting while you are talking) something has happened. Your loved one may have suddenly become very detail conscious (concrete thinking), or perhaps she is focusing on external events, such as where she was and what other people were doing (teleological thinking). Or perhaps she is being dismissive of or unresponsive to you or to the feelings of other people, or making gross assumptions about you. She may be offering trite explanations for her behavior, such as "You wouldn't understand," or "That's the way I am," and explanations of interactions or situations that lack continuity. These scenarios indicate that something has probably triggered your loved one in the moment and mentalization has stopped. When a person loses the ability to mentalize, other problems may manifest (like cutting or using drugs), explaining how people with BPD can seem to act "as if" they are fine, "apparently competent," until they are triggered or dysregulated.

What if you can see that the situation has gone beyond the momentary rupture, the original incident that triggered the reaction, and a full-blown eruption is upon you? Or what if your loved one walks through the front door and is already extremely dysregulated? He is misperceiving and misinterpreting everything, everything is about him, and everything is negative. Whatever response you exhibit causes him to escalate. He may respond by becoming abusive and destructive, or avoid and dissociate. Cause and effect, reciprocity, another's perspective, and thinking logically have become more difficult for him than scaling Mount Everest. Inflexibility, the rigid behavior that is a hallmark of the disorder, rises to the occasion, and he seems to need to control you and the situation. At these times, you will probably have your own problems mentalizing, making it most difficult to be able to repair relationships, get his prefrontal cortex back on line, find solutions to problems, stay attuned to one another, and think in wise mind. What do you do?

When you sense a break in mentalization has occurred, the first thing to do is to *stop* and suspend the interaction. The break has to be dealt with in the moment. If you keep going and ignore the rift, you are on a slippery slope heading toward more escalation.

The next step will depend on whether the break in mentalizing that you are sensing is mild (amber alert), moderate (orange alert), or extreme (red alert). The intensity of his response will determine the next actions you take. Try to figure out not only what he is feeling but also how intensely he is feeling it in the moment, and how you are feeling. With a supportive and empathetic attitude, explore and identify the exact moment when the rupture occurred, the precise context when mentalization broke down. Observe his mental state and validate his feelings. How dysregulated is he? Think of what you did, or what else may have contributed to the break; what may have been misinterpreted? What triggered this reaction? Talk about your perception, feelings, and intentions while asking questions about his feelings and offering alternative perspectives. Explore the specifics while exploring whether there are broader, general themes or patterns underlying the rupture.

Mild Dysregulation (Amber Alert): Stop, Listen, and Look

Stop and investigate by challenging your loved one with Columbo-like questions to clarify or explore the emotional feelings between you. "I can see you are feeling hurt, upset, and angry. What just happened?" *Look* at the situation from multiple perspectives. Challenge trite explanations, generalizations, or automatic thoughts. Express curiosity about how each of you arrived at your own perspective of the interaction. *Listen* attentively to his response. Discern how his perspective is preventing him from moving forward in the moment. Persistently offer alternative perspectives. Explain what you are feeling. When you sense the rift has been repaired, you can continue on. "I can see you are feeling hurt. Let's wait a moment and try to figure out what happened that made you so upset with me. How do you explain why I did that? Do you think there is another explanation? Why would I have done something to make you feel bad? What do you think other people would think about this? How did working that out with me make you feel?"

If he says, "You wouldn't understand," ask with humility, "Why wouldn't I understand? I would really like to know what happened. Can you help me out here?"

Moderate Dysregulation (Orange Alert): Stop, Rewind, and Explore

Stop the discussion and be clear that you will not ignore the break nor proceed until it has been repaired. It is crucial that your "S*top* tone of voice be compassionate lest it be misconstrued as confrontational or aggressive. Say, "Wait a minute, hold on, I'm confused, I don't get what just happened." If exploring feelings at this point does not get results, as may be the case when your loved one is moderately dysregulated, you must *rewind*, with humility, to the moment of rupture, the moment you realized mentalization went off track. Go back to the moment when you were both able to think about each other and communicate openly. What happened to close off that communication? Rewind frame by frame. Search for details to find the moment of misinterpreting and misunderstanding. A misunderstanding occurs when what was said is not understood, meanings were attributed or explained wrongly so that the intention of what was said was misconstrued or made personal. Try to understand the process that contributed to the error or to the rupture. Rewind by discussing the details, identifying your role in triggering the incident, and each of your interpretations of what happened in the moment. What you are doing is an in-the-moment, on-site, chain analysis as the event is being experienced.

- I can see you're feeling hurt. I wonder how come? Let's rewind and see where we went off track.
- Let's try to figure out how this came about. At first you seemed to understand what was going on but then . . . How did that come about? When did it happen?
- Hold on, let's rewind and see if we can figure out what is going on between us. What was going on in your mind at that time? What did you think I was thinking? What did you think I was trying to say?
- I think I said the wrong thing and hurt your feelings. What I can't understand is how I came to say it. Can you help me go back to what we were talking about before I seem to have put my foot in my mouth and things went wrong between us?

Be curious and inquisitive, *explore* the incident in detail, including the emotions each of you felt. Think about what could have triggered a sense of badness, shame, humiliation, or feelings of rejection, loss, hurt, panic, or abandonment. Remember that the feeling of shame is generally the common denominator of most BPD reactions.

- Is there something I said or did that might have made you feel like that?
- Have I missed the point in what you told me? It was not my intention to get it wrong. Can you help me out here by clarifying what happened? I really want to know.
- I think we might be able to sort this out if I can tell you what I was thinking about what you were saying, and then you can let me know if I'm on the right track.

Extreme Dysregulation (Red Alert): Stop and Stand

Communicate your intention to *stop* the dialogue in the moment by raising your hand, palm forward, in a STOP gesture known as the *mentalizing hand*, or by actually saying "Stop." The stop gesture and/or word *stop* is an explicit signal to your loved one that you are aware of the disconnect. The occurrence of a rupture in your relationship is an indication of a breakdown in mentalization—for you, for her, or for both of you.

Stand fast and stay persistently and mindfully focused on exploring the rupture. You can kick start mentalization by challenging and confronting your loved, one by creating doubt, by jolting her with an alternative perception, a question regarding your intention, or a response in an irreverent tone. Challenge his perspective, unwarranted beliefs, and assumptions, especially those referring to you, as well as his decisions that are based on erroneous assumptions. Do so with radical genuineness, humility, and honesty.

Do not validate the invalid or be deflected. Focusing on the rupture will give you both a chance to catch your breath and evaluate what has happened between you. You are not doing a cognitive analysis of the logic of the dialogue but rather an exploration of feelings and assumptions in the moment. This is the most difficult of the confrontations, yet is an opportunity to really explore unaddressed feelings. This approach takes courage and the ability to take risks. The key is to be nonjudgmental, compassionate, and empathic in tone.

- Bear with me; I think we need to figure out what just happened.
- I can't be sure but, it seems to me that we don't see this quite the same way. Can you help me out here? It never occurred to me that you were seeing the situation this way.
- I am getting the impression that you believe . . . however, that was not what I was thinking. How did we arrive at such different points of view?

It is also possible that you will run into an impasse and have to take a break.

Coping with Impasses

Stop and *stand* can easily lead to an impasse, as you will not allow yourself to be deflected, cave in, or reinforce maladaptive behavior. The failure to mentalize will evoke your loved one's characteristic rigidity. Sometimes the time, the situation, or the degree of arousal makes resolution of a rupture in the moment impossible. At these times, it is okay to retreat and regroup, as long as you express this in a supportive and empathic way. Many famous generals retreated, losing the battle but going on to win the war. Agree to disagree and take a break. Timing matters. What was difficult to deal with in the moment may be easier to resolve when emotions have had a chance to cool down.

- How does repeating the same sentence over and over again get us to move on toward a resolution of this problem?
- As far as I can tell, we are just going around and around in circles. Maybe we can agree to talk about this later on?
- We seem to have hit a speed bump and stalled. When I say something, you dismiss my response as stupid. I admit that sometimes I do respond stupidly, but I cannot accept that my responses are always stupid. What do you think?
- If we can't get past this, I may have to conclude that this discussion has hit a stone wall and is over for now. Perhaps we can talk about it later? What do you think?
- I can see that this conversation is frustrating for both of us, yet at the same time I feel that I am not being heard. What can I do to explain myself? What can we do to get past this? Maybe we have to agree to disagree for now

When you have hit a wall and realize you and your loved one are no longer resonating or reflecting each other's experience, that your minds are no longer meeting, it may be appropriate to have a "time out" so that you can regroup and "strike when the iron is *cool.*" Being effective does not mean you have to become a doormat. At these times, especially, you can send an e-mail. It is sometimes easier for your loved one to "hear" what you have to say, to move from explicit to implicit thinking, if she is reading a letter or e-mail instead of talking to you face to face. E-mails can remove the triggering effect of voice tone and facial expressions and clarify misinterpretation and ambiguity. Use validating language to cool down and restore mentalization.

Dr. Bateman reminds us that sometimes it is okay to walk away, giving emotions time to cool off. You do not have to stay in the moment if your loved one is behaving in an abusive or hurtful manner.

Sometimes it is okay to walk away, giving emotions time to cool off.

10

Putting It All Together

Integrating Skills for Acceptance and Change

> Most successful people do not have fewer obstacles; they just get up
> after falling down more often than unsuccessful people do.
>
> –Marsha Linehan

PROGRESS IMPLEMENTING CHANGE SKILLS AND IMPROVING YOUR relationship is a process, not an event. The skills discussed throughout this book will take time to internalize and to put into practice; remember that learning these skills is akin to learning a new language. You cannot learn French in a day, can you?

This final chapter is a mini-guide of sorts to the skills discussed in this book and is organized into a checklist of techniques and tips for you to keep in mind during your daily interactions with your loved one. If one technique does not work, move on to another. There is no hard-and-fast rule on when to use which technique, and no single technique can be guaranteed to work every time. None of these techniques will be effective if they are not implemented with compassion. Every person with borderline personality disorder is different, and every situation will evoke a different response from them. This chapter is meant to help you respond to your loved one with spontaneity, flexibility, and compassion, so that you do not maintain or exacerbate the problem.

CHIRP for Relationship Repair

CHIRP (Compassion, Humility, Intuition, Restraint, Persistence) is a handy mnemonic for practicing the skills needed for repairing and improving your relationship with your loved one. Compassion, humility, intuition, and restraint, and being persistent, will help your family on the road to healing. As you adapt new attitudes and skills into your daily life (accepting the neurobiology underlying BPD while mindfully observing, describing, and validating the emotions you sense in your loved one's responses), you will start to see positive changes come about.

It may seem as though applying for contemporary sainthood would be easier than learning to CHIRP. You must practice willingness, giving up your own ego-focused responses and expectations of "normal" relationship reciprocity. Difficult as it may seem, CHIRPing may be easier to learn than you might imagine because your love and concern for your loved one are such strong motivators. As you incorporate these new ways of communicating into your daily interactions and practice them, the improvements you see will encourage you to keep up your efforts.

Compassion. Your loved one is suffering. Cultivating compassion for her pain means you have accepted that she is doing the best she can. Her intention is not to make you suffer. No one chooses to be as unhappy and uncomfortable in her own skin as your loved one with BPD. Acceptance is pivotal for relationship repair and for the process of reconciliation that takes time to evolve, in baby steps. Keep reminding yourself that acceptance is a process, not an event.

Humility. Do you have the humility to admit to yourself and to your loved one that, without intending to, you have said or done things in the past that may have caused harm? Can you accept that you may have done the wrong things for the right reasons? If you can be humble and accept responsibility for your own actions or errors, your loved one will begin to trust you and your relationship will improve.

State the Acceptance-Acknowledgment Declaration in your own words and style. By being genuinely humble and radically genuine, you validate your loved one's painful experiences of not being heard or understood for so much of his life. He will come to see and appreciate the effort you are making to really hear him. Although it may be extremely difficult for you to admit that you have inadvertently hurt the person you love because you did not understand his pain, your acknowledgment will help decrease his suffering. The positive effects on your relationship of being radically genuine will surely outweigh your own feelings of guilt and distress.

Acceptance-Acknowledgement Declaration

I never knew how much pain you were in. I never knew how much you suffered. I must have said and done so many things to hurt you because I did not understand or acknowledge your pain. I am so sorry. It was never my intention to cause you pain. What can we do now to improve our relationship?

Intuition. Trust your feelings and act on them. If you make a mistake, you can always go back and repair it. Only those who do nothing make no mistakes. When you sense that you have said something to upset your loved one or that her emotions have changed, trust your intuitions and act on them. Do not invalidate your own emotional responses or hers because you are afraid of negative emotions or blowups. Even when you are dealing with supposed experts, trust your intuitions. Remember the adage, buyer beware. If your doctor recommends a medication or treatment for your child such as electric shock therapy or residential treatment, ask, "Where can I read about this treatment or this medication? How do I know that it is effective? What's the source of this information? Were clinical trials conducted for this treatment? What were the results?" When in doubt, say "No." Do not let yourself be pressured by professionals or by your loved one into doing something your instincts tell you not to do. Trust yourself. When your loved one asks for something you feel may not be effective, such as moving to another state, it is okay to trust your intuition and voice your disagreement. Do not "rubber stamp" her request; instead, be authentic and tell your loved one that you are worried about what she is asking for. When your friends tell you to practice "tough love," saying that this is the best way to deal with your loved one, trust your intuition. In the end, however, whatever any adult decides to do is his choice, and you must accept that it is his choice to make. If you constantly prevent him from making mistakes, how will he ever develop confidence in his own decision making or learn consequences? At these times, you must give up your efforts to control and tolerate your own distress.

Restraint. During interactions, resolutely focus on long-term goals rather than on short-term peace. As a family member, you probably have an extremely strong desire to fix, rescue, or save the person you love. This desire is heightened when you have experienced the consequences of his drug abuse, eating disorders, self-injury, suicide attempts, and other impulsive behaviors. If you are always jumping into the problem pool with your loved one and trying to fix things, you are not helping him build his own sense of competence or sense of self. Sometimes, especially for family members who are used to solving problems and giving advice, restraint can be more effective than action. Are you solving his problems so as to make yourself feel better? You must tolerate the pain, fear, discomfort, and distress you feel when your loved one makes the mistakes that will inevitably occur as he learns how to solve his own problems. Do you remember how you felt the first time your watched your child cross a busy street alone? Remind yourself of your feelings when you brought your child to school for the first time and how you were able to tolerate that distress. You can do this because you can do hard things. To become competent adults we must gain mastery of important life skills. By allowing your loved one to experience the consequences of his own behaviors as he learns, you are helping him develop mastery, whereas solving his problems disables him and reinforces his sense of incompetence.

> Are you solving his problems so as to make yourself feel better? You must tolerate the pain, fear, discomfort, and distress you feel when your loved one makes the mistakes that will inevitably occur as he learns how to solve his own problems.

Persistence. Balance restraint with persistence. Successful family implementation and reinforcement of change skills depend on your ability to persist until your loved one trusts your sincerity. Your loved one is like a little mouse hiding in its burrow that ventures out for a few minutes and, at the first sign of trouble, scurries back into its nest. Trust develops as you persistently reassure the little mouse. Even if there are no visible signs of success or of decreases in abusive behaviors in the moment, persist in your efforts. If your loved one continues to reject or insult you, continue validating and ask questions such as, "How do you think I feel when you talk to me this way?" "How do you think speaking to me this way encourages me to want to help you?" "How does this get you to your goal or solve the immediate problem or change the situation?" Above all, do not personalize their responses. Be willing to give to get.[1] No matter how your loved one responds to your efforts, do not give up and or tell yourself it will not work. Have faith. Helen Keller said, "We can do anything we want as long as we stick to it long enough." Be relentless in your focus on long-term goals rather than on short-term peace. Use distress tolerance skills to keep yourself going. Your persistence will ultimately bring about changes.

A DBT Tool Kit

Using your newly learned change skills is a bit like playing tennis. This unpredictable, fast-paced game is an apt metaphor for Dialectical Behavior Therapy readiness. When you are playing tennis, you do not know where next the ball will come from, yet you must be ready to respond immediately when it comes across the net, no matter where it lands or how fast it is going. If you really want to win the match, you would not dream of throwing up your hands and tossing the racquet away in the middle of the court, saying, "This is just too hard; that ball was too fast." No matter what is thrown at you, you have to be ready with a DBT response or skill, in the moment. You cannot hesitate and you cannot give up. The following skills and methods can be used to deescalate situations and solve problems. There is no correct order for using these skills. Think of them as your DBT tool kit.

Make an Acceptance-Acknowledgment Declaration. As noted in previous chapters, for you and your loved one this declaration often opens the door to healing and change. Do not assume that making this declaration once is enough; repeat it over and over if necessary. Write your own version but try to keep the focus on the unacknowledged pain you may have caused your loved one. Remind your loved one that you never intended to do any harm, but that you may have been doing the wrong thing for what you thought was the right reason. Acknowledge and validate her pain. Apologize.

---

[1] Linehan, 1993b.

Take your loved one's emotional temperature. Observe your loved one, pay attention, get the lay of the land. Try to sense what emotion she is feeling. Observe body language, gestures, and facial expressions. Determine what is going on, what to validate, and what voice tone to use. It is okay to ask questions so as to get a better sense of what she is feeling.

Mind-read. Since you know your loved one so well, you are in the best position to read his responses. When trying to interpret behaviors, remind yourself that shame is the unarticulated common denominator of most BPD responses. Imagine being your loved one by

---

Barriers to Family Effectiveness

A number of attitudes, habits, and opinions can easily thwart your efforts to support your loved one in an effective, compassionate, and nonjudgmental way. To recap, try to avoid:

- Denying your loved one has BPD
- Making it about you by personalizing, defending, or justifying yourself
- Over-apologizing
- Expressing anger
- Expressing disappointment
- Being over-controlling
- Capitulating to demands
- Being inconsistent
- Feeling hopeless, or believing that nothing will help
- Stuffing down your emotions, fearing your own feelings, avoiding experiencing your feelings
- Willfulness, or focusing on being right rather than being effective
- Focusing on being liked rather than being effective

Furthermore, you must learn to tolerate your own distress, especially when you must say *no* to your loved one. Finally, it is important to radically accepting BPD and its effect on you and the members of your family. Inability to do so leads to invalidated and inhibited grief.

looking at the current situation from his perspective, given his dysregulations and past experiences. Assume shame and a sense of isolation are involved in how he responds or interprets the interaction and try to figure out what triggered the present situation. Validate and normalize his response. Validating shame responses can prevent or diminish emotional escalations or crises in the moment. Do not expect him to be able to articulate what he is feeling. If you get it wrong, try again and state that you are really trying to understand.

When trying to interpret behaviors, remind yourself that shame is the unarticulated common denominator of most BPD responses.

Describe. Describe what you see, what you feel, what your intuition tells you. Take a risk and ask him if you got it right. Reflect back what he is saying, "So, you are telling me that you feel like a loser. Is that what you are feeling? Help me out, I really want to understand."

Validate. Have courage and validate the emotion you sense your loved one is feeling. Try to identify her primary emotion. Be mindful; if your loved one is being abusive toward you, do not take it personally. Keep your own emotion out of it, it is not about you. Do not react to what you are validating. Understand your loved one's experience within the context of her life, her biology, her past experiences, her beliefs, and her relationships. Imagine her wearing the TARA tiara (see Chapter 2). Validate her inner capabilities and wisdom, how hard she is trying, as well as her inherent ability to overcome difficulties and obstacles so as to create a better life for herself.

Validation is the key to improving communication but it is only half a sentence. It needs to be followed by a change strategy. If you are constantly validating without asking for any changes, you will soon be appeasing and disabling. You will not earn your loved one's trust and eventually she will sense that you are patronizing her and not being genuine. Do not validate the invalid by accepting or reinforcing your loved one's abusive behaviors toward you or herself. This only serves to normalize pathology.

Be fully present in the moment. During the interaction, stop doing what ever you were doing and focus all your attention on your loved one. Be sure to make eye contact. Do not do two or more things at once. Put away your cell phone and your BlackBerry. Ask, "What happened?" Say, "I don't understand, can you explain?" "Tell me more!" "What were you thinking at that point? What then?"

Understand the experience within its context. Be the facilitator of exploration. Multitasking is interpreted as your failure to see your loved one or take him seriously, and is a sure-fire way to escalate negative emotions.

Identify and prevent triggers. Now that you have learned how people with BPD think and the emotional pain they live with, it is time to practice predicting their reactions by identifying possible behavioral triggers in various situations, especially those relating to interactions with other people, most likely you. Think of your loved one as a beautiful vase on a pedestal. Your do not want the vase to fall and smash into pieces. What might cause a vibration that would jeopardize the stability of this fragile vase and how could you prevent it? This requires you to mind-read so as to identify possible behavioral triggers and try to prevent emotional escalations by validating emotions and suggesting alternative behaviors. Identifying triggers will help you maintain harmony or allow you to quickly repair damages, especially when they were triggered by experiences with other people over whom you have no control. It is hoped that compassionate understanding and acceptance of your loved one will empower you to focus your attention on the vase of your own relationship so that it will not shatter, rather than repairing the emotional escalations you may have triggered.

Script a DEAR CCC. When you want to ask for something or to explain why you cannot do something, plan what you will say in advance by writing out a structured, clear, and concise script using the DEAR CCC format (see Chapter 8). This will help you to reduce misinterpretations of simple, uncomplicated situations or neutral statements (such as "pass the butter" into "why me? I'm not the maid!"). Remind yourself that BPD is like emotional dyslexia because your loved one seems to experience a disconnect between actual words spoken and her interpretation of the words. The intention of what you say is often misconstrued or made personal. Using DEAR CCC as a guide can prevent triggering maladaptive BPD responses and decrease the possibility of misinterpretations, thereby averting stressful, aversive interactions and improving communication.

E-mail. It is sometimes easier for your loved one to "hear you" when what you are saying is written rather than said face to face. Brain areas that process written words are different from the areas used in interpreting conversations, faces, and gestures, especially

when the conversation is with someone with whom there is an emotional relationship. Reading decreases the potential misinterpretation
of voice tones and facial expressions. Try sending short, validating
e-mails as often as you can. Analyze each and every word you use to
be sure it is nonjudgmental, nondemanding, noncritical, and non-
blaming. Do not start any sentences with the word "you" as this can
be interpreted as an accusation or judgment. If you do not get an
immediate response, do not be discouraged. Think of what you are
doing as planting seeds. If e-mail is not used, try leaving notes in
conspicuous places or sending postcards so that your loved one gets
your message without having to open an envelope.

Cheerlead. Be a coach, not a codependent. Encourage your loved
one by reminding him that he can do hard things, that he has done
hard things in the past, and that he is capable of tolerating distress.
Communicate that you believe in your loved one, in his ability to
overcome difficulties and obstacles and to achieve his goal. Offering
encouragement can build a sense of competence that will help him
handle future problems. Remind him that you believe in his inner
capabilities and wisdom as well as his ability to make decisions, control his own future, and lead a meaningful life. Refer to past accomplishments. You can ask, "What can I say right now that would make
you feel better?" Or ask, "What would you say to a friend who had
the same problem?"

Develop a scale. Help your loved one to evaluate his experiences,
to rate his own emotional intensity or the difficulty of his problem.
Try to find visual means that demonstrate comparisons, such as this
measuring cup technique: Hearing your loved one saying something
like, "This is the worst day of my life, I am in so much pain, I feel so
bad, I have to die," is frightening. Do
not panic. At these times you will
have to first cope with your own distress. Take a deep breath and proceed
as follows: "Wow, I can see how upset
you are. It must feel awful to have
had such a bad day. However, was this

"Many of life's failures are people who did not realize how close they were to success when they gave up." –Thomas Edison

day as bad as the day when you lost your wallet at the mall and couldn't
get home? Or as bad as the day when Judy broke up with you? When
you didn't get a date for the prom?" Take out measuring cups, Russian
nesting dolls, or a set of graduated gift boxes. Set them in a row in

front of your loved one and ask, "Was getting stuck at the mall after it closed as bad as today's crisis? How would you rate today's problem on a scale of 1 to 10? Which cup compares to this problem? Where would you put this problem compared to how you felt when you got stuck at the mall?" Remind him of how he overcame prior problems. Then add another problem he experienced and overcame.

You can also try pouring water from one cup to another and say, "I can see how angry you are right now. Does your anger fill this cup or do you need a larger cup to hold your anger?" As he thinks about how to rate his present feelings, comparing them to prior experiences of anger, he is distracting himself and activating different parts of his brain, allowing his emotional intensity to decrease. By getting him to think in this visual way, you are not only distracting him but are also helping build mastery by reminding him of past accomplishments.

Remember the power of WOW. WOW stands for *Wait, Observe, Wing It*. If, before you respond, you use a strong word that conveys emotion such as *wow*, you buy yourself a little time to think of how best to respond. Wow is also a word that conveys an emotional reaction, an exclamation of surprise or concern .

Be a magnifying glass. People with BPD do not see the world the way you do because their thinking has a strong negative bias. They generally interpret their own lives as a perpetually half-empty cup. Call attention to the positive aspects of situations by reframing actions your loved one has taken and discussing alternative interpretations of events. Guide her toward thinking about the other person's point of view and considering his or her possible intentions. By pointing out the overlooked positive in her life you are being her magnifying glass, helping her see the world and her own accomplishments in a more positive light.

Find the nugget of truth. Find the nugget of truth in whatever it is that your loved one says or feels. There is usually something valid at the bottom of his feelings or actions. It is your job to find and validate it. Remember, this does not mean you are approving of his reactions or behavioral choices. Accept that he feels what he feels. Normalize by reminding him that anyone might feel this way in this situation, including you. Explain the validity of his insight and then offer alternative explanations. "I can see why you would think I was angry when I didn't say good morning; however, I had a headache and was feeling grouchy." This confirms that he read the situation correctly, but depersonalizes it.

Do not encourage fragility. When you avoid facing truths, discussing the reality of situations, or experiencing the natural consequences of certain actions, you are allowing a herd of elephants to take up residence in your living room and you are fragelizing your loved one. This contributes to his feelings of shame. Do not treat your loved one with kid gloves by behaving in a patronizing or condescending manner. This communicates that you believe he is incompetent and too fragile to hear the truth. Raise the bar, assume he can rise to the occasion and do something he has not done before. Acknowledge how hard he is trying and his inherent capacity to change. Be radically genuine.

Build competency and self-respect. To feel competent, a person must succeed at doing something, even if it is just a small thing. Competence, or mastery, is the feeling a person gets when she has accomplished something hard, a difficult challenge she thought perhaps she could not do, like running a marathon, solving a difficult problem, cooking a great meal, making the last payment on a car, getting good grades in a difficult course, giving a well-received speech, or repairing a relationship with a friend. Competency is feeling proud of yourself because you have achieved something you wanted to do. As a result you feel proficient, capable, and effective. You have overcome barriers, both external and internal, and are not living your life passively. You are not too fragile to do difficult things.

Point out that your loved one deserves to feel really good about himself because he has achieved a goal he did not think he could achieve. In your interactions, try to validate the effort your loved one is making, his inherent capacity to change, and the positives in the situation. By discouraging him from meeting challenges because you fear he might fail, you are reinforcing passivity and hopelessness. Give your loved one the benefit of the doubt by chasing the elephant out of your living room, convey that you believe he is equal to hearing the truth. Say things like, "You're the kind of person who . . ." As he develops a sense of his own competency, he will realize that this sense was not within him to begin with but is there now because of the efforts he has made, the actions he took, the things he did, and the obstacles he overcame.

Achieving competency, in "psychobabble" terminology, means developing self-esteem. People with BPD need to feel they have control of their lives, can stand up for themselves, express their own opinions, and say "no" to demands. Dependency is the antithesis of competency. Instead of solving every problem for your loved one, respond with a version of these questions: "How do you think you can solve this problem? What do you think you can do to make things better? I can see how hard you are trying to resolve this problem; what else do you think you can do? How does doing this get you to your goal?" These questions throw the ball back into your loved one's court, telling her implicitly that you believe in her ability to solve her own problems, decrease her dependency, and develop a sense of her own competence. Other helpful statements are "You must be so proud of yourself. Wow, you accomplished a lot; you can do hard things."

This may seem counterintuitive, but do not say "I am proud of you," because this conveys that you are bestowing approval upon her behavior and that what she is thinking or doing does not count without your approval. Likewise, do not say "We are proud of you." BPD is a disorder of interpersonal relationships, and it is hard enough for your loved one to appraise the reactions of and cope with one person; dealing with a "we" situation is even more difficult and confusing. Saying, "We're proud of you," creates a two-on-one situation in which two people are communicating their "approval" of your loved one or her behavior. This presents an even greater obstacle to developing a sense of mastery.

Also, try asking your loved one for advice. Ask her for her opinion. This demonstrates that you respect and trust her opinion and have confidence in her competency. You can ask, "What advice would you give your best friend in this situation?" Encourage her to give herself advice as if she were her own best friend.

Be irreverent. Use humor, make challenging statements, or say things that are irreverent. Mary says, "I must be a real loser if I can't set up this computer by myself." John challenges her statement: "Oh, is everyone supposed to be able to install their own computer? If that were true, why are there so many computer installation companies? I couldn't install my own computer and I had to hire a company to do it. My brother hired his roommate to install his computer. Everyone needs computer help. Why do you think you are supposed to be able to do this by yourself?" It is important to keep your tone of voice light and validating so that these statements are not interpreted as sarcasm.

Learn to live with failure. If you protect your loved one from experiencing failure, how will she ever learn how to overcome it? If you never get a chance to solve a problem, to test yourself against life, how will you ever find out that you can do hard things? An enabling environment is detrimental for everyone but is especially crippling for a person lacking a strong sense of their own capacity to be effective.

When a child is learning to walk he is expected to fall down. The child falls, gets up, falls down again and again, but keeps getting up until he can walk. Can a parent prevent a child from falling as he is learning to walk? What would happen to a child who was prevented from falling as he learned to walk? Is falling down an indication that the child is a failure, or is it a part of the process of learning? Failure is as much a part of life as is success. Getting up creates competency. Sooner or later, we all fail at something. Donald Trump went bankrupt, Hillary Clinton lost the Democratic primary, and John McCain lost his bid for the presidency. Not every meal a chef prepares is perfect, not every painting is a masterpiece—even Wall Street fails sometimes. Every year, there are four actors and actresses who do not win the Oscar. Are they failures?

Accentuate the positive. Remember the old adage, "Is the glass half full or half empty?" People with BPD tend to see themselves and their life experiences as persistently "half empty." They view their lives through a lens focused on their incompetence. They seek confirmation from the world around them supporting their negative beliefs, so that they become self-fulfilling prophecies. They interpret negative outcomes of events as proof of the result they predicted. If she breaks up with a boyfriend after the fifth date, she will pick a fight with a new boyfriend on the fifth date as she is convinced it will be their last. If someone does not say good morning to him, this is a sign that he is a loser. Life seems to conspire to produce the negatives. If you imagine a situation and are sure it will have a negative outcome, you increase the likelihood that the outcome will be negative. Everything depends on how you choose to frame things, the spin you put on events.

> "Success is not forever and failure isn't fatal."
> —Don Shula

Ron's first job was working on a major prime-time network TV series. It ran for seven episodes, then the network dropped the show. Was Ron a loser who worked on a lousy show or was he lucky to have gotten his first shot at a network series? A retrospective of most great artists shows that their early paintings were usually mediocre. How many rejection slips do most writers receive before being published? Persistence is often more important than innate talent. It takes courage to keep going. Courage is not the absence of fear but the ability to keep going in spite of it.

Be your loved one's memory. When a person with BPD is in emotion mind (see Chapter 6), she will hold herself up to impossible, unrealistic standards; compare herself to others; and feel as if the world has conspired to cast her as a failure. She seems to have a memory deficit that prevents her from remembering her own accomplishments, difficulties she overcame, and happy times when she felt competent and secure. You can be helpful by being your loved one's biographer, reminding her of past accomplishments and good times. You are the repository of her achievements, positive experiences, and successes. When you share your own positive memories, you help her develop competency and self-respect. Remind her that a feeling is not a fact—just because she feels like a failure does not mean she is. There were times when she felt as hopeless, sad, or incompetent as she does now, yet those feelings eventually changed. You can cheerlead with statements such as "You can do hard things. Do you remember when you got the only A in science class? Came in second in the swimming race? Got the lead in the school play? Broke up with Frank and met Ken three days later? Lost your job and were sure you would never get another one, and then landed a better job?" Mental health professionals treating your loved one do not have this reservoir of past experiences to tap into that can be so helpful in developing competency.

Because people with BPD seem to have difficulty accessing their own happy memories, provide your loved one with concrete, physical evidence of his positive experiences. For a birthday or any occasion, make small memory books with pictures to remind him of happy times. If you have childhood mementos or keepsakes, include them in the memory books. Write descriptions of the pictures. Give framed photos as gifts. If your loved one is not living with you, send photos in e-mails.

Manage contingencies. Anticipate how your loved one might react or feel in a situation. If a family function such as a wedding, funeral, or holiday dinner is coming up and she is going to be with all her relatives, you can count on anxiety escalating as she ruminates over what might happen. Try asking questions about potentially difficult situations that are sure to arise and help her find ways to deal with them ahead of time. Rehearse what others might ask your loved one and work out responses that would deescalate or change the subject. Ask her how she would feel if confronted about certain topics. Anticipate her feelings of shame. Try to help her reframe others' actions and intentions so as to decrease her self-referential interpretations. Rehearse strategies so that she has an exit plan ready if she is unable to tolerate a situation, such as, "I would really like to tell you what I am doing now but I have to go to the ladies' room." Rehearse how to change the subject when someone asks intrusive questions. She can respond by saying, "By the way, how is Aunt Mary's divorce coming along?" Or, "I ran into Fred the other day."

Empower your loved one. Your loved one's rigid and inflexible attitudes toward new experiences, change, or doing anything you might ask him to do has probably caused you much angst. How can you motivate someone to do something you want him to do, and have him think all along that it was his own idea? Your loved one needs to feel that any decision is his own to make, that he has total control over what he does. You must be willing to cede control and accept the decisions your loved one makes, even if they are not the ones you wanted.

Talk about goals. Ask, "How does doing this or making this choice get you to your goal?" You will have to "sell" your choice by presenting the positive reasons for making this choice. Present alternative solutions. Call attention to the pros and cons of a choice and suggest writing them down. Discuss the negatives of a choice while validating the difficulties of the situation and repeating, over and over again, "Whatever you decide to do is your choice." Ask your loved one, "How will you get from here to there?" ending every statement, like a broken record, with "It's your choice!" If a choice is made that you do not approve of, you must respect it without judging or threatening your loved one with statements such as "If you don't do this, I will . . ." Do not offer arbitrary choices. Be flexible, not willful. Would you rather be right, or effective?

Almost any new situation in which your loved one feels out of control, judged, compared to others, criticized, incompetent, or embarrassed will produce anxiety. Remind her of past achievements in similar difficult situations. Instead of telling her what to do, ask your loved one challenging questions. Play devil's advocate by making her defend her choice or decision. "I know you really liked that gym in our old neighborhood, but why go all the way across town to a gym when there is one close by?" Bring out the negatives of a choice by asking, "What would you do if . . ." then present contingencies.

"Door in the Face" is a technique in which you ask for something "bigger" than what you really want, such as "How about coming over for the weekend?" When the person says no, you keep reducing your requests to something smaller and more manageable, such as "Well, how about coming over for dinner?" Keep negotiating down: "Would you consider meeting for lunch? Brunch? A cup of coffee?" Always provide an exit strategy by saying, "If you are uncomfortable, you can always leave." Be a broken record; keep offering alternatives while repeating the message that the ultimate decision is their choice.

"Foot in the Door" reverses this procedure. Start out by making an easy, small request, then follow it up with a harder or bigger request. Keep "upping the ante" while repeating, "it is your choice." When you select a strategy and it does not get results, try an alternative strategy. This is a process, not an event. Remember to respect your loved one's goals and ideas.

Reconcile and synthesize. Both you and the person with BPD must radically accept that each one of you did the best you could and never realized or understood the effect your behaviors and responses had on the other person. To achieve a synthesis between acceptance and change it is essential that you forgive one another. Although each of you may have reacted in ways that hurt or invalidated one another, this was not your intention. Each of you must accept the difficulty of the problems you are facing, as well as the idea that the problems can be overcome. With compassion, you can achieve the dialectic balance of acceptance with change.

Accept the premises of DBT. Progress in DBT is not an "ah ha! moment"; rather it is a slow, ongoing process. It requires setting realistic goals and readjusting expectations. BPD is a chronic disorder, not an infection that gets better with a shot of antibiotics. Progress is a decrease in the severity of episodes and an increase in the length of time between episodes. Prioritize; you do not have to hit a home run every time. Winning is not as important as staying in the game. Keep trying. Progress depends on the priorities you set for yourself and your loved one. Ask yourself, is it more important that he graduate from college, or that he stay alive, stop self-injuring, and improve the quality of his life? Try to tolerate your own fears, frustrations, disappointments, and sense of powerlessness. Your loved one's emotional difficulties are invisible handicaps that impede his achievement of competency and self-respect. If your goal is improving or repairing your relationship, the rest will follow. Focus on changing yourself so that you can be willing, open, radically genuine, authentic, and compassionate.

To achieve a synthesis between acceptance and change it is essential that you forgive one another.

Afterword: For Clinicians

RESEARCH SHOWS US THAT 70% OF PEOPLE WITH BORDERLINE PERSONALITY DISORDER drop out of treatment. According to John Gunderson, medical director of the Center for the Treatment of Borderline Personality Disorder at McLean Hospital, in Boston, Massachusetts, failure to involve the family as support for treatment of BPD makes patients' involvement in therapy superficial and is a major reason for premature dropout. Family members or partners consult clinicians for help in coping with someone with BPD because they care, and are frightened, frustrated, and feeling helpless. This is someone they love. As a clinician you have an opportunity to guide these families toward reconciliation and repair. Family members spend more time with the person with BPD than anyone else and are in a key position to provide ongoing help and guidance, prevent escalations, and motivate their loved one to participate in evidence-based treatment.

Here is a compilation of what families need from clinicians based on hundreds of TARA helpline calls, reports from family skills group participants, and from the work of John Gunderson.

Accurate information. Knowledge of the biological basis of BPD can help families reframe the behavior of their loved one in the light of current science and accept that evidence-based treatment works. Accurate information can dispel the stigma that colors attitudes toward people with BPD.

Understanding that the person with BPD is doing the best he can and does not intend to harm others or himself. Discourage viewing the person with BPD as "manipulative," as the enemy, or as hopeless. Understanding can melt anger and cultivate compassion.

Acceptance that the person with BPD has a disability and has special needs. Help the family accept their loved one as someone with a chronic illness. They may continue to be financially and emotionally dependent on the family and be vocationally impaired. BPD is a deficit or handicap that can be overcome. Help families to reconcile to the long-term course of BPD and accept that progress will be slow. There are no short-term solutions.

Compassion. Do not assume that every family is a "dysfunctional family." Emotions are contagious. Living with someone with BPD can make any family dysfunctional. Family members have been recipients of rages as well as abusive and irrational behaviors. They live in perpetual fear and feel manipulated. They often react by either protecting and rescuing or rejecting and avoiding. Reframe their points of view with compassion. Families are doing the best they can. They need support and acceptance. "Bad parents" are usually uninformed, not malevolent. They did the wrong things for the right reasons (the "allergic to milk syndrome"). Anyone can have a disturbed child. Keep reminding the family of the neurobiological dysregulations of BPD, and of the pain their loved one is coping with each day.

Collaboration for change. Accept that families can help, can learn effective skills and become therapeutic partners. They can reinforce treatment. The IQ of a family member is not reduced if a loved one has BPD. Do not patronize or fragelize family members. Family members are generally well-educated, intelligent people who are highly motivated to help. Respect their commitment. When you provide them with effective skills to help their loved one, they can become therapeutic parent or partners. You can help them.

Stay in the present. Do not focus on past painful experiences when the person with BPD cannot cope with aversive feelings and has no distress tolerance skills. Avoid shame-inducing memories. If you induce arousal and the patient cannot cope with the arousal, therapy becomes unacceptable, giving her additional pressure and stress and undermining cognitive control. This is a sure-fire way to get her to drop out of therapy.

Be nonjudgmental. Respect that families are doing the best they can, in the moment, without any understanding of the underlying disorders or the ability to translate their loved one's behaviors. Although they may have done the wrong thing in the past, it was probably for the right reasons. Their intention was not to hurt their loved one.

Teach awareness of nonverbal communication. Teach them limbic language so they can learn to speak to the amygdala, to communicate emotionally through validation. Teach families to be aware of body language, voice tones, gestures, and facial expressions. Especially avoid neutral faces. Teach effective coping skills based on cognitive behavior therapy, DBT, and mentalization.

Corroborate allegations. Try not to assume the worst, and corroborate allegations. Remember that your perception of an event or experience may be different from what actually happened.

Remember, families have rights. When families are paying for therapy, they have rights, beyond confidentiality regulations such as the Health Insurance Portability and Accountability Act (HIPAA). This reality must be acknowledged. Excluding parents completely jeopardizes the feasibility of continuation of therapy. They need to help decide if investment in therapy is worthwhile and have a right to know about attendance, motivation, and benefits from therapy. What is confidential in therapy is what is talked about. Let them know about the therapy, prognosis, and course of the illness

Avoid boundaries, limits, contracts, and tough love. These methods are not effective with people with BPD. Be sure that families understand that boundaries are generally viewed as punishment by the person with BPD. Be sure they understand how to change behavior by explaining reinforcement, punishment, shaping, and extinction so that they do not reinforce maladaptive behaviors

Discourage "we." Encourage family members to nurture individual relationships with the person with BPD, not the united front of "we." Although both parents can have the same goals for their loved one, they must express these goals in their own style, in one-on-one relationships. Focus on developing individual relationships and trust, not solving individual problems. This will discourage "splitting."

Encourage family involvement. When a person with BPD resists family involvement, this should not be automatically accepted. Resistance is symptomatic of the person with BPD devaluing his loved ones. If you participate in devaluing the family, difficulties are intensified when treatment comes to an end, especially when the person is financially dependent on his family. Remember that the family loves this person and will be there for him when you are no longer involved.

Resources

Treatment and Research Advancements National Association for
Personality Disorder (TARA NAPD)
23 Greene Street
New York, NY 10013
Phone: (212) 966-6514
Email: taraapd@aol.com

Behavioral Tech LLC
2133 Third Avenue
Suite 205
Seattle, WA 98121
Phone: (206) 675-8588
Email: information@behavioraltech.org

National Education Alliance for Borderline Personality Disorder
(NEA-BPD)
PO Box 974
Rye, NY 10580
www.neabpd.org

Middle Path
www.middle-path.org

Florida Borderline Personality Disorder Association
PO Box 756
St. Petersburg, FL 33731
Email: amanda.smith@fbpda.org

Bibliography

American Psychiatric Association. *Diagnostic and Statistical Manual of Mental Disorders* (4th ed.; DSM-IV). Washington, DC: American Psychiatric Association, 1994.

American Psychiatric Association. *Diagnostic and Statistical Manual of Mental Disorders* (4th ed., text rev.). Washington, DC: American Psychiatric Association, 2000.

Anais Nin. Personal Communication, New York. 1970.

Aron, Elaine N. *The Highly Sensitive Person. How to Thrive When the World Overwhelms You.* New York: Broadway Books, 1996.

Ayduk, O., V. Zayas, G. Downey, A. B. Cole, Y. Shoda, and W. Mischel. "Rejection Sensitivity and Executive Control: Joint predictors of Borderline Personality features." *J Res Pers* 42.1 (2008): 151–168.

Balas, E. A., and S. A. Boren. "Managing Clinical Knowledge for Health Care Improvement." *Yearbook of Medical Informatics*. Maryland: International Medical Informatics Association (2000): 65–70.

Baldwin James, Chappaqua: NY Readers Digest, August 1971.

Bastien, Célyne H., et al. "Cognitive-Behavioral Therapy for Insomnia: Comparison of Individual Therapy, Group Therapy, and Telephone Consultations." *Journal of Consulting and Clinical Psychology* 72.4 (2004): 653–9.

Bastien, Célyne H., A. Vallières, and C. M. Morin. "Precipitating Factors of Insomnia." *Behavioral Sleep Medicine* 2.1 (2004): 50–62.

Bateman, A., and P. Fonagy. *Psychotherapy for Borderline Personality Disorder Mentalization-Based Treatment*. Oxford: Oxford University Press, 2004.

Battle, C. L., et al. "Childhood Maltreatment Associated with Adult Personality Disorders: Findings from the Collaborative Longitudinal Personality Disorders Study." *Journal of Personality Disorders* 18.2 (2004): 193–211.

Baumeister, Roy F., T. F. Heatherton, and D. Tice. *Losing Control: How and Why People Fail At Self-Regulation*. San Diego: Academic Press, 1994.

Baumeister, Roy F., J. M. Twenge, and D. Tice. *The Social Self*, 2003.

Beblo, T., M. Driessen, M. Mertens, K. Wingenfeld, M. Piefke, N. Rullkoetter, A. Silva-Saavedra, C. Mensebach, L. Reddemann, H. Rau, H. J. Markowitsch, H. Wulff, W. Lange, C. Berea, I. Ollech, F. G. Woermann. "Functional MRI correlates of the recall of unresolved life events in borderline personality disorder." *Psychol Med* 36.6 (2006):845–56.

Beck, Aaron T., *Prisoners of Hate: The Cognitive Basis of Anger, Hostility and Violence*. New York: HarperCollins, 1999.

Beck, Aaron T., Arthur Freeman, and Associates. *Cognitive Therapy of Personality Disorder*. New York: Guilford Press, 1990.

Beck, Aaron T., A. Freeman, D. D. Davis, and Associates. *Cognitive Therapy of Personality Disorder* (2nd ed.). New York: Guilford Press, 2004.

Berenson, K. R., A. Gyurak, O. Ayduk, G. Downey, M. J. Garner, K. Mogg, B. P. Bradley, D. S. Pine. "Rejection Sensitivity and Disruption of Attention by Social Threat Cues." *J Res Pers* 43.6 (2009): 1064–1072.

Berlin, H. A., E. T. Rolls. "Time Perception, Impulsivity, Emotionality, and Personality in Self-Harming Borderline Personality Disorder Patients." *J Personal Disord* 18.4 (2004): 358–78.

Biederman, J., D. R. Hirshfeld-Becker, J. F. Rosenbaum, C. Herot, D. Friedman, N. Snidman, J. Kagan, and S. V. Faraone. "Further Evidence of Association between Behavioral Inhibition and Social Anxiety in Children." *American Journal of Psychiatry* 158.10 (2001): 1673–9.

Bockian, Neil R., V. Porr, and N. E. Villagram. *New Hope for People with Borderline Personality Disorder*. New York: Three Rivers Press, 2002.

Bohus, M., et al. "Effectiveness of Inpatient Dialectical Behavioral Therapy for Borderline Personality Disorder: A Controlled Trial." *Behaviour Research and Therapy* 42.5 (2004): 487–99.

Bohus, M., C. Schmahl, and K. Lieb. "New Developments in the Neurobiology of Borderline Personality Disorder." *Current Psychiatry Reports* 6.1 (2004): 43–50.

Brambilla, P., et al. "Anatomical MRI Study of Borderline Personality Disorder Patients." *Psychiatry Research* 131.2 (2004): 125–33.

Bridget, F. G., Ph.D., Ph.D., F. S. Stinson, Ph.D., D. A. Dawson, Ph.D., S. P. Chou, Ph.D., W. J. Ruan, M.A., and R. P. Pickering, M.S. "Co-Occurrence of 12-Month Alcohol and Drug Use Disorders and Personality Disorders in the United States Results From the National Epidemiologic Survey on Alcohol and Related Conditions." *Archives of General Psychiatry* 61(April 2004): 361–368. http://pubs.niaaa.nih.gov/publications/arh29–2/121–130.htm

Brodsky, B. S., and B. Stanley. "Dialectical Behavior Therapy for Borderline Personality Disorder." *Psychiatric Annals* 32.6 (2002): 347–56.

Brown, M. Z., K. A. Comtois, and M. M. Linehan, "Reasons for Suicide Attempts and Nonsuicidal Self-injury in Women with Borderline Personality Disorder." *Journal of Abnormal Psychology* 111.1 (2002): 198–202.

Burns, D., *The Feeling Good Handbook*. New York: Plume, 1999.

Caspi, A., K. Sugden, T. E. Moffitt, A. Taylor, I. W. Craig, H. Harrington, J. McClay, J. Mill, J. Martin, A. Braithwaite, and R. Poulton. "Influence of Life Stress on Depression: Moderation by a Polymorphism in the 5-HTT." *Science* 301.5631 (July 18, 2003): 386–9.

Cauwels, J. M. *Imbroglio: Rising to the Challenges of Borderline Personality Disorder*. New York: Norton, 1992.

Chodron, P. *The Place That Scares You: A Guide to Fearlessness in Difficult Times*, Boston: Shambhala, 2002.

Cleary, T. F., *Teachings of Zen (YING AN)*, Boston, MA:Shambhala, 1998.

Coccaro, E. F., R. J. Kavoussi. "Fluoxetine and Impulsive Aggressive Behavior in Personality-Disordered Subjects". *Arch Gen Psychiatry* 54.12 (1997): 1081–8.

Cornelius, J. R., et al. "Fluoxetine in Depressed AUD Adolescents: A 1-Year Follow-Up Evaluation." *Journal of Child and Adolescent Psychopharmacology* 14.1 (2004): 33–8.

Cornelius, J. R., et al. "Acute Phase and Five-Year Follow-Up Study of Fluoxetine in Adolescents with Major Depression and a Comorbid Substance Use Disorder: A Review." *Addictive Behaviors* 30.9 (2005a): 1824–33.

Cornelius, J. R., et al. "Fluoxetine in Adolescents with Comorbid Major Depression and an Alcohol Use Disorder: A 3-Year Follow-Up Study." *Addictive Behaviors* 30.4 (2005b): 807–14.

Cornelius, J. R., et al. "Treatment of Co-Occurring Alcohol, Drug, and Psychiatric Disorders." *Recent Developments in Alcoholism* 17 (2005c): 349–65.

Covert, M. V., et al. " Shame-Proneness, Guilt-Proneness, and
   Interpersonal Problem Solving: A Social Cognitive Analysis." *Journal of
   Social and Clinical Psychology* 22.1 (2003): 1–12.

Cummings E.E., Poems 1923–1054, NY: W.W. Norton, 1923.

Dalai Lama, and D. Goleman, *Destructive Emotions, How Can We
   Overcome Them*. New York: Bantam Books, 2003.

Dalai Lama, and D. Goleman, *Healing Emotions*. Boston: Shambala, 2003.

Damasio, H., T. Grabowski, R. Frank, A. M. Galaburda, A. R. Damasio. "The
   Return of Phineas Gage: Clues about the Brain from the Skull of a
   Famous Patient." *Science* 264.5162 (1994): 1102–5.

Damasio, A. *Descarte's Error*. New York: Penguin Putnam, 1994.

Damasio, A. *The Feeling of What Happens. Body and Emotion in the
   Making of Consciousness*. Orlando, FL: Harcourt, 1999.

Damasio, A. *Looking for Spinoza: Joy, Sorrow and the Feeling Brain*.
   Orlando, FL: Harcourt, 2003.

Dearing, R. L., J. Stuewig, and J. P. Tangney. "On the Importance of
   Distinguishing Shame from Guilt: Relations to Problematic Alcohol and
   Drug Use." *Addictive Behaviors* 30.7 (2005) : 1392–404.

Dimeff, L. A., and K. Koerner (eds). *Dialectic Behavior Therapy in Clinical
   Practice, Applications Across Disorders and Settings*. New York:
   Guilford Press, 2003.

Didion, J. *The Year of Magical Thinking*. New York: Alfred A. Knopf,
   2005.

Doka, K .J., and R. Aber. "Psychological Loss and Grief." In K. J. Doka (Ed.),
   Disenfranchised Grief: Recognizing Hidden Sorrow (187–98).
   Lexington, MA: Lexington Books,1989.

Donegan, N. H., et al. "Amygdala Hyperreactivity in Borderline
   Personality Disorder: Implications for Emotional Dysregulation."
   Biological Psychiatry 54.11 (2003): 1284–93.

Downey, G., V. Mougios, O. Ayduk, B. E. London, Y. Shoda. "Rejection
   Sensitivity and The Defensive Emotional System, Insights from the
   Startle Response to Rejection Cues." *Psychological Science* 15.10:
   668–673.

Dutton, D. G. *The Abusive Personality: Violence and Control In Intimate
   Relationships*. New York: Guilford Press, 1998.

Ebner-Priemer, U. W., S. S. Welch, P. Grossman, T. Reisch, M. M. Linehan,
   M. Bohus. "Psychophysiological Ambulatory Assessment of Affective
   Dysregulation in Borderline Personality Disorder." *Psychiatry Res*
   150.3 (2007): 265–75.

Ekman, P. *Emotions Revealed*. New York: Times Books/Henry Holt, 2003.

Ekman, P., and Dalai Lama. *Emotional Awareness*. New York: Henry Holt
   & Co, 2008.

Ellis, T. E., and C. F. Newman. *Choosing to Live. How to Defeat Suicide through Cognitive Therapy.* Oakland, CA: New Harbinger, 1996.

Ellis, A. *Anger: How To Live With And Without It.* New Jersey: Citadel Press, 1977.

Erkwoh, R., S. Herpertz, and H. Sass. "Personality Disorders and Schizophrenic Psychoses." *Nervenarzt* 74.9 (2003): 740–7.

Fertuck, E. A., A. Jekal, I. Song, B. Wyman, M. C. Morris, S. T. Wilson, B. S. Brodsky, B. Stanley. "Enhanced 'Reading the Mind in the Eyes' in Borderline Personality Disorder Compared to Healthy Controls." *Psychol Med* 39.12 (2009): 1979–88.

Fertuck, E. A., M. F. Lenzenweger, J. F. Clarkin, S. Hoermann, B. Stanley. "Executive Neurocognition, Memory Systems, and Borderline Personality Disorder." *Clin Psychol Rev* 26.3 (2006): 346–75.

Fossati, P., et al. "In Search of the Emotional Self: An FMRI Study Using Positive and Negative Emotional Words." *American Journal of Psychiatry* 160.11 (2003): 1938–45.

Fossati, P., et al. "Distributed Self in Episodic Memory: Neural Correlates of Successful Retrieval of Self-Encoded Positive and Negative Personality Traits." *NeuroImage* 22.4 (2004): 1596–604.

Fox, T. "Integrating Dialectical Behavioral Therapy into a Community Mental Health Program." *Psychiatric Services* 49.10 (1998): 1338–40.

Friedel, R. O. *Borderline Personality Disorder Demystified: An Essential Guide for Understanding and Living with BPD.* New York: Marlowe, 2004.

Fruzzetti, A. E., J. Waltz, and M. Linehan. "Supervision in DBT." In C. E. Watkins (Ed), *Handbook of Psychotherapy Supervision.* New York: Guilford Press, 1997.

Gordon, F. W., I. Lombardo, A. S. New, M. Goodman, P. S. Talbot, Y. Huang, D. Hwang, M. Slifstein, S. Curry, A. Abi-Dargham, M. Laruelle, and L. J. Siever. "Brain Serotonin Transporter Distribution in Subjects with Impulsive Aggressivity: A Positron Emission Study." *American Journal of Psychiatry* 162.5 (2005): 915–23.

Gibran, K. *The Prophet.* New York: Alfred A. Knopf, 1923.

Girolamo, G. de, and J. H. Reich. *Personality Disorder.* Geneva, Switzerland: World Health Organization, 1993.

Gladwell, M. *Blink: The Power of Thinking without Thinking.* New York: Little, Brown, 2005.

Goleman, D. *Emotional Intelligence.* New York: Bantam,1995.

Goleman, D. *Social Intelligence.* New York: Bantam 2006.

Goodman, M., et al. "The Role of Childhood Trauma in Differences in Affective Instability in Those with Personality Disorders." *CNS Spectrums* 8.10 (2003): 763–70.

Gordon, J. *Stress Management, 21st Century Health And Wellness,* New York: NY Chelsea House, 1990.

Grandin, T. *Thinking in Pictures and Other Reports from My Life with Autism.* New York: Vintage Books, 1995.

Grant, B. F., S. P. Chou, R. B. Goldstein, B. Huang, F. S. Stinson, T. D. Saha, S. M. Smith, D. A. Dawson, A. J. Pulay, R. P. Pickering, W. J. Ruan. "Prevalence, Correlates, Disability, and Comorbidity of DSM-IV Borderline Personality Disorder: Results from the Wave 2 National Epidemiologic Survey on Alcohol and Related Conditions." *J Clin Psychiatry* 69.4 (2008): 533–45.

Grant, J. E., S. Correia, T. Brennan-Krohn, P. F. Malloy, D. H. Laidlaw, S. C. Schulz. "Frontal White Matter Integrity in Borderline Personality Disorder with Self-Injurious Behavior." *J Neuropsychiatry Clin Neurosci* 19.4 (2007): 383–90.

Grilo, C. M., C. A. Sanislow, and T. H. McGlashan. "Co-Occurrence of DSM-IV Personality Disorders with Borderline Personality Disorder." *Journal of Nervous and Mental Disease* 190.8 (2002): 552–4.

Gunderson, J. G., I. Weinberg, M. T. Daversa, K. D. Kueppenbender, M. C. Zanarini, M. T. Shea, A. E. Skodol, C. A. Sanislow, S. Yen, L. C. Morey, C. M. Grilo, T. H. McGlashan, R. L. Stout, I. Dyck. "Descriptive and longitudinal observations on the relationship of borderline personality disorder and bipolar disorder." *Am J Psychiatry* 163.7 (2006): 1173–8.

Gunderson, J. *Borderline Personality Disorder, A Clinical Guide, Second Edition*, Virginia: American Psychiatric Publishing Inc, 2008.

Gurvits, I. G., H. W. Koenigsberg, and L. J. Siever. "Neurotransmitter Dysfunction in Patients with Borderline Personality Disorder." *Psychiatric Clinics of North America* (Special Issue: Borderline Personality Disorder) 23.1 (2000): 27–40.

Hanh, T. N. *The Miracle of Mindfulness.* Boston MA: Beacon Press, 1975.

Hanh, T. N. *Being Peace.* Berkeley, CA: Parallax Press, 1987.

Hanh, T. N. *Peace in Every Step.* New York: Bantam, 1991.

Hanh, T. N. *Teachings on Love.* Berkeley, CA: Parallax Press, 1998.

Hanh, T. N. *Anger.* New York: Berkley Publishing Group, 2001.

Hanh, T. N. *Joyfully Together.* Berkeley, CA: Parallax Press, 2003.

Hare, R. D., and J. W. Jutai. "Psychopathy and Cerebral Symmetry in Semantic Processing." *Personality and Individual Differences* 9.2 (1988): 329–37.

Hazlett, E. A., A. New, R. S. Newmark, M. M. Haznedar, J. N. Lo, L. J. Speiser, A. D. Chen, V. Mitropoulou, M. Minzenberg, L. J. Siever, and M. S. Buchsbaum. "Reduced Anterior and Posterior Cingulate Gray Matter in Borderline Personality Disorder." *Biol Psychiatry* 58.8 (2005): 614–23.

Hazlett, E. A., J. Levine, M. S. Buchsbaum, J. M. Silverman, A. New, E. M. Sevin, L. A. Maldari, and L. J. Siever. "Deficient Attentional Modulation of the Startle Response in Patients with Schizotypal Personality Disorder." *American Journal of Psychiatry* 160.9 (2003) :1621–6.

Hazlett, E. A., L. J. Speiser, M. Goodman, M. Roy, M. Carrizal, J. K. Wynn, W. Williams, M. Romero, M. J. Minzenberg, L. J. Siever, A. S. New. "Exaggerated Affect-Modulated Startle during Unpleasant Stimuli in Borderline Personality Disorder." *Biol Psychiatry* 62.3 (2007): 250–5. Epub: Jan 29, 2007.

Hebebrand, J., et al. "Binge-Eating Episodes Are Not Characteristic of Carriers of Melanocortin-4 Receptor Gene Mutations." *Molecular Psychiatry* 9.8 (2004): 796–800.

Heinlein, R. A., *Assignment in Eternity*, Riverdale, NY: Baen Books, 1991.

Henry, C., V. Mitropoulou, A. S. New, H. W. Koenigsberg, J. Silverman, and L. J. Siever. "Affective Instability and Impulsivity in Borderline Personality and Bipolar II Disorders: Similarities and Differences." *Journal of Psychiatric Research* 35.6 (2001): 307–12.

Herpertz, S., et al. "Affective Instability and Impulsivity in Personality Disorder: Results of an Experimental Study." *Journal of Affective Disorders* 44.1 (1997): 31–7.

Herpertz, S., H. Sass, and A. Favazza. "Impulsivity in Self-Mutilative Behavior: Psychometric and Biological Findings." *Journal of Psychiatric Research* 31.4 (1997): 451–65.

Herpertz, S., and H. Sass. "Impulsiveness and Impulse Control. on the Psychological and Psychopathological Conceptualization. "*Nervenarzt* 68.3 (1997): 171–83.

Herpertz, S. C., T. M. Dietrich, B. Wenning, T. Krings, S. G. Erberich, K. Willmes, A. Thron, and H. Sass. "Evidence of Abnormal Amygdala Functioning in Borderline Personality Disorder: A Functional MRI Study." *Biological Psychiatry* 50.4 (2001): 292–8.

Hoffman, P. D., et al. "Family Members' Knowledge about Borderline Personality Disorder: Correspondence with Their Levels of Depression, Burden, Distress, and Expressed Emotion." *Family Process* 42.4 (2003): 469–78.

Hoffman, P., and T. McGlashan. *A Development Model of Borderline Personality Disorder*, Virginia, Amer: Psychiatric Publishing, 2003.

Hooley, J. "Family 'Overinvolvement' Aids Borderline Patient's Recovery." *Emotional Environmental Matters*, Clinical Psychiatry News 30.12 (2002).

Hooley, J. M., S. A. Gruber, H. A. Parker, J. Guillaumot, J. Rogowska, D. A. Yurgelun-Todd. "Neural Processing of Emotional Overinvolvement in Borderline Personality Disorder." *J Clin Psychiatry.* Department of Psychology, Harvard University (2010).

Hooley, J. M., and J. B. Hiller. "Personality and Expressed Emotion." *Journal of Abnormal Psychology* 109.1 (2000): 40–4.

Hooley, J. M., and P. D. Hoffman. "Expressed Emotion and Clinical Outcome in Borderline Personality Disorder." *American Journal of Psychiatry* 156.10 (1999): 1557–62.

Judd, P. H., and T. H. McGlashan. *A Developmental Model of Borderline Personality Disorder. Understanding Variations in Course and Outcome.* Washington, DC: American Psychiatric Publishing, 2003.

Juengling, F. D., C. Schmahl, B. Hesslinger, D. Ebert, J. D. Bremner, J. Gostomzyk, M. Bohus, and K. Lieb. "Positron Emission Tomography in Female Patients with Borderline Personality Disorder." *Journal of Psychiatric Research* 37.2 (2003): 109–115.

Kabat-Zinn, J. *Full Catastrophe Living: Using the Wisdom of Your Body and Mind to Face Stress, Pain, and Illness.* New York: Delta Books, 1990.

Kagan J., N. Snidman, M. McManis, and S. Woodward. Temperamental Contributions to the Affect Family of Anxiety." *Psychiatric Clinics of North America* 24.4 (2001): 677–88.

Kandel, E. R. *Psychiatry, Psychoanalysis, and the New Biology of Mind.* Washington, DC: American Psychiatric Publishing, 2005.

Kandel, E. R. *In Search of Memory: The Emergence of a New Science of Mind.,* New York: Norton, 2006.

Kandel, E. R., J. H. Schwartz, and T. M. Jessell. *Principles of Neural Science* (4th ed.). New York: McGraw-Hill, 2000.

Kaysen, S. *Girl Interrupted.* New York: Vintage Books, 1994.

Keller, H. *The Story of My Life,* Kansas: Digireads Publishing, January 2007.

Kemperman, I., M. J. Russ, C. W. Crawford, T. Kakuma, E. Zanine, and K. Harrison. "Pain Assessment in Self-Injurious Patients with Borderline Personality Disorder Using Signal Detection Theory." *Psychiatry Research* 70.3 (1997): 175–83.

Kemperman, I., M. J. Russ, and E. Shearin. "Self-Injurious Behavior and Mood Regulation in Borderline Patients." *Journal of Personality Disorders* 11.2 (1997): 146–57.

Kiehl, K. A., A. M. Smith, A. Mendrek, B. B. Forster, R. D. Hare, and P. F. Liddle. "Temporal Lobe Abnormalities in Semantic Processing by Criminal Psychopaths as Revealed by Functional Magnetic Resonance Imaging." *Psychiatry Research* 130.3 (Apr 30, 2004): 297–312. Corrected and republished from: *Psychiatry Research* 130.1 (Jan 15, 2004): 27–42.

Kingsley, E. P., *Welcome to Holland.* 1987.

Klosterman, L. "Endorphins: The Gift You Give Yourself." *Chronogram* 11 (Nov. 2005).

Koenigsberg, H. W., P. D. Harvey, V. Mitropoulou, A. New, M. Goodman, and L. J. Siever. "Affective Instability in Personality Disorders." *American Journal of Psychiatry* 160.2 (2003): 395.

Koenigsberg, H. W., P. D. Harvey, V. Mitropoulou, J. Schmeidler, A. S. New, M. Goodman, J. M. Silverman, M. Serby, F. Schopick, and L. J. Siever. "Characterizing Affective Instability in Borderline Personality Disorder." *American Journal of Psychiatry* 159.5 (2002): 784–8.

Koenigsberg, H. W., L. J. Siever, X. Guo, A. S. New, M. Goodman, H. Cheng, and I. Prohovnik. "Cerebral Processing of Negative Emotion in Borderline Personality Disorder: An fMRI Perspective." *Biological Psychiatry* 57.85 (2005): 2015–16.

Korfine, L., and J. M. Hooley. "Directed Forgetting of Emotional Stimuli in Borderline Personality Disorder." *Journal of Abnormal Psychology* 109.2 (2000): 214–21.

Kramer, H. *Liberating the Adult Within: How to be a Grown-Up for Good.* New York: Simon and Schuster, 1994.

Kreisman, J. J., and H. Strauss. *I Hate You—Don't Leave Me: Understanding the Borderline Personality.* New York: Avon Books, 1991.

Kubler-Ross, E., D. Kessler. *Grief and Grieving: Finding the meaning of grief through the five stages of loss.* New York: Scribner, 2005.

Kuchinke, L., A. M. Jacobs, C. Grubich, M. L. Vo, M. Conrad, and M. Herrmann. "Incidental Effects of Emotional Valence in Single Word Processing: An fMRI Study." *Neuroimage* 28.4 (2005): 1022–32.

Kumbier, E., K. Haack, and S. Herpertz. "Considerations on the Work of the Neuropsychiatrist Gabriel Anton (1858–1933)." *Nervenarzt* 76.9 (2005): 1132–6.

Kuperberg, G. R., P. K. McGuire, E. T. Bullmore, M. J. Brammer, S. Rabe-Hesketh, I. C. Wright, D. J. Lythgoe, S. C. Williams, and A. S. David. "Common and Distinct Neural Substrates for Pragmatic, Semantic, and Syntactic Processing of Spoken Sentences: An fMRI Study." *Journal of Cognitive Neuroscience* 12.2 (2000): 321–41.

Lacoboni, M. *Mirroring People, The New Science of How We Connect With Others.* Farrar Strauss and Giroux: New York, 2008.

Lafond, V. *Grieving mental Illness: A guide for Patients and their Caregivers.* Toronto: Univ. Of Toronto Press, 1994.

Lane, R. D., G. L. Ahern, G. E. Schwartz, R. J. Davidson, K. J. Friston, L. S. Yun, and K. Chen. "Neuroanatomical Correlates of Externally and Internally Generated Human Emotion." *American Journal of Psychiatry* 154.7 (1997): 918–25.

Lane, R. D., G. R. Fink, P. M. Chau, and R. J. Dolan. "Neural Activation during Selective Attention to Subjective Emotional Responses." *Neuroreport* 8.18 (1997): 3969–72.

Lane, R. D., E. M. Reiman, G. L. Ahern, G. E. Schwartz, and R. J. Davidson. "Neuroanatomical Correlates of Happiness, Sadness, and Disgust." *American Journal of Psychiatry* 154.7 (1997): 926–933.

Lane, R. D., E. M. Reiman, M. M. Bradley, P. J. Lang, G. L. Ahern, R. J. Davidson, and G. E. Schwartz. "Neuroanatomical Correlates of Pleasant and Unpleasant Emotion." *Neuropsychologia* 35.11 (1997): 1437–44.

Lawson, C. A. *Understanding the Borderline Mother: Helping Her Children Transcend the Intense, Unpredictable, and Volatile Relationship.* Northvale, NJ: Jason Aronson, 2002.

LeDoux, J. *The Amygdala and Emotion: A View through Fear.* In Aggleton J. P. (Ed). Oxford: Oxford University Press, 2000.

LeDoux, J. *The Emotional Brain: The Mysterious Underpinnings of Emotional Life.* New York: Touchstone, 1996.

Lehrer, J. *Proust Was a Neuroscientist.* Boston: Houghton Mifflin Company, 2007.

Leith, K. P., and R. F. Baumeister. "Empathy, Shame, Guilt, and Narratives of Interpersonal Conflicts: Guilt-Prone People Are Better at Perspective Taking." *Journal of Personality* 66.1 (1998): 1–37.

Levenkron, S. *Cutting: Understanding and Overcoming Self-Mutilation.* New York: Norton, 1998.

Leyton, M., H. Okazawa, M. Diksic, J. Paris, P. Rosa, S. Mzengeza, S. N. Young, P. Blier, C. Benkelfat. "Brain Regional alpha-[11C]methyl-L-tryptophan Trapping in Impulsive Subjects with Borderline Personality Disorder." *Am J Psychiatry* 158.5 (2001): 775–82.

Linehan, M. M. *Cognitive Behavioral Treatment of Borderline Personality Disorder.* New York: Guilford Press, 1993a.

Linehan, M. M. *Skills Training Manual for Treating Borderline Personality Disorder.* New York: Guilford Press, 1993b.

Linehan, M. "Validation and Psychiatric." In A. Bohart and U. L. Greenberg (Eds.), *Empathy Reconsidered: New Directions.* Washington, DC: American Pyschiatric Association, 1997: 353–92.

Linehan, M., H. Schmidt III, L. A. Dimeff, and J. C. Craft. "Dialectical Behavior Therapy for Patients with Borderline Personality Disorder and Drug-Dependence." *American Journal on Addictions* 8 (1999): 279–92.

Liston, C., and J. Kagan. "Brain Development: Memory Enhancement in Early Childhood." *Nature* 419.6910 (2002): 896.

Low, A. *Peace versus Power in the Family: Domestic Discord and Emotional Distress.* (previously titled: Lectures to Relatives of Former Patients). Glencoe, IL: Willet, 1943.

Low, A. Selections from Dr. Low's Works, 1950–1953. Chicago: Recovery Inc, 1950.

Low, A. A. *Mental Health through Will Training.* Glencoe, IL: Willet, 1950.

Ludascher, P., M. Bohus, K. Lieb, A. Philipsen, A. Jochims, C. Schmahl. "Elevated Pain Thresholds Correlate with Dissociation and Aversive Arousal in Patients with Borderline Personality Disorder." *Psychiatry Res* 149.(1–3) (2007): 291–6.

Ludascher, P., W. Greffrath, C. Schmahl, N. Kleindienst, A. Kraus, U. Baumgartner, W. Magerl, R. D. Treede, M. Bohus. "A Cross-sectional Investigation of Discontinuation of Self-injury and Normalizing Pain Perception in Patients with Borderline Personality Disorder." *Acta Psychiatr Scand* 120.1 (2009): 62–70.

Lundberg, G., and J. Lundberg. *I Don't Have to Make Everything All Better.* New York: Penguin Group, 1995.

Lynch, T. R., M. Z. Rosenthal, D. S. Kosson, J. S. Cheavens, C. W. Lejuez, R. J. Blair. "Heightened Sensitivity to Facial Expressions of Emotion in Borderline Personality Disorder." *Emotion* 6.4 (2006): 647–55.

Lyon, G. R., S. E. Shaywitz, and B. A. Shaywitz. "A Definition of Dyslexia." *Annals of Dyslexia* 53 (2003): 1–14.

MacFarlane, M. M. *Family Treatment of Personality Disorders: Advances in Clinical Practice.* Binghampton, NY: Haworth Clinical Practice Press, 2004.

MacGregor, P. "Grief: The Unrecognized Parental Response to Mental Illness in a Child." *Social Work* 39.2 (1994):160–166.

MacKinnon D. F., F. Dean, and R. Pies. "Affective Instability as Rapid Cycling: Theoretical and Clinical Implications for Borderline Personality and Bipolar Spectrum Disorders." *Bipolar Disorder* 8.1 (2006): 1–14.

Mason, M. S., T. Paul, and R. Kreger. *Stop Walking on Eggshells: Taking Your Life Back When Someone You Care About Has Borderline Personality Disorder.* Oakland, CA: New Harbinger Publications, 1998.

Mauchnik, J., C. Schmahl, and M. Bohus. "New Findings in the Biology of Borderline Personality Disorder." *Directions in Psychiatry* 25.3 (2005): 197–215.

McFarlane, W. B. *Multifamily Group in the Treatment of Severe Psychiatric Disorders.* New York: Guilford Press, 2002.

McWilliams, P., *Life 101.* Los Angeles, California: Prelude Press, 1994.

Meekeren, Erwin van. *Starry Starry Night: Life and Psychiatric History of Vincent Van Gogh.* Amsterdam: Benecke, 2003.

Meloy, J. R. *The Psychology of Stalking: Clinical and Forensic Perspectives.* San Diego, CA: Academic Press, 1998.

Miklowitz, D., and M. Goldstein. *Bipolar Disorder: A Family-focused Treatment Approach.* New York: Guilford Press, 1997.

Miller, A. L., J. Rathus, M. Linehan, *Dialectic Behavior for Suicidal Adolescents.* New York: Guilford Press, 2007.

Miller, D. *Women Who Hurt Themselves: A Book of Hope and Understanding.* New York: Basic Books, 1994.

Miller, F., J. Dworkin, M. Ward, and D. Barone. "A Preliminary Study of Unresolved Grief in Families of Seriously Mentally Ill Patients." *Hospital and Community Psychiatry* 41.12 December (1990): 1321–1325.

Millon, T., and R. D. Davis. *DSM-IV and Beyond (2nd ed.).* New York: Wiley, 1996.

Minzenberg, M. J., J. Fan, A. S. New, C. Y. Tang, L. J. Siever. "Frontolimbic Structural Changes in borderline personality disorder." *J Psychiatr Res.* Sep 6 2007.

Mirmiran, M. "The Function of Fetal/Neonatal Rapid Eye Movement Sleep." *Behavioural Brain Research* 69.1–2 (1995): 13–22.

Mitropoulou, V., R. L. Trestman, A. S. New, J. D. Flory, J. M. Silverman, and L. J. Siever. "Function and Temperament in Subjects with Personality Disorders." *CNS Spectrums* 8.10 (2003): 725–30.

Mogel, W. *The Blessing of a Skinned Knee.* New York: Scribner, 2001.

Moskovitz, R. A. *Lost in the Mirror: An Inside Look at Borderline Personality Disorder.* Dallas, TX: Taylor, 1996.

National Institute of Mental Health (NIMH). *Neuroscience of Mental Health II.* Washington, DC: U.S. Department of Health and Human Services, 1995.

Neviaser, D. S., *The Inner View*, California: Mach 4 Press, December 2000.

New, A. S., et al. "Blunted Prefrontal Cortical 18 fluorodeoxyglucose Positron Emission Tomography Response to Meta-Chlorophenylpiperazine in Impulsive Aggression." *Archives of General Psychiatry* 59.7 (2002): 621–9.

New, A. S., et al. "Serotonergic Function and Self-Injurious Behavior in Personality Disorder Patients." *Psychiatry Research* 69.1 (1997): 17–26.

New, A. S., M. S. Buchsbaum, E. A. Hazlett, M. Goodman, H. W. Koeigsberg, J. Lo, L. Iskander, R. Newmark, J. Brand, K. O'Flynn, and L. J. Siever. "Fluoxetine Increases Relative Metabolic Rate in Prefrontal Cortex in Impulsive Aggression." *Psychopharmacology* 176.3–4 (2004): 451–58.

New, A. S., R. F. Trestman, V. Mitropoulou, M. Goodman, Harold H. Koenigsberg, J. Silverman, and L. J. Siever. "Low Prolactin Response to

Fenfluramine in Impulsive Aggression." *Journal of Psychiatric Research* 38.3 (2004): 223–30.

New, A. S. , E. Hazlett, M. S. Buchsbaum, M. Goodman, H. W. Koenigsberg, L. J. Siever. "M-CPP PET and Impulsive Aggression in Borderline Personality Disorder." Abstract in 41st Annual Meeting of the American College of Neuropsycholopharmacology 2003: 257.

New, A. S., E. A. Hazlett, M. S. Buchsbaum, M. Goodman, S. A. Mitelman, R. Newmark, R. Trisdorfer, M. M. Haznedar, H. W. Koenigsberg, J. Flory, L. J. Siever. "Amygdala-Prefrontal Disconnection in Borderline Personality Disorder." *Neuropsychopharmacology* (2007).

New, A. S., J. Triebwasser, D. S. Charney. "The Case for Shifting Borderline Personality Disorder to Axis I." *Biol Psychiatry* 64.8 (2008): 653–9.

Norman, A. S. F. , Z. V. Segal, H. Mayberg, J. Bean, D. McKeon, F. Zainab, A. K. Anderson. "Attending to the Present: Mindful meditation reveals distinct Neural modes of self-reference." *Soc Cogn Affect Neurosi.* 2.4(DEC 2007): 313–322.

Norra, C., M. Mrazek, F. Tuchtenhagen, R. Gobbele, H. Buchner, H. Sass, and S. C. Herpertz. "Enhanced Intensity Dependence as a Marker of Low Serotonergic Neurotransmission in Borderline Personality Disorder." *Journal of Psychiatric Research* 37.1 (2003): 23–33.

Northoff, G., A. Heinzel, M. de Greck, F. Bermpohl, H. Dobrowolny, J. Panksepp. "Self-referential Processing in Our Brain—A Meta-analysis of Imaging Studies on The Self." *Neuroimage* 31.1 (2006): 440–57.

Oldham, J. M. *Personality Disorders: New Perspectives on Diagnostic Validity.* Washington, DC: American Psychiatric Publishing, 1991.

Oldham, J. M., and L. B. Morris. *Personality Self-Portrait: Why You Think, Work, Love, and Act the Way You Do.* New York: Bantam, 1990.

Paladin, L. S. *Ceremonies for Change: Creating Personal Rituals to Heal Life's Hurts.* New Hampshire: Stillpoint Publishing Inernational, 1991.

Philipsen, A. A., B. Feige, A. Al-Shajlawi, C. Schmahl, M. Bohus, H. Richter, U. Voderholzer, K. Lieb, D. Riemann, et al. "Increased Delta Power and Discrepancies in Objective and Subjective Sleep Measurements in Borderline Personality Disorder." *Journal of Psychiatric Research* 39.5 (2005): 489–98.

Philipsen, A., et al. "Clonidine in Acute Aversive Inner Tension and Self-Injurious Behavior in Female Patients with Borderline Personality Disorder." *Journal of Clinical Psychiatry* 65.10 (2004): 1414–9.

Philipsen, A., C. Schmahl, and K. Lieb. "Naloxone in the Treatment of Acute Dissociative States in Female Patients with Borderline Personality Disorder." *Pharmacopsychiatry* 37.5 (2004): 196–9.

Poldrack, R. A., A. D. Wagner, M. W. Prull, J. E. Desmond, G. H. Glover, and J. D. Gabrieli. "Functional Specialization for Semantic and Phonological

Processing in the Left Inferior Prefrontal Cortex." *Neuroimage* 10.1 (1999): 15–35.

Porr, V. *A Family Guide to Validation*. New York: TARA, 1999.

Porr, V. "From Grief to Advocacy, A Mother's Journey." *Journal of the California Alliance for the Mentally Ill* 8.1 (1997): 7–9.

Porr, V. How Advocacy is Bringing Borderline Personality Into the Light T*E*N November 2001 70–73v.

Porr, V. CD: Creating a Therapeutic Family Environment for People with Borderline Personality Disorder Nami Convention, Washington, DC.

Porr, V. CD: Borderline Personality Disorder From the Family Point of View, Adolescent Needs American Society of Adolescent Psychiatry (2005), Houston, TX.

Porr, V., M. Linehan, F. Goodwin, S. B. Smith. *The Infinite Mind*. Lichtenstein Creative media.

Post, R. M. "Stress Sensitization, Kindling, and Conditioning." *Behavioral Brain Science* 8.2 (1985): 372–3.

Post, R. M., K. D. Chang, R. L. Findling, B. Geller, R. A. Kowatch, S. P. Kutcher, and G. S. Leverich. "Prepubertal Bipolar I Disorder and Bipolar Disorder NOS Are Separable from ADHD." *Journal of Clinical Psychiatry* 65.7 (2004): 898–902.

Post, R. M., S. R. B. Weiss, H. Li, M. A. Smith, L. X. Zhang, G. Xing, E. A. Osuch, and U. D. McCann. "Neural Plasticity and Emotional Memory." *Developmental Psychopathology* 10.4 (1998): 829–55.

Post, R. M., S. Weiss, G. S. Leverich, and M. S. George. "Developmental Psychobiology of Cyclic Affective Illness: Implications for Early Therapeutic Intervention." *Developmental Psychopathology* 8.1 (1996): 273–305.

Pryor, K. *Don't Shoot the Dog! : The New Art of Teaching and Training*. New York: Bantam. 1984.

Pugh, K. R., et al. "Neurobiological Studies of Reading and Reading Disability." *Journal of Communication Disorders* 34.6 (2001a): 479–92.

Pugh, K. R., et al. "Neuroimaging Studies of Reading Development and Reading Disability." *Learning Disabilities Research and Practice* (Special Issue: Emergent and Early Literacy: Current Status and Research Directions) 16.4 (2001b): 240–9.

Pukrop, R., et al. "Special Feature: Personality and Personality Disorders. A Facet Theoretical Analysis of the Similarity Relationships." *Journal of Personality Disorders* 12.3 (1998): 226–46.

Rando, T. A. "Death of an Adult Child." In K. J. Doka (Ed.), *Disenfranchised Grief: Recognizing Hidden Sorrow*. Champaign. IL: Research Press, 1986a (221–38).

Rando, T. A. "Individual and Couple Treatment following the Death of a Child." In K. J. Doka (Ed.), *Disenfranchised Grief: Recognizing Hidden Sorrow*. Champaign, IL: Research Press, 1986b (341–414).

Rando T. A. "The Unique Issues and Impact of the Death of a Child." In K. J. Doka (Ed.), *Disenfranchised Grief: Recognizing Hidden Sorrow*. Champaign, IL: Research Press, 1986c (5–44).

Rando, T. A. "Creating Therapeutic Rituals in the Psychotherapy of the Bereaved." *Psychotherapy: Theory, Research, Practice, Training* 22.2 (1985): 236–40.

Remen, R. N. *Kitchen Table Wisdom*. New York: Riverhead Books, 1996.

Reiman, E. M., R. D. Lane, G. L. Ahern, et al. "Neuroanatomical Correlates of Externally and Internally Generated Human Emotion." American Journal of Psychiatry 154.7 (1997): 918–25.

Rickenbacker, E. V., Ohio: Hendricks Magazine, 1997.

Rinne, T., et al. "SSRI Treatment of Borderline Personality Disorder: A Randomized, Placebo-Controlled Clinical Trial for Female Patients with Borderline Personality Disorder." *American Journal of Psychiatry* 159.12 (2002): 2048–54.

Rinne, T., E. R. de Kloet, L. Wouters, J. G. Goekoop, R. H. de Rijk, and W. van den Brink. "Fluvoxamine Reduces Responsiveness of HPA Axis in Adult Female BPD Patients with a History of Sustained Childhood Abuse." *Neuropsychopharmacology* 28.1 (2003): 126–32.

Rusch, N., et al. "A Voxel-Based Morphometric MRI Study in Female Patients with Borderline Personality Disorder." *NeuroImage* 20.1 (2003): 385–92.

Rusch, N., K. Lieb, I. Gottler, C. Hermann, E. Schramm, H. Richter, G. A. Jacob, P. W. Corrigan, M. Bohus. "Shame and Implicit Self-Concept in Women with Borderline Personality Disorder." *Am J Psychiatry* 164.3 (2007): 500–8.

Rusch, N., P. W. Corrigan, M. Bohus, G. A. Jacob, R. Brueck, K. Lieb. "Measuring Shame and Guilt by Self-Report Questionnaires: A Validation Study." *Psychiatry Res* 150.3 (2007): 313–25.

Rusch, N., A. Holzer, C. Hermann, E. Schramm, G. A. Jacob, M. Bohus, K. Lieb, P. W. Corrigan. "Self-stigma in Women with Borderline Personality Disorder and Women with Social Phobia." *J Nerv Ment Dis* 194.10 (2006): 766–73.

Rusch, N., M. Weber, K. A. Il'yasov, K. Lieb, D. Ebert, J. Hennig, L. T. van Elst. "Inferior Frontal White Matter Microstructure and Patterns of Psychopathology in Women with Borderline Personality Disorder and Comorbid Attention-Deficit Hyperactivity Disorder." *Neuroimage* 35.2 (2007): 738–47.

Russ, M. J., et al. "Pain and Self-Injury in Borderline Patients: Sensory Decision Theory. Coping Strategies. and Locus of Control." *Psychiatry Research* 63.1 (1996): 57–65.

Schmahl, C., and M. Bohus. "Symptom-Focused Drug Therapy in Borderline Personality Disorder [Review]." *Fortschritte der Neurologie-Psychiatrie* 69.7 (2001): 310–21.

Schmahl, C. G., et al. Magnetic Resonance Imaging of Hippocampal and Amygdala Volume in Women with Childhood Abuse and Borderline Personality Disorder. *Psychiatry Research: Neuroimaging* 122.3 (2003a): 193–98.

Schmahl, C. G., et al. "Neural Correlates of Memories of Abandonment in Women with and without Borderline Personality Disorder." *Biological Psychiatry* 54.2 (2003b): 142–51.

Schmahl, C., et al. "Differential Nociceptive Deficits in Patients with Borderline Personality Disorder and Self-Injurious Behavior: Laser-Evoked Potentials, Spatial Discrimination of Noxious Stimuli, and Pain Ratings." *Pain* 110.1–2 (2004a): 470–9.

Schmahl, C. G., et al. "Psychophysiological Reactivity to Traumatic and Abandonment Scripts in Borderline Personality and Posttraumatic Stress Disorders: A Preliminary Report." *Psychiatry Research* 126.1 (2004b): 33–42.

Schmahl, C. G., et al. "A Positron Emission Tomography Study of Memories of Childhood Abuse in Borderline Personality Disorder." *Biological Psychiatry* 55.7 (2004c): 759–65.

Schmahl, C. G., T. H. McGlashan, and J. D. Bremner. "Neurobiological Correlates of Borderline Personality Disorder [Review]." *Psychopharmacology Bulletin* 36.2 (2002): 69–87.

Schmahl, C., M. Meinzer, A. Zeuch, M. Fichter, M. Cebulla, N. Kleindienst, P. Ludascher, R. Steil, M. Bohus. "Pain Sensitivity is Reduced in Borderline Personality Disorder, but not in Posttraumatic Stress Disorder and Bulimia Nervosa." *World J Biol Psychiatry* 11(2 Pt 2): 364–71.

Schnell, K., T. Dietrich, R. Schnitker, J. Daumann , S. C. Herpertz. "Processing of autobiographical memory retrieval cues in borderline personality disorder." *J Affect Disord* 97.1–.3 (2007): 253–9.

Schultz, R. T. "Developmental Deficits in Social Perception in Autism: The Role of the Amygdala and Fusiform Face Area." *International Journal of Developmental Neuroscience* (Special Issue: Autism: Modeling Human Brain Abnormalities in Developing Animal Systems) 23.2–3 (2005): 125–41.

Schwartz, C. E., and S. L. Rauch. „Temperament and Its Implications for Neuroimaging of Anxiety Disorders." *CNS Spectrums* 9.4 (2004): 284–91.

Schwartz, C. E., N. Snidman, and J. Kagan. "Adolescent Social Anxiety as an Outcome of Inhibited Temperament in Childhood." *Journal of the American Academy of Child and Adolescent Psychiatry* 38.8 (1999): 1008–15.

Schwartz, C. E., et al. "Inhibited and Uninhibited Infants "Grown Up": Adult Amygdalar Response to Novelty." *Science* 300.5627 (2003): 1952–3.

Schwartz, C. E., C. I. Wright, L. M. Shin, J. Kagan, P. J. Whalen, K. G. McMullin, and S. L. Rauch. "Differential Amygdalar Response to Novel versus Newly Familiar Neutral Faces: A Functional MRI Probe Developed for Studying Inhibited Temperament." *Biological Psychiatry* 53.10 (2003): 854–62.

Segal, Z. V., J. M. G. Williams, J. D. Teasdale. *Mindfulness-Based Cognitive Therapy for Depression*, New York: Guilford Press, 2002.

Seligman, M. E. P. *Learned Optimism: How to Change Your Mind and Your Life*. New York: Pocket Books, 1990.

Shaywitz, B. A., et al. "Disruption of Posterior Brain Systems for Reading in Children with Developmental Dyslexia." *Biological Psychiatry* 52.2 (2002): 101–10.

Shaywitz, B. A., et al. "Development of Left Occipitotemporal Systems for Skilled Reading in Children after a Phonologically Based Intervention." *Biological Psychiatry* 55.9 (2004): 926–33.

Shaywitz, S. E. *Neurobiological Indices of Dyslexia*. New York: Guilford Press, 2003a.

Shaywitz, S. *Overcoming Dyslexia. A New and Complete Science-Based Program for Reading Problems at Any Level*. New York: Alfred A. Knopf, 2003b.

Shaywitz, S. E., and B. A. Shaywitz. "Dyslexia (Specific Reading Disability)." *Biological Psychiatry* 57.11 (2005): 1301–9.

Shula, D. *Everyone's a Coach: Five Business Secrets for High Performance Coaching*, New York, NY: Harper Collins, June 1996.

Siever, L. "Neurobiology and Genetics of Borderline Personality Disorder." *Psychiatric Annals* 32.6 (2002): 329–36.

Siever, L. J., and W. Frucht. *The New View of Self: How Genes and Neurotransmitters Shape Your Mind, Your Personality and Your Mental Health*. New York: Macmillan, 1997.

Siever, L., and H. Koenisberg. *Cerebrum*. New York: DANA Press, 2000.

Siever, L. J., H. W. Koenigsberg, and D. Reynolds. "Neurobiology of Personality Disorders: Implications for a Neurodevelopmental Model." In Dante Cicchetti and Elaine Walker (Eds.), *Neurodevelopmental Mechanisms in Psychopathology*. New York: Cambridge University Press, 2003 (405–27).

Siever, L. J., S. Torgersen, J. G. Gunderson, W. J. Livesley, and K. S. Kendler, "The Borderline Diagnosis III: Identifying Endophenotypes for Genetic Studies." *Biological Psychiatry* 51.12 (2002): 964–8.

Siever, L. J., M. Buchsbaum, A. New, J. Spiegel-Cohen, T. Wei, E. Hazlett, E. Sevin, M. Nunn, V. Mitropoulou. "d,l-fenfluramine Response in Impulsive Personality Disorder Assessed with 18F-deoxyglucose Positron Emission Tomography." *Neuropsychopharmacology* 20.5 (1999): 413–423.

Silbersweig, D., J. F. Clarkin, M. Goldstein, O. F. Kernberg, O. Tuescher, K. N. Levy, G. Brendel, H. Pan, M. Beutel, M. T. Pavony, J. Epstein, M. F. Lenzenweger, K. M. Thomas, M. I. Posner, E. Stern. "Failure of Frontolimbic Inhibitory Function in the Context of Negative Emotion in Borderline Personality Disorder." *Am J Psychiatry* 164.12 (2007): 1832–41.

Skodol, A. E., et al. "The Collaborative Longitudinal Personality Disorders Study (CLPS): Overview and Implications." *Journal of Personality Disorders* 19.5 (2005): 487–504.

Smith, S. B. *Diana in Search of Herself*. New York: Times Books, 1999.

Soloff, P. H. "Algorithms for Pharmacological Treatment of Personality Dimensions: Symptom-Specific Treatments for Cognitive-Perceptual, Affective, and Impulsive-Behavioral Dysregulation." *Bulletin of the Menninger Clinic* 62.2 (1998): 195–214.

Soloff, P. H. "Psychopharmacology of Borderline Personality Disorder." *Psychiatric Clinics of North America* 23.1 (2000): 169–92.

Soloff, P. H., et al. "Gender Differences in a Fenfluramine-Activated FDG PET Study of Borderline Personality Disorder." *Psychiatry Research* 138.3 (2005): 183–95.

Soloff, P. H., et al. "Impulsivity and Prefrontal Hypometabolism in Borderline Personality Disorder." *Psychiatry Research* 123.3 (2003): 153–63.

Soloff, P. H., C. C. Meltzer, P. J. Greer, D. Constantine, T. M. Kelly. "A Fenfluramine-activated FDG-PET Study of Borderline Personality Disorder." *Biol Psychiatry* 47 (2000): 540–547.

Stanley, B., L. Sher, S. Wilson, R. Ekman, Y. Y. Huang, J. J. Mann. "Non-suicidal Self-injurious Behavior, Endogenous Opioids and Monoamine Neurotransmitters." *J Affect Disord* 2009.

Stanley, B., L. Siever. "The interpersonal Dimension of Borderline Personality Disorder: Toward a Neuropeptide Model." *Am J Psychiatry* 167(2010): 24–39.

Stanley, B., and B. Brodsky. "Suicidal and Self-Injurious Behavior in Borderline Personality Disorder: A Self-Regulation Model." In John G. Gunderson and Perry D. Hoffman (Eds.), *Understanding and Treating Borderline Personality Disorder: A Guide for Professionals and Families*. Washington, DC: American Psychiatric Publishing, 2005 (43–63).

Stanley, B., M. J. Gameroff, V. Michalsen, and J. J. Mann. "Are Suicide Attempters Who Self-Mutilate a Unique Population?" *American Journal of Psychiatry* 158.3 (2001): 427–32.

Stiglmayr, C., T. Grathwol, and M. Bohus, "States of Aversive Tension in Patients with Borderline Personality Disorder: A Controlled Field Study." In J. Fahrenberg and M. Myrtek (Eds.), *Progress in Ambulatory Assessment: Computer-Assisted Psychological and Psychophysiological Methods in Monitoring and Field Studies*. Ashland, OH: Hogrefe and Huber, 2001(135–41).

Stiglmayr, C. E., T. Grathwol, M. M. Linehan, G. Ihorst, J. Fahrenberg, and M. Bohus. "Aversive Tension in Patients with Borderline Personality Disorder: A Computer-Based Controlled Field Study." *Acta Psychiatrica Scandinavica* 111.5 (2005): 372–9.

Stiglmayr, C. E., D. A. Shapiro, R. D. Stieglitz, M. Limberger, and M. Bohus. "Experience of Aversive Tension and Dissociation in Female Patients with Borderline Personality Disorder: A Controlled Study." *Journal of Psychiatric Research* 35.2 (2001): 111–18.

Szalavitz, M. *Help At Any Cost*. New York, Penguin books, 2006.

Tangney, J. P., and D. J. Mashek. *In Search of the Moral Person: Do You Have to Feel Really Bad to Be Good?* New York: Guilford Press, 2004.

Tangney, J. P., and D. J. Mashek. *Handbook of Experiment Existential Psychology*. New York: Guilford Press, 2004.

Tangney, J. P., D. Mashek, and J. Stuewig. "Shame, Guilt, and Embarrassment: Will the Real Emotion Please Stand Up?" *Psychological Inquiry* 16.1 (2005): 44–8.

Tangney, J. P., et al. "Assessing Individual Differences in Constructive versus Destructive Responses to Anger across the Lifespan." *Journal of Personality and Social Psychology* 70.4 (1996a): 780–96.

Tangney, J. P., et al. "Relation of Shame and Guilt to Constructive versus Destructive Responses to Anger across the Lifespan." *Journal of Personality and Social Psychology* 70.4 (1996b): 797–809.

Tangney, J. P., R. F. Baumeister, and A. L. Boone. "High Self-Control Predicts Good Adjustment, Less Pathology, Better Grades, and Interpersonal Success." *Journal of Personality* 72.2 (2004): 271–324.

Tannen, D. *You're Wearing That? Understanding Mothers and Daughters in Conversation*. New York: Random House, 2006.

Tebartz, van E. L., B. Hesslinger, T. Thiel, E. Geiger, K. Haegele, L. Lemieux, K. Lieb, M. Bohus, J. Hennig, and D. Ebert. "Frontolimbic Brain

Abnormalities in Patients with Borderline Personality Disorder: A Volumetric Magnetic Resonance Imaging Study." *Biological Psychiatry* 54.2 (2003): 163–71.

Tebartz van E. L., P. Ludaescher, T. Thiel, M. Buchert, B. Hesslinger, M. Bohus, N. Rusch, J. Hennig, D. Ebert, K. Lieb. "Evidence of Disturbed Amygdalar Energy Metabolism in Patients with Borderline Personality Disorder." *Neurosci Lett* 417.1 (2007): 36–41.

Thatcher, D. L., J. R. Cornelius, and D. B. Clark. "Adolescent Alcohol Use Disorders Predict Adult Borderline Personality." *Addictive Behaviors* 30.9 (2005): 1709–24.

Torgersen, S., S. Lygren, P. A. Oien, I. Skre, S. Onstad, J. Edvardsen, K. Tambs, E. Kringlen. "A Twin Study of Personality Disorders." *Compr Psychiatry* 41.6 (2000): 416–25.

Torgerson, S. "Genetics." In Michael Hersen and Alan S. Bellack (Eds.), *Psychopathology in Adulthood (2nd ed.)*. Needham Heights, MA: Allyn and Bacon, 2000 (55–76).

Trestman, R. L. "Behind Bars: Personality Disorders." *Journal of the American Academy of Psychiatry and the Law* 28.2 (2000): 232–5.

Trestman, R., J. Ford, Hogan, and S. Quarti. "Epidemiology of Personality Disorders in Connecticut Jails." Presented at annual meeting, International Society for the Study of Personality Disorders, Buenos Aires, Argentina, April 23, 2005.

Twenge, J. M., R. F. Baumeister, C. N. Dewall, N. J. Ciarocco, and J. M. Bartels. "Social Exclusion Decreases Prosocial Behavior." *Journal of Pers. & Soc Psychology* 92 (2007): 56–66.

Vallières, A., H. Ivers, C. H. Bastien, S. Beaulieu-Bonneau, and C. M. Morin. "Variability and Predictability in Sleep Patterns of Chronic Insomniacs." *Journal of Sleep Research* 14.4 (2005): 447–53.

Vollrath, M., R. Alnaes, and S. Torgerson. "Coping and MCMI-II Personality Disorders." *Journal of Personality Disorders* 8.1 (1994): 53–63.

Wagner, A. W., and M. M. Linehan. "Facial Expression Recognition Ability among Women with Borderline Personality Disorder: Implications for Emotion Regulation?" *Journal of Personality Disorders* 13.4 (1999): 329–44.

Walker, A. *The Courtship Dance of the Borderline.* Lincoln, NE: Writer's Showcase. 2002.

Walker, A. *Siren's Dance: My Marriage to a Borderline: A Case Study.* Emmaus, PA : Rodale, 2003.

Whalen, P. J., J. Kagan, R. G. Cook, F. C. Davis, H. Kim, S. Polis, D. G. McLaren, L. H. Somerville, A. A. McLean, J. S. Maxwell, and T.

Johnstone. "Human Amygdala Responsivity to Masked Fearful Eye Whites." *Science* 306.5704: (2004): 2061.

Wright, C. I., L. M. Shin, J. Kagan, and S. L. Rauch. "Inhibited and Uninhibited Infants 'Grown Up': Adult Amygdalar Response to Novelty." *Science* 300.5627 (2003): 1952–3.

Witting W., D. van der Werf, and M. Mirmiran."An On-Line Automated Sleep-Wake Classification System for Laboratory Animals." *Journal of Neuroscience Methods* 66.2 (1996): 109–12.

Yen, S., et al. "Recent Life Events Preceding Suicide Attempts in a Personality Disorder Sample: Findings from the Collaborative Longitudinal Personality Disorders Study." *Journal of Consulting and Clinical Psychology* 73.1 (2005): 99–105.

Young, J. E., J. S. Klosko, and M. E. Weishaar. *Schema Therapy: A Practitioner's Guide*. New York: Guilford Press, 2003.

Young, J. E., and J. S. Klosko. *Reinventing Your Life: How to Break Free from Negative Life Patterns and Feel Good Again*. New York: Plume. Penguin New York, May 1994.

Zetzsche, T., T. Frodl, U. W. Preuss, G. Schmitt, D. Seifert, G. Leinsinger, C. Born, M. Reiser, H. J. Moller, E. M. Meisenzahl. "Amygdala Volume and Depressive Symptoms in Patients with Borderline Personality Disorder." *Biol Psychiatry* 60.3 (2009):302–10.

Zimmerman, M., C. Ruggero, I. Chelminski, D. Young. "Psychiatric Diagnosis in Patients Previously Overdiagnosed with Bipolar Disorder." *J Clinical Psychiatry*, 2009.

Valerie Porr, M.A., is a mental health educator and advocate trained in Dialectical Behavior Therapy, and the founder and president of the Treatment and Research Advancements National Association for Personality Disorder (TARA NAPD). She conducts psycho-educational training seminars for family members of those with BPD in New York and elsewhere.

Index

Abandoning ship, 236
Abuse
    BPD misdiagnosis and, 28
    misconceptions regarding, 225
    National Institute on Alcohol
        Abuse and Alcoholism
        and, 10
    parents and, 224–25
Accentuate positive, 341–42
Acceptance. *See also* Radical
        acceptance
    clinicians regarding, 348
    of mistakes, 257–58
    nonjudgment and, 202
    struggle for, 216
Acceptance-acknowledgment
        declaration
    as DBT tool, 333
    difficulty of, 181–82
    humility and, 330–31
    sample of, 180–81
    sincerity regarding, 180
    as starting point, 181
    taking responsibility/apologizing
        via, 314

Accurate reflection. *See* Reflection,
        accurate
Acknowledgment, families and, 24
ADHD. *See* Attention-deficit
        hyperactivity disorder
Adolescents with BPD, 17
Advise
    avoiding, 183
    iatrogenic, 29–30
Affective dysregulation
    amygdala and, 47–48
    aversive arousal and, 48
    awareness of, 274
    behaviors indicating, 3, 252–53
    bipolar disorder and, 51–52
    cede control to prevent, 275
    cognitive dysregulation and,
        57–58
    emotion regulation skills and,
        272–79
    features of, 45–46
    impaired mentalization and, 299,
        301
    manifestations of, 272–73
    mini-respites relieving, 275–76

Affective dysregulation (*cont'd*)
  normalization and, 162–65
  nurturing relationships and,
    252–53
  opposite actions and, 277–78
  respect negative emotions
    lessening, 278–79
  shame and, 48–50
  stage two targets regarding, 122,
    124–25
  suicide and, 52
  trigger avoidance for preventing,
    275
Affective mentalization, 292
Alcohol, shame and, 50
Alcoholism
  BPD misdiagnosis and, 28
  National Institute on Alcohol
    Abuse and Alcoholism, 10
Alternate perspectives
  acceptability of, 320
  example illustrating, 319–20
  mentalization and, 318–20
  questions facilitating, 318–19
Alzheimer's disease, 222
Amygdala
  affective dysregulation and, 47–
    48
  described, 47
  emotion mind and, 190–91
  hypervigilance and, 48
  implicit mentalization and, 296–
    97
  memory and, 68–71
  validation and, 132
Anger
  assertiveness and, 254–55
  compassion and, 137, 277–78
  failure/shame and, 230
  grief becoming, 229–30
  opposite action and, 277–78
  validation and, 173–74

Anterior cingulate, 59
Anxiety
  behaviors indicating, 5
  disorder, 28
  impulsivity/mood disorders
    and, 72
Apology, 313–14
Apparent competence
  as common to BPD sufferers,
    11–12
  Princess Diana and, 12
  raised eyebrow effect and, 12–13
Approval, radical acceptance *vs.*, 240
Asking for what you want
  assert element of, 267
  benefits of, 265
  compromise element of, 269–70
  concentrate element of, 268
  confidence element of, 269
  DEAR CCC and, 264–72
  DEAR MAN and, 264, 265
  describe element of, 266
  example, 270–71
  express element of, 266–67
  overview of, 264–65
  pointers on, 271–72
  reinforce element of, 267–68
Asking questions
  details and, 309
  examples of, 311
  as mentalization technique, 309–
    11
  motivation and, 310–11
  not knowing attitude when, 310
Assert element of DEAR CCC, 267
Assertiveness
  defining goals and, 251–52
  developing, 254–55
Assumptions, DBT
  DBT can fail although
    clinicians do not, 113–14
    families do not, 118

DBT clinicians
  can fail, 113–14
  need support, 114
  relate as equals, 113
  family members
    are doing the best they can,
      115
    are equals, 117–18
    must be self-motivated,
      115–16
    must be willing to change, 116
    need support, 116–17
    need to accept BPD loved
      one's, 117
  people with BPD
    are doing best they can,
      110–11
    cannot fail in DBT, 111–12
    currently suffer unbearable
      lives, 113
    must be self-motivated,
      112–13
    must learn new behaviors, 111
    must solve problems in the
      moment, 112
    want to improve, 111
Attachment
  impaired mentalization and,
    300–301
  infancy and, 299–300
  mentalization and, 299–301
  parental grief and, 223–24
  sense of self and, 300
Attention, paying
  describing what you observe
    and, 146–47
  hints for, 146
  just the facts regarding, 147
  as validation mode, 145–47
Attention-deficit hyperactivity
    disorder (ADHD), 28
Auditory processing disorder, 56–57

Authenticity, 321–22
Autism
  facial perception and, 57
  as impaired mentalization,
    298–99
Aversive arousal
  affective dysregulation and, 48
  attachment and, 301
  defining goals and, 250
Aversive control, 15

Barriers to family effectiveness, 334
Bastien, Celyne, 63
Bateman, Anthony, 287
Behavioral aspects of BPD
  anxiety, 72
  cognitive dysregulation, 55–62
  color key of, 42
  genetics and, 41–42
  impulsivity, 42–45
  inconsistencies, 216
  juggler analogy illuminating,
    40–42
  memory dysregulation, 67–71
  mood/affective dysregulation,
    45–52
  pain dysregulation, 64–67
  sensitivity dysregulation, 53–54
  sleep dysregulation, 62–64
Behavior change
  CBT and, 77–78, 79–104
  CBT techniques for, 82–104
  difficulty of, 78
  extinction for, 98–100
  normalization and, 162–63
  psychodynamic therapy vs. CBT,
    80–82
  punishment and, 97–98
  reframing for, 82–88
  reinforcement for, 88–97
  shaping for, 100–104
  validation for, 165–66

Beliefs, validation of, 166
Billing codes, Medicare, 28
Bipolar disorder
    BPD vs., 51–52
    misdiagnosis and, 28, 51–52
Black grieving stones, 234
Blame
    on mothers, 216, 220
    parents and, 16
    validation and, 159, 169
Bohus, Martin, 44, 66
    aversive arousal and, 48
    BPD as described by, 46
    intense emotional reaction and,
        48–49
    shame and, 49
Borderline personality disorder
        (BPD). See also
        Adolescents with BPD;
        Assumptions, DBT;
        Behavioral aspects of BPD;
        Children of those with
        BPD; Children with BPD;
        Parents of those with
        BPD; Science of BPD;
        Siblings of those with
        BPD; Skills for behavior
        change, DBT; Spouses of
        child with BPD; Spouses
        of spouse with BPD
    apparent competence and, 11–13
    bipolar disorder vs., 51–52
    characteristics/traits associated
        with, 3–6
    chronic nature of, 239
    denial and, 228–29
    diagnostic criteria for, 8, 9
    Linehan describing, 8, 45–46
    misdiagnosis and, 28
    public ignorance of, 10
    stigma of, 30–33, 219–22
    what it is, 7–14

Bower, Gordon, 264
BPD. See Borderline personality
        disorder
Brain
    affective dysregulation and,
        47–48
    auditory processing disorder
        and, 56
    autism and, 57
    cognitive dysregulation and,
        55–57
    dyslexia and, 55–56
    emotion processing and, 57–58
    Gage and, 40
    impulsivity and, 43–45
    miswiring of, 55
    pain dysregulation and, 64
    self-referential processing and,
        58–60
Buddhism. See Zen Buddhism
Building mastery, 263–64
Bullshitting, 303–4

Calming breaths, 283, 284
Candles, 234
Cause/effect, understanding, 256–57
CBT. See Cognitive behavior
        therapy
CD. See Conduct disorder
Cede control, 275
Change. See also Behavior change
    as constant, 247–48
    nurturing relationships
        regarding, 252
    past, validation of, and, 158–60
    radical acceptance balanced with,
        241–42, 244
    Reeve, Christopher, and, 241–42
    validation and, 135, 158–60,
        165–66, 246, 335
    willingness to, 116
Cheerlead, 337

Children, of those with BPD
    attachment and, 223–24
    issues facing, 23–24
Children with BPD
    attachment and, 223–24
    diagnosis regarding, 17
    spouses of, 225–26
CHIRP
    compassion and, 330
    humility and, 330–31
    intuition and, 331
    persistence and, 332–33
    restraint and, 332
Choice, 240
Clinicians
    accurate information from, 347
    assumptions about DBT, 113–14
    avoid boundaries/limits/
        contracts/tough love, 349
    certification of, 128
    DBT training and, 127–28
    diagnosis and, 26–27
    encourage family involvement,
        349–50
    families as adjuncts to treatment
        and, 34–35
    family education and, 217, 347–50
    iatrogenic advise given by, 29–30
    judgment and, 202
    pretreatment targets and, 119–21
    questions to ask potential, 127
    role of, 120
    stigma and, 30–33
    those without BPD regarding, 247
    understanding/acceptance/
        compassion from, 348
    what families need from, 347–50
Cognitive behavior therapy (CBT).
        See also Dialectical
        Behavior Therapy
    effectiveness of, 80
    extinction for, 98–100

overview of, 79–80, 82, 107
pervasiveness of, 77–78
vs. psychodynamic therapy,
    80–82
punishment, 97–98
reframing, 82–88
reinforcement, 88–97
shaping, 100–104
techniques, 82–104
types of behavior and, 79
Cognitive distortions
    behaviors indicating, 5
    reframing, 82–84
Cognitive dysregulation
    attachment and, 301
    auditory processing disorder
        and, 56
    autism regarding, 57
    dyslexia and, 55–56
    emotion processing and, 57–58
    miscommunication and, 54–55
    neutral faces and, 60–62
    self-referential processing and,
        58–60
Cognitive mentalization, 292
Collaboration, clinicians
        regarding, 348
Color key, 42
Columbo (Television character), 309
Commitment to accept, 241
Communication, nonverbal, 349
Compassion
    anger and, 137, 277–78
    CHIRP and, 330
    clinicians regarding, 348
    cultivating, 136–37
    DBT and, 107–8
    defining, 136
    mentalization and, 308–9
    opposite action and, 277–78
    validation and, 136–37
Competency, 339–40

Compromise element of DEAR
CCC, 269–70
Concentrate element of DEAR
CCC, 268
Concrete thinking, 305–6
Conduct disorder (CD), 28
Confidence element of DEAR
CCC, 269
Conflict resolution, 259–61
Consequences, natural, 239
Consistency, 314–15
Contingencies, managing, 343
Contracts, 142–44
Control
aversive, 15
ceding, 275
of emotion, 273
radical acceptance and, 238–39
validation do nots regarding, 170
Counterintuitive
DBT as, 107
validation as, 177–78
Criticism, 169

Dalai Lama, 141
Damasio, Antonio, 40
DBT. See Dialectical Behavior
Therapy
DEAR CCC
assert element of, 267
benefits of, 265
compromise element of, 269–70
concentrate element of, 268
confidence element of, 269
as DBT skill, 336
describe element of, 266, 335
example, 270–71
express element of, 266–67
overview of, 264–65
pointers, 271–72
reinforce element of, 267–68
TARA and, 264, 265

DEAR MAN, 264, 265
Decision making, difficulty
with, 3–4
Declarative memory, 71
Defining goals
assertiveness and, 251–52
aversive feelings and, 250
as DBT skill, 250–52
wants and, 250–51
Delay
as DBT skill, 282
reframing, 85–86
Denial
BPD facilitating, 228–29
development of, 227–28
grief becoming, 227–29
normalizing pathology and, 228
pain and, 242
physical health affected by, 229
as therapeutic, 228
Depression
BPD misdiagnosis and, 28
as common, 10
Describe element of DEAR CCC,
266, 335
Describing, 197–98
Devotion, 222
Diagnosis, 7–8
adolescents/children with BPD
and, 17
bipolar disorder and, 28, 51–52
challenges of, 26–27
criteria for, 8, 9
lack of instruments for, 27
mis-, 28–29, 51–52
Diagnostic and Statistical Manual
of Mental Disorders
(DSM) (American
Psychiatric Association)
adolescents/children with BPD
and, 17
BPD diagnostic criteria in, 8, 9

mental disorder classification in,
51–52
overview of, 7–8
Dialectical Behavior Therapy (DBT).
See also Assumptions,
DBT; Skills for behavior
change, DBT; Treatment,
DBT
assumptions: DBT can fail
although
clinicians do not, 113–14
families do not, 118
assumptions: DBT clinicians
can fail, 113–14
need support, 114
relate as equals, 113
assumptions: family members
are doing the best they can, 115
are equals, 117–18
must be self-motivated,
115–16
must be willing to change, 116
need support, 116–17
need to accept BPD loved
one's, 117
need to accept present
reality, 117
assumptions: people with BPD
are doing best they can,
110–11
cannot fail in DBT, 111–12
currently suffer unbearable
lives, 113
must be self-motivated,
112–13
must learn new behaviors, 111
must solve problems in the
moment, 112
want to improve, 111
balance regarding, 245–46
change as constant and, 247–48
as collaborative, 108

compassion and, 107–8
counterintuitive nature of, 107
dialectics and, 105–6
ensuring efficacy of, 127–28
goals, 118
history of, 105
how it is practiced, 126–28
implementing, 107–9
improvisation and, 109
method *vs.* principle, 109–10
neurogenesis and, 74
overview of, 105–6
patient participation required
in, 109
phone coaching, 123–24
pretreatment targets of, 119–21
principles of, 108–9
questions to ask potential
therapists, 127
radical acceptance and, 235–36
stage four targets, 126
stage one targets, 121–22
stage three targets, 125
stage two targets, 122, 124–25
states of mind and, 190–92
team treatment in, 126
tool kit, 333–45
Dialectics
DBT and, 105–6
what it is, 106–7
Zen Buddhism and, 107
Diana, Princess, 12
Difficulty with decision making,
3–4
Discourage "we," 349
Disenfranchised grief, 218–19
Distraction
as DBT skill, 280–81
validation and, 169–70
Distress tolerance skills, 279–84
calming breaths, 283, 284
delay, 282

Distress tolerance skills (cont'd)
    distraction, 280–81
    focus on present, 283
    ice, 282–83
    introduction to, 279–80
    moment improvement, 282–84
    soothing activity, 281–82
Divorce
    spouses, of children with BPD,
        and, 225–26
    spouses, of spouse with BPD,
        and, 21–22
Donegan, Nelson, 60
Door in the Face, 344
Downey, Geraldine, 50
DSM. See Diagnostic and
        Statistical Manual of
        Mental Disorders
Dyslexia, 55–56
Dysregulation. See Affective
        dysregulation; Cognitive
        dysregulation; Extreme
        dysregulation; Memory
        dysregulation; Mild
        dysregulation; Moderate
        dysregulation; Mood
        dysregulation; Pain
        dysregulation; Sensitivity
        dysregulation; Sleep
        dysregulation

Eating disorder, 28
Education
    families and, 25, 34, 217, 347–50
    selectivity regarding, 26
Ego, letting go of, 212–13
Ekman, Paul, 312
Ekman Faces, 60–61
E-mail, 336–37
Emotion. See also Affective
        dysregulation
    accurate reflection and, 148

awareness of, 274
as contagious, 298
control of, 273
cooling of, 327
excessive, 285
facts and, 200
identification of, 163–64
implicit mentalization and,
        296–98
integrated mind and, 194–95
intense emotional reaction,
        48–49, 178
labeling, 318
matching voice tones and,
        148–50
memory dysregulation and,
        70–71
mentalization and, 291–92
mind, 190–91, 194–95
mindfulness and, 190–91, 208–9
normalization and, 162–63
processing in brain, 57–58
regulation skills, 272–79
respecting negative, 278–79
scale of, 337–38
society and, 193
stage two targets and, 122, 124–25
take temperature of, 334
validation and, 165, 166,
        168–69, 178
Emotion regulation skills
    cede control, 275
    introduction to, 272–74
    mini-respites, 275–76
    opposite actions, 277–78
    respect negative emotions, 278–79
    trigger avoidance, 275
Empathy
    alternate perspectives and, 319
    developing, 140
    mentalization and, 292–93,
        308–9

validation and, 137–40
validation *vs.*, 138–39
what it is, 137–38
Empower your loved one, 343
Empty nest syndrome, 218
Endorphins, 65
Environment, 285–86
Excessive emotions, 285
Explicit memories, 69, 72
Explicit mentalization, 298, 305–6
Exploring, moderate dysregulation and, 325
Express element of DEAR CCC, 266–67
Extinction
    bursts, 100
    examples of, 99–100
    explained, 98–99
Extreme dysregulation
    stand fast and, 236
    stopping and, 325

Facial perception, 57
Facts
    feelings and, 200
    judgment and, 200–201
    just, 147
Failure
    admission of, 313–14
    anger and, 230
    clinicians', 113–14
    living with, 341
    to mentalize, 307
    pain and, 242
Falk, Peter, 309
Families
    as adjuncts to treatment, 33–35
    anger and, 229–30
    assumptions about, 114–18
    barriers to effectiveness of, 334
    children, of those with BPD, 23–24

concrete thinking and, 305
DBT failure and, 113–14
DEAR CCC and, 264–72
denial and, 227–29
diagnosis and, 26–27
education of, 25, 34, 217, 347–50
ego and, 212–13
emotionality and, 208–9
getting help for, 25
grief of, 217–19
guilt and, 230–31
humility and, 212
iatrogenic advise given to, 29–30
invalidated grief of, 218–19
involvement of, 349–50
method *vs.* principle, 110
mindfulness and, 193–95, 208–12
needs and, 24–25
overview of, 14–15
parents, of those with BPD, 15–19
partners/spouses, of those with BPD, 21–23
radical acceptance and, 237–38
rights of, 349
siblings, of those with BPD, 19–21
stigma of BPD and, 30–33, 219–22
suicide stigma and, 220–21
TARA workshop for, 247
willfulness and, 209–11
willingness and, 211
Fantasy, 302–3
Feelings. *See* Affective dysregulation; Emotion
Fibromyalgia, 67
Flexibility, 290
Focus
    on being right, 175
    on other person, 182–83
    on present, 205–6, 283

Fonagy, Peter, 287
Foot on the Door, 344
Fragility, discourage, 339
Future mentalization, 292

Gage, Phineas, 40
Gaslight syndrome
    described, 13
    of parents, 16–17
Genetics
    abuse *vs.*, 225
    behavioral aspects of BPD and,
        41–42
Goals, DBT, 118. *See also* Defining
        goals
Grief
    acknowledgment of, 231–32
    becoming anger, 229–30
    becoming denial, 227–29
    becoming guilt, 230–31
    examples of, 218
    of families, 217–19
    invalidated, 218–19
    overview regarding, 215–17
    parental, 222–26
    rituals to relieve, 231–35
    society and, 221–22
    spousal/partner, 226–27
    stigma and, 219–22
    what it is, 217–18
Grieving ritual, TARA's
    black stones/candles in, 234
    elements of, 233–35
    hope expressed in, 234–35
    need for, 232–33
    opportunities for, 233
    outcomes of, 235
Grilo, Carlos, 65
Guilt
    grief becoming, 230–31
    shame *vs.*, 49–50
Gunderson, John, 347

Herpertz, Sabine, 74
Hippocampus, 69, 70
Hochschild, Russell, 221
Holland analogy, 243–44
Honesty, 321–22
Hooley, Jill M., 61
Hope, 234–35
Humility
    alternate perspectives and, 319
    CHIRP and, 330–31
    as mentalization technique, 313
    mindfulness and, 212
Hypersensitivity
    attachment and, 301
    behaviors indicating, 4
Hypervigilance
    amygdala and, 48
    attachment and, 301
    behaviors indicating, 4
    sleep dysregulation and, 63

IAPS. *See* International Affective
        Picture System
Iatrogenic advise, 29–30
Ice, 282–83
Ice box mothers, 216
IED. *See* Intermittent explosive
        disorder
Impaired mentalization
    affective dysregulation and, 299,
        301
    attachment and, 300–301
    autism and, 298–99
Impasses, coping with, 326–27
Implicit memories, 69, 72
Implicit mentalization, 296–98
    amygdala and, 296–97
    concrete thinking *vs.*, 305–6
    as reading minds, 297
Improvisation, 109
Impulsivity
    anxiety and, 72

as behavioral aspect, 42–45
behaviors indicating, 3, 43
medication and, 45
nature of, 42
prefrontal cortex and, 43–44
prison population and, 43
serotonin and, 44–45
suicide and, 52
Indecision about priorities, 285
Individual perceptions, reframing,
84–85
Inflexible thinking, 3–4
Insanity, 236
Insight therapy. *See* Psychodynamic
therapy
Insomnia, 62. *See also* Sleep
dysregulation
Insurance, misdiagnosis and, 28
Integrated mind
emotion and, 194–95
what it is, 192
willingness and, 211
Intellect, 298
Intermittent explosive disorder
(IED), 28
International Affective Picture
System (IAPS), 59
Interpersonal effectiveness skills
accepting mistakes, 257–58
asking for what you want,
264–72
assertiveness, 254–55, 267
balancing priorities/demands,
258–63
balancing wants/shoulds, 263
cause/effect and, 256–57
compromise element of, 269–70
concentrate element of, 268
confidence element of, 269
DBT, 248–72
defining goals, 250–52
describe element of, 266

express element of, 266–67
intimate *vs.* peripheral
relationships and, 249
key components of, 250
mastery, building, 263–64
nurturing relationships, 252–54
pointers, 271–72
purpose of, 248–49
reinforce element of, 267–68
requirements of, 249
self-respect, building, 255–56
Interpersonal relationship
problems, 4
Intimacy, 226
Intuition, 331. *See also*
Counterintuitive
Intuitive insight, 289, 290
Intuitive understanding. *See also*
Understanding
developing, 157–58
mind reading and, 156
overview of, 155–56
responding to your, 156–57
validation and, 155–58
Invalid, validation of, 175–77
Invalidated grief, 218–19
Irreverence, 340–41

Judgment
clinicians regarding, 202, 349
examples regarding, 203
fact and, 200–201
non-, 200–203
vs. preference, 201–2
validation and, 169
Juggler analogy, 40–42
Just the facts, 147

Kagan, Jerome, 54
Kandel, Eric, 74
Keep it simple, 316
Keller, Helen, 130

Kenji, Miyazawa, 243
Kingsley, Emily, 243
Koenigsberg, Harold, 59
Kübler-Ross, Elisabeth, 233

Label feelings, 318
Lability, 3. *See also* Affective
    dysregulation
Lack of skill, 285
Language
    examples of use of, 317
    impact of, 316–17
    as mentalization technique,
        316–18
LeDoux, Joseph, 71, 72
Letters of validation
    avoid advice/soapbox in, 183
    focus on other person in, 182–83
    normalizing in, 183–84
    one event at a time for, 182
    sample, 184–86
    writing, 182–84
Limbic system, 47–48
Linehan, Marsha
    BPD as described by, 8, 45–46
    on clinician effectiveness, 27
    DBT history and, 105
    DEAR MAN and, 264
    on insomnia, 62
    neutral faces and, 60–61
    on pain, 242
    on reality, 160
    on success, 329
    suicide and, 52
    on unconditional love, 141
    on validation, 131
Listening
    mentalization and, 311–13
    mild dysregulation and, 324
Logic, 171–73
Logical mind, 191–92
Looking, 323–24

Loss, 222–23
Love
    acceptance and, 117, 140–41,
        167–68
    unconditional, 21, 140–41,
        167–68
    validation is not, 167–68
Lying, 303

Magnifying glass, 338
Maintaining mentalization
    alternate perspectives for,
        318–20
    ask questions, 309–11
    be consistent, 314–15
    be humble, 313
    be supportive/empathic/
        compassionate, 308–9
    in heat of moment, 322–27
    honesty/authenticity for, 321–22
    keep it simple, 316
    label feelings for, 318
    language for, 316–18
    listen/observe/validate for,
        311–13
    overview of, 307–8
    taking responsibility/
        apologizing, 313–14
    techniques for, 308–22
    vulnerability for, 320–21
Manage contingencies, 343
Manipulation, reframing, 86–88
Mastery, building, 263–64
Matching voice tones, 148–50
MBT. *See* Mentalization-Based
    Therapy
Medeeiros, Marilaine, 63
Medicare billing codes, 28
Memory
    amygdala and, 68–71
    be your loved one's, 342
    declarative, 71

hippocampus and, 68–69, 70
validation of, 160–61
workings of, 67–70
Memory dysregulation
behaviors indicating, 5
emotion and, 70–71
memory discrepancies and, 67
shame and, 71
Mental illness
classification, 51–52
common types of, 10
living with, 215–17
onset of, 215
Mentalization
alternate perspectives and,
318–20
asking questions, 309–11
attachment and, 299–301
benefits of, 289–90, 292–93
concrete thinking and, 305–6
consistency and, 314–15
as emotional knowing, 291–92
empathy and, 292–93, 308–9
explicit, 298
extreme dysregulation impeding,
325–26
in heat of moment, 322–27
honesty/authenticity and, 321–22
humbleness and, 313
identifying breaks in, 322
impaired, 298–99, 300–301
impasses and, 326–27
implicit, 296–98, 305–6
intuitive insight and, 289, 290
keep it simple, 316
labeling feelings in, 318
language for, 316–18
listen/observe/validate, 311–13
maintaining, 307–22
mental states and, 290–91
mild dysregulation impeding,
323–24

misuse of, 306
moderate dysregulation
stopping, 324
neuroscience and, 291
of others, 295
overview of, 288–89
prementalizing and, 302–6
pretend thinking and, 303–4
pseudomentalizing and, 304–5
psychic equivalences and, 302–3
recognizing failures of, 307
of relationships, 295–96
of self, 293–95
steps to reestablish, 323–26
supportive/empathic/
compassionate, 308–9
suspension of, 323
taking responsibility/
apologizing, 313–14
teleological thinking and, 304
types of, 292
vulnerability and, 320–21
Mentalization-based therapy
(MBT)
attachment theory and, 299–300
elements of, 287
overview of, 287–88
Micro Expression Training Tool, 312
Mild dysregulation
listening and, 324
looking and, 323–24
stopping and, 323
Mindfulness
being nonjudgmental and,
200–203
as DBT tool, 335–36
ego and, 212–13
emotionality and, 208–9
emotion mind and, 190–91
families and, 193–95, 208–12
feelings/facts and, 200
how of effective, 206–8

Mindfulness (*cont'd*)
humility and, 212
integrated mind and, 192
logical mind and, 191–92
one problem at a time and,
204–5
origin of, 190
overview of, 189–90
participation and, 198–99
perceiving/observing and, 195–97
portraying/describing and, 197–98
practicing, 199–206
present focus and, 205–6
prioritizing and, 204
relationship maintenance and,
207–8
skills, 195–99
states of mind described by,
190–92
tips for, 208
willfulness and, 209–11
willingness and, 211
Mind-read, 334–35
Mini-respites, 275–76
Misattribution, validation reducing,
132–34
Misdiagnosis, 28–29, 51–52
Misinterpretation, validation
reducing, 132–34
Mistakes
acceptance of, 257–58
past, 161–62
Misuse of mentalization, 306
Moderate dysregulation
exploring and, 325
rewinding and, 324–25
stopping and, 324
Modes of validation
describing what you observe
and, 146–47
find nugget of truth, 154–55
intuitive understanding, 155–58

memories, validation of, 160–61
overview of, 144
past, validation of, 158–62
past mistakes and, 161–62
paying attention, 145–47
present, validation of, 162–65
reflection, accurate, 147–54
reflection in action, 150–54
voice tone matching, 148–50
Moment improvement skills
calming breaths, 283, 284
delay, 282
example of using, 283–84
ice, 282–83
Mood dysregulation, 45–52.
See also Affective
dysregulation
anxiety and, 72
Mothers, blame and, 216, 220
Motivation
asking questions and, 310–11
self-, 112–13, 115–16
Mourning, 231

Narcissism, 28
National Institute on Alcohol Abuse
and Alcoholism, 10
Natural consequences, 239
Negative
emotions, respect, 278–79
ignoring, 94–95
reinforcement, 90–91
Neurogenesis, 74–75, 246
Neuroplasticity, 74
Neuroscience, social, 291
Neutral faces, 60–62
New, Antonia, 44
Nonjudgment
acceptance and, 202
mindfulness and, 200–203
Nonverbal communication, 349
Normalizing

behavior *vs.* feelings and, 162–63
identification of feeling and,
    163–64
pathology, 228
present, validation of, and,
    162–65
in validation letter, 183–84
Not knowing attitude, 310
Nugget of truth, finding, 154–55,
    338–39
Nurturing relationships. *See also*
    Relationships
affective dysregulation and,
    252–53
change and, 252
DBT skills for, 252–54
validation and, 253–54

Observation
as mentalization technique,
    311–13
obstacles to, 196–97
paying attention via, 146–47
practicing, 195–96
prerequisites for, 195
WOW and, 338
ODD. *See* Oppositional defiant
    disorder
One at a time
problems, 204–5
shaping attributes, 101–2
One problem at a time, 204–5
Opioids, 65–66, 67
Opposite action, 277–78
Oppositional defiant disorder
    (ODD), 28
Others, mentalization of, 295
Oxytocin, 300

Pain
acceptance of, 242–43
delay and, 282

distraction and, 280–81
distress tolerance skills and,
    279–84
focus on present and, 283
ice and, 282–83
moment improvement and,
    282–84
soothing activity and, 281–82
Pain dysregulation
brain and, 64
fibromyalgia and, 66–67
opioids and, 64–65, 66
perception and, 65
self-injurious behavior and,
    65–66
Parental grief, 222–26
abuse and, 224–25
attachment and, 223–24
devotion and, 222
loss and, 222–23
unrealistic expectations and, 223
Parents, of those with BPD
abuse and, 224–25
attachment and, 223–24
aversive control of, 15
blame and, 16
children/adolescent diagnosis
    regarding, 17
coping styles of, 15–16
devotion and, 222
Gaslight syndrome of, 16–17
guilt and, 230–31
ineffective therapies and, 17–18
loss and, 222–23
older (senior), 18–19
unconditional love of, 21
unrealistic expectations and, 223
Participation, 198–99
Partners, of child with BPD
challenges faced by, 225–26
grief and, 222–26
separation of, 226

Partners, of partner with BPD
abandoning ship, 236
"contagious" experience of, 22
divorce and, 21–22
grief and, 226–27
reciprocal relationships and, 21
Past, validation of
blame and, 159
for change, 158–60
memories and, 160–61
past mistakes and, 161–62
reality and, 159–60
suitable behavior and, 158–59
Past mentalization, 292
Paying attention. See Attention, paying
Peele, Roger, 52
Perceiving
facial, 57
mentalization and, 291
obstacles to, 196–97
pain dysregulation and, 65–66
practicing, 195–96
prerequisites for, 195
reframing individual, 84–85
Persistence, 332–33
Personalization, 174
Philipsen, Alexandra, 63
Phone coaching, 123–24
Physical health, denial affecting, 229
Portraying, 197–98
Positive accentuation, 341–42
Positive reinforcement, 89–90
Posttraumatic stress disorder (PTSD), 28
Practicing validation
examples of, 179–80
with strangers, 178–79
Praise, validation vs., 168
Preference, judgment vs., 201–2
Prefrontal cortex

explicit mentalization and, 298
Gage and, 40
impulsivity and, 43–44
logical mind and, 191–92
Prementalizing
concrete thinking and, 305–6
misuse of mentalization and, 306
modes of, 302
pretend thinking and, 303–4
pseudomentalizing and, 304–5
psychic equivalence and, 302–3
teleological thinking and, 304
Present
clinicians regarding, 348
focus on, 205–6, 283
need to accept, 117
Present, validation of
behavior vs. feelings and, 162–63
identification of feeling and, 163–64
normalizing and, 162–65
Present mentalization, 292
Pretend thinking, 303–4
Pretreatment targets, 119–21
Princess Diana, 12
Priorities
indecision about, 285
mindfulness and, 204
Priorities/demands, balancing
conflict resolution and, 259–61
as DBT skill, 258–63
defining your own, 261–62
doing nothing and, 259
overcommitment and, 258
realistic expectations and, 262–63
Prison population, impulsivity of, 43
Problems
fixing/solving, 170–71
interpersonal relationship, 4
not jumping into, 171

one at a time, 204–5
solving in the moment, 112
Pseudomentalizing, 304–5
Psychic equivalence, 302–3
Psychodynamic therapy
   vs. CBT, 80–82
   ineffectiveness of, 81
   overview of, 80–81
   present science regarding, 82
PTSD. *See* Posttraumatic stress
      disorder
Punishment, 97–98

Radical acceptance
   alternatives to, 236
   approval *vs.*, 240
   change balanced with, 241–42,
      244
   choice and, 240
   chronic condition and, 239
   commitment and, 241
   control and, 238–39
   DBT and, 235–36
   family members and, 237–38
   Holland analogy and, 243–44
   implications of, 236–38
   "is" and, 238
   natural consequences and, 239
   origin of concept of, 235
   of pain, 242–43
   Reeve, Christopher, and, 241–42
   turning the mind for, 240–41
   understanding *vs.*, 239
   vulnerability and, 320–21
   Wynn and, 237
Raised eyebrow effect, 12–13
Rapid eye movement (REM) sleep,
      63, 64
Reading minds, 297
Reality
   concrete thinking and, 305–6
   pretend thinking and, 303–4

pseudomentalizing and, 304–5
psychic equivalence *vs.*, 302–3
teleological thinking and, 304
Reciprocity, 293
Reconcile, 344
Reeve, Christopher, 241–42
Reeve, Dana, 242
Reflection, accurate
   in action, 150–54
   being a mirror, 147–48
   matching voice tones for,
      148–50
Reframing
   cognitive distortions, 82–84
   delays, 85–86
   individual perceptions, 84–85
   manipulation, 86–88
   overview of, 82
   rejection, 86
   social interactions, 85
Refrigerator mothers, 216
Reinforce element, DEAR CCC,
      267–68
Reinforcement
   emphasize positive/ignore
      negative, 94–95
   frequency of, 92
   harmful behaviors and, 95–97
   negative, 90–91
   overview of, 88–89
   positive, 89–90
   relative to situation, 92–93
   self-, 93–94
Rejection, reframing, 86
Relationships. *See also* Nurturing
      relationships
   behaviors indicating problems
      in, 4
   intimate *vs.* peripheral, 249
   maintenance of, 207–8
   mentalization of, 295–96
   reciprocal, 21

REM. *See* Rapid eye movement
    sleep
Research
    current state of, 38–39
    future, 73–74
Respect negative emotions, 278–79
Responsibility, 313–14
Restraint, 332
Rewinding, 324–25
Rituals
    cultural examples of, 232
    grieving, 231–35
    significance of, 231
    TARA's grieving, 232–35
Roshoman (Japanese tale), 134

Sangha, 188, 232, 235
Scale of emotional intensity,
    337–38
Schizophrenogenic mothers, 216
Schmahl, Christian, 63, 66
Schultz, Robert T., 57
Science of BPD. *See also* Behavioral
    aspects of BPD
    brain and, 40
    current state of research, 38–39
Security, 293
Selective serotonin reuptake
    inhibitors (SSRIs), 45
Self-injurious behavior
    pain perception and, 65
    stage one targets regarding, 121
Self mentalization, 293–95
Self-referential processing, 58–60
Self-reinforcement, 93–94
Self-respect, building, 255–56,
    339–40
Sensitive discussions, 170
Sensitivity dysregulation, 53–54.
    See also Hypersensitivity
Sensory processing disorder, 53
Serotonin, 44–45

Shame
    affective dysregulation and,
        48–50
    alcohol and, 50
    anger and, 230
    guilt *vs.*, 49–50
    memory dysregulation and, 71
    suicide and, 49
Shaping
    breakthroughs, 102–4
    hints, 104
    one attribute at a time, 101–2
    overview of, 100–101
Shaywitz, Bennett A., 56
Shaywitz, Sally, 55–56
Shoulds/wants, balancing, 263
Siblings, of those with BPD
    coping by, 20–21
    issues faced by, 19–20
    research and, 19
Siever, Larry, 44, 45, 53, 66
Sincerity, 180
Skills
    CHIRP, 330–33
    DBT tool kit of, 333–45
    integrating/internalizing, 329
    lack of, 285
    mini-guide of, 330–45
Skills, mindfulness
    participation, 198–99
    perceiving/observing, 195–97
    portraying/describing, 197–98
    two sets of, 195
Skills for behavior change, DBT
    accept DBT premises, 344–45
    accepting mistakes, 257–58
    asking for what you want,
        264–72
    assertiveness, 254–55
    balance regarding, 245–46
    balancing priorities/demands,
        258–63

balancing wants/shoulds, 263
building mastery, 263–64
calming breaths, 283, 284
cause/effect, understanding, 256–57
cede control, 275
cheerlead, 337
competency/self-respect, 339–40
DEAR CCC, 336
defining goals, 250–52
delay, 282
describe, 335
difficulty of, 284–86
distraction, 280–81
distress tolerance, 279–84
e-mail, 336–37
emotion regulation, 272–79
empower your loved one, 343
failure, learning to live with, 341
focus on present, 283
fragility, discourage, 339
ice, 282–83
interpersonal effectiveness, 248–72
irreverence, 340–41
magnifying glass, 338
manage contingencies, 343
memory, be your loved one's, 342
mind-read, 334–35
mini-respites, 275–76
modules, 246
moment improvement, 282–84
neurogenesis and, 246
nugget of truth, 338–39
nurturing relationships, 252–54
opposite actions, 277–78
positive accentuation, 341–42
reconcile/synthesize, 344
respect negative emotions, 278–79
scale of emotional intensity, 337–38
self-respect, building, 255–56

soothing activity, 281–82
take emotional temperature, 334
those without BPD regarding, 246–47
tool kit of, 333–45
trigger avoidance, 275, 336
validate, 335
WOW, 338
Sleep dysregulation, 62–64
behaviors indicating, 5–6
hypervigilance and, 63
REM sleep and, 62, 63
Soap box, avoiding, 183
Social interactions
invalidated grief and, 218–19
reframing, 85
rituals and, 221, 232
rules of, 221
understanding and, 288
Solitary confinement, 130
Soothing activity, 281–82
Spouses, of child with BPD
challenges faced by, 225–26
grief and, 222–26
Spouses, of spouse with BPD
abandoning ship, 236
"contagious" experience of, 22
divorce and, 21–22
grief and, 226–27
reciprocal relationships and, 21
SSRIs. *See* Selective serotonin reuptake inhibitors
Stage four targets, 126
Stage one targets, 121–22
Stage three targets, 125
Stage two targets, 122, 124–25
Stand fast, 236
Stanley, Barbara, 65
States of mind
emotion mind, 190–91
integrated mind, 192
logical mind, 191–92

Steiner, Hans, 45
Stigma
    clinicians and, 30–33
    mental *vs.* physical disorder
        and, 220
    societal, 219–22
    suicide and, 220–21
    unsubstantiated theories and, 32
Stopping
    extreme dysregulation and, 325
    impasse and, 326
    mild dysregulation and, 323
    moderate dysregulation and, 324
Substance abuse, 28
Suffering, 242
Suicidal ideation, 221
Suicide
    impulsivity and, 52
    shame and, 49
    stage one targets regarding, 121
    stigma and, 220–21
    terror of dealing with, 221
Support
    clinicians need, 114
    families needing, 24, 25, 116–17
    mentalization and, 308–9
Sympathy, 135–36
Synthesize, 344

Talk therapy. *See* Psychodynamic
        therapy
Tangney, June Price, 50
TARA. *See* Treatment and Research
        Advancements National
        Association for
        Personality Disorder
Tara (Buddhist goddess of
        compassion), 137
Targets
    pretreatment, 119–21
    stage four, 126
    stage one, 121–22

stage three, 125
stage two, 122, 124–25
suicide/self-injurious behaviors
        and, 121
therapy/life interfering
        behaviors and, 122
Team treatment, 126
Teleological thinking, 304
Temperature, emotional, 334
Theory
    attachment, 299–300
    unsubstantiated, 32
Therapists. *See* Clinicians
Therapy. *See specific therapy*
Tiara, TARA, 73
Tool, Micro Expression Training, 312
Tool kit, DBT, 333–45
Tough love, 29–30
Treatment, DBT
    ensuring efficacy of, 127–28
    how it is practiced, 126–28
    phone coaching, 123–24
    pretreatment targets, 119–21
    questions to ask potential
        clinicians, 127
    stage four targets, 126
    stage one targets, 121–22
    stage three targets, 125
    stage two targets, 122, 124–25
    team, 126
Treatment and Research
        Advancements National
        Association for
        Personality Disorder
        (TARA)
    apparent competence and, 12
    DEAR CCC and, 264, 265
    family workshops and, 247
    grieving ritual of, 232–35
    tiara, 73
Trestman, Robert, 43
Trigger avoidance, 275, 336

Trust
    mentalization and, 293, 320–21
    vulnerability and, 320–21
Truth, finding nugget of, 154–55,
        338–39
Turning the mind, 240–41

Ultimatums, 142–44
Unconditional acceptance
    rules/ultimatums/contracts *vs.*,
        142–44
    vs. unconditional love, 140–41
    what it is, 141
Unconditional love
    of parents, 21
    vs. unconditional acceptance,
        140–41, 167–68
Understanding. *See also* Intuitive
        understanding
    cause/effect, 256–57
    clinicians regarding, 348
    radical acceptance *vs.*, 239
    social intelligence and, 288
    validation *vs.*, 167
Unrealistic expectations, 223
Unsubstantiated theories, 32

Validation
    absence of, 129–30
    acceptance-acknowledgement
        declaration and, 180–82
    bypassing reason, 134
    change and, 135, 158–60,
        165–66, 246, 335
    compassion and, 136–37
    as counterintuitive, 177–78
    as DBT tool, 335
    defining, 130–32
    difficulty of, 181–82
    do not(s), 169–77
        be distracted, 169–70
        criticize/judge/blame, 169

example of, 184–85
fix/solve problems, 170–71
focus on being right, 175
personalize, 174
respond with anger, 173–74
respond with logic, 171–73
validate invalid, 175–77
empathy and, 137–40
essentials of, 135–40
of feelings, 165, 166, 168–69, 178
find nugget of truth for, 154–55
intense emotion and, 178
intuitive understanding and,
        155–58
key concepts summary, 187–88
letters of, 182–86
Linehan on, 131
love *vs.*, 167–68
of memories, 160–61
as mentalization technique,
        311–13
misconceptions about, 167–69
misinterpretation/misattribution
        and, 132–34
modes of, 144–65
nurturing relationships and,
        253–54
of past, 158–62
past mistakes and, 161–62
practicing, 178–80
vs. praise, 168
prerequisites for, 134–35
of present, 162–65
reflection, accurate, and, 147–54
reflection in action for, 150–54
rules/ultimatums/contracts *vs.*,
        142–44
of self, 188
of specific behaviors, 165–66
sympathy and, 135–36
as unconditional acceptance,
        140–44

Validation (*cont'd*)
   vs. unconditional love, 140–41,
      167–68
   vs. understanding, 167
   voice tone matching for, 148–50
Voice tones, matching, 148–50
Vulnerability, 226, 320–21

Wagner, Amy, 61
Wait, observe, wing it (WOW), 338
Wants/shoulds, balancing, 263
Weissman, Myrna, 220
"Welcome to Holland" (Kingsley),
   243
Willfulness
   example of, 210
   getting past, 209–10
   mindfulness and, 209–11

risk and, 211
   what it is, 209
Willingness
   to change, 116
   mindfulness and, 211
Wise mind
   emotional communication and,
      194–95
   what it is, 192
   willingness and, 211
Worry thoughts, 285
WOW. *See* Wait, observe, wing it
Wynn, Steve, 237

Zen Buddhism
   dialectics and, 107
   radical acceptance and, 235
Zimmerman, Marc, 51